# ENRICHMENT IN THE LAW OF UNJUST ENRICHMENT AND RESTITUTION

Enrichment is key to understanding the law of unjust enrichment and restitution. This book provides a comprehensive analysis of the concept of enrichment and its implications for restitutionary awards. Dr Lodder argues that enrichment may be characterised either factually or legally, and explores the consequences of that distinction. In factual enrichment cases, the measure of enrichment is the objective value received. This is the basis of many awards of money had and received, quantum meruit, quantum valebat and money paid. In legal enrichment cases, the benefit is the acquisition of a specific right or the release of a specific obligation. The remedy is restitution of that right or reinstatement of that obligation. It is demonstrated that specific restitution of the defendant's legal enrichment is often the basis for resulting trusts, rescission, rectification and subrogation. This book has profound implications for understanding restitutionary awards and the relationship between the enrichment inquiry and other aspects of the law of unjust enrichment, including the 'at the expense of' inquiry and the defence of change of position.

**Volume 3 in the series Hart Studies in Private Law**

# Enrichment in the Law of Unjust Enrichment and Restitution

AVM Lodder

•HART•
PUBLISHING

OXFORD AND PORTLAND, OREGON
2012

Published in the United Kingdom by Hart Publishing Ltd
16C Worcester Place, Oxford, OX1 2JW
Telephone: +44 (0)1865 517530
Fax: +44 (0)1865 510710
E-mail: mail@hartpub.co.uk
Website: http://www.hartpub.co.uk

Published in North America (US and Canada) by
Hart Publishing
c/o International Specialized Book Services
920 NE 58th Avenue, Suite 300
Portland, OR 97213-3786
USA
Tel: +1 503 287 3093 or toll-free: (1) 800 944 6190
Fax: +1 503 280 8832
E-mail: orders@isbs.com
Website: http://www.isbs.com



British Library Cataloguing in Publication Data
Data Available

ISBN: 978-1-84946-329-4

Typeset by Compuscript Ltd, Shannon
Printed and bound in Great Britain by
TJ International Ltd, Padstow, Cornwall

# ACKNOWLEDGMENTS

I owe a great debt to the many individuals and organisations that have supported me throughout the writing of *Enrichment in the Law of Unjust Enrichment and Restitution* and the D Phil thesis on which it is based. First and foremost, this book could not have been written without the constant direction and keen interest of my D Phil supervisor, Justice James Edelman, who first introduced me to the law of unjust enrichment and restitution as an undergraduate at the University of Western Australia in 2004 and who has guided my development in the subject ever since. My thanks also to the Rhodes Trust for funding my studies and to Magdalen College for the ongoing support that I received during my time at Oxford. I am extremely grateful to Richard Hart for backing this project and to everyone at Hart Publishing for making it a reality.

A number of people read and commented on various drafts of my manuscript and D Phil thesis. In particular, I benefitted from a most precise and careful proof-reader in Ben Spagnolo, who changed my mind more than once and whose astute comments often saved me from error. Also, I am grateful to my fellow members of the Oxford Obligations Discussion Group, especially Eli Ball, Tatiana Cutts, Andy Dyson, Dave Winterton and Fred Wilmot-Smith, for our regular lively discussions on all aspects of private law and their insightful comments on my work. Thanks to Eric Heenan, who has argued with me about unjust enrichment and restitution since we first encountered the subject and, in one of those many arguments in 2005, helped me reach the view that would form the central thesis of this book.

On a personal level, my thanks to my family, Corrie, Vere and Wil, for their ongoing encouragement throughout this process, and to Giulia, for her love and support.

# CONTENTS

# TABLE OF ABBREVIATIONS

| | |
|---|---|
| **BCCA** | British Columbia Court of Appeal |
| **BCSC** | British Columbia Supreme Court |
| **Cal App** | Court of Appeal of California |
| **DCAC** | District Court of Appeal of California |
| **FMCA** | Federal Magistrates Court of Australia |
| **HCA** | High Court of Australia |
| **Idaho App** | Court of Appeals of Idaho |
| **MBCA** | Manitoba Court of Appeals |
| **MBQB** | Manitoba Court of Queen's Bench |
| **NH** | New Hampshire Supreme Court |
| **NLCA** | Newfoundland and Labrador Court of Appeal |
| **NSWCA** | Court of Appeal of Supreme Court of New South Wales |
| **NSWSC** | Supreme Court of New South Wales |
| **NZCA** | Court of Appeal of New Zealand |
| **NZDC** | District Court of New Zealand |
| **NZHC** | High Court of New Zealand |
| **ONCA** | Court of Appeal for Ontario |
| **ONCJ** | Ontario Court of Justice |
| **ONHC** | Ontario High Court |
| **ONSC** | Ontario Superior Court of Justice |
| **Ont Ch** | Ontario Court of Chancery |
| **SASC** | South Australian Supreme Court |
| **Sask QB** | Saskatchewan Court of Queen's Bench |
| **SCC** | Supreme Court of Canada |
| **SCT** | Supreme Court of Tasmania |
| **USCC** | United States Court of Claims |
| **VSC** | Supreme Court of Victoria |
| **WASCA** | Court of Appeal of Supreme Court of Western Australia |

# TABLE OF CASES

# TABLE OF STATUTES

# 1

# Introduction

Enrichment is perhaps the most under-theorised aspect of the law of unjust enrichment but it is arguably the most important element for the future direction and consolidation of the subject. As Buxton LJ said in *Deutsche Morgan Grenfell plc v IRC*, enrichment is 'not merely material to success, but the whole essence of the action'.[1] In recent years, the enrichment inquiry has attracted greater scholarly attention and a number of excellent attempts have been made to give more precise content to various parts of the enrichment inquiry.[2] However, the aim of this book is broader: to understand the theoretical structure and role of enrichment in the law of unjust enrichment and to propose a comprehensive model for the enrichment inquiry that is consistent with these theoretical foundations and explains and justifies the cases. The central thesis is that a defendant's enrichment can be characterised in two different ways—*factually*, in terms of economic value, and *legally*, in terms of rights and obligations—and that this theoretical bifurcation has important substantive implications for determining when a defendant is enriched and, accordingly, the form restitution will take.

The division of enrichment into factual and legal enrichment challenges the prevailing orthodoxy in a fundamental way. It shows that enrichment is not a unitary element satisfied by a single test; rather, the *same benefit may be understood in two different ways*: (i) by the value of the benefit received ('factual enrichment'); or (ii) by the change in the legal relations of the defendant effected by the acquisition of a right or the release of an obligation ('legal enrichment'). For instance, the transfer of title to a car may be characterised factually—as the receipt of the value of the title to the car—or legally—by the change in the defendant's rights and obligations. While a defendant who receives value as a result of a mistake, duress or failure of consideration is now commonly recognised as having an obligation

[1] *Deutsche Morgan Grenfell plc v IRC* [2005] EWCA Civ 78, [2006] Ch 243 [294] (Buxton LJ).

[2] See in particular M McInnes, 'Enrichment Revisited' in J Neyers, M McInnes and S Pitel (eds), *Understanding Unjust Enrichment* (Oxford, Hart, 2004); R Stevens, 'Three Enrichment Issues' in A Burrows and A Rodger (eds), *Mapping the Law: Essays in Memory of Peter Birks* (Oxford, Oxford University Press, 2006); R Chambers, 'Two Kinds of Enrichment' in R Chambers, C Mitchell and J Penner (eds), *Philosophical Foundations of the Law of Unjust Enrichment* (Oxford, Oxford University Press, 2009); J Edelman, 'The Meaning of Loss and Enrichment' in R Chambers, C Mitchell and J Penner (eds), *Philosophical Foundations of the Law of Unjust Enrichment* (Oxford, Oxford University Press, 2009); McGhee, 'The Nature of the Enrichment Enquiry' in J Edelman and S Degeling (eds), *Unjust Enrichment in Commercial Law* (Sydney, Lawbook Co, 2009).

to make restitution for unjust enrichment, the same analysis has not traditionally been applied to a defendant who, on precisely the same grounds, is required to make restitution specifically by way of resulting trust, rescission, rectification or subrogation.

The recognition of two kinds of enrichment reveals the connection between enrichment and the nature of the claim for restitution of an unjust enrichment. Rather than asking whether the defendant is enriched and then determining whether restitution should be monetary or proprietary, it is necessary to ascertain whether the claimant is asserting:

(i) that the defendant is enriched by the value of the benefit received and seeks monetary restitution of that value; or
(ii) that the defendant is enriched by the acquisition of a right (or release of an obligation) at the claimant's expense and seeks specific restitution of that right (or reinstatement of that obligation) in law.

In other words, the distinction between monetary and 'proprietary' restitution is not an open choice of remedies following a finding that the defendant is abstractly enriched; rather, the characterisation of the enrichment and the claim for restitution are linked. Specific restitution is the reversal of a legal enrichment, not by the payment of money, but in law. The value of the right or release is simply irrelevant to proof of enrichment in a claim framed in this way, although value may otherwise be relevant to the primary claim or defences.

Far from being a mere exercise in taxonomy or theoretical elegance, it will be shown that accepting this approach has wide-ranging substantive consequences for the enrichment inquiry and the law of unjust enrichment and restitution. The first consequence of accepting this division is that it illuminates the superficial understanding of 'restitution' in present analyses. Existing theories of restitution differentiate between monetary and 'proprietary' restitution,[3] but this distinction insufficiently appreciates the varieties of specific restitution. This book suggests that restitution is better divided into monetary restitution, which is a claim-right to the value received by the defendant at the claimant's expense, and 'specific restitution', which takes several different forms, including the power to obtain a specific right, the power to cancel a right, the power to create or modify a right and the reinstatement of a liability. All these responses share the same purpose and effect: to reverse a legal enrichment.

The second substantive consequence of bifurcating the enrichment inquiry is that it reveals that the freedom of choice concerns usually incorporated into the enrichment inquiry pertain only to factual enrichment cases. When transfers of value are properly understood, it becomes clear that 'subjective devaluation'[4]

[3] See ch 3, s III.C.
[4] See ch 6, s I.

must be rejected in favour of an objective enrichment model. It is suggested that a defendant is enriched by the value of a benefit received whenever:

(i) there is a transfer of value to the defendant at the claimant's expense; and
(ii) the defendant chose the benefit or it is 'incontrovertibly enriching'.[5]

This model addresses freedom of choice concerns in factual enrichment cases directly through the 'choice of benefit' test, affording much-needed clarity as to when holding a defendant to be enriched by the value of a benefit in kind will infringe her freedom of choice. By contrast, in legal enrichment cases, it is shown that the defendant's enrichment is established simply by proving that the defendant has obtained a right or the release of an obligation at the expense of the claimant.

Third, the bifurcation of enrichment proposed in this book clarifies the point at which enrichment occurs. The traditional approach, conflating factual and legal enrichment, confuses immediate and extant enrichment, as courts assess enrichment sometimes at the point of receipt and sometimes at the date of judgment. Once the two kinds of enrichment are properly understood separately, it becomes clear that the enrichment inquiry is always concerned with the immediate enrichment received by the defendant. In value cases, it will be shown that, subject to the limitations imposed by the requirement of proof of choice of the benefit or incontrovertibility, the defendant is enriched by the immediate value transferred, not the value surviving in the defendant's hands. In legal enrichment cases, the defendant is enriched by the right at the moment it is acquired or the release of the obligation at the moment it is released. As the claimant is seeking restitution of the specific right or reinstatement of the specific obligation and not the value of these benefits, no question of valuation arises. Until now, the failure to apprehend the difference in characterisation by value or in law has often led to the point of enrichment being confused with specific restitution of a right still held at the date of judgment.

Finally, such a radical reappraisal of the enrichment inquiry has wide-ranging implications for the relationship between enrichment and other aspects of the law of unjust enrichment. In particular, the 'at the expense of' requirement and the change of position defence are two aspects of the law of unjust enrichment that will need to be carefully reassessed in light of the theory of enrichment presented in this book. Although these questions fall beyond the strict scope of this book, the implications of accepting the factual–legal distinction are adumbrated in chapter eight. In relation to 'at the expense of', it is suggested that the bifurcation of enrichment does not necessarily entail the bifurcation of the 'at the expense of' inquiry and that understanding transfers of value in the manner proposed in this book may resolve several vexing questions in three-party cases. In relation

[5] See ch 6, s III.

to the change of position defence, it is suggested that accepting that enrichment is focused on immediate, as opposed to extant, enrichment provides a bright line between the enrichment inquiry and the defence: enrichment is directed to the defendant's immediate enrichment in the defective transaction, whereas the change of position defence concerns occurrences extraneous to the defective transaction. In addition, it is suggested that the defence may operate differently in factual and legal enrichment cases and that the enrichment model advanced here helps to identify the different issues that apply in each case.

As the goal of this book is to provide a coherent theoretical structure and comprehensive doctrinal account of the enrichment inquiry, it forms part of the broader debates concerning the principle of unjust enrichment and the response of restitution. It is helpful in this chapter to situate this book within those debates. Section I explains the principle of unjust enrichment and sets out the theoretical framework for the discussion in this book. Section II then addresses the restitutionary response to unjust enrichment and outlines a broader definition of restitution encompassing the two different kinds of enrichment that may be reversed by restitution. Section III then outlines the methodology applied in, and scope of, this book, while section IV outlines the structure and the key points that will be defended in each chapter.

# I. Unjust Enrichment

## A. A Theoretical Framework

All legal rights are responses to causative events.[6] These causative events can be divided into the categories of consent,[7] wrongs,[8] unjust enrichment[9] and 'other events'[10] in what is often referred to as the 'Birksian taxonomy' of private law.

[6] J Austin, *Lectures on Jurisprudence or the Philosophy of Positive Law*, 5th edn (London, John Murray, 1885) 760; P Birks, 'Equity in the Modern Common Law: An Exercise in Taxonomy' (1996) 26 *University of Western Australia Law Review* 1; P Birks, *Unjust Enrichment*, 2nd edn (Oxford, Clarendon Press, 2005) 20.

[7] Eg contracts, declarations of trust, gifts, conveyances and wills.

[8] Eg torts, equitable wrongs, breach of contract and breach of statutory duty.

[9] Enrichment at the expense of the claimant that is prima facie reversible due to the presence of an unjust factor: *Pavey & Matthews v Paul* (1987) 162 CLR 221 (HCA) 256–57 (Deane J); *Portman BS v Hamlyn Taylor Neck* [1998] 4 All ER 202 (CA) 206 (Millett LJ); *Banque Financiere de la Cité v Parc (Battersea) Ltd* [1999] 1 AC 221 (HL) 227 (Lord Steyn) 234 (Lord Hoffmann); *Roxborough v Rothmans of Pall Mall Australia Ltd* [2001] HCA 68, (2001) 208 CLR 516, 568 fn 257 (Kirby J); *Rowe v Vale of White Horse DC* [2003] EWHC 388 (Admin), [2003] 1 Lloyd's Rep 418 [11] (Lightman J); *Filby v Mortgage Express (No 2) Ltd* [2004] EWCA Civ 759, [2004] 2 P&CR DG16 [62] (May LJ); P Birks, *An Introduction to the Law of Restitution*, revised edn (Oxford, Clarendon Press, 1989) 21; G Virgo, *The Principles of the Law of Restitution*, 2nd edn (Oxford, Oxford University Press, 2006) 9; A Burrows, *The Law of Restitution*, 3rd edn (Oxford, Oxford University Press, 2010) 26–27. See, eg *Kelly v Solari* (1841) 9 M&W 54, 152 ER 24.

[10] Eg finder's rights, specification, accession and mixing.

Each category of 'causative event' comprises different causes of action that share common features. For example, all of the causes of action in the category of wrongs rely on the characterisation of the facts as a breach of duty in determining a legal response.[11] Further, each of these legally relevant events gives rise to certain responses such as compensation, restitution and disgorgement. This model has become a dominant taxonomy of private law and it serves as an heuristic for analysing the interaction between causative events and legal responses.

While the Birksian model has become an influential taxonomy of private law, there is considerable debate about which events give rise to which responses. For the most part, this book need not touch on this debate, but there is a critical schism that must be addressed at the outset. 'Quadrationists' insist that restitution is only ever a response to unjust enrichment.[12] Although quadration takes different forms, quadrationists tend to divide the concept of unjust enrichment into unjust enrichment by wrongdoing, meaning unjust enrichment consequent upon a breach of duty, and autonomous unjust enrichment, which is not characterised by a breach of duty. In contrast, Birks[13] and other 'multi-causalists'[14] deny that restitution is confined to unjust enrichment and insist that including restitution for wrongs under the umbrella of unjust enrichment is unhelpful. They also argue that restitution is a response to various events besides unjust enrichment and wrongs. Following recognition that wrongs-based liability in 'knowing-receipt' claims is restitutionary,[15] it is clear that the multi-causalist position is in

[11] J Edelman, *Gain-Based Damages: Contract, Tort, Equity and Intellectual Property* (Oxford, Hart, 2002) 25, 33.

[12] See *Halifax BS v Thomas* [1996] Ch 217 (CA) 224 (Peter Gibson LJ); K Mason and J Carter, *Restitution Law in Australia* (Sydney, Butterworths, 1996) 56–57; A Tettenborn, 'Misnomer—A Response to Professor Birks' in R Nolan (ed), *Restitution: Past, Present and Future* (Oxford, Hart, 1998); A Burrows, 'Quadrating Restitution and Unjust Enrichment: A Matter of Principle?' (2000) 8 *RLR* 257 *cf* Burrows, *The Law of Restitution* (2011) (n 9) 9–12, which adopts a nuanced middle position, insisting that the *principle* of unjust enrichment underpins all claims for restitution while recognising that restitution is a response to both wrongs and unjust enrichment.

[13] P Birks, 'Property and Unjust Enrichment: Categorical Truths' [1997] *New Zealand Law Review* 623, 626–27, 658–59; P Birks, 'Misnomer' in Cornish (ed), *Restitution: Past, Present and Future* (Oxford, Hart, 1998) 1–29; P Birks, 'Equity, Conscience and Unjust Enrichment' (1999) 23 *Melbourne University Law Review* 1, 4–17; P Birks, 'Unjust Enrichment and Wrongful Enrichment' (2001) 79 *Texas Law Review* 1767; Birks, *Unjust Enrichment* (2005) (n 6) 11–16.

[14] L Smith, 'The Province of the Law of Restitution' (1992) 71 *Canadian Bar Review* 672; I Jackman, *The Varieties of Restitution* (Sydney, Federation Press, 1998); R Grantham and C Rickett, *Enrichment and Restitution in New Zealand* (Oxford, Hart, 2000) 471; J Edelman, 'Unjust Enrichment, Restitution and Wrongs' (2001) 79 *Texas Law Review* 1869; Edelman, *Gain-Based Damages* (2002) (n 11) 36–41; P Millett, 'Proprietary Restitution' in S Degeling and J Edelman (eds), *Equity in Commercial Law* (Sydney, Thomson LBC, 2005) 312; Virgo, *The Principles of the Law of Restitution* (2006) (n 9) 6–8, 10; Chambers, 'Two Kinds of Enrichment' (2009) (n 2) 242–43; C Mitchell, P Mitchell and S Watterson, *Goff & Jones The Law of Unjust Enrichment*, 8th edn (London, Sweet & Maxwell 2011) §§1-01–1-05.

[15] *Royal Brunei Airlines Sdn Bhd v Tan* [1995] 2 AC 378 (PC) 386 (Lord Nicholls); *Jeffrey Lorne Gold v Primary Developments Ltd* [1997] 3 SCR 767 (SCC) [41]–[49] (La Forest, Cory & Iacobucci JJ); *Koorootang Nominees Pty Ltd v Australia and New Zealand Banking Group Ltd* [1998] 3 VR 16 (VSC) 78–105 (Hansen J) *cf Farah Constructions Pty Ltd v Say-Dee Pty Ltd* [2007] HCA 22, (2007) 203 CLR 89 [140]–[158] (Gleeson CJ, Gummow, Callinan, Heydon and Crennan JJ).

the ascendancy,[16] and it has been accepted by the Supreme Court of Canada[17] and the House of Lords.[18] Restitution is a response both to unjust enrichment and wrongs,[19] and may arguably be a response to consent[20] and other events.[21] In light of the recognition that restitutionary awards are not confined to unjust enrichment, quadration cannot be sustained and this book adopts the dominant multi-causalist position.

## B. The Elements of a Claim in Unjust Enrichment

Unjust enrichment is concerned with the reversal of normatively defective transactions enriching the defendant at the claimant's expense.[22] It is a category comprising various causes of action for restitution of a benefit obtained by the defendant, rather than compensation for losses suffered by the claimant.[23] It is now generally accepted in English law that a claim in unjust enrichment requires the satisfaction of four elements:[24]

(i) that the defendant is enriched;
(ii) that the enrichment is at the claimant's expense;
(iii) that the enrichment is unjust; and,
(iv) that no recognised defence applies.

This book concerns the first of these four elements for a successful claim in unjust enrichment. Where a claim satisfies these elements, the law's response is usually restitutionary, although it will not always be.[25] The meaning of restitution is considered in section II below.

[16] See A Burrows, E McKendrick and J Edelman, *Cases and Materials on the Law of Restitution*, 2nd edn (Oxford, Oxford University Press, 2007) 2–3.

[17] *Kingstreet Investments v New Brunswick (Department of Finance)* [2007] 1 SCR 3 (SCC) [33].

[18] *Sempra Metals Ltd v IRC* [2007] UKHL 34, [2008] 1 AC 561 [116] (Lord Nicholls) [132]–[146] (Lord Scott) [230]–[231] (Lord Mance).

[19] Eg *United Australia Ltd v Barclays Bank Ltd* [1941] AC 1 (HL); *Strand Electric and Engineering Co Ltd v Bristol Entertainments Ltd* [1952] 2 QB 246 (CA); *Inverugie v Hackett* [1995] 1 WLR 713 (PC).

[20] Eg Birks argues that a loan contract where the borrower consents to make restitution of the loan amount is restitution in the category of consent, see Birks, *An Introduction to the Law of Restitution* (1989) (n 9) 44–46; Birks, *Unjust Enrichment* (2005) (n 6) 11.

[21] Eg *vindicatio* claims, see *Macmillan Inc v Bishopsgate Investment Trust Plc (No 3)* [1996] 1 WLR 387 (CA); *Westdeutsche Landesbank Girozentrale v Islington LBC* [1996] AC 669 (HL) 707 (Lord Browne-Wilkinson).

[22] *Gribbon v Lutton* [2001] EWCA Civ 1956, [2002] QB 902 [60] (Robert Walker LJ); *Kingstreet Investments v New Brunswick (Department of Finance)* [2007] 1 SCR 3 (SCC) [32]. See L Smith, 'Unjust Enrichment: Big or Small?' in S Degeling and J Edelman (eds), *Unjust Enrichment in Commercial Law* (Sydney, Lawbook Co, 2008) 49–52.

[23] *Sempra Metals Ltd v IRC* [2007] UKHL 34, [2008] 1 AC 561 [28] (Lord Hope); *Haugesund Kommune v Depfa ACS Bank* [2010] EWHC 227, [2010] 1 All ER 1109 [18] (Tomlinson J).

[24] See n 9. A fifth question is sometimes added as to what right the claimant obtains, eg whether it is personal or proprietary: P Millett, 'Restitution and Constructive Trusts' (1998) 114 *LQR* 399, 408; Birks, *Unjust Enrichment* (2005) (n 6) 39.

[25] Mitchell, Mitchell and Watterson, *Goff & Jones The Law of Unjust Enrichment* (2011) (n 14) §§1-03, 36-28–36-37 *cf* Burrows, *The Law of Restitution* (2010) (n 9) 9. Goff & Jones takes the view that

## II. Restitution

This book takes the view that restitution is *the reversal of the defendant's enrichment*. Restitution is a 'gains-based' response. It takes the form of a right or power to reverse the defendant's enrichment at the claimant's expense. Restitution is not restricted to giving that enrichment back *to the claimant*; it includes remedies that cancel or negate the enrichment *received by the defendant*.[26] This conclusion follows from the thesis advanced here that restitution can take two forms mirroring the two characterisations of enrichment: (i) the reversal of transfers of value in money; and (ii) the reversal of the acquisition of a right or release of an obligation in law.[27] Nonetheless, the purpose and effect of both kinds of restitution is the same: the reversal of the defendant's enrichment.

The definition of 'restitution' adopted above is controversial. The orthodox definition is that restitution refers to the 'reversal of a transfer of value' from the claimant to the defendant.[28] However, it will be shown that this definition only covers some of the cases that form part of the law of restitution. Value is not the measure of restitution in legal enrichment cases: the value of the right transferred or the obligation released at the time of the defective transaction may be very different from the value of that right or release at some later date, depending on the myriad factors that may influence the value of any given right or obligation. Nonetheless, it is generally accepted that 'proprietary restitution' cases are instances of restitution and this book argues that the restitution of specific rights is part of the law of restitution. Furthermore, this book suggests that the reinstatement of obligations is also part of the law of restitution. As such, definitions of restitution that are restricted to the reversal of transfers of value are inadequate. This book prefers a modified version of Birks's original definition in *An Introduction to the Law of Restitution*, which covers both factual and legal enrichment: 'Restitution

preventative remedies are a response to unjust enrichment, citing exonerative relief, declaratory relief, and insurers' subrogation rights as examples. In ch 5, s IV.A of this book, it is argued that prophylactic subrogation arises to prevent unjust enrichment.

[26] *Cf* Virgo, *The Principles of the Law of Restitution* (2006) (n 9) 4–5.

[27] See ch 3, s III.C.

[28] *Commissioner of State Revenue (Victoria) v Royal Insurance Australia Ltd* (1994) 182 CLR 51 (HCA) 75; *Westdeutsche Landesbank Girozentrale v Islington LBC* [1996] AC 669 (HL) 681 (Lord Goff); *Roxborough v Rothmans of Pall Mall Australia Ltd* [2001] HCA 68, (2001) 208 CLR 516 [20]–[26] (Gleeson CJ, Gaudron and Hayne JJ); L Smith, 'Restitution: The Heart of Corrective Justice' (2001) 79 *Texas Law Review* 2115, 2142; Edelman, *Gain-Based Damages* (2002) (n 11) 66; E Weinrib, 'The Normative Structure of Unjust Enrichment' in C Rickett and R Grantham (eds), *Structure and Justification in Private Law* (Oxford, Hart, 2008); E Weinrib, 'Correctively Unjust Enrichment' in R Chambers, C Mitchell and J Penner (eds), *Philosophical Foundations of the Law of Unjust Enrichment* (Oxford, Oxford University Press, 2009) 39; E Bant, *The Change of Position Defence* (Oxford, Hart, 2009) 13; Mitchell, Mitchell and Watterson, *Goff & Jones The Law of Unjust Enrichment* (2011) (n 14) §4-01.

is the response which consists in causing one person to give up … *an enrichment received at [the claimant's] expense or its value in money*' (emphasis added).[29]

Restitution must be distinguished from disgorgement.[30] A restitutionary award reverses an enrichment of the defendant obtained at the claimant's expense; a disgorging award, by contrast, extends to all of the defendant's gains causally attributable to the cause of action, whether from the claimant or not.[31] The distinction between factual and legal enrichment helps to avoid confusion of the two gains-based awards. For example, specific restitution of rights is often confused with disgorgement because the claimant may obtain a right that has increased in value by the date of judgment.[32] On the approach articulated in this book, these cases are properly classified as restitutionary: the remedy specifically reverses a legal enrichment, rather than disgorging profits. In chapter seven, it is explained that the unjust enrichment defendant is enriched by the value immediately transferred (subject to proof of choice or incontrovertibility), or the right or release immediately obtained, in the defective transaction (or its traceable substitute). This is a restitutionary response.

In this book, therefore, 'restitution' refers to the reversal of a defendant's enrichment. The purpose and effect of restitution is to reverse benefits conferred in defective transactions, either by reversing value transferred or by reversing the acquisition of a right or release of an obligation in that transaction. This can be achieved by means other than the payment of money, for example by way of resulting trust, rescission, rectification or subrogation. The restitutionary operation of these doctrines is explored in detail in chapter five, where it is explained that restitution extends to those responses where the defendant's acquisition of a right or release from an obligation is reversed in law.

## III. Methodology and Scope

The book seeks to develop a theoretical model for the enrichment inquiry in the modern law of unjust enrichment that is drawn from an analysis of the cases. The approach is explicitly 'bottom-up', rather than 'top-down', attempting to distil the principles of enrichment from the cases and the historical development of the

[29] Birks, *An Introduction to the Law of Restitution* (1989) (n 9) 13.

[30] *Sempra Metals Ltd v IRC* [2007] UKHL 34, [2008] 1 AC 561 [32] (Lord Hope). See Smith, 'The Province of the Law of Restitution (1992) 696; Edelman, *Gain-Based Damages* (2002) (n 11) 65–91; M McInnes, 'The Measure of Restitution' (2002) 52 *University of Toronto Law Journal* 163, 185; J Edelman, 'Gain-Based Damages: Development and Reflections' in A Burrows and A Rodger (eds), *Mapping the Law: Essays in Memory of Peter Birks* (Oxford, Oxford University Press, 2006) *cf* Birks, 'Equity in the Modern Common Law: An Exercise in Taxonomy' (1996) (n 6) 28; Virgo, *The Principles of the Law of Restitution* (2006) (n 9) 5–6.

[31] Eg *Reading v Attorney General* [1951] AC 507 (HL); *Boardman v Phipps* [1967] 2 AC 46 (HL).

[32] See R Chambers, 'Resulting Trusts' in A Burrows and A Rodger (eds), *Mapping the Law: Essays in Memory of Peter Birks* (Oxford, Oxford University Press, 2006) 250–51.

law. It is shown that the various common counts in *indebitatus assumpsit* from which the modern law of unjust enrichment emerged did not bequeath causes of action, but rather a response to causes of action. Where the basis of the award was unjust enrichment, the common counts did no more than categorise restitutionary awards by the nature of the defendant's enrichment, that is money, services, goods or the release of obligations. As these awards were historically similar in origin and purpose and responded to the same grounds for liability, their artificial segregation yielded to the recognition of unjust enrichment as the organising principle in English law. Furthermore, both at law and in equity, transactions were reversed on similar grounds by rescission and, in equity, by way of resulting trusts, rectification and subrogation. Although these responses have not traditionally been conceptualised as restitution for unjust enrichment, this book contends that, following the abolition of the forms of action and the fusion of the administration of law and equity, similar responses to identical grounds for restitution should be understood together.

Chapters two and three of the book set out a theoretical framework for the enrichment inquiry, while chapters four, five, six and seven set out the doctrine and application of the enrichment model in the cases. Although the theory of enrichment is outlined before the analysis of the cases, this is for the purposes of exposition only. It will be clear that the theoretical model is developed from an analysis of the cases and the historical development of the law of unjust enrichment. This book does not attempt a full examination of the individual causes of action in unjust enrichment or the law of resulting trusts, rescission, rectification and subrogation, each of which is another book in itself; rather, the aim is to show that each of these doctrines may reverse unjust enrichment. The focus of the analysis is on identifying the enrichment in each case and understanding the operation of the enrichment inquiry across the law of unjust enrichment.

It is helpful to define the scope of the analysis by noting a number of limitations on this book at the outset. First, it does not provide an extended analysis of enrichment in restitution for wrongs cases. Although it is suggested in chapter eight that the enrichment model proposed here can generally be extrapolated to wrongs cases, restitution for wrongs cases are otherwise considered in this book only to the extent that they shed light on unjust enrichment. Second, the discussion in this book is limited to bilateral two-party scenarios involving the claimant and an immediate enrichee from the claimant. The implications of bifurcating the enrichment inquiry for the 'at the expense of' requirement in more complex situations are outlined in chapter eight. Third, this book is not concerned with identifying when specific restitution of a legal enrichment will be granted, only establishing that the characterisation of the enrichment is different in these cases. The availability of specific restitution for unjust enrichment is evidently more constrained than monetary restitution, but this book does not seek to determine when a claimant will be prevented from seeking specific restitution. As such, questions of when the involvement of third parties, particularly in circumstances of insolvency, will preclude specific restitution of a legal enrichment are not considered in this work. Nevertheless, it is suggested in chapter eight that the bifurcated enrichment model advanced here is key to resolving the question of when specific restitution is available.

## IV. Structure of the Book

The first part of the book, comprising chapters two and three, is predominantly theoretical. Chapter two sets out the conceptual building blocks of the enrichment inquiry: value, rights and obligations. These concepts form the basis of the distinction between factual and legal enrichment developed in the rest of the book. It is shown that value in the law is an objectively ascertained, relational concept, which can, and should, be distinguished from idiosyncratic conceptions of valuation arising from an individual's personal preferences and priorities. Value, understood in this way, is contrasted with rights, powers and obligations, which are juridical constructs that form the basis of legal enrichment. In addition, the chapter examines the concept of wealth, which is a concept often employed in the definition of enrichment in academic writing. It is argued that wealth is an unhelpful and confusing concept that should be eschewed in enrichment analysis. Finally, the chapter outlines the relationship between all of these concepts in the law of unjust enrichment.

Chapter three proposes an alternative theoretical model of enrichment in the law of unjust enrichment. It is a broad outline of the theory presented in this book that a defendant's enrichment can be characterised factually or legally and that different considerations pertain in each case. The chapter outlines the purpose of the enrichment inquiry and the justification for the label 'enrichment', before presenting a theoretical framework for factual and legal enrichment cases. It is shown that factual enrichment cases involve objectively ascertaining the value transferred to the defendant in the defective transaction, while legal enrichment cases involve identifying the legal characterisation of the benefit received.

The remainder of the book adopts a doctrinal approach by reference to the cases, justifying the theoretical model defended in chapter three in the manifold different circumstances in which a defendant could be said to be enriched. Chapter four examines factual enrichment in the cases. The common counts in *indebitatus assumpsit* are assimilated into the law of unjust enrichment under the rubric of enrichment by the receipt of value. It is shown that the factual enrichment model can explain enrichment by the receipt of money (including awards of money had and received), services (quantum meruit), goods (quantum valebat), land and the discharge and release of obligations (including those cases formerly categorised under the money paid count). The award of monetary restitution in these cases is subject to the limitations imposed by the protection of the defendant's freedom of choice, which is examined in chapter six.

Chapter five then applies the enrichment model developed in chapter three to legal enrichment cases. It is argued that a defendant can be enriched by the acquisition of contractual rights, property rights and other rights by their nature capable of assignment, as well as by the release of obligations. Where the claimant seeks specific restitution of a right acquired or an obligation released at the claimant's expense in circumstances that are unjust, the law's response is to award a *power* to obtain restitution. It is shown that this can be achieved through resulting trusts, rescission, rectification or subrogation.

Chapter six recognises that the freedom of choice problems that arise in establishing enrichment are confined to factual enrichment cases where the defendant is required to make restitution in money for a benefit in kind. The chapter rejects the prevailing 'subjective devaluation' orthodoxy in favour of an objective 'choice of benefit' test. It is argued that a defendant will be enriched by the receipt of value where the defendant is either incontrovertibly enriched by the value received or has chosen the benefit in which the value inheres. The requirements for a choice of a benefit to be effective are closely examined and it is contended that the defendant must have a choice to accept or reject the benefit and acceptance of the benefit must constitute an assumption of responsibility to pay for it.

Chapter seven focuses on identifying the point of enrichment, arguing that the moment of enrichment is the relevant point of valuation in all cases. In factual enrichment cases, enrichment is the immediate value transferred in the defective transaction, subject to the limitations imposed by the requirement of choice of the benefit or incontrovertibility. In legal enrichment cases, the defendant is enriched by the right created or obligation released in the defective transaction. The chapter examines and rejects various extant enrichment approaches, concluding that liability in unjust enrichment is normatively limited to the enrichment received in a defective transaction. Enrichment is concerned, therefore, with the value received or right or release obtained in the defective transaction, not what the defendant still holds. While the law of unjust enrichment takes account of what survives in the defendant's hands, this represents the principled distinction between the enrichment inquiry and the defence of change of position. Furthermore, it is argued that the focus on immediate enrichment is mandated by the 'at the expense of' requirement, which connects the two parties to the defective transaction.

Finally, chapter eight summarises the conclusions of the book and examines six key implications for the law of unjust enrichment and restitution. The first implication of the factual and legal enrichment distinction is that it will help clarify when specific restitution of a legal enrichment is available. Although this book does not resolve this vexed question, the distinction between factual and legal enrichment simplifies the problem and suggests the beginnings of an answer to when specific restitution should be available. Second, the factual and legal enrichment distinction raises the question of when monetary and specific restitution claims can be combined. The chapter suggests that the proper principle is that both types of claim may be combined, except where it would involve double recovery. Third, this chapter examines whether or not the factual and legal enrichment distinction is replicated in the 'at the expense of' requirement. It is concluded that it is not, but that the proper identification of enrichment clarifies the question of what must be at the expense of the claimant. The fourth implication of the analysis in this book is that it exposes difficulties with Birks's 'absence of basis' approach in legal enrichment cases, particularly rescission. Fifth, it is shown that the immediate enrichment thesis clarifies the operation of the most important defence to unjust enrichment claims, change of position. Finally, it is suggested that the same factual and legal enrichment distinction applies in the law of restitution for wrongs, subject to possible limitations on the appeal to freedom of choice.

# 2

# Value, Rights and Obligations

This book suggests that a claimant's enrichment may be conceptualised in two different ways: (i) as the receipt of value; or (ii) as the acquisition of a right or release of an obligation. The central concepts in defining enrichment are therefore value, rights and obligations. In the cases and literature on enrichment, there are three competing approaches to these concepts: 'the value approach',[1] which focuses on the abstract receipt of value by the defendant; 'the rights approach',[2] which focuses on the acquisition of a right by the defendant; and 'the wealth approach',[3] which elides the concepts of value and rights in the umbrella concept of 'wealth'. Problematically, the concepts are often used in tandem or interchangeably, which confuses the analysis of enrichment in unjust enrichment.

It is helpful to set out in detail what is meant by the various labels and the relationship between these concepts, which is the task attempted in this chapter. Section I considers the meaning of value in the law of unjust enrichment in order to give content to notions such as 'benefit', 'wealth' and 'gain' that are employed, usually without any precise definition or content, to describe the receipt of value by the defendant. Section II then explores the concepts of rights and obligations in the context of enrichment, applying a Hohfeldian approach and setting out the relationship between personal rights, property rights and equitable property rights. Section III considers and rejects the usefulness of the concept of wealth, while section IV examines the relationship between these concepts in the law of unjust enrichment.

## I. The Concept of Value

Value is one of the two pillars of the enrichment inquiry. The most common response to a cause of action in unjust enrichment is monetary restitution: reversal of the 'value' received by the defendant. Unfortunately, value is a concept little

[1] See, eg L Smith, 'Restitution: The Heart of Corrective Justice' (2001) 79 *Texas Law Review* 2115, 2142; E Weinrib, 'The Normative Structure of Unjust Enrichment' in C Rickett and R Grantham (eds), *Structure and Justification in Private Law* (Oxford, Hart, 2008); E Weinrib, 'Correctively Unjust Enrichment' in R Chambers, C Mitchell and J Penner (eds), *Philosophical Foundations of the Law of Unjust Enrichment* (Oxford, Oxford University Press, 2009) 39.

[2] See, eg W Swadling, 'Rescission, Property and the Common Law' (2005) 121 *LQR* 123.

[3] See, eg P Birks, *Unjust Enrichment*, 2nd edn (Oxford, Clarendon Press, 2005).

explained in the literature on unjust enrichment,[4] which is a grave lacuna in an area where recovery usually turns upon, and is measured by, the receipt of value. This section attempts to remedy this gap in the literature by elucidating the concept of value in the law of unjust enrichment through economic and philosophical theories of value. While it is impossible to do justice to value theory within the confines of this work, it is shown that restitution of value in unjust enrichment can be better understood in light of the existing economic and philosophical literature.

## A. Monetary and Non-Monetary Value

Value is not necessarily a monetary concept. We understand things as having, for example, sentimental value, academic value, cultural value or emotional value. However, the law does not allow claims for sentimental, academic, cultural or emotional value.[5] The law of unjust enrichment is only concerned with these alternative concepts of value to the extent that non-monetary value affects, and is quantifiable as, monetary value. For instance, *Brenner v First Artists' Management Pty Ltd*[6] concerned claims for restitution by the managers of the singer, Daryl Braithwaite, for services conferred in a campaign to revive his career. One of the benefits he received was the encouragement and support of his managers,[7] but this emotional benefit was only relevant to the extent that it could be quantified in money. As McLachlin J held in *Peter v Beblow*, the law 'has consistently taken a straightforward economic approach'[8] to the concept of value. The Supreme Court of Canada made the same point in *(Peel) Regional Municipality v Canada*, concluding that 'without a benefit … which can be restored to the donor in specie or by money, no recovery lies for unjust enrichment'.[9] The right to restitution of value is the right to restitution of money's worth and the claim is restricted to value quantifiable in money terms. The discussion of the concept of value in this chapter is thus restricted to the concept of monetary value.

[4] With notable exceptions, such as R Chambers, 'Two Kinds of Enrichment' in R Chambers, C Mitchell and J Penner (eds), *Philosophical Foundations of the Law of Unjust Enrichment* (Oxford, Oxford University Press, 2009) and Weinrib, 'The Normative Structure of Unjust Enrichment' (2008) (n 1).

[5] See *Single v Macharski Estate* [1996] 3 WWR 23 (MBCA) [24]–[27] (Helper JA); *Barnaby v Petersen Estate* (1996) 15 ETR (2d) 138 (BCSC) [63]–[81] (Taylor J); *Stanhope v Stanhope* (1998) 166 Sask R 293 (Sask QB) [44]–[55] (Zarzeczny J); C Mitchell, P Mitchell and S Watterson, *Goff & Jones The Law of Unjust Enrichment*, 8th edn (London, Sweet & Maxwell, 2011) §4-03.

[6] *Brenner v First Artists' Management Pty Ltd* [1993] 2 VR 221 (VSC).

[7] Ibid 265. This example is used in Mitchell, Mitchell and Watterson, *Goff & Jones The Law of Unjust Enrichment* (2011) (n 5) §4-03.

[8] *Peter v Beblow* [1993] 1 SCR 980 (SCC) 990 (McLachlin J). See also *Garland v Consumers' Gas Co* [2004] SCC 25, [2004] 1 SCR 629 (SCC) [31]; *Pacific National Investments Ltd v City of Victoria* [2004] SCC 75, [2004] 3 SCR 545 (SCC) [15].

[9] *Peel (Regional Municipality) v Canada* [1992] 3 SCR 762 (SCC).

## B. Idiosyncratic and Relational Value

The cases and commentary on enrichment often elide two competing conceptions of value. The first conception of value, here called 'idiosyncratic value', postulates that value is simply the 'subjective and particular valuation a given individual places on an object in light of his or her actual particular needs, interests and purposes'.[10] The second concept, here called 'relational value', is the concept by which particular things are 'reducible to some single dimension or substance—to one and the same thing—notwithstanding their diversity'.[11] That single dimension is 'value': the concept by which we are able to say that an amount of *x* is 'worth' the same as another amount of *y*, irrespective of the particularities of *x* and *y*. Money, it will be shown, is the typical measure of relational value. It is argued that the relational concept of value underpins the enrichment inquiry in the law of unjust enrichment.

### *(i) Idiosyncratic Value*

On the idiosyncratic value approach, 'value' does not abstract either from the particular right or benefit or the particular individual in question; rather, it is inherently bound up in that individual's idiosyncratic measure of what a particular right or benefit is worth to them. To quote a memorable passage from Birks' *Unjust Enrichment*:[12]

> We all have our likes and dislikes, and we match our available resources to our own sense of priorities. The market price is thus often very different from the price at which you or I would buy. There are many marketable things that we would not buy at all, not at any price. There are canine beauty parlours at which the price of a dog's haircut can run to more than £100. There is a market for that service. Some people hate the very idea. They prefer their poodles shaggy. Asked to pay for an unrequested perm, they would counterclaim for damage.

While £100 may be the market value for a dog's haircut at a canine beauty parlour, the 'price at which you or I would buy' is our idiosyncratic valuation of that service. Idiosyncratic values are not relational, as that concept will be described below. A comparison between two idiosyncratic valuations is not a comparison between two things of value, but a comparison between the qualities I value and the qualities you value. The comparison is really between your values and mine. This is why the idiosyncratic values you or I attach to the same thing, such as a haircut for a poodle, will usually differ.

Of course, we have the right subjectively to value things differently from other people or the market; this follows from our freedom of choice. However,

[10] P Benson, 'The Unity of Contract Law' in P Benson (ed), *The Theory of Contract Law: New Essays* (Cambridge, Cambridge University Press, 2001) 195. See, eg C Langdell, *Summary of the Law of Contracts*, 2nd edn (Boston, Little, Brown & Co, 1880) 70–71.

[11] Benson, 'The Unity of Contract Law' (2001) (n 10) 188.

[12] Birks, *Unjust Enrichment* (2005) (n 3) 53.

while it may be a manifestation of freedom of choice, the law is not interested in idiosyncratic valuations.[13] As Birks went on to say, the law 'does not pretend to attempt the impossible task of finding out at which price the particular recipient of an unrequested benefit would have bought it'.[14] A commitment to the 'idiosyncratic value' approach would necessarily involve an inquiry into the unexpressed state of mind of the defendant which, as we shall see, is never relevant to a claim in unjust enrichment.

The importance of identifying the idiosyncratic value approach is to avoid it. No major theory of enrichment or subjective devaluation depends upon a strong commitment to the idiosyncratic value approach. However, many leading theories, including those of Birks, Burrows and Virgo, highlight the role of 'subjectivity' of value and 'subjective' devaluation in the enrichment inquiry and, on occasion, the language of subjectivity elides a concern to protect the defendant's freedom of choice with idiosyncratic valuation. This is addressed in detail in chapter six.[15] For the purposes of this chapter, it is enough to identify the concept of idiosyncratic value to distinguish it from relational value, but the pitfalls of the idiosyncratic value approach will become apparent in the analysis of 'subjective devaluation' in this book.

### *(ii) Relational Value*

The law of unjust enrichment adopts a relational conception of value. Value, so understood, is an abstract standard for the comparison and exchange of qualitatively heterogeneous things in quantitatively comparable and equivalent terms.[16] This idea of value is explicitly Hegelian, building on the *Elements of the Philosophy of Right*, where Hegel argues that 'In property, the quantitative character which emerges from the qualitative is value'.[17] As Weinrib explains, goods and services have:[18]

> [B]oth a qualitative and a quantitative aspect. The qualitative aspect, the use that a person makes or might want to make of the thing focuses on the particular qualities of the thing in question and on the role of those qualities in satisfying the particular wants and needs of the person using the thing. Thus the qualitative aspect connects the particularity of the thing to the particularity of the person using it. In contrast, the quantitative aspect abstracts from the specific usefulness of the thing to a general conception of usefulness in which things are quantitatively comparable with other things. This quantitative aspect is value.

[13] *Benedetti v Sawiris* [2010] EWCA Civ 1427 [145] (Etherton LJ).

[14] Birks, *Unjust Enrichment* (2005) (n 3) 54.

[15] See ch 6, fns 51–52 and accompanying text.

[16] Weinrib, 'The Normative Structure of Unjust Enrichment' (2008) (n 1) 27; Weinrib, 'Correctively Unjust Enrichment' (2009) (n 1) 34–35.

[17] G Hegel, *Elements of the Philosophy of Right* (Cambridge, Cambridge University Press, 1991) §63. See P Benson, 'Abstract Right and the Possibility of a Nondistributive Concept of Contract: Hegel and Contemporary Contract Theory' (1989) 10 *Cardozo Law Review* 1077, 1187–96.

[18] Weinrib, 'The Normative Structure of Unjust Enrichment' (2008) (n 1) 27.

On this approach, value is necessarily relational and abstract, not idiosyncratic and particular: it is concerned not with what makes a thing 'valuable' to the person who has it, but with its relative value as compared with other things.

The most common relational value is 'market value', which refers to the determination of value under competitive conditions through the medium of exchange. Anything that can be exchanged in a market can be reduced to a value and thereby related to anything else that can be exchanged in a market, divorced from the particular needs of individual participants and the particular uses of that which is exchanged. Value 'reflects the possibility of equalizing all things of value with one another, and equating any given thing of value with all other things of value'.[19] While the exchange value in a given market is a function of numerous idiosyncratic valuations, the aggregation of those innumerable individual value judgments abstracts from any one individual's subjective preferences or values.[20] As Benson explains, a competitive market price:[21]

> [M]ay result from and be realized in innumerable particular transactions, [but] it cannot be affected by any one of these transactions or by the particular needs, purposes, and interests of those who transact. All must take as given the same identical price, irrespective of their differences and particularities.

The market price therefore abstracts from the qualitative reasons underpinning the subjective judgments of any individual market participant to a quantitatively heterogeneous and comparable value for exchange. Consequently, although market value derives from subjective value judgments, it is not 'subjective' in the idiosyncratic sense.

Value is thus relational whenever it is abstracted from the particular thing of value and the particular individual who values it. The corollary of this point is that a wide range of relational values are possible depending on how one abstracts from the particular to the general in order to compare different things. Any abstract value by which two different things can be compared in heterogeneous terms is relational in the Hegelian sense. For example, while Weinrib's discussion of relational value focuses on the value which can be obtained in a market,[22] a 'relational' value is not necessarily market value. Exchange value is simply one relational measure of the monetary value of a thing.[23] It is perfectly possible to place a relative value on something for which there is no market. For example, the value of a non-transferable asset, such as an unassignable lease, may be measured by the present future value of the income that will be generated from its

[19] Weinrib, 'Correctively Unjust Enrichment' (2009) (n 1) 36.

[20] In relation to uncompetitive markets, see ch 3, fns 90–92 and accompanying text.

[21] Benson, 'The Unity of Contract Law' (2001) (n 10) 189–90.

[22] See criticism in R Chambers, C Mitchell and J Penner, *Philosophical Foundations of the Law of Unjust Enrichment* (Oxford, Oxford University Press, 2009) 4–5.

[23] J Beatson, *The Use and Abuse of Unjust Enrichment* (Oxford, Clarendon Press, 1991) 30–31; Chambers, 'Two Kinds of Enrichment' (2009) (n 4) 244; Mitchell, Mitchell and Watterson, *Goff & Jones The Law of Unjust Enrichment* (2011) (n 5) §4–04.

use.[24] Alternatively, a thing may be valued by the capital value of its component parts.[25] The difference between these valuation approaches can be demonstrated by the valuation of share capital, which can be measured by its exchange value, the present value of its future dividend income or the capital value of the asset share on dissolution of the company.[26] The important point for our purposes is that all these measures of value are relational rather than idiosyncratic: they allow a quantitative comparison between the value of a share in company *x* and a share in company *y*, irrespective of the shareholder.

The distinction between idiosyncratic and relational value is not always easy to draw. This point is illustrated by *Sempra Metals v IRC*.[27] The claimant's case turned on establishing that the IRC was enriched by the use value of the advanced corporate tax payments it received. However, the House of Lords did not require the Revenue to make restitution at commercial rates of interest because it had instead discharged public sector borrowing at government rates. On one interpretation,[28] the House of Lords held that the 'value' received by the Revenue was not the market value of the borrowing, but rather its *value to the Revenue*. In his speech, Lord Nicholls pointed out that 'A benefit is not always worth its market value to a particular defendant'.[29]

The better view is that *Sempra* is not a rejection of relational value in favour of idiosyncratic value. Both the ordinary commercial rate and the public sector borrowing rate are relational values, not idiosyncratic values. No attempt was made to find out what value the Revenue itself attached to the borrowing. For example, it was irrelevant whether the Government needed to borrow funds at the time and the rate which it would have been willing to pay for marginal borrowing. Instead, the House of Lords applied the current market rate for discharging Government borrowing, which was the rate the market charged for public sector borrowing rather than the value the IRC placed on the borrowing in question. Values arrived at by markets, whether they be primitive or complex, perfect or imperfect, are relational because they abstract from the particular individual and the particular thing being valued to arrive at a relative price. *Sempra* simply turns on how that abstraction is to be done in a particular case.

Accordingly, the concept of value in this book is relational in the Hegelian sense and idiosyncratic valuation is rejected in chapter six.[30] For present purposes, two important points follow from the relational conception. First, value is an abstract

[24] Chambers, 'Two Kinds of Enrichment' (2009) (n 4) 244.

[25] Ibid 244.

[26] *Guinness Peat Group plc v British Land Co plc* [1998] EWCA Civ 1956, [1999] BCC 536 as discussed in Chambers, 'Two Kinds of Enrichment' (2009) (n 4) 244.

[27] *Sempra Metals Ltd v IRC* [2007] UKHL 34, [2008] 1 AC 561.

[28] The decision may also be explicable as an application of the change of position defence, see ibid [119] (Lord Nicholls). See also [233] (Lord Mance) and the discussion of change of position in the text accompanying ch 8, fns 20–21.

[29] Ibid [119] (Lord Nicholls).

[30] See ch 6, section I.

standard for the comparison and exchange of qualitatively heterogeneous things in quantitatively comparable terms, not a measure of the utility of a particular thing to a particular individual. Second, the relational conception of value encompasses any of a number of different abstract standards for the comparison or exchange of things of value, not simply market value.

### *(iii) Relational Value and Money*

The concept of relational value is fundamental to the concept of 'money'.[31] Money has the unique characteristic of being a universal medium of exchange and therefore functions as the standard numerical measure of relative value. In other words, the way in which we usually say how much a given quantity of *x* is worth in terms of a given quantity of *y* is by saying, for example, that *x* is worth £10 while *y* is worth £50. In this way, money abstracts from the particularities of the thing and the person purchasing the thing to a numerical system for the measurement of the relative value of things. Moreover, money is more than simply the measure of value: it is also a store of value. Money has the property of intrinsic and incontrovertible value: anyone who values anything that can be purchased with money must value money. Therefore, money is both a measure of value and a store of value, but it is not synonymous with value.

However, it is important not to conflate the concepts of money and relational value. Money is a measure of value, not the conceptual equivalent of value. As outlined above, there is a wide range of relational values depending on how one abstracts from the specific individual and commodity to the general comparison between things of value. It is perfectly possible to conceive of relational values that eschew the concept of money altogether and compare a given amount of *x* with a given amount of *y* without adopting an external standard of measurement. To take one example, in a game of marbles, it may be accepted by the participants that one black marble is worth three white marbles and seven gold marbles, although some individual participants may idiosyncratically value white marbles more highly than black marbles. The values in the game are relational, although money plays no part.

## C. Transfers of Value

### *(i) The Meaning of 'Transfer'*

The law of unjust enrichment is sometimes said to concern the reversal of 'transfers of value'.[32] However, the use of the term 'transfer' often conceals that which

[31] For a detailed discussion of the nature and function of money in the law see C Proctor, *Mann on the Legal Aspect of Money*, 6th edn (Oxford, Oxford University Press, 2005); D Fox, *Property Rights in Money* (Oxford, Oxford University Press, 2008).

[32] See ch 1, fn 28 and accompanying text.

is transferred. Hohfeld identified this ambiguity in 'Some Fundamental Legal Conceptions':[33]

> If X says that he has transferred his watch to Y, he may conceivably mean, quite literally, that he has physically handed over the watch to Y; or, more likely, that he has 'transferred' his legal interest, without any delivery of possession—the latter, of course, being a relatively figurative use of the term.

So, Hohfeld explains, the 'transfer' of the watch from X to Y may refer either to the delivery of the watch itself or the acquisition of X's right to the watch by Y. In addition to the first two ways of understanding the transfer of the watch, the notion of a 'transfer of value' introduces a third way of understanding the 'transfer' between X and Y. It asks us to reduce the right to the watch and the consideration for the watch (if any) to the same quantitative dimension and to consider the movement of value between X and Y by reason of either the delivery of the watch to Y or the acquisition of the right to the watch by Y. To the extent that unjust enrichment is concerned with reversing transfers of value (and it is not always), it is this third way of understanding the transfer that is relevant. By abstracting from the particular individuals and the particular good being transferred, the transfer between X and Y can be understood relationally as the movement of value between the parties. This is simply an abstract way of conceptualising the same transfer.

It is important to understand that the notion of a 'transfer of value' is not meant to imply that value is itself a thing;[34] value is a quality of things and it is a nonsense to talk of a transfer of value in the absence of a benefit that possesses value, such as money, rights, release from an obligation, the performance of a service or valuable forbearance. In other words, a transfer of value is an abstract way of conceptualising the conferral of a benefit. In the case of the watch, it is the right to the watch or the use of the watch that has a value but we can analyse the purchase of a watch at a higher level of abstraction as the exchange of one thing of value (money) for another thing of value (the right to the watch). The same is true where a transaction concerns the provision of a service: the performance of the service has a value and the receipt of that service can be conceptualised as transferring value.

However, it is also critical to understand what 'transfer' does not mean. First, the idea of 'transfer' or 'transaction' employed in this book is not intended to suggest an intended or conscious action by the participants. The terms are used in a technical sense to describe the receipt of value by the defendant through the conferral of a benefit by the claimant. So the terms 'transfer' and 'transaction' include unconscious transfers of value in circumstances where there is an absence of consent and unintended transfers of value in circumstances where consent is vitiated, as well as circumstances where the transfer of value is intended. Second, the notion of 'transfer' is not meant to imply a corresponding loss of value from

[33] W Hohfeld, 'Some Fundamental Legal Conceptions as Applied in Judicial Reasoning' (1913) 23 *Yale Law Journal* 16, 24.

[34] See Hegel, *Elements of the Philosophy of Right* (1991) (n 17) §77; Weinrib, 'Correctively Unjust Enrichment' (2009) (n 1) 33.

the claimant, which is arguably a requirement of the 'at the expense of' inquiry.[35] As we shall see, the enrichment is the value *received by the defendant* at the claimant's expense, not the value given up by the claimant, which may often differ.[36]

### *(ii) Net Transfers of Value and* Saldotheorie

If we accept the relational conception of value, then all transactions between persons can be reduced to quantitatively comparable movements of value between the parties and these can be netted. In other words, we can describe a transaction by the relative gain or loss to each party. When I exchange a thing of value for something else of equal value, no net value is transferred: I have a different thing of the same value. Logically, the same analysis must be possible when the 'thing' transferred is the performance of a service. If I exchange something of value for the performance of a service of equal value, then the transaction involves no net transfer of value.

However, Benson[37] and Weinrib[38] misleadingly characterise a transaction at market price as a transaction involving *no transfer of value*. As Weinrib puts it, 'Only to the extent that the transfer is gratuitous ... does the transfer of a thing of value involve a transfer of value as well'.[39] This is not correct. An exchange of equivalent values does involve a transfer of value: it involves two equal and opposite transfers of value. What Benson and Weinrib mean to say is that there is no *net* transfer of value in such a transaction. Therefore, a competitive market price is that measure of value at which a transaction will involve *no net transfer of value*, that is the price at which there will be an exchange of equivalent values. As markets are seldom perfect or stable, most exchanges will involve at least a negligible net transfer of value as the price paid will usually only approximate the exchange of equivalent values. Nonetheless, 'market value' or a range of market values is a convenient economic and juridical proxy for a value-neutral transfer.

The possibility of netting transfers of value in this way raises an important question as to whether the law of unjust enrichment responds to transfers of value or net transfers of value. For example, does each party to a defective transaction in which there is performance on both sides have an independent claim for unjust enrichment against the other or is there one claim for the difference? The '*Saldotheorie*', which arguably represents the position in German law,[40] nets the value transferred by the claimant against the value received. Thus, a transfer of

[35] See generally, Birks, *Unjust Enrichment* (2005) (n 3) 78–82; G Virgo, *The Principles of the Law of Restitution*, 2nd edn (Oxford, Oxford University Press, 2006) 112–15; A Burrows, *The Law of Restitution*, 3rd edn (Oxford, Oxford University Press, 2010) 64–65.

[36] J Edelman, 'The Meaning of Loss and Enrichment' in R Chambers, C Mitchell and J Penner (eds), *Philosophical Foundations of the Law of Unjust Enrichment* (Oxford, Oxford University Press, 2009).

[37] Benson, 'The Unity of Contract Law' (2001) (n 10) 189.

[38] Weinrib, 'Correctively Unjust Enrichment' (2009) (n 1) 36.

[39] Weinrib, 'The Normative Structure of Unjust Enrichment' (2008) (n 1) 28.

[40] See J Dawson, 'Erasable Enrichment in German Law' (1981) 61 *Boston University Law Review* 217, 295; T Krebs, *Restitution at the Crossroads: A Comparative Study* (London, Cavendish, 2001) 101–104; R Zimmerman and J Du Plessis, 'Basic Features of the German Law of Unjustified Enrichment' [1994] *RLR* 14, 38–42.

value occurs when a transaction involves a net gain or loss of value, that is 'when one transfers a thing of value without the reciprocal receipt of a thing of equivalent value'.[41] If this position were adopted in English law, the focus in factual enrichment cases would be on identifying the receipt of value by the defendant in circumstances where reciprocal value has not been given back to the claimant. This is identical to the approach recently taken by Weinrib in a series of articles explaining unjust enrichment as an instance of corrective justice.[42]

However, this is not the English law of unjust enrichment.[43] Although the net value approach was arguably adopted by Hobhouse J at first instance in *Kleinwort Benson v Sandwell BC*,[44] the better view is that English law is concerned with an independent transfer of value 'at the expense of the claimant', subject to an independent claim for counter-restitution. First, as will be detailed in chapter seven, a claim in unjust enrichment arises immediately at the point of receipt; it is not a claim to the extant or surviving enrichment in the defendant's hands. English law's immediate enrichment approach is inconsistent with restricting the claim to the net enrichment still surviving, which is the approach embodied in para 818(3) of the Bürgeriches Gesetzbuch (Civil Code) (BGB) in German law.[45] Second, the English law of rescission is inconsistent with *Saldotheorie*. As will be explained in relation to the requirement of *restitutio in integrum* in rescission cases in chapter five,[46] rescission is best understood as a power to obtain restitution subject to a requirement of counter-restitution, rather than a single claim for the difference. Finally, following from the theoretical discussion of transfers of value above, it is incorrect to say there is no transfer of value in transactions at market value: there is a transfer of value from the claimant to the defendant, which, if defective, can be reversed, and there is an equal and opposite transfer of value from the defendant to the claimant. There is no theoretical or practical justification for reducing two independent transfers of value to the net difference between them if the receipt of value is an enrichment that may be unjust. As will be demonstrated in chapters four and five of this book, the approach in English law recognises the two separate transfers of value and rejects *Saldotheorie* in favour of independent claims for restitution and counter-restitution.

[41] Weinrib, 'Correctively Unjust Enrichment' (2009) (n 1) 37.

[42] See Weinrib, 'The Normative Structure of Unjust Enrichment' (2008) (n 1); Weinrib, 'Correctively Unjust Enrichment' (2009) (n 1).

[43] See E Bant, *The Change of Position Defence* (Oxford, Hart, 2009) 281; Burrows, *The Law of Restitution* (2010) (n 35) 570–71 *cf* Birks, *Unjust Enrichment* (2005) (n 3) 225–29.

[44] *Kleinwort Benson Ltd v Sandwell BC* [1994] 4 All ER 890 (QB) 941 (Hobhouse J) *cf* Bant, *The Change of Position Defence* (2009) (n 43) 96–102.

[45] Zimmerman and Du Plessis, '*Basic Features of the German Law of Unjustified Enrichment* (1994) 38–39; P Birks, 'Change of Position and Surviving Enrichment' in W Swadling (ed), *The Limits of Restitutionary Claims: A Comparative Analysis* (Glasgow, The United Kingdom Committee of Comparative Law, 1997) 58–59; Krebs, *Restitution at the Crossroads: A Comparative Study* (2001) (n 40) 280.

[46] See ch 5, fns 88–104 and accompanying text.

# II. The Concepts of Rights and Obligations

This book suggests that restitution of value is only one part of the law of unjust enrichment. In chapters three and five, it will be shown that many cases of restitution involve the restitution of rights, rather than value, and it is contended that, in these cases, the relevant enrichment may also be characterised as the right itself rather than its value. Another group of cases involve release from an obligation. In these cases, the defendant's benefit may also be characterised legally (as the release of an obligation) or factually (by the value received by the defendant). This section provides a theoretical framework for analysing the 'rights' and 'obligations' that underpin a legal conception of enrichment, as well as the 'right' a claimant obtains to restitution. In addition, it outlines a number of key concepts in understanding legal enrichment by rights and specific restitution: personal rights, property rights, assignable rights and persistent powers.

## A. Rights and Powers, Duties and Liabilities

In his influential essay, 'Some Fundamental Legal Conceptions as Applied in Judicial Reasoning',[47] Hohfeld outlined four meanings of 'right': a claim-right; a liberty (or privilege);[48] a power; and, an immunity.[49] For this book, the distinction between claim-rights and powers is the most important.[50] In addition, there are two important meanings of 'obligation' that emerge from Hohfeld's categorisation of rights: duties and liabilities. This book employs the Hohfeldian terminology whenever it is important to distinguish between the different meanings. However, throughout the book, 'obligation' is used to refer generically to both duties and liabilities and 'right' is also used as an umbrella term for rights and powers when this meaning appears from the context.

### *(i) Claim-Rights and Duties*

A is said to have a 'claim-right' against B only where B has a correlative duty to A to do, or refrain from doing, a particular act.[51] As such, claim-rights correlate with duties on a Hohfeldian approach. For example, where A transfers title to a watch to B by mistake, B obtains a 'claim-right' to the watch. In addition, A's right to restitution of the value of the watch is a 'claim-right' and B has a correlative 'duty' to pay the value to A. It will be seen in chapter three that claim-rights constitute benefits capable

[47] Hohfeld, 'Some Fundamental Legal Conceptions as Applied in Judicial Reasoning' (1913) (n 33).

[48] A will have a 'liberty' to act or refrain from acting when B has no claim-right to prevent A so acting: ibid 32–33.

[49] A will have an 'immunity' as against B where A is free from the exercise of a power by B: ibid 55.

[50] See B McFarlane and R Stevens, 'The Nature of Equitable Property' (2010) 4 *Journal of Equity* 1, 12–13.

[51] Hohfeld, 'Some Fundamental Legal Conceptions as Applied in Judicial Reasoning' (1913) (n 33) 31–32; *Howley Park Coal v L & N W Ry* [1913] AC 11 (HL) 25 (Viscount Haldane) 27 (Lord Shaw).

of enriching a defendant either factually or legally, and that the response to a factual enrichment claim is always a claim-right to restitution of value. In addition, the release of a duty is a benefit capable of enriching a defendant factually or legally.[52]

### *(ii) Powers and Liabilities*

A will have a 'power' against B where A has the ability to effect 'a change in a given legal relation' binding on B.[53] B will come under a corresponding 'liability' to A, as A has the power to change B's legal relations. For instance, A will have a power where B has fraudulently misrepresented the quality of a motor vehicle and A has the option to rescind the contract and revest title.[54] Until A exercises the power, B retains title to the car and the obligations contained in the contract remain valid, but B is under a liability. At common law, A's decision to rescind changes the legal relationship between A and B by revesting title to the car in A. As with claim-rights and duties, the acquisition of a power and the release of a liability are both benefits capable of enriching a defendant factually or legally.

## B. Rights, Powers and Property

The relationship between unjust enrichment and property is fraught with controversy,[55] but much of the debate suffers from terminological confusion and conceptual ambiguity about the meaning of 'property'. As this book suggests a

[52] While the release of a duty is *capable* of being characterised as a legal enrichment, we will see in ch 3 that, in practice, specific restitution of obligations is limited to reinstatement of liabilities, not duties: ch 3, s III.B.

[53] Hohfeld, 'Some Fundamental Legal Conceptions as Applied in Judicial Reasoning' (1913) (n 33) 44.

[54] Eg *Car & Universal Finance Co Ltd v Caldwell* [1963] 1 QB 525 (CA).

[55] See, eg P Birks, 'Restitution and Resulting Trusts' in S Goldstein (ed), *Equity and Contemporary Legal Developments* (Jerusalem, Harry and Michael Sacher Institute for Legislative Research and Comparative Law, 1992); P Birks, 'Trusts Raised to Reverse Unjust Enrichments: The *Westdeutsche* Case' [1996] *RLR* 3; R Grantham and C Rickett, 'Restitution, Property and Ignorance—A Reply to Mr Swadling' [1996] *LMCLQ* 463; W Swadling, 'A Claim in Restitution?' [1996] *LMCLQ* 63; W Swadling, 'A New Role for Resulting Trusts' (1996) 16 *LS* 110; P Birks, 'Property and Unjust Enrichment: Categorical Truths' [1997] *New Zealand Law Review* 623; R Grantham and C Rickett, 'Restitution, Property and Mistaken Payments' [1997] *RLR* 83; R Grantham and C Rickett, 'Property and Unjust Enrichment: Categorical Truths or Unnecessary Complexity?' [1997] *New Zealand Universities Law Review* 668; W Swadling, 'Property and Unjust Enrichment' in J Harris (ed), *Property Problems: From Genes to Pension Funds* (London, Kluwer Law International, 1997); P Millett, 'Restitution and Constructive Trusts' (1998) 114 *LQR* 399; L Smith, 'Unjust Enrichment, Property and the Structure of Trusts' (2000) 116 *LQR* 412; W Swadling, 'Property: General Principles' in P Birks (ed), *English Private Law*, 1st edn (Oxford, Oxford University Press, 2000); P Birks, 'Property, Unjust Enrichment and Tracing' (2001) 54 *CLP* 231; A Burrows, 'Proprietary Restitution: Unmasking Unjust Enrichment' (2001) 117 *LQR* 412; R Grantham and C Rickett, 'Property Rights as a Legally Significant Event' (2003) 62 *CLJ* 717; C Rotherham, 'Tracing Misconceptions in *Foskett v McKeown*' [2003] *RLR* 57; L Smith, 'Unravelling Proprietary Restitution' [2004] *Canadian Business Law Journal* 317; P Millett, 'Proprietary Restitution' in S Degeling and J Edelman (eds), *Equity in Commercial Law* (Sydney, Thomson LBC, 2005); Swadling, 'Rescission, Property and the Common Law' (2005) (n 2); L Smith, 'Philosophical Foundations of Proprietary Remedies' in R Chambers, C Mitchell and J Penner (eds), *Philosophical Foundations of the Law of Unjust Enrichment* (Oxford, Oxford University Press, 2009); McFarlane and Stevens, 'The Nature of Equitable Property' (2010) (n 50).

novel understanding of the relationship between unjust enrichment and specific restitution, it is helpful to define the key concepts in characterising rights and powers as an enrichment and as a response to unjust enrichment. This section considers and defines four common categories of right for the analysis that follows: personal rights, property rights, assignable rights and proprietary powers.

### *(i) Personal Rights*

Personal rights are claim-rights against persons with correlative duties to act that do not persist against third parties.[56] Personal rights can both constitute an enrichment and be the response to a claim in unjust enrichment. Where A transfers £1 million into B's bank account with X Bank, B obtains a claim-right to payment of £1 million by X Bank.[57] The right B obtains against X Bank is a 'personal right': B cannot assert the right to payment of the £1 million in his bank account with X Bank against anyone other than X Bank; B cannot assert this right against A and, if X Bank becomes insolvent, B will have to share with the other creditors of the bank. The right will not persist against a third party to whom X Bank transfers the money: B's claim is against X Bank and X Bank alone.

### *(ii) Property Rights*

Property rights are defined in this book as rights in corporeal things exigible against all the world.[58] Unlike personal rights, property rights—as defined here—may only be an enrichment and not a response to a claim in unjust enrichment. If we change the example in the preceding paragraph so that, instead of depositing £1 million in B's bank account, A transfers his car to B and title is effectively transferred into B's name,[59] the right B obtains to the car is different from the personal right to payment of £1 million against X bank: it is a 'property right'. While it is generally accepted that personal rights are to be distinguished from property rights, the definition and structure of property rights is an intensely complicated and contentious subject.[60] As Stevens points out in *Torts and Rights*:[61]

> Property rights … have a number of characteristics, not one of which is a necessary characteristic of all rights so described. A simple definition of what this family of rights have in common which would accord with all usages is therefore unobtainable. Further,

[56] B McFarlane, *The Basic Structure of Property Law* (Oxford, Hart, 2008) 21–22.

[57] See, eg *Chase Manhattan Bank NA Ltd v Israel-British Bank (London) Ltd* [1981] Ch 105 (Ch).

[58] See *Yanner v Eaton* (2000) 201 CLR 351 (HCA) 365–66 (Gleeson CJ, Gaudron, Kirby and Hayne JJ) 376 (McHugh J); J Penner, *The Idea of Property in Law* (Oxford, Clarendon Press, 1997) 23–31; McFarlane, *The Basic Structure of Property Law* (2008) (n 56) 22; R Chambers, *An Introduction to Property Law in Australia*, 2nd edn (Sydney, Lawbook Co, 2008) 5–7.

[59] See, eg *McDonald v Coys of Kensington* [2004] EWCA Civ 47, [2004] 1 WLR 2775.

[60] See, eg W Hohfeld, *Fundamental Legal Conceptions as Applied in Judicial Reasoning* (New Haven, Yale University Press, 1923); J Penner, 'The Bundle of Rights Picture of Property' (1996) 43 *UCLA Law Review* 711; J Harris, *Property and Justice* (Oxford, Clarendon Press, 1996); P Eleftheriadis, 'The Analysis of Property Rights' (1996) 16 *OJLS* 31; Penner, *The Idea of Property in Law* (1997) (n 58).

[61] R Stevens, *Torts and Rights* (Oxford, Oxford University Press, 2007) 5.

> a single litmus test cannot be given by which property rights can be differentiated from other forms of right.

However, while no one definition can encompass 'all usages' of property rights, it is possible to identify the different meanings of 'property rights' and employ different labels to keep these different usages apart. Indeed, given the impossibility of a clear litmus test for proper use of the term, using the term 'property rights' without further elucidation is likely only to obfuscate.

Chambers suggests there are three different meanings of 'property'.[62] The first is the misleading reference to the subject matter of property rights as 'property', that is if I own a car, the car can be described as my 'property'. This is what Chambers describes as the 'popular, non-legal meaning of property as things'.[63] However, since Bentham it has been observed that referring to a person's 'property' rather than the subject of a person's property rights erroneously conflates rights to a thing with the thing itself.[64] Subjects of property rights are best described as 'things' or 'subject matter'. It is critical to keep property rights and the subject matter of property rights separate and for this reason this first usage of 'property' is eschewed in this book.

The second meaning of property, and the usage that will be employed in this book, is property rights as rights in things, specifically corporeal things.[65] A property right is a right in a corporeal thing enforceable against an indeterminate class of people: 'all the world'.[66] It is a single impersonal right in a thing,[67] not a multitude of personal rights against every other individual.[68] The correlative duty is owed by an indeterminate class of people in respect of the thing. This is 'the duty of non-interference' we all owe: the duty not to interfere with things in a manner that is inconsistent with the property rights of others.[69] It is not a personal duty owed to the right-holder, but a single impersonal duty each person owes to the holders of property rights generally.[70] The consequence of this definition of property rights is that the right–duty relationship is mediated by the thing: an individual right-holder has a right in a thing exigible against the world, while the rest of society owes a duty of non-interference to the holders of property rights. This definition therefore excludes rights enforceable against all the world that are not rights in things, such as the right to bodily integrity or intellectual property rights, which have 'no subject matter independent of the right itself'.[71]

[62] Chambers, 'Two Kinds of Enrichment' (2009) (n 4) 254.

[63] Ibid.

[64] J Bentham, *An Introduction to the Principles of Morals and Legislation* (London, Athlone Press, 1970) 211; Penner, 'The Bundle of Rights Picture of Property' (1996) (n 60) 801; Harris, *Property and Justice* (1996) (n 60) 10–13, 142; Swadling, 'Property: General Principles' (2000) (n 55) §4.02.

[65] See n 58.

[66] McFarlane, *The Basic Structure of Property Law* (2008) (n 56) 22–23.

[67] Penner, *The Idea of Property in Law* (1997) (n 58) 23–25.

[68] *Cf* Hohfeld, *Fundamental Legal Conceptions as Applied in Judicial Reasoning* (1923) (n 60) 72.

[69] Penner, *The Idea of Property in Law* (1997) (n 58) 29. See *Fowler v Hollins* (1872) 7 QB 616 (Ex) 639 (Cleasby B); *RH Willis & Son v British Car Auctions* [1978] 1 WLR 438 (CA).

[70] Penner, *The Idea of Property in Law* (1997) (n 58) 27–29.

[71] Stevens, *Torts and Rights* (2007) (n 61) 6.

However, leaving aside rare exceptions not relevant to this book, the private law does not have actions against things, only actions against persons. A thing cannot sue or be sued. Instead, the law concerns itself with the circumstances in which a right in relation to a thing gives rise to a personal right exigible against a specific person or when the duty of non-interference owed by an indeterminate class of persons is breached by a specific person. In other words, the private law is primarily concerned with events that generate personal rights out of these property right–duty relationships.

### *(iii) Assignable Rights*

Chambers refers to a third meaning of 'property rights' that must be kept separate from the usage in this book. This is the enlarged category that follows when the criterion for identifying property rights is assignability.[72] Many personal rights are assignable and therefore can be enforced not only by the right-holder but by their assignee, such as debts and other choses in action. This is a quality that most (though not all) property rights share and it defines a much broader category of 'property' than the stipulative usage adopted throughout this work. However, whatever the usefulness of labelling assignable rights as 'property rights' in other contexts, it serves only to confuse the distinction between personal and property rights in the law of unjust enrichment. Therefore, this book avoids this 'property' terminology and uses 'assignable rights' to refer to personal rights and property rights that have the quality of being assignable.

### *(iv) Persistent Powers*

A fourth usage of 'property' emerges from what is traditionally understood by the label 'equitable property rights'.[73] The notion of 'equitable property' most often refers to a beneficiary's rights under a private trust, which are often (and unfortunately) understood as a property right recognised in equity but not at law.[74] However, 'equitable property rights' are not property rights for two reasons. First, the beneficiary does not have a right in a corporeal thing exigible against the world;[75] rather, the beneficiary has a right or power in relation to *the trustee's rights or powers*, which is exigible against anyone acquiring the rights or powers held on trust.[76] An 'equitable property right' to land held on trust is not a parallel

[72] Ibid 6–7; Chambers, 'Two Kinds of Enrichment' (2009) (n 4) 254.

[73] See McFarlane and Stevens, 'The Nature of Equitable Property' (2010) (n 50); R Nolan, 'Equitable Property' (2006) 122 *LQR* 232.

[74] A Scott, 'The Nature of the Rights of the "Cestui Que Trust"' (1917) 17 *Columbia Law Review* 269, 275; S Worthington, *Personal Property: Cases and Materials* (Oxford, Hart, 2000) 44; R Goode, *Commercial Law* (London, Penguin, 2004) 38 cited in McFarlane and Stevens, 'The Nature of Equitable Property' (2010) (n 50) 2 fn 3.

[75] Smith, 'Unravelling Proprietary Restitution' (2004) (n 55); Smith, 'Philosophical Foundations of Proprietary Remedies' (2009) (n 55).

[76] See McFarlane, *The Basic Structure of Property Law* (2008) (n 56) 23–26; Chambers, *An Introduction to Property Law in Australia* (2008) (n 58) §13.90; McFarlane and Stevens, 'The Nature of Equitable Property' (2010) (n 50) *cf* Nolan, 'Equitable Property' (2006) (n 73).

property right to the land recognised by Chancery, but rather a right or power in respect of the rights or powers held by the trustee. This is highlighted by the decision in *Webb v Webb*,[77] where the European Court of Justice held that a claim that real property is held on resulting trust is not a claim *in rem*, but rather a personal claim against the titleholder. Although the beneficiary's equitable right persisted against third parties, the European Court rightly recognised that the beneficiary's right was against the trustee, not the land.

Second, 'equitable property rights' are not necessarily rights. In a private trust for persons, the beneficiary does not always have a 'right against a right',[78] but the beneficiary will always have a *power* to obtain a right or power. Where T is a trustee for B, B will generally have various rights and powers, one of which is the power to collapse the trust and require T to transfer the right or power held on trust to B. This power of the beneficiary is an incident of the institution of a private trust itself, which is why it can override the trust instrument when certain conditions are met, as recognised in *Saunders v Vautier*.[79] Indeed, following *Citibank NA v QVT Financial*,[80] it may be the only core, irreducible element of a private trust in English law.[81] Critically for present purposes, until B chooses to exercise the power to collapse the trust, T is not under a duty to transfer the legal rights to B, but rather under a liability to do so. This liability correlates with the power of B to acquire the rights or powers held by T. Thus, although B may have various rights against T, B does not have a 'property right' in the subject matter of the trust. For ease of exposition and terminological clarity, the language of 'equitable property rights' will therefore be avoided.

This book need not resolve the nature of the trust in English law. The essential point is that the beneficiary of a private trust has a power to collapse the trust, which is the reason why a resulting trust effects restitution.[82] The power to collapse a trust is what is described in this book as a 'persistent power'.[83] It is fundamental to the idea of the trust as 'property' that rights and powers are held by the trustee subject to the beneficiary's power to collapse the trust. For this reason, the beneficiary of a private trust is said to have a 'property right' in the subject matter of the trust,[84] whereas the beneficiary of a discretionary trust does not.[85] The power is 'persistent' because it will bind third parties who acquire the rights and powers

[77] *Webb v Webb* [1994] 3 WLR 801 (ECJ).

[78] *Cf* McFarlane and Stevens, 'The Nature of Equitable Property' (2010) (n 50).

[79] *Saunders v Vautier* (1841) 4 Beav 115, 49 ER 482.

[80] *Citibank NA v QVT Financial LP* [2007] EWCA Civ 11, [2007] 1 All ER (Comm) 475.

[81] See A Trukhtanov, 'The Irreducible Core of Trust Obligations' (2007) 123 *LQR* 342, 346.

[82] See ch 5, s I.

[83] *Cf* B Häcker, 'Rescission and Third Party Rights' [2006] *RLR* 1; B Häcker, *Consequences of Impaired Consent Transfers* (Tübingen, Mohr Siebeck, 2009); B Häcker, 'Proprietary Restitution After Impaired Consent Transfers: A Generalised Power Model' (2009) 68 *CLJ* 324.

[84] *Westdeutsche Landesbank Girozentrale v Islington LBC* [1996] AC 669 (HL) 705 (Lord Browne-Wilkinson).

[85] *Gartside v IRC* [1968] AC 553 (HL).

held on trust (subject to defences).[86] Anyone (other than a bona fide purchaser for value without notice) who acquires rights or powers in breach of trust will take subject to the claimant's power to obtain specific restitution of those rights or powers. As we shall see, all of the powers to obtain restitution of a specific right or power examined in chapter five bind third parties. For instance, the power of rescission is enforceable against volunteers[87] and those taking with notice,[88] but not bona fide purchasers for value without notice.[89] As Häcker[90] and Chambers[91] point out, this persistent quality of powers is common in English law.

As the power to collapse a trust requires the existence of a trust, it is necessary to confront the argument that a trust requires the trustee's 'conscience' to be affected, as suggested by Lord Browne-Wilkinson in *Westdeutsche*:[92]

> [T]he equitable jurisdiction to enforce trusts depends upon the conscience of the holder of the legal interest being affected, he cannot be a trustee … until he is aware that he is intended to hold the property for the benefit of others in the case of an express or implied trust, or, in the case of a constructive trust, of the factors which are alleged to affect his conscience.

This knowledge requirement has been heavily criticised.[93] It is clear that a trustee does not have to know of the trust or the circumstances giving rise to the trust in order for a trust to come into existence.[94] It may be the case that certain positive fiduciary and non-fiduciary duties of the trustee depend on the trustee's acquiring knowledge of the circumstances giving rise to the trust, but the liability to give up the right upon the exercise of the power of the beneficiary unequivocally arises at the moment of receipt. This book is concerned with the existence of this power–liability relationship, not whether it can or should be described as a 'trust'.

[86] McFarlane and Stevens, 'The Nature of Equitable Property' (2010) (n 50) 5–6.

[87] See, eg *Gould v Okeden* (1731) 4 Brown 198, 2 ER 135; *Small v Atwood* (1832) You 407, 535–38; 159 ER 1051, 1103–04.

[88] *Dunbar v Tredennick* (1813) 1 B&B 304, 318–19 (Lord Manners); *Addis v Campbell* (1841) 4 Beav 401, 49 ER 394.

[89] *Hawes v Wyatt* (1790) 2 Cox 263, 265; 30 ER 122, 123; *Bowen v Evans* (1844) 1 J&Lat 178, 263–64; *Bellamy v Sabine* (1857) 1 De G&J 566, 44 ER 842; *Phillips v Phillips* (1861) 4 De GF&J 208, 218; 45 ER 1164, 1167.

[90] Häcker, 'Proprietary Restitution After Impaired Consent Transfers: A Generalised Power Model' (2009) (n 83) 335–42.

[91] Chambers, 'Two Kinds of Enrichment' (2009) (n 4) 257.

[92] *Westdeutsche Landesbank Girozentrale v Islington LBC* [1996] AC 669 (HL) 705 (Lord Browne-Wilkinson). See also McFarlane, *The Basic Structure of Property Law* (2008) (n 56) 305–06.

[93] *Box v Barclays Bank plc* [1998] Lloyd's Rep Bank 185 (Ch); *Twinsectra v Yardley* [1999] Lloyd's Rep Bank 438 (CA); *Bank of America v Arnell* [1999] Lloyd's Rep Bank 399 (QB) 462–63 (Potter LJ); *Shalson v Russo* [2003] EWHC 1637 (Ch), [2005] Ch 281 [106]–[127] (Rimer J). See J Edelman and E Bant, *Unjust Enrichment in Australia* (Oxford, Oxford University Press, 2006) 57–58.

[94] *Lonrho plc v Fayed (No 2)* [1992] 1 WLR 1 (Ch) 13 (Millett J); R Chambers, *Resulting Trusts* (Oxford, Clarendon Press, 1997) 203–09; Chambers, 'Two Kinds of Enrichment' (2009) (n 4) 273. See, eg *Smith v Wheeler* (1671) 1 Lev 279, 83 ER 406; *Birch v Blagrave* (1755) Amb 265, 27 ER 176; *Siggers v Evans* (1855) 5 E&B 367, 119 ER 518; *Childers v Childers* (1857) 1 De G&J 482, 44 ER 810; *Mallott v Wilson* [1903] 2 Ch 494 (Ch); *Re Vinogradoff* [1935] WN 68 (Ch).

Therefore, an 'equitable property right' is not a right to a thing or even a claim-right at all; it is a power in relation to a specific right or power held by the defendant. Moreover, this power is not exigible against all the world; it is illogical for a power in relation to a specific right or power to be exigible against anyone besides the person holding the specified right or power. However, because the power will bind third parties,[95] McFarlane labels such rights 'persistent rights'.[96] Nonetheless, this book prefers the terminology of 'persistent powers' to McFarlane's 'persistent rights' for two reasons. First, the claimant obtains a power, not a right. Until the power is exercised by the claimant, the defendant has no correlative duty but is subject only to a liability. Second, 'persistent rights' is linguistically a category that includes all property rights, as these rights also have the quality of persistence. The label 'persistent powers' accurately describes the fourth category of 'property rights' without this ambiguity.

## III. The Concept of Wealth

Some analyses of enrichment equate enrichment with wealth or otherwise rely upon the concept of wealth in defining enrichment.[97] 'Wealth' is a difficult concept to distinguish from rights and value. The concepts are intimately related but not identical and it is important to analyse them separately. This section suggests that 'wealth' refers to the net accumulation of things having a value, whether through exchange, the production of income or otherwise. In sub-section A, it is argued that wealth may be conceptualised in either a discrete or an abstract way and that wealth is distinct from value and rights on either conception. Sub-section B then defines wealth according to the value-possessing and value-producing qualities of items of wealth. It is contended that the most useful conception of a person's wealth is as an abstract fund netting tangible and intangible assets held against valuable obligations owed to others.

### A. Discrete and Abstract Conceptions of Wealth

Birks explained in *Unjust Enrichment* that the law embraces two differing conceptions of wealth, the discrete and the abstract:[98]

> The first sees the person's wealth as a list of particular assets, some corporeal, some incorporeal. ... [W]ealth as an inventory of distinct items such as a house, car, jewels,

[95] McFarlane, *The Basic Structure of Property Law* (2008) (n 56) 23–25. See also Stevens, *Torts and Rights* (2007) (n 61) 5–6.

[96] McFarlane, *The Basic Structure of Property Law* (2008) (n 56) 23–25.

[97] Eg P Birks, *An Introduction to the Law of Restitution*, 1st edn (Oxford, Clarendon Press, 1985) 13; Birks, *Unjust Enrichment* (2005) (n 3) 50–55; Beatson, *The Use and Abuse of Unjust Enrichment* (1991) (n 23) 21–44.

[98] Birks, *Unjust Enrichment* (2005) (n 3) 69. See also B Rudden, 'Things as Things and Things as Wealth' (1994) 14 *OJLS* 81; L Smith, 'Tracing' in A Burrows and A Rodger (eds), *Mapping the Law:*

> money, bank accounts, bonds, shares, and so on. The other conception envisages an individual's wealth as a single fund with a money value. When a celebrity is said to be worth millions, the speaker is thinking in terms of an abstract fund.

In the discrete conception of wealth, wealth is simply the accumulation of things of value, and is therefore easily distinguished from value itself: assets and the value of those assets are distinct ideas. The discrete conception of wealth also holds when, instead of viewing wealth as the accumulation of things or assets, we more accurately view wealth as the rights to those things or assets.[99] We then have an inventory of rights: a right to a house, a right to a car, rights to jewellery and so on. The discrete conception of wealth is a simplistic conception of wealth as it does not net assets and liabilities to arrive at a concept of net wealth, but instead lists only one side of an individual's balance sheet. As such, this conception of wealth does not reflect the concept of enrichment because a defendant can be enriched either by the receipt of rights or the release of obligations.[100] For instance, where a mistaken payment is made into an overdrawn account, this is no less an enrichment than if the account had been in credit.[101]

The abstract conception of wealth, on the other hand, allows us to take liabilities into account to arrive at a conception of net wealth in balance sheet terms. As Chambers explains, 'A man with £10 million in assets might appear to be wealthy, but if he also has £20 million in debts, he is in reality hopelessly bankrupt'.[102] In this way, the abstract conception shares some features of the relational concept of value advanced in this book, insofar as it abstracts from particular things of value to a net fund with a money value. Nonetheless, the relationship between the abstract conception of 'wealth' and the idea of value is that an abstract fund *has a value*. A celebrity's wealth is measured in millions. Thus, even when wealth is viewed as the net of assets and liabilities in an abstract fund, 'wealth' is not synonymous with value.

## B. Defining Wealth

So far we have only defined 'wealth' negatively by distinguishing it from the concept of value. What qualities define wealth itself? Birks and Beatson provide the most extensive discussion of the meaning of wealth in the literature on unjust enrichment. In his last work, *Unjust Enrichment*, Birks rejects his initial view equating wealth with enrichment and instead defines wealth at a higher level of generalisation:[103]

> '[W]ealth received' embraces both enrichments to be reversed and enrichments prevented.... [T]he reason why the generalisation ... stops at enrichment is that if it went

*Essays in Memory of Peter Birks* (Oxford, Oxford University Press, 2006) 126–27; Chambers, 'Two Kinds of Enrichment' (2009) (n 4) 251.

[99] Eg A Berle and G Means, *The Modern Corporation and Private Property*, revised edn (New York, Harcourt, Brace & World, 1968) 305.

[100] Chambers, 'Two Kinds of Enrichment' (2009) (n 4) 251.

[101] Ibid.

[102] Ibid.

[103] Birks, *Unjust Enrichment* (2005) (n 3) 52.

> higher to 'thing' it would reach the receipt of non-wealth ... And, if it went slightly less high, to 'wealth', it would cross the line between ... the creation of new rights to reverse enrichments, and the assertion of pre-existing property rights, the survival of which prevents the recipient's enrichment.

As this passage shows, Birks views wealth as a factual rather than a legal question: 'wealth' extends to anything with a monetary value, including assets in which someone else holds a property right. As such, the term 'wealth' captures the receipt of value and rights, but excludes what Birks terms 'not-wealth', which is anything that a court will not turn into money, such as other human beings.[104]

However, excepting 'not-wealth' does not offer much guidance as to what positively constitutes 'wealth'. Beatson's essay on 'Benefit, Reliance and the Structure of Unjust Enrichment'[105] provides a more detailed definition. Relying extensively on economic literature, Beatson argues that 'exchange-value, transferability, or capacity to produce income are the hallmarks of wealth'.[106] Wealth therefore includes those things that have a value, either in exchange or in use, except for particular things that, for policy reasons, the law excludes from monetary valuation, including human beings. To put this more technically, the term 'wealth' captures rights that have an exchange value or produce income through use (ie assets). When combined with the abstract conception of wealth, wealth can therefore be defined as an abstract fund netting tangible and intangible assets held against valuable obligations owed to others.

## IV. The Relationship between the Concepts

### A. Value, Rights and Obligations

The significance of understanding value relationally is that it 'distinguish[es] between things that have value and value itself'.[107] Value should therefore be distinguished from 'rights' and 'obligations', which may have value, but are not synonymous with value. We shall see in chapter three that a defendant may be enriched by the acquisition of a claim-right or power at the claimant's expense, or by the release of a duty or a liability. These rights and obligations may or may not have value, but they are not the same as value. This point can be proved by the existence of valueless rights or rights that have a negative value. Chambers points to rights to things with only a sentimental value, such as a child's artwork or 'a ticket stub kept as a reminder of a special event', or rights to property that

[104] Ibid 51.
[105] Beatson, *The Use and Abuse of Unjust Enrichment* (1991) (n 23) 21–44.
[106] Ibid 31.
[107] Weinrib, 'The Normative Structure of Unjust Enrichment' (2008) (n 1) 27.

are in fact a liability, such as the right to possess toxic waste.[108] The same point can be made in respect of obligations, which need not have an economic value, such as a duty to give up a valueless right. Indeed, an obligation may have a positive value, such as a liability under an option contract where the price is higher than market value. It is therefore important to distinguish between value, rights and obligations and recall that the relationship between them is that, rather than constituting value, rights and obligations are capable of having value.

## B. Value and Wealth

The law of unjust enrichment is concerned with transfers of value: what matters for prima facie liability is that value has been received by the defendant, not that value is retained by the defendant as wealth.[109] Transfers of value do not necessarily equate to increases or decreases in wealth. A defendant may have received value, for example a pure service, which does not result in a marketable residuum. In such a case, the defendant has received value without an increase in wealth. Conversely, immediately after purchasing a valuable asset, the asset acquired may be worth less, as usually happens upon purchasing a new car. Even though the exchange occurs at market value, the purchaser's net wealth has declined without a net transfer of value to the vendor. Value and wealth are not equivalent terms. The critical point is that, although a person's wealth has a value, the receipt of value does not necessarily import an increase in wealth or vice-versa.

One difficulty with Chambers's analysis of the relationship between value and wealth is his view that 'Enrichment is measured by its effect on the defendant's wealth, but the enrichment is value, not wealth'.[110] Birks identifies the same relationship between value and wealth, arguing that enrichment is 'value measured by money'[111] but that 'An enrichment, or gain, is an addition to wealth'.[112] This approach confuses the relationship between value and wealth because it suggests that there is a necessary relationship between the receipt of value and an accretion to wealth when this is not the case. Enrichment is not measured by its effect on the defendant's wealth because, where enrichment is the receipt of value, the value received does not necessarily alter the abstract fund of rights and assets held by the defendant that have an exchange value or income-producing capacity. Pure services have an exchange value in the market and the right to a pure service, like a haircut, may be an item of wealth, but the receipt of a valuable haircut, of itself, does not alter the defendant's stock of rights or assets. Enrichment is measured by value, not wealth. The concept of wealth serves only to confuse the enrichment received by the defendant.

108 Chambers, 'Two Kinds of Enrichment' (2009) (n 4) 255.
109 *Cf* ibid. 247–49, 267–69.
110 Ibid 252.
111 Birks, *Unjust Enrichment* (2005) (n 3) 52.
112 Ibid 69.

## C. 'Benefit' and 'Gain'

The same problems that are presented by the concept of 'wealth' often arise from the use of the concepts of 'benefit' and 'gain' in discussion of the enrichment of a defendant. 'Benefit' and 'gain' are often used interchangeably with either or all of 'value', 'rights' and 'wealth'. For example, the first *Restatement of the Law of Restitution* equivocates between all three concepts in the use of the term 'benefit':[113]

> A person is enriched if he has received a benefit … A person confers a benefit upon another if he gives to the other possession of or some interest in money, land, chattels, or choses in action, performs services beneficial to or at the request of the other, or in any way adds to the others' security or advantage.

'Benefit' is thus used to refer to the receipt of discrete rights and assets ('possession of or some interest in money, land, chattels or choses in action') or the receipt of value, whether or not it increases the defendant's abstract wealth ('services beneficial to or at the request of the other') or, apparently, to encompass what Birks would term 'not-wealth' ('any way adds to the others' security or advantage'). 'Benefit' is also the term used in the Law Reform (Frustrated Contracts) Act 1943,[114] which caused Lord Wright to differentiate the principles of 'unjust enrichment' and 'unjust benefit' in *Fibrosa*.[115]

The term 'gain' is often similarly abused. Where D acquires a share from C for £10,000, but the market value is £12,000 and the share increases in value to £14,000 the day after the transfer, the transaction may involve a 'gain' to D in three distinct senses. The first possible 'gain' is that D has a right that has value: the right to the share adds a discrete item of wealth to D's inventory. The second possible 'gain' is the profit made in the transaction with C. Used in this sense, D's gain is the £2,000 he paid below market value for the shares at the time of purchase. Gain here refers to the value received by D, not its ultimate effect on the surviving stock of rights and assets of D. Lastly, the third possible 'gain' is the abstract accretion to D's net wealth as a result of the transaction. D's gain is then the £4,000 increase in the value of the right acquired.

It is important, therefore, to be clear by what we mean by 'benefit' and 'gain' in the enrichment inquiry. First, the term 'benefit' will be used in this book to refer to anything that has the quality of value. As outlined above, 'value' does not have a separate existence; it is not a thing in itself, it is a quality of things. The term 'benefit' is best used to describe something that has a monetary value, whether that be a right or the performance of a service or otherwise. It is therefore not restricted to the acquisition of rights or the release of obligations, but extends to

[113] American Law Institute, *Restatement of the Law of Restitution*, 1st edn (Minnesota, American Law Institute, 1937) 12.

[114] Law Reform (Frustrated Contracts) Act 1943.

[115] *Fibrosa Spolka Akcynja v Fairbairn Lawson Combe Barbour Ltd* [1943] AC 32 (HL) 61 (Lord Wright). See Virgo, *The Principles of the Law of Restitution* (2006) (n 35) 62.

abstract benefits like services, valuable forbearance and so on. Used in this way, the transfer of value requires the receipt of a benefit that has a value. 'Benefit' is not to be confused with an accretion to wealth because, as explained above, value and wealth are not equivalent terms and something that is a benefit in the sense described here, such as a haircut or the performance of an opera, may have no effect on wealth.

Second, the term 'gain' will be used exclusively to refer to an accretion to the defendant's net wealth. So, in the share example above, while 'gain' could mean: (i) D's right to the shares; (ii) the net profit made by D in the transaction (£2,000); or (iii) the net increase in D's wealth (£4,000), it is the last of these three senses of 'gain' that is preferred in this book. In this way, 'gain' is distinct from 'value received'. As we shall see, restitution reverses the acquisition of a 'benefit' in a defective transaction, either specifically or by value, whereas disgorgement reverses the defendant's 'gain' causally attributable to the transaction.

## D. Transfers of Value and Transfers of Rights

As a 'benefit' is a broad concept that incorporates both rights and not-rights, the transfer of value should be understood and analysed separately from the transfer of an underlying right of value. There are two reasons for this. First, although a transfer of value *may* involve the acquisition of a right by the defendant, this is not necessary for the transfer of value. For example, the performance of a service and the release of an obligation do not involve the acquisition of a right by the defendant. Second, focusing on the right is apt to mislead. There may be a bilateral transfer of value between C and D in the absence of a bilateral transfer of a right between C and D. The transfer of value is necessarily transactional and therefore bilateral: it occurs when a benefit of value is received by the defendant at the claimant's expense.[116] However, it does not require a bilateral 'transfer' of the right. Although D may acquire the right from X, if it is at C's expense there is a bilateral transfer of value between C and D. The movement of value does not entail the movement of an underlying right; it requires merely that a benefit of value is transferred to the defendant at the claimant's expense.

As we shall see in chapter three, the possibility of two different characterisations of a transfer of a right is crucial. The nature of the claim depends upon whether the transfer of a right is characterised factually or legally. In legal enrichment cases, it is enough that the defendant has acquired the right. This effects a change in his juridical right–duty relations that constitutes an enrichment to be reversed. However, when the transfer of a right is analysed in terms of value, the transfer of value is limited to the *value of the right acquired by the defendant*, not the value given up by the claimant. For instance, where the defendant acquires a right to a chattel, but the chattel is never delivered or other circumstances diminish the

[116] Weinrib, 'Correctively Unjust Enrichment' (2009) (n 1) 39.

exchange value of the right at the moment acquired by the defendant, the value *transferred* can be no more than that value received by the defendant. Similarly, where the defendant acquires a right as trustee of a valid trust, there is no transfer of value to the defendant, but rather a transfer of value to the beneficiary. The important point is that, even though value inheres in benefits and rights constitute a benefit in the law of unjust enrichment, the transfer of a right and the receipt of value are distinct concepts that must be analysed separately.

## V. Conclusion

This chapter is preliminary in nature. The discussion of enrichment in the cases and literature often relies upon the concepts of 'value', 'rights', 'obligations' and 'wealth' without further definition, which has a tendency to confuse the analysis of enrichment. It was argued that value is to be understood relationally as an abstract standard for the comparison and exchange of qualitatively heterogeneous things in quantitatively comparable and equivalent terms. Relational value was distinguished from idiosyncratic value, which is the value a particular individual attaches to a particular good or service. On the approach in this book, a 'transfer of value' involves the abstract movement of value *to the defendant* by receipt of a 'benefit' that has a value. By contrast, rights and obligations are not synonymous with value; rights and obligations are benefits that may or may not *have* a value. It is therefore possible to characterise a transfer both by the change in the defendant's juridical relations and by value. Finally, it was shown that the law of unjust enrichment does not rely upon the concept of wealth. 'Wealth' was defined as an abstract fund netting tangible and intangible assets held against valuable obligations owed to others. A person's wealth is therefore something that has value, rather than being synonymous with value, and the concept of 'wealth' does not usefully explain restitution, which is based on either the receipt of value or the legal effect of acquiring rights or being released from obligations.

# 3

# Bifurcating the Enrichment Inquiry

Chapter three introduces the central argument of this book that there are two concepts of enrichment in the law of unjust enrichment: (i) factual enrichment, that is the receipt of value by the defendant at the claimant's expense; and (ii) legal enrichment, that is the acquisition of a right, or the release of an obligation, at the claimant's expense. Although both the 'factual' and 'legal' enrichment inquiries are *legal* inquiries, the language is intended to highlight the distinction drawn in chapter two between the economic concept of value and the legal constructs of rights and obligations. The purpose of this chapter is to propose a bifurcated model for the enrichment inquiry that will be tested and justified against the case law in chapter four, which deals with factual enrichment cases, and chapter five, which deals with legal enrichment cases. As such, the project undertaken here is essentially conceptual and the chapter engages predominantly with the academic and theoretical literature, while discussion of the cases is largely postponed to the remaining chapters of the book.

Section I explains the generalisation 'enrichment'. It advances the thesis that there are two different kinds of enrichment captured by the term and justifies the choice of this terminology over 'wealth', 'value', 'rights', 'assets', 'things received' and other candidate terms. Section II then outlines a theoretical model for factual enrichment cases. It suggests an objective approach to identifying and valuing the enrichment received by the defendant. Section III provides a theoretical framework for legal enrichment cases. It is argued that value is not relevant to establishing legal enrichment.

## I. The Meaning of Enrichment

In *Unjust Enrichment*, Birks asks why the generalisation from the core case of money 'stops at enrichment' rather than 'things received' or 'wealth' or 'assets'.[1] The term 'enrichment' indeed requires justification. It is argued here that enrichment is an umbrella concept that encompasses both the factual and legal characterisations of the receipt of a benefit by the defendant at the claimant's expense.

[1] P Birks, *Unjust Enrichment*, 2nd edn (Oxford, Clarendon, 2005) 52.

In addition, the need to protect freedom of choice in factual enrichment cases makes a different generalisation, such as 'wealth', 'assets' or 'things received' inappropriate. Sub-section A contends that there are two types of enrichment captured by the term 'enrichment' and sub-section B explains why the generalisation 'enrichment' is preferable to the alternatives. It is contended that 'enrichment' is not synonymous with either 'value' or 'rights' because it is a broader concept than both of these; nor is it synonymous with 'things received', 'assets' or 'wealth' because it is a different concept from each of these.

## A. Two Kinds of Enrichment

### *(i) Factual and Legal Enrichment*

The first notable attempt to distinguish between two types of enrichment is Birks's distinction between factual and legal enrichment.[2] Birks noted that, in most unjust enrichment cases, the defendant receives a right at the claimant's expense. For example, in Birks's core case of *Kelly v Solari*,[3] the mistaken payment was effective to pass title to Solari, who therefore had a legal right to the money. However, in cases where title does not pass, Birks proposed that the recipient may be *factually* enriched:[4]

> [I]f I receive money from you but the money remains yours, technically I am no better off, but factually and realistically I am now in control of the buying power represented by your money.

In this way, Birks sought to draw a distinction between legal enrichment and factual enrichment, which he conceptualised in terms of exchange value. Nonetheless, Birks never developed a rigorous distinction between factual and legal enrichment; instead, he defined enrichment as the receipt of 'value measured by money'[5] and 'an addition to wealth',[6] regarding 'factual enrichment' as a pragmatic answer to reach cases where title does not pass.

Birks's proposed notion of 'factual' enrichment has been roundly criticised by those who take the view that the defendant is not enriched if title does not pass because enrichment is legal, not factual, and the defendant has received no legal

[2] P Birks, 'On Taking Seriously the Difference between Tracing and Claiming' (1997) 11 *Trusts Law International* 2, 7–8; P Birks, 'Property and Unjust Enrichment: Categorical Truths' [1997] *New Zealand Law Review* 623, 654–56. See also G Virgo, *The Principles of the Law of Restitution*, 2nd edn (Oxford, Oxford University Press, 2006) 134–35; A Burrows, 'The Relationship between Unjust Enrichment and Property: Some Unresolved Issues' in J Edelman and S Degeling (eds), *Unjust Enrichment in Commercial Law* (Sydney, Lawbook Co, 2008) 334–38; A Burrows, *The Law of Restitution*, 3rd edn (Oxford, Oxford University Press, 2010) 55 fn 47.

[3] *Kelly v Solari* (1841) 9 M&W 54, 152 ER 24.

[4] Birks, 'On Taking Seriously the Difference between Tracing and Claiming' (1997) (n 2) 7–8.

[5] Birks, *Unjust Enrichment* (2005) (n 1) 52.

[6] Ibid 69.

right.[7] The merits of these arguments are considered in chapter four.[8] However, this book will show that it is not necessary for the defendant to acquire a right to be enriched, for example in the case of quantum meruit for services rendered or where the defendant is enriched by the release of an obligation. Unfortunately, Birks never elaborated the idea of factual enrichment in any detail; this is what is attempted in this book. The factual enrichment model advanced here aims to give precise content to Birks's idea of factual enrichment and to demonstrate that every monetary restitution case should be understood as turning on the receipt of value, rather than the acquisition of a right.

### *(ii) The Chambers Thesis*

Chambers attempts to draw a similar distinction in enrichment between value and rights. Although no reported case explicitly draws a distinction between value- and rights-based enrichment, a number of commentators have expressed the view that there is a difference between cases where the claimant asserts that the defendant is enriched by the value of the benefit he has received and those cases where the claimant insists that the defendant is enriched by a specific right. Burrows,[9] Edelman[10] and Smith[11] have all expressed versions of this view without exploring the implications in detail. However, Chambers is the most prominent advocate of distinguishing the two different types of enrichment in his essay, 'Two Kinds of Enrichment'.[12]

Chambers argues that the reversal of transfers of value only captures part of the law of unjust enrichment. The other part of the subject is those cases where the defendant has acquired a specific right in circumstances that are unjust and the claimant seeks restitution of the right, rather than its value. In these cases, 'the value of the enrichment is wholly irrelevant to its status as enrichment'.[13] On his view, this occurs in three common situations: rescission, rectification and resulting trusts. Thus, Chambers's theory is that there are two kinds of enrichment that can be unjust for the same sorts of reasons (mistake, duress, undue influence and

[7] Eg W Swadling, 'A Claim in Restitution?' [1996] *LMCLQ* 63, 65; R Grantham and C Rickett, 'Restitution, Property and Ignorance—A Reply to Mr Swadling' [1996] *LMCLQ* 463, 465; R Grantham and C Rickett, 'Restitution, Property and Mistaken Payments' [1997] *RLR* 83, 87.

[8] See ch 4, fns 175–84 and accompanying text.

[9] A Burrows, *The Law of Restitution*, 2nd edn (London, Butterworths, 2002) 16 *cf* Burrows, *The Law of Restitution* (2010) (n 2) 55 fn 47.

[10] J Edelman, 'The Meaning of Loss and Enrichment' in R Chambers, C Mitchell and J Penner (eds), *Philosophical Foundations of the Law of Unjust Enrichment* (Oxford, Oxford University Press, 2009) 226–27. See also J Edelman and E Bant, *Unjust Enrichment in Australia* (Oxford, Oxford University Press, 2006) 53–54.

[11] L Smith, 'Tracing' in A Burrows and A Rodger (eds), *Mapping the Law: Essays in Memory of Peter Birks* (Oxford, Oxford University Press, 2006) 126–29; L Smith, 'Unjust Enrichment: Big or Small?' in S Degeling and J Edelman (eds), *Unjust Enrichment in Commercial Law* (Sydney, Lawbook Co, 2008) 40.

[12] R Chambers, 'Two Kinds of Enrichment' in R Chambers, C Mitchell and J Penner (eds), *Philosophical Foundations of the Law of Unjust Enrichment* (Oxford, Oxford University Press, 2009). See also R Chambers, 'Resulting Trusts' in A Burrows and A Rodger (eds), *Mapping the Law: Essays in Memory of Peter Birks* (Oxford, Oxford University Press, 2006) 256–59.

[13] Chambers, 'Two Kinds of Enrichment' (2009) (n 12) 261.

so forth) and result in one kind of restitution: the reversal of the enrichment. In value cases, this means monetary restitution; in rights cases, restitution of the relevant right.

While this book accepts that there is a distinction between the two kinds of enrichment Chambers identifies, it departs from Chambers's theory in four fundamental ways, which it is convenient to identify at the outset. The first departure is the broadening of the category of rights-based enrichment to reach the release of an obligation. As will be shown in chapter five,[14] the release of an obligation is an enrichment specifically reversed by subrogation, which is recognised by the House of Lords as a response to unjust enrichment. Thus, this book prefers the terminology of 'legal enrichment', which includes both rights acquired, and obligations released, at the claimant's expense.

The second departure is the thesis advanced in chapter seven: that unjust enrichment is concerned with immediate enrichment rather than the subsequent or surviving enrichment. Chambers argues that distinguishing between value- and rights-based enrichment shifts the focus from 'value received' to 'value surviving'.[15] While Chambers notes that the shift to surviving value 'depends primarily on the defence of change of position',[16] his analysis links the defence with the enrichment inquiry in a way that muddies the waters. For instance, Chambers regards enrichment as posing a 'different question' from simply asking whether the defendant has received value, instead concluding that the enrichment inquiry concerns both whether 'the defendant has received value *and is better off financially as a result*' (emphasis added).[17] The other editors of *Philosophical Foundations of the Law of Unjust Enrichment* argue that Chambers's thesis 'strongly suggests that the change of position defence is not really a defence … and the purpose of the "defence" is to reflect how much the defendant *remains* enriched'.[18] As Millett LJ said in *Portman BS v Hamlyn Taylor Neck*, the cause of action 'does not depend on the continued retention of the money by the defendant'.[19] This book will demonstrate that there is no necessary connection between accepting the distinction between factual and legal enrichment and a focus on what survives in the defendant's hands in the enrichment inquiry. On the contrary, the distinction allows for a strict approach to identifying the enrichment as the value received, right acquired or obligation released at the moment of enrichment, tempered by the change of position defence.

Third, Chambers adopts a subjective approach to value, embracing the notion of 'subjective devaluation'. In contrast, chapter two explained that the concept of value that underpins the private law is 'relational'. Relational value is the concept by

[14] See ch 5, s IV.A.

[15] Chambers, 'Two Kinds of Enrichment' (2009) (n 12) 247–49.

[16] Ibid 247.

[17] Ibid.

[18] R Chambers, C Mitchell and J Penner, *Philosophical Foundations of the Law of Unjust Enrichment* (Oxford, Oxford University Press, 2009) 16.

[19] *Portman BS v Hamlyn Taylor Neck* [1998] 4 All ER 202 (CA) 207 (Millett LJ).

which particular things are 'reducible to some single dimension or substance—to one and the same thing—notwithstanding their diversity'.[20] That single dimension is a thing's 'value': the concept by which we are able to say that an amount of *x* is 'worth' the same as another amount of *y*, irrespective of the particularities of *x* and *y*. By contrast, Chambers' approach adopts Birks' 'subjective devaluation' thesis and is ultimately reliant on an 'idiosyncratic value' premise that permits the value to the defendant to determine liability. In chapter six, this book rejects the notion of 'subjective devaluation' and advances an alternative thesis based upon objective valuation and proof of choice of the benefit by the defendant.

Finally, the fourth point of departure is in relation to Chambers' assertion that, although there are two kinds of enrichment, there is only 'one kind of restitution'.[21] In relation to value cases, this book concurs with Chambers that the restitutionary response is a right to the value transferred. However, in relation to legal enrichment, the claimant does not obtain a *right* to restitution. As will be explained in section III of this chapter, the claimant obtains a *persistent power* to obtain specific restitution, whether that be a power to rescind, a power to rectify, a power to collapse a resulting trust or a power under a subrogated security. Rather than two kinds of enrichment and one kind of restitution, there are two kinds of enrichment that entail two different kinds of restitution.

### *(iii) Why Distinguish Two Kinds of Enrichment?*

Enrichment is not defined solely by the economic value received by the defendant or solely by the legal effect of the defective transaction on the defendant's rights and obligations, but is a generalised concept that encompasses both factual and legal characterisations of the same benefit. This proposition can be demonstrated by proving two converse propositions: first, that the law awards restitution where the defendant has acquired neither a right nor the release of an obligation; and, second, that the law awards restitution where the defendant has not received value.

The first proposition—that the law awards restitution of value where the defendant does not receive a valuable right or release of an obligation—is best shown by reference to cases where the defendant is enriched by a service. As will be shown in chapter four,[22] there is now little doubt that pure services can be enriching.[23] So, where you request a haircut from me, you are enriched by the provision of that service even though you acquire no valuable right. This was the case in *Craven-Ellis v Canons Ltd*,[24] where the claimant provided valuable management services

[20] P Benson, 'The Unity of Contract Law' in P Benson (ed), *The Theory of Contract Law: New Essays* (Cambridge, Cambridge University Press, 2001) 188.

[21] Chambers, 'Two Kinds of Enrichment' (2009) (n 12) 267.

[22] See ch 4, fns 119–47 and accompanying text.

[23] Eg *Brenner v First Artists' Management Pty Ltd* [1993] 2 VR 221 (VSC); *Rowe v Vale of White Horse DC* [2003] EWHC 388 (Admin), [2003] 1 Lloyd's Rep 418; *Chief Constable of Greater Manchester Police v Wigan Athletic FC* [2008] EWCA Civ 1449, [2009] 1 WLR 1580.

[24] *Craven-Ellis v Canons Ltd* [1936] 2 KB 403 (CA).

to the defendant company under a contract of employment that was void because he did not obtain his qualification shares within two months as required by the articles of association. It was accepted that the defendant company received a valuable service for which it had to pay quantum meruit, but it had no right to the services provided by the claimant as the contract was void.[25] The same obtained in *Sempra Metals*,[26] where it was accepted that the IRC had no right to the use of the money but had to pay restitution of the value of that use nonetheless.

The second proposition, that the law awards restitution of rights where the defendant has not received value, is apparent from the approach to specific restitution in the cases. In chapter five, it is shown that specific restitution may be achieved by rescission.[27] An example is *Car & Universal Finance v Caldwell*.[28] The defendant, Caldwell, had sold his Jaguar to a rogue who had sold it on, through various hands, to the claimant in good faith and for value. As a result of the fraud, Caldwell had a power to rescind the contract and revest the title to the Jaguar, which he exercised by reporting the fraud. The sale to the claimant, Car & Universal Finance, was thus ineffective as title had already been revested in Caldwell and the claimant could not obtain good title. Caldwell's power to rescind and obtain the right to the Jaguar is a form of 'specific restitution', as he had the power to obtain restitution of the right acquired by the rogue.[29] Importantly, this is restitution of a right, not a thing: by rescinding Caldwell obtained the right to immediate possession of the car, not the car itself.[30]

While the right to the car in *Car & Universal Finance v Caldwell* was undoubtedly a valuable right, there is no reason this must be so. There is no suggestion in the judgments that the outcome turned on the value of the Jaguar or that Caldwell could not have obtained title to the Jaguar by rescission of the contract of sale if the Jaguar had been in an accident and was worth less than the cost of making it roadworthy. As Chambers explains:[31]

> [N]ot all rights have value. … For example, things may have only sentimental value, such as a child's primary school artwork or a ticket stub kept as a reminder of a special event. … [T]here is no doubt that the rights to possess them are property rights. A property right may even be a liability, such as possession of hazardous waste or contaminated land. Assignable personal rights may have no value whatsoever, such as a debt due from a hopelessly bankrupt person or shares in a hopelessly insolvent company.

The logic of the claim for rescission does not depend on the right's being valuable. The better view is that specific restitution of a right may have the effect of, but does not depend upon, reversing a transfer of value.

25 See also *Rowe v Vale of White Horse DC* [2003] EWHC 388 (Admin), [2003] 1 Lloyd's Rep 418.
26 *Sempra Metals Ltd v IRC* [2007] UKHL 34, [2008] 1 AC 561.
27 See ch 5, s II.
28 *Car & Universal Finance Co Ltd v Caldwell* [1963] 1 QB 525 (CA).
29 *Cf* W Swadling, 'Rescission, Property and the Common Law' (2005) 121 *LQR* 123.
30 Chambers, 'Two Kinds of Enrichment' (2009) (n 12) 256.
31 Ibid 255.

An example of the irrelevance of value is provided by undue influence cases. Where an agreement is set aside for undue influence, the claim for restitution of the specific right does not depend on the value of the right. In *CIBC Mortgages v Pitt*,[32] the House of Lords rejected any requirement to prove manifest disadvantage in cases of actual undue influence. A mortgage at market value can thus be set aside for undue influence. In *Pitt*, the husband borrowed money against the matrimonial home and, under pressure, his wife signed the loan application. When the husband's investment of the loan in stocks soured as a result of a market crash, the claimant mortgagee applied for possession of the matrimonial home and the wife claimed that the mortgage should be set aside due to undue influence exercised by her husband. There is no suggestion that the claimant, CIBC Mortgages, had not given full value for that mortgage. The wife's claim was not that CIBC had received value from her and must make restitution of the value; rather, it was that CIBC had acquired a right against her home that she wanted undone. The House of Lords emphasised this point in *Royal Bank of Scotland v Etridge (No 2)*,[33] where Lord Nicholls and Lord Scott made it clear that the right to rescind the transaction did not depend on the transaction being disadvantageous. The value of the right is simply not relevant to a claim for specific restitution. Burrows makes this point in *The Law of Restitution*: 'where the claimant is seeking a revesting of the legal title, no valuation is required'.[34]

## B. The Terminology of 'Enrichment'

The choice of the term 'enrichment' is deliberate. While this book has defined several other terms to make sense of the enrichment inquiry, the label 'enrichment' as a generalisation for the overall inquiry is preferable to alternative terms such as 'value', 'rights', 'wealth', 'benefit', 'gain', 'things received' and other similar candidates. There are three main reasons for adopting the language of enrichment: first, the label is a term of art that has found broad acceptance in the cases; second, the label adequately encompasses both the receipt of value and the acquisition of rights or release from obligations; and, third, the label can linguistically accommodate the requirement of freedom of choice.

The first and dominant reason for settling upon the term enrichment is that the label is a term of art. Historically, the term can be traced to Pomponius[35] and

[32] *CIBC Mortgages plc v Pitt* [1994] 1 AC 200 (HL). As Chambers explains, value may be relevant to other elements of the cause of action in presumed undue influence cases, such as the unjust factor: Chambers, 'Two Kinds of Enrichment' (2009) (n 12) 259–60.

[33] *Royal Bank of Scotland v Etridge (No 2)* [2001] UKHL 44, [2002] 2 AC 773 [12] (Lord Nicholls) [156] (Lord Scott).

[34] Burrows, *The Law of Restitution* (2010) (n 2) 55. See also C Mitchell, 'Restitutionary Claims for Services: Principles of Quantification' in J Edelman and S Degeling (eds), *Unjust Enrichment in Commercial Law* (Sydney, Lawbook Co, 2008); B McFarlane, *The Basic Structure of Property Law* (Oxford, Hart, 2008) D4.

[35] *Jure naturae aequum est, neminem cum alterius detrimento et injuria ¢eri locupletiorem* ('it is natural justice that no-one should unjustly enrich himself to the detriment of another'): J Edelman, 'Review: The Law and Ethics of Restitution' (2006) 69 *MLR* 131, 131.

the terminology of 'enrichment' was then picked up by Professor Ames in the late nineteenth century.[36] Ames vacillated between the terms 'benefit' and 'enrichment', but appeared to settle on the term 'enrichment', famously describing the category as premised on 'the fundamental principle that no one ought unjustly to enrich himself at the expense of another'.[37] Following Ames, Professor Keener also used the term 'enrichment',[38] although the *Restatement* later preferred the term 'benefit'.[39] Eventually, English law settled upon the term 'enrichment' and it is suggested here that the label is apt to describe the inquiry undertaken in the modern law of unjust enrichment as to what the defendant has received at the claimant's expense.

The second reason for preferring 'enrichment' is that, if the distinction between factual and legal enrichment defended in this book is correct, then it is clear that any generalisation must encompass both the receipt of value and the legal effect of acquiring a right or being released from an obligation. As a result, we can immediately dismiss 'value' and 'rights' as candidate generalisations. Although it is regularly said that unjust enrichment concerns reversals of transfers of value,[40] this is misleading: unjust enrichment is only sometimes about the reversal of transfers of value. 'Enrichment' is a broad enough generalisation to encompass both the receipt of value and the acquisition of rights or release of obligations.[41] Furthermore, unlike terms such as 'wealth' or 'assets', the term 'enrichment' is not tied to an extant benefit. As defined in chapter two, 'wealth' refers to an abstract fund netting the tangible and intangible assets a person holds against the valuable obligations they owe to others. 'Assets' is a related term that refers to rights that have value.[42] Both terms are tied to the retention of an extant benefit and therefore fail sufficiently to account for the receipt of value in cases where it does not increase the defendant's wealth, such as pure services, which leave no marketable residuum. The performance of a service is not an item of wealth; only the right to the performance of a service or the end-product of a service count as wealth. However, as described in chapter four, the law of unjust enrichment extends to restitution of the value of pure services. Hence, enrichment is synonymous with neither 'wealth' nor 'assets'.

[36] Edelman and Bant, *Unjust Enrichment in Australia* (2006) (n 10) 82.

[37] JB Ames, 'The History of Assumpsit: Implied Assumpsit' (1888) 2 *Harvard Law Review* 53, 64. See also JB Ames, *Lectures on Legal History and Miscellaneous Legal Essays* (Cambridge, Harvard University Press, 1913) 162.

[38] W Keener, *A Treatise on the Law of Quasi-Contracts* (Massachusetts, Baker and Voorhis & Co, 1893) 19.

[39] American Law Institute, *Restatement of the Law of Restitution*, 1st edn (Minnesota, American Law Institute, 1937) §1 cmt b.

[40] See ch 1, fn 28 and accompanying text.

[41] *Cf* L Fuller and W Perdue, 'The Reliance Interest in Contract Damages' (1936) 46 *Yale Law Journal* 52, 72; Virgo, *The Principles of the Law of Restitution* (2006) (n 2) 63; Burrows, *The Law of Restitution* (2010) (n 2) 44–45.

[42] Chambers, 'Two Kinds of Enrichment' (2009) (n 12) 255.

Virgo challenges the argument that 'enrichment' adequately encompasses both factual and legal conceptions of benefit. He observes that 'unjust benefit' may be 'the more accurate expression' because 'enrichment' is linguistically 'limited to those benefits which can be assessed only in terms of monetary value' such that 'a defendant will only be enriched where he or she has received something which has an exchange value'.[43] A similar interpretation seems to have been adopted by Fuller and Perdue, who took the view that 'enrichment' is a 'stricter' term than 'benefit'.[44] If 'enrichment' does indeed connote the stricter economic interpretation Virgo suggests, he takes this terminology to imply that pure services are excluded because nothing with an exchange value survives in the defendant's hands. As we shall see in chapter seven, this particular concern about the linguistic implications of the terminology of 'enrichment' is only valid if we confuse immediate and extant value: at the time of performance, pure services do have a monetary exchange value. Nor is there a basis for the linguistic connection Virgo observes between enrichment and economic value. Although enrichment is a more technical term than 'benefit', it does no violence to natural and ordinary meaning to say that a defendant who has acquired a right (or been released from an obligation) is enriched irrespective of the value of that right (or release). She has a right she did not have before the defective transaction and she is being asked to give up the right, not pay its value. As such, 'enrichment' is an appropriate label to encompass the legal characterisation of a benefit received by the defendant at the claimant's expense.

Finally, the third reason for preferring the terminology of enrichment is that, as explained in chapter six, the protection of the defendant's freedom of choice is achieved, in part, through the enrichment inquiry. In factual enrichment cases, the defendant's freedom of choice is part of the assessment of whether the defendant is enriched. A generalisation that cannot incorporate the requirement of choice of the relevant benefit will not do. Technical economic or accounting terms like 'value', 'wealth' and 'assets' cannot easily accommodate a requirement of choice. A car is valuable, an 'asset' and a component of 'wealth' whether or not the defendant chooses it. Likewise, terms such as 'gains' and 'things received' are over-generalisations that incorporate benefits not chosen by the defendant. But whether someone is 'enriched' by the receipt of a car contemplates an inquiry specific to the particular defendant. Of the possible generalisations, 'benefit' and 'enrichment' are the only candidates that easily accommodate a concern for the particular defendant, and 'enrichment' is the term the law has settled upon. For these reasons, the generalisation 'enrichment' is accurate and appropriately

[43] Virgo, *The Principles of the Law of Restitution* (2006) (n 2) 63. Burrows also seems to prefer 'benefit', although—like Virgo—he uses the terms interchangeably: Burrows, *The Law of Restitution* (2010) (n 2) Ch 3.

[44] Fuller and Perdue, 'The Reliance Interest in Contract Damages' (1936) (n 41) 72. Virgo also cites R Goff and G Jones, *The Law of Restitution*, 6th edn (London, Sweet & Maxwell, 2002) 17 in support of the same point.

adapted to the task of determining whether the defendant has received a benefit for which he must make restitution.

## II. Overview of Factual Enrichment

On the approach in this book, the enrichment inquiry is either about identifying the legal effect of a benefit obtained by the defendant or its economic effect as a transfer of value. It is suggested here that, when the claimant seeks monetary restitution, only the latter is relevant. The relevant enrichment *is* value. As outlined in chapter two, value is a quality of things, not a thing itself, and therefore the defendant must have received a benefit (ie something that has a value), whether that benefit be a right, the use of an asset, the performance of a service or something else. However, it is the receipt of value by the defendant in the defective transaction that constitutes the enrichment, not the particular benefit(s) by which a transfer of value is effected.

An additional problem arises in factual enrichment cases because a requirement to make restitution in money for the value of a benefit in kind may infringe the defendant's freedom of choice. The paradigm case of factual enrichment is the receipt of money, which is a measure of value and therefore incontrovertibly enriching,[45] but a defendant can also be enriched by the value of goods, services or anything else that has a monetary value. The difficulty with non-money cases is that the conferral of a benefit may have taken place without the defendant's consent or choice. Even though the defendant may undoubtedly have received a valuable benefit, this is not enough to say that the particular defendant is enriched. The law is concerned to protect the defendant's freedom to choose the benefits he wants.[46] A towing company that mistakenly tows the wrong car has provided the owner with a benefit valued by the market, but the owner cannot be said to be enriched by it. As claimants must prove their losses in a tort claim, so they must prove the defendant's enrichment in an unjust enrichment claim.

To accommodate freedom of choice concerns, it is contended here that factual enrichment requires proof that the defendant chose the relevant benefit or that the benefit is incontrovertibly enriching. This is not to be confused with 'subjective devaluation'. This section outlines an objective two-stage analysis of factual enrichment in sub-section A and an objective approach to the measure of monetary restitution in sub-section B. The aim is simply to set out the model; the argument that this represents the true position in English law is postponed until the analysis of the cases in chapter four and the freedom of choice requirement in chapter six.

[45] *BP Exploration Co (Libya) Ltd v Hunt (No 2)* [1979] 1 WLR 783 (QB) 789 (Robert Goff J); *Garland v Consumers' Gas Co* [2004] SCC 25, [2004] 1 SCR 629 (SCC) [36] (Iacobucci J).

[46] *BP Exploration Co (Libya) Ltd v Hunt (No 2)* [1979] 1 WLR 783 (QB) 799 (Robert Goff J).

## A. The Two Stage Inquiry

Proving the defendant's enrichment is not a straightforward exercise and there is considerable disagreement about the manner in which enrichment is to be established. Indeed, the leading commentators have suggested a variety of different approaches to enrichment and the case law has not settled the question. It is argued in this book that factual enrichment is a two-stage inquiry that requires proof that:

(i) the defendant received value; and
(ii) the defendant chose the benefit or it is 'incontrovertibly enriching'.

While these two limbs are often conflated in the discussion of enrichment and 'subjective devaluation' in the literature,[47] it is critical for analytical clarity that they be separately analysed. There is a distinction between describing something as a benefit and describing a defendant as 'enriched' by that benefit.[48] Indeed, much of the difficulty with enrichment has arisen from confusing 'benefit' and 'benefit *to the defendant*', rather than separately analysing the value received and whether the defendant chose the benefit. Accordingly, as explained in chapter two,[49] the term 'benefit' is used in this book exclusively to refer to things of value (ie things that are capable of being enriching), whereas 'enrichment' is used exclusively to refer to a benefit that actually enriches the defendant in question.

### *(i) Receipt of Value*

In chapter two,[50] a transfer of value was explained as a 'transactional' concept, which involves the movement of value to the defendant in a defective transaction. The focus in factual enrichment cases is therefore on identifying the receipt of a benefit by the defendant in circumstances where value is transferred to the defendant at the claimant's expense. The 'first limb' in claims for monetary restitution is therefore to identify objectively the receipt of value by the defendant. It is submitted that this has much in common with the first step in the approaches adopted by Burrows and Virgo of identifying an 'objective benefit' received by the defendant at the claimant's expense, but that the emphasis on the receipt of value rather than the underlying benefit in which that value resides is critical.

[47] *Cf* Virgo, *The Principles of the Law of Restitution* (2006) (n 2) 62–64 and Burrows, *The Law of Restitution* (2010) (n 2) 45–47 where, although not embracing a purely objective approach, identification of an objective benefit is clearly distinguished from 'subjective devaluation'.

[48] Virgo analyses a different distinction between 'benefit' and 'enrichment' that follows from an economic definition of 'enrichment' that is not employed here, see Virgo, *The Principles of the Law of Restitution* (2006) (n 2) 62–63.

[49] See ch 2, s IV.C.

[50] See ch 2, s I.C.

Burrows and Virgo both maintain that the first step in the enrichment inquiry is to identify an 'objective benefit' received by the defendant.[51] Virgo offers four reasons for starting the inquiry with the identification of an objective benefit received by the defendant:[52]

(i) it makes sense for the claimant to prove that the defendant has received an objective benefit and for the burden to then shift to the defendant to disprove this, rather than requiring the claimant to show at the outset that the defendant valued the benefit;
(ii) the subjective aspect of the enrichment inquiry is usually expressed as 'subjective devaluation' of a benefit received, which only makes sense if the defendant is shown to have received an objective benefit that can be devalued;
(iii) the objective test is generally relied on to value the enrichment; and
(iv) several cases provide support for the adoption of an objective test, including *BP Exploration v Hunt (No 2)*[53] and *Leigh v Dickeson.*[54]

Although this book rejects the subjective devaluation approach in chapter six, Virgo's points about the structure of the enrichment inquiry are well made in respect of cases of factual enrichment: it is logical first to establish the receipt of a benefit by the defendant and, second, to consider whether the particular defendant can be regarded as enriched by that benefit. The adoption of an objective choice of benefit test at the second stage as advocated in this book does not detract from Virgo's case for first identifying the receipt of a valuable benefit.

However, this book departs from Burrows and Virgo's focus on an objective *benefit* in favour of the objective identification of the receipt of *value.* This may seem a minor distinction, but it is more precise in three important ways. First, a focus on the benefit rather than the transfer of value wrongly identifies the defendant's enrichment: instead of the value received from the claimant, it treats the enrichment as the thing in which that value inheres. For example, where the claimant provides a service increasing the value of the defendant's chattel, there are two potential benefits—the service and the improved chattel—but only one transfer of value from the claimant. So, in *Greenwood v Bennett*,[55] Harper provided £226 worth of labour and materials to repair Bennett's car, but the increase in the value of the car when subsequently sold was £325. As a result of focusing on the benefit held by the defendant (the chattel) rather than the value transferred from the claimant, Virgo reaches the conclusion that the defendant's enrichment is the £325 increase in the value of the car.[56] However, the Court of Appeal rightly

[51] Burrows, *The Law of Restitution* (2010) (n 2) 45–47; Virgo, *The Principles of the Law of Restitution* (2006) (n 2) 64–65.
[52] Virgo, *The Principles of the Law of Restitution* (2006) (n 2) 64–65.
[53] *BP Exploration Co (Libya) Ltd v Hunt (No 2)* [1979] 1 WLR 783 (QB) 802 (Robert Goff J).
[54] *Leigh v Dickeson* (1884) 15 QBD 60 (CA).
[55] *Greenwood v Bennett* [1973] QB 195 (CA).
[56] Virgo, *The Principles of the Law of Restitution* (2006) (n 2) 99.

awarded £226, which is the value received from the claimant. Title to the car is a benefit held by the defendant, but it is not the benefit by which value was transferred from the claimant.

Second, as articulated in chapter seven,[57] focusing on the benefit itself rather than its value may confuse the 'at the expense of' inquiry.[58] It is the value received by the defendant that must come at the claimant's expense, not the benefit in which that value inheres. In *Greenwood v Bennett*, the increase in the value of the car is not only due to the repairs carried out by Harper, but also to reasons extraneous to the transaction such as the intrinsic potential value of the car. The entire £325 increase in the value of the car is not 'at the expense of' Harper.

Finally, an approach that focuses on the benefit obtained, rather than the value transferred, may confuse immediate and extant enrichment, as explained in chapter seven. For instance, where the claimant mistakenly gives his paint to the defendant, who needs it to finish a painting, the right to the paint no longer exists as it accedes to the painting.[59] However, even though the benefit (the right to the paint) does not survive, what matters is that the defendant received value at the claimant's expense. The enrichment is the value received by the defendant, not the right to the paint. The same will apply in cases of pure services where there is by definition no benefit retained by the defendant. If the immediate enrichment thesis in chapter seven is correct, enrichment is always concerned with the receipt of value, not the retention of a benefit.

For these reasons, the first stage of the enrichment inquiry in factual enrichment cases is the objective identification of a receipt of value by the defendant. It will be demonstrated in section B below that the correct test is to assess the value to a reasonable person of the benefit conferred in the defective transaction. While a transfer of value will necessarily be effected by the conferral of a benefit on the defendant, the term 'benefit' directs attention away from the movement of value and may lead to a focus on the surviving enrichment and confuse the 'at the expense of' inquiry. If monetary restitution for unjust enrichment reverses a transfer of value from the claimant to the defendant, it must be the case that the enrichment is the value received by the defendant. Whether the particular defendant can be regarded as enriched by that value is a question of protecting the defendant's freedom of choice.

### *(ii) Protection of Freedom of Choice*

This book takes the view that enrichment is an objective question concerned with the value to a reasonable person in the position of the defendant. 'Subjective devaluation' is rejected in chapter six in favour of identifying and valuing the

[57] See ch 7, s I.B.

[58] See generally E Ball, '"At the Expense of the Claimant": Unpacking the Requirement' (M Phil thesis, University of Oxford 2011).

[59] *Appleby v Myers* (1867) 2 CP 651 (Ex) 659, 660; *Gough v Wood & Co* [1894] 1 QB 713 (CA) 719, 721; *Reynolds v Ashby & Son* [1904] AC 466 (HL) 475 (Lord Lindley).

benefit to the defendant objectively. However, the law must confront the problem of forcing defendants to pay for benefits that they may not have chosen.[60] It is argued in this book that the second limb of the enrichment inquiry in factual enrichment cases is concerned, not with subjective value, but with direct protection of the defendant's freedom of choice. The rationale underpinning the enrichment inquiry was explicitly said to be 'the principle of freedom of choice'[61] by the Supreme Court of Canada in *Peel (Regional Municipality) v Canada*. In England, the classic statement of the law's approach to freedom of choice is this dictum of Collins LJ from *Sumpter v Hedges*: 'the circumstances must be such as to give an option to the defendant to take or not to take the benefit of the work done'.[62] Likewise, in *Miles v Wakefield MDC*,[63] which involved employees' intentionally performing only part of their contractual obligations in an industrial action, Lord Brightman and Lord Templeman emphasised that the employees were entitled to be paid quantum meruit only where the employer chose to 'accept' the non-conforming work.[64] It is only those benefits *chosen* by the defendant that count in the assessment of factual enrichment.

There are two important caveats. First, as defended in chapter six,[65] where a benefit is 'incontrovertibly enriching', then it is not necessary for the claimant to prove that the defendant chose the benefit. This has much in common with the position originally adopted in the *Restatement* in 1937: '[a] person confers a benefit if he … performs services *beneficial to or at the request* of the other' (emphasis added).[66] The incontrovertible enrichment test is 'not the antithesis of freedom of choice' but applies where 'freedom of choice as a problem is absent'.[67] Where the benefit received by the defendant is money or its equivalent, finding the defendant to be enriched does not infringe the defendant's freedom of choice. In other words, the second limb of the enrichment inquiry is rendered otiose. This reflects the historical position: in an action for money had and received (an action restricted to money),[68] there was no request requirement.[69] The 'incontrovertible enrichment' test is discussed in detail in chapter six, but it suffices for the moment to note that it only extends to those benefits where the defendant's freedom of choice is never infringed by his being required to pay the value.

[60] See *Peel (Regional Municipality) v Canada* [1992] 3 SCR 762 (SCC) [42]–[46] (McLachlin J); *Damberg v Damberg* [2001] NSWCA 87, (2001) 52 NSWLR 492 [186]–[190] (Heydon JA).

[61] *Peel (Regional Municipality) v Canada* [1992] 3 SCR 762 (SCC) [43], [50] (McLachlin J).

[62] *Sumpter v Hedges* [1898] 1 QB 673 (CA).

[63] *Miles v Wakefield MDC* [1987] AC 539 (HL).

[64] Ibid 552–53 (Lord Brightman) 561 (Lord Templeman).

[65] See ch 6, s III.

[66] American Law Institute, *Restatement of the Law of Restitution* (1937) (n 39) §1 cmt b.

[67] *Peel (Regional Municipality) v Canada* [1992] 3 SCR 762 (SCC) [43] (McLachlin J) citing JRM Gautreau, 'When Are Enrichments Unjust?' (1988–89) 10 *Advocates' Quarterly* 258, 270–71.

[68] *Nightingall v Devisme* (1770) 2 Wm Bl 684, 96 ER 401.

[69] H Stephen, *A Treatise on the Principles of Pleading in Civil Actions*, 2nd edn (London, Joseph Butterworth & Son, 1827) 312. See P Birks, *An Introduction to the Law of Restitution*, revised edn (Oxford, Clarendon Press, 1989) 111–12.

Second, it is important to realise that, while the strict liability regime in unjust enrichment must protect the defendant's freedom of choice, it need not do so at the enrichment stage of the inquiry. The orthodox view—that the defendant's freedom of choice is protected through the definition of enrichment—requires justification. As Lord Nicholls suggested in *Sempra Metals*,[70] it may be that the defendant's freedom of choice is protected by the defence of change of position. The role of freedom of choice is explored in chapter six, but it suffices at this juncture to note that freedom of choice is relevant to liability in two ways: first, the defendant's freedom of choice is relevant to his prima facie liability to make restitution; and, second, it is relevant to what the defendant chooses to do in reliance on the receipt or anticipated receipt of a benefit. As such, the law protects the defendant's freedom of choice in two ways: (i) by the second limb of the enrichment inquiry in factual enrichment cases, that is proving that the particular defendant chose the relevant benefit; and (ii) by the defence of change of position. It is suggested that this dual role ensures that the defendant's freedom of choice is robustly protected by a system that takes an objective approach to enrichment.

Accordingly, on the factual enrichment model examined in chapter four, the claimant must prove an objective receipt of value by the defendant and the choice or incontrovertibility of the benefit. The choice is objectively ascertained. If the application of the objective test reveals a transfer of value to the defendant through the conferral of a benefit by the claimant but the evidence is that the defendant did not choose the benefit and it is not incontrovertibly enriching, then the defendant is not enriched. The content of the choice of benefit test and what constitutes a choice is examined in detail in chapter six.

## B. Objective Valuation

This book contends that the value of the enrichment received by the defendant should be understood objectively as *the value to a reasonable person in the position of the defendant*. The defendant's idiosyncratic valuation of the benefit received is not relevant; nor should the valuation process take into account the defendant's personal priorities and preferences. The question then is to what extent the reasonable person's valuation is to be tailored to 'the position of the defendant'. This section sets out the considerations that should be relevant, but—much like the calculation of compensatory damages—factual enrichment is ultimately a question of fact to be established by evidence before the court as to the most appropriate measure of value, industry rates and practice, the relevant market, its scope and competitiveness and other relevant factors.

[70] *Sempra Metals Ltd v IRC* [2007] UKHL 34, [2008] 1 AC 561 [119] (Lord Nicholls). See also [232] (Lord Mance).

### (i) The Purpose of Valuation

The starting point in valuation is to identify the purpose of the valuation exercise. It is contended in this book that the goal of valuation is to determine the value to a reasonable person in the position of the defendant. The reasonable person test has not received much consideration in the literature on unjust enrichment as the existing commentary is dominated by analysis of a subjective test of value; however, Virgo considers this question in some detail. In his view, the objective benefit test at the first stage is 'whether reasonable people would consider the defendant to have received something of value' or 'whether reasonable people would have been prepared to pay money for the benefit which the defendant received'.[71] Leaving aside the possibility of subjective devaluation, the valuation should be objective, argues Virgo:[72]

> The general test of valuation which should be adopted is an objective test, namely the reasonable value of the benefit in kind, since this is the basic test which is relied on when identifying whether or not the defendant has actually been enriched. This reasonable value is usually ascertained by reference to the market value, which is the sum 'a willing supplier and buyer would have agreed upon' for the provision of the benefit in kind.

While Virgo thinks the objective value is subject to the possibility of subjective devaluation or revaluation, his starting point is similar to the test suggested in this book. The objective test is the reasonable value of the benefit in kind to a reasonable person, not to the defendant in particular.

However, this book suggests that the test is more specific than 'the reasonable value of the benefit in kind'. As Etherton LJ explained in *Benedetti v Sawiris*, the test is the value to a 'reasonable person in the defendant's position'.[73] This should be clear from the usual reference to market values to determine the objective value of the benefit: the market value depends on the position of the defendant. The scope of the market (eg local, national or global) and the position of the defendant within that market will be relevant to calculating the reasonable value of the benefit. This is demonstrated by *Sempra Metals*, where the reasonable value to a person in the position of the defendant was not the commercial borrowing rate, but the public sector borrowing rate. The House of Lords did not apply the subjective value of the Revenue, but instead the value of a reasonable person in the position of the Revenue, that is a public sector borrower. In the same way that issues of market scope and definition bedevil the law of competition, there is no escaping the need to assess the reasonable value by reference to the relevant market in the law of unjust enrichment. It is therefore critical to define the relevant market and the position of the defendant in order to ask what value the benefit in kind would have for a reasonable person in the same position.

[71] Virgo, *The Principles of the Law of Restitution* (2006) (n 2) 64–65.
[72] Ibid 98.
[73] *Benedetti v Sawiris* [2010] EWCA Civ 1427 [140] (Etherton LJ). See also Edelman, 'The Meaning of Loss and Enrichment' (2009) (n 10) 231 *cf* Burrows, *The Law of Restitution* (2010) (n 2) 61.

However, the reasonable value to a person in the position of the defendant does not mean a reasonable person with the same subjective preferences and priorities as the defendant.[74] Instead, as Etherton LJ explained in *Benedetti v Sawiris*, what is relevant is 'the existence of conditions increasing or decreasing the objective value of the benefit to any reasonable person in the same (unusual) position as the defendant'.[75] As we shall see in chapter six,[76] taking into account the defendant's subjective preferences and priorities is the error in *Ministry of Defence v Ashman*[77] and *Ministry of Defence v Thompson*.[78] In both cases, the court defined the market as alternative low-cost housing for someone in the position of the defendants. While this approach suggests a concern to find an objective value in a relevant market (the defendants' idiosyncratic valuations were rightly not considered relevant), the relevant benefit to be valued was the particular military partnered accommodation in question, not alternative low-cost housing. As we will see in chapter six, the defendants' economic circumstances, expenditure priorities and idiosyncratic valuations should have been irrelevant. The test should have been the reasonable rental value of the partnered accommodation in question, not the reasonable rental value of entirely different accommodation.

With the exception of *Ashman* and *Thompson*, in those cases where the courts have been called on to value the benefit to the defendant, they have adopted an objective approach, usually by reference to the relevant market value. For example, in the vast preponderance of quantum meruit awards for unjust enrichment examined in chapter four,[79] the courts awarded the claimant the market value of the benefit conferred on the defendant. The courts are explicit that the usual method for assessing the reasonable value of services is by reference to the necessary costs incurred in doing the work plus a reasonable profit margin assessed by reference to the relevant industry rates and practices.[80] The same objective approach extends to quantum valebat awards, where the value of the goods is typically assessed by reference to the relevant market value.[81] Chapter four will demonstrate that the approach to valuation in the cases is objective, not subjective, and that the courts will typically award the market value, not the idiosyncratic value that the defendant happens to attach to the benefit.

### *(ii) Alternative Methods of Valuation*

As outlined in chapter two, there are many different ways of arriving at relational values besides market valuation. Any abstraction from the particular thing being valued and the particular person who values it to a quantitative standard for

[74] *Benedetti v Sawiris* [2010] EWCA Civ 1427 [145] (Etherton LJ).
[75] Ibid.
[76] See ch 6, fns 31–37 and accompanying text.
[77] *Ministry of Defence v Ashman* (1993) 66 P&CR 195 (CA).
[78] *Ministry of Defence v Thompson* (1993) 25 HLR 552 (CA).
[79] See ch 4, fns 70–88 and accompanying text.
[80] See text to nn 83–88 below.
[81] *BP Exploration Co (Libya) Ltd v Hunt (No 2)* [1979] 1 WLR 783 (QB) 839 (Robert Goff J).

comparison will be relational in this sense. Fixed values for necessities in communist systems are relational values; values in monopolistic and oligopolistic markets are relational too. As outlined above, the courts typically assess value by reference to the market price, but market valuation is not always possible and, even where it is possible, it is not always the best method of objective valuation. Furthermore, settling on the appropriate 'market value' is a difficult task that depends on a host of factors, including defining the scope of the relevant market and taking account of its competitiveness. Hence, in complex cases, valuation is a question on which a court must consider evidence as to the appropriate valuation method to apply and the relevant factual questions to take into consideration in quantifying the value transferred. This is similar in some respects to the process the court will engage in to determine compensatory damages in tort.

This point is demonstrated by the quantification of quantum meruit in cases where the relevant benefit is the provision of services, considered in detail in chapter four.[82] The practical reality is that the available evidence of the market value will differ between cases and, further, that there will be different ways of assessing value that may be appropriate in particular cases. Calculating the reasonable value of a service is a difficult question and the method of valuation applied by the courts depends on the relevant industry, market and service. For example, there is an emerging consensus, applied by Lord Scott in the recent decision in *Yeoman's Row Management v Cobbe*,[83] that the award is to be calculated on a 'cost-plus' basis,[84] that is the cost to the claimant of the work plus a reasonable profit margin. What constitutes a 'reasonable profit margin' will vary according to the circumstances, including the margins typical in the industry, the nature and quality of the work and the level of competition. In some cases, it may be appropriate to dispense with cost-plus and value the services by the hour,[85] by way of commission or profit-share,[86] by reference to industry rates[87] or by some combination of valuation methods.[88] A quantum meruit is thus calculated, not by reference to the

[82] See ch 4, fns 70–88 and accompanying text.

[83] *Yeoman's Row Management Ltd v Cobbe* [2008] UKHL 55, [2008] 1 WLR 1752 [42] (Lord Scott).

[84] See ch 4, fn 81.

[85] See, eg *Countrywide Communications Ltd v ICL Pathway Ltd* [2000] CLC 324 (QB) 352–53; *MacKenzie v Thompson* [2005] 3 NZLR 285 (NZHC) [14]–[15]; *Chief Constable of Greater Manchester Police v Wigan Athletic FC* [2007] EWHC 3095 (Ch) [131] (Mann J); *Spencer v S Franses Ltd* [2011] EWHC 1269 (QB) [239]–[244] *cf Brenner v First Artists' Management Pty Ltd* [1993] 2 VR 221 (VSC) 263 (Byrne J).

[86] See, eg *Way v Latilla* [1937] 3 All ER 759 (HL) 764–65 (Lord Atkin) 766 (Lord Wright); *Upjay Pty Ltd v MJK Pty Ltd* [2001] SASC 62, (2001) 79 SASR 32 [79]–[81] (Wicks J); *Andrew Shelton & Co v Alpha Healthcare* [2002] VSC 248, [2003] 5 VR 577; *Vedatech Corp v Crystal Decisions (UK) Ltd* [2002] EWHC 818 (Ch) [86]–[96]; *MacKenzie v Thompson* [2005] 3 NZLR 285 (NZHC) [16]–[17]; *Benedetti v Sawiris* [2009] EWHC 1330 (Ch) [247] (Patten J).

[87] See, eg *Brenner v First Artists' Management Pty Ltd* [1993] 2 VR 221 (VSC) 263–64 (Byrne J).

[88] Ibid 263 (Byrne J).

loss suffered by the claimant or the actual gain to the defendant,[89] but by reference to the reasonable market value of the service received by the defendant.

More difficult problems of valuation may arise where the market is not competitive.[90] This is a problem that could have arisen in *Rowe v Vale of White Horse DC*[91] and *Chief Constable of Greater Manchester Police v Wigan Athletic FC*,[92] as the relevant services were provided by monopoly service providers. Although the difficulty of market valuation in these circumstances was ultimately not considered in either case, reliance upon the market value may not accurately reflect the objective value transferred to the recipient of such services. In such circumstances, the court may prefer to adopt a different valuation method or to discount the market price to quantify the reasonable objective value of the service conferred. However, there is no suggestion that the courts should resort to idiosyncratic valuations in these circumstances and it suffices to observe that there are different methods of objective valuation that can be employed where the market value is not an accurate guide.

In chapter two, it was explained that exchange value is simply one relative measure of the monetary value of a thing.[93] The absence of a market or the existence of a market in which the conditions of competition are not met does not preclude the objective calculation of a relative value. It is readily observed that there are a host of alternative valuation methods that may be appropriate, including the present future value of the income that will be generated from the benefit (eg rental income) or the capital value of its component parts. The important point for our purposes is that all these measures of value are objectively ascertainable and relational rather than idiosyncratic. The courts are well placed to examine evidence on the appropriate method of valuation in particular cases and calculate the appropriate award of monetary restitution.

## III. Overview of Legal Enrichment

The second approach to enrichment in the law of unjust enrichment is legalistic: the enrichment is characterised as the acquisition of a right, or the release of an obligation owed, by the defendant. In certain circumstances, the claimant may

[89] There are some US authorities which award the amount of the defendant's gain: *George v Double D Foods Inc*, 155 Cal App 3d 36, 47, 201 (1984); *Hartwell Corp v Smith*, 107 Idaho 134, 140–42 (1984) (Idaho App); *R Zoppo Co v City of Dover*, 124 NH 666, 666 (1984) (NH). See C Kovacic, 'A Proposal to Simplify Quantum Meruit Litigation' (1985) 35 *American University Law Review* 547, 556.

[90] See *Transpower New Zealand Ltd v Meridian Energy Ltd* [2001] 3 NZLR 700 (NZHC) [58]–[63]; C Mitchell, P Mitchell and S Watterson, *Goff & Jones The Law of Unjust Enrichment*, 8th edn (London, Sweet & Maxwell, 2011) §5-37.

[91] *Rowe v Vale of White Horse DC* [2003] EWHC 388 (Admin), [2003] 1 Lloyd's Rep 418.

[92] *Chief Constable of Greater Manchester Police v Wigan Athletic FC* [2008] EWCA Civ 1449, [2009] 1 WLR 1580.

[93] See ch 2, fns 23–26 and accompanying text.

reverse that enrichment specifically in law rather than by an award of the value of the right or release. This is an alternative to the claim articulated in section II above: if the benefit is valuable and there is no objection on freedom of choice grounds, the defendant's enrichment can also be characterised factually as the value of the right or release. However, the law of unjust enrichment admits both claims, which is the basis of the distinction between factual and legal enrichment in this work.

Sub-section A considers whether specific restitution cases form part of the law of unjust enrichment, principally by confronting Virgo's contrary position that many of these cases involve vindication of property rights and the argument that unjust enrichment never generates 'proprietary restitution'. Sub-section B then examines the legal characterisation of benefits, arguing that a defendant is enriched where the defendant acquires a right or is released from an obligation at the expense of the claimant. Finally, sub-section C examines specific restitution of a legal enrichment, arguing that restitution takes the form of a power, rather than a claim-right, to obtain restitution.

## A. Are Legal Enrichment Cases Part of Unjust Enrichment?

Legal enrichment treats the legal construct of a right (or the release from an obligation) as the relevant enrichment. Where the benefit received is identified as a right or the release from an obligation, the defendant is enriched in a characteristically legal sense. If specific restitution of a legal enrichment is part of the law of unjust enrichment, the law of unjust enrichment is not limited to the reversal of transfers of value; it extends to the reversal of the acquisition of rights or release of obligations. A formidable challenge to this analysis is posed by Virgo, who argues that restitution of property rights is not part of the law of unjust enrichment. In Virgo's view, these cases are best explained as the vindication of pre-existing property rights.[94] Virgo thinks that unjust enrichment cannot explain the recovery of property in which the claimant has a proprietary interest unless:[95]

> '[U]njust enrichment' is used in a trivial, descriptive sense to indicate that the defendant has property which it is just for him or her to return to the claimant. 'Unjust enrichment' in its substantive sense is completely irrelevant in this context because the action to vindicate property rights forms part of the law of property and has nothing to do with the principle of reversing unjust enrichment.

Virgo goes on to explain that this view has been endorsed by the House of Lords in *Foskett v McKeown*[96] and to criticise the notion that property rights ever arise in unjust enrichment. This book rejects Virgo's position, suggesting that the vindication of pre-existing property rights, while it may explain many cases of specific

[94] Virgo, *The Principles of the Law of Restitution* (2006) (n 2) Chs 20–21.
[95] Ibid 11–12.
[96] *Foskett v McKeown* [2001] 1 AC 102 (HL).

restitution, cannot explain those cases where the defendant acquires a right or the release of an obligation at the claimant's expense. Further, while *property rights* are never a response to unjust enrichment, a *persistent power* to obtain a right is regularly available in unjust enrichment.

### (i) Unjust Enrichment or Vindication of Pre-existing Property Rights?

While acknowledging that the restitution of property based on pre-existing property rights is not part of the law of unjust enrichment, this book differs from Virgo as to which cases fall into the category of vindication of pre-existing property rights. Three important points must be made. First, property rights are, without more, inert. As defined in chapter two, property rights are rights to corporeal things and the right corresponds to a duty on members of society generally not to interfere with such rights. Crucially, some further event must occur to generate legal rights *in personam*. The right–duty relationship is mediated by the thing and it is only through an interference with that right that an *in personam* right and correlative duty emerges between the right-holder and a person who interferes with the thing. For example, the various torts of interference with property rights generate *in personam* rights against the meddler. In the same way, 'property' should not be understood as the causative event in cases where the claimant seeks restitution of a thing in which he holds a property right. As Birks explains,[97] the true causative event is the receipt of property to which another is entitled, an event classified in the miscellany of other causative events. If the property right is itself the causative event, then the *in personam* right against the defendant to restitution exists even when the thing is in the hands of the owner, which is plainly nonsense.

Second, property rights are exclusively a response to events.[98] For Birks, property rights may be a response to consent,[99] wrongs,[100] unjust enrichment[101] or other events.[102] In contrast, Grantham and Rickett—who elaborate an alternative version of the vindication of rights thesis adopted by Virgo—contend that property rights have a dual role in this taxonomy as both an event and a response to events.[103] For example, Grantham and Rickett say that the right to compensation

[97] Birks, 'Property and Unjust Enrichment: Categorical Truths' (1997) (n 2) 657; P Birks, 'Property, Unjust Enrichment and Tracing' (2001) 54 *CLP* 231, 251; P Birks, 'Unjust Enrichment and Wrongful Enrichment' (2001) 79 *Texas Law Review* 1767; Birks, *Unjust Enrichment* (2005) (n 1) 27. See also L Smith, 'Restitution: The Heart of Corrective Justice' (2001) 79 *Texas Law Review* 2115, 2140–41.

[98] *Cf* Birks, 'Property, Unjust Enrichment and Tracing' (2001) (n 97) 245, 251.

[99] Most commonly, property rights arise from a conveyance: C Rickett, 'Old and New in the Law of Tracing' in J Edelman and S Degeling (eds), *Equity in Commercial Law* (Sydney, Lawbook Co, 2005).

[100] For a possible example, see *Attorney General for Hong Kong v Reid* [1994] 1 AC 324 (PC).

[101] For a possible example, see *Chase Manhattan Bank NA Ltd v Israel-British Bank (London) Ltd* [1981] Ch 105 (Ch).

[102] Eg *specificatio*, *accessio* or mixing, see *Appleby v Myers* (1867) 2 CP 651 (Ex).

[103] R Grantham and C Rickett, 'Property and Unjust Enrichment: Categorical Truths or Unnecessary Complexity?' [1997] *New Zealand Universities Law Review* 668; R Grantham and C Rickett, 'Property Rights as a Legally Significant Event' (2003) 62 *CLJ* 717, 727ff; Rickett, 'Old and New in the Law of

for conversion is properly attributable to the event of 'property',[104] not to wrongful interference with property rights.[105] However, their analysis is only supportable at a different level of abstraction from the meaning of 'event' in the Birksian taxonomy as it is presented in this book. It is equivalent to saying that the rights generated by interference with the person (eg the right to compensation for battery) are attributable to the event of 'personhood' or 'bodily integrity', and not to wrongful interference with the person. A property right, like the right to bodily integrity, is a prerequisite for certain causes of action, but some other event must intercede to generate legal responses.[106] It is a definitional error to consider property rights as events in the same sense as the other events in the Birksian taxonomy and this book rejects the category of 'property' as a causative event in private law.[107]

Third, the right to restitution is a *new* right, not the vindication of a pre-existing right. Although Virgo cites Grantham and Rickett's views on this debate with seeming approval,[108] his position is more nuanced. He takes the view, accepted in this book, that 'the use of the phrase "property rights" is neutral' and accepts that it must be 'that the defendant has interfered with the claimant's property rights by not allowing the claimant the exclusive benefit of his or her rights … which justifies the award'.[109] As such, the interference is the relevant event. However, if we apply a Hohfeldian analysis of rights and duties to Virgo's position, it is clear that new personal rights arise in the claimant against the defendant. All the claimant previously held was a property right in the thing; now she has a personal right against the defendant. In cases of wrongdoing, the event is the breach of a duty; where the claim is not a wrong but a vindication claim, there must likewise be some event generating this new right.

Thus, the essence of a vindication claim is that one person has a right to the thing *and* it is in the hands of another: the event is the receipt of property to which another is entitled. In contrast, the logic of a legal enrichment claim is not the vindication of the pre-existing property rights of the claimant but rather that the defendant is unjustly enriched by *rights acquired or obligations released* at the expense of the claimant. The claimant seeks the restitution of the specific legal enrichment acquired by the defendant in the defective transaction. Accordingly, although Virgo is right to insist on a distinction between the vindication of

Tracing' (2005) (n 99) 675–84. See also P Jaffey, 'Two Theories of Unjust Enrichment' in J Neyers, M McInnes and S Pitel (eds), *Understanding Unjust Enrichment* (Oxford, Hart, 2004) 146–49.

[104] Rickett, 'Old and New in the Law of Tracing' (2005) (n 99).

[105] J Penner, *The Idea of Property in Law* (Oxford, Clarendon Press, 1997) 24, 31.

[106] See L Smith, 'Unjust Enrichment, Property and the Structure of Trusts' (2000) 116 *LQR* 412, 421.

[107] See also W Swadling, 'Property and Unjust Enrichment' in J Harris (ed), *Property Problems: From Genes to Pension Funds* (London, Kluwer Law International, 1997); Smith, 'Unjust Enrichment, Property and the Structure of Trusts' (2000) ibid; D Fox, 'Legal Title as a Ground of Restitutionary Liability' [2000] *RLR* 465; A Burrows, 'Proprietary Restitution: Unmasking Unjust Enrichment' (2001) 117 *LQR* 412; Smith, 'Unjust Enrichment: The Heart of Corrective Justice' (2001) (n 97) 2128.

[108] Virgo, *The Principles of the Law of Restitution* (2006) (n 2) 15 fn 65.

[109] Ibid 15.

pre-existing property rights and restitution for unjust enrichment, this is not the same as drawing a line between specific restitution and unjust enrichment.

### *(ii) Proprietary Responses to Unjust Enrichment*

The relationship between the law of unjust enrichment and property rights is highly controversial and the above discussion forms part of a long-standing dispute as to whether or not unjust enrichment ever generates 'proprietary' responses.[110] On the one hand, Swadling and Lord Millett have argued that the common law should follow the civilian approach, which denies proprietary responses to unjust enrichment,[111] an approach apparently favoured by the House of Lords in *Foskett v McKeown*.[112] On the other, Birks and Chambers have been at the forefront of a more robust view of the circumstances in which unjust enrichment will generate property rights (which they define more broadly than the restrictive definition employed in this book).[113] The approach taken in this book suggests that both approaches are unsatisfactory. Swadling and Lord Millett are right that unjust enrichment never generates property rights in the strict sense of a claim-right to a corporeal thing, but it is also true that the response to unjust enrichment is not restricted to monetary restitution. As we shall see in chapter five, while property rights are never a response to unjust enrichment, the power to obtain specific rights (including property rights) is regularly awarded in unjust enrichment. Unjust enrichment is thus not limited to claims for value.

Two further points should be observed in respect of the connection between the 'proprietary restitution' debate and the legal enrichment model advanced here. First, if Swadling and Lord Millett are correct in suggesting that unjust enrichment only ever results in orders for restitution of value, then the characterisation of a benefit as a legal enrichment is otiose. However, this book accepts that unjust enrichment can generate specific restitution and relies upon the existing case law on rescission, rectification, resulting trusts and subrogation to support that conclusion. Second, the precise limits of specific restitution for unjust enrichment are beyond the scope of this work. The legal enrichment thesis is compatible with various different views as to the availability of specific restitution in unjust enrichment but, as the focus here is on enrichment, this book need not adjudicate on the precise conditions for the award of specific restitution in unjust enrichment.

[110] See ch 2, fn 55.

[111] Swadling, 'Property and Unjust Enrichment' (1997) (n 107) 130; P Millett, 'Proprietary Restitution' in S Degeling and J Edelman (eds), *Equity in Commercial Law* (Sydney, Thomson LBC, 2005); W Swadling, 'Unjust Delivery' in A Burrows and A Rodger (eds), *Mapping the Law: Essays in Memory of Peter Birks* (Oxford, Oxford University Press, 2006).

[112] *Foskett v McKeown* [2001] 1 AC 102 (HL).

[113] See, eg Birks, *Unjust Enrichment* (2005) (n 1) 304–07; Chambers, 'Resulting Trusts' (2006) (n 12).

## B. Legal Enrichment

Legal enrichment cases do not involve the same two-stage inquiry as factual enrichment cases. Instead, it is necessary simply to prove that the defendant has acquired a right ('enrichment by rights'), or the release of an obligation ('enrichment by release'), at the expense of the claimant. As will be explained below, the defendant's freedom of choice is not an *enrichment issue* where the claim is brought in this form, so there is no need to establish choice of the benefit or incontrovertibility. The response in legal enrichment cases is specific restitution to reverse the enrichment in law.

### *(i) Enrichment by Rights*

This book shows that the law allows specific restitution of rights where the defendant is enriched by the acquisition of a right. However, what rights count? What kind of right must the defendant obtain in order to be 'enriched by rights'? Chapter two introduced a number of distinctions within the category of rights.[114] First, personal rights and property rights were distinguished: personal rights were defined as rights exigible only against a particular person and property rights were prescriptively defined as rights to corporeal things. Second, the definition of property rights adopted in this book was distinguished from a broader meaning of property rights that extends the label 'property' to assignable personal rights, such as debts and other choses in action. Finally, 'persistent powers' were defined as powers to obtain specific rights or powers prima facie exigible against anyone who obtains those rights or powers. It is contended here that a defendant will be legally enriched by the acquisition of any right or power by its nature capable of assignment, including property rights, assignable personal rights and persistent powers.

A defendant may be factually or legally enriched by the acquisition of any right. Legal enrichment is not restricted to property rights or 'equitable property rights' or even to assignable rights. While the defendant in *Car & Universal Finance v Caldwell*[115] was enriched by a property right (the right to the Jaguar), the defendant bank in *Chase Manhattan*,[116] was enriched by a personal right (the right to US$2 million mistakenly transferred to the Israel-British Bank in London).[117] A defendant may be enriched by a contractual right,[118] as occurs when a mistaken payment is made into a bank account and the defendant receives a contractual right to claim against the bank for that amount.[119] Likewise, contractual rights

[114] See ch 2, s II.B.

[115] *Car & Universal Finance Co Ltd v Caldwell* [1963] 1 QB 525 (CA).

[116] *Chase Manhattan Bank NA Ltd v Israel-British Bank (London) Ltd* [1981] Ch 105 (Ch).

[117] See also *Vandervell v IRC* [1967] 2 AC 291 (HL).

[118] E Bant, *The Change of Position Defence* (Oxford, Hart, 2009) 91 *cf Criterion Properties plc v Stratford UK Properties LLC* [2004] UKHL 28, [2004] 1 WLR 1846 [27] (Lord Scott); Virgo, *The Principles of the Law of Restitution* (2006) (n 2) 29 fn 140.

[119] Eg *Jones & Sons (a firm) (Trustee) v Jones* [1997] Ch 159 (CA).

can be held on trust,[120] so where an attempt to declare a trust of a contractual right fails, the intended trustee's enrichment is a contractual right. Any legal right is capable of constituting a legal enrichment.

In his essay 'Two Kinds of Enrichment', Chambers suggests that 'Specific restitution means restitution of assignable rights'.[121] However, it is probably wrong to confine legal enrichment to assignable rights. For instance, it is possible to hold an unassignable right on trust,[122] and a resulting trust could effect specific restitution of that unassignable right.[123] Likewise, many contractual rights are unassignable, but nonetheless constitute a legal enrichment that can be reversed by rescission.[124] A claimant may, as a consequence of a fraudulent misrepresentation, confer an unassignable lease interest on the defendant. If the claimant exercises the power to rescind the lease, the right to immediate possession of the land will revest in the claimant. As such, the correct line seems to be that a defendant will be enriched by any right that by its nature is ordinarily capable of assignment, even if the particular right in question is unassignable.

One reason Chambers offers for restricting enrichment by rights to the category of 'assignable rights' is that it prevents the recovery of rights beyond the scope of unjust enrichment, 'such as … human body parts and abducted children'.[125] However, this does not require restricting legal enrichment to assignable rights. It is perfectly consistent to recognise enrichment extends to some non-assignable rights and yet exclude the recovery of rights to human body parts, children, bodily integrity and the like from the law of unjust enrichment. A system that does not recognise rights to human body parts will not suddenly do so because unjust enrichment admits restitution of rights. 'There is nothing preventing us from simply choosing to exclude'[126] certain rights from the law of unjust enrichment. Therefore, Chambers' restriction of rights-based enrichment to assignable rights is not necessary to avoid claims for the recovery of some rights from the law of unjust enrichment.

Nevertheless, while a defendant may be enriched by certain non-assignable rights, the utility of asserting legal enrichment is confined to the situation where the claimant can obtain restitution of a specific right. Where it is not possible to obtain specific restitution of the relevant right because it is non-assignable, then restitution of rights is not possible. One example may be an untransferable right to run a market.[127] If the defendant's enrichment is untransferable, the claimant will not be entitled to restitution of the right if this would be impossible. The claimant

[120] Eg *Don King Productions Inc v Warren (No 1)* [2000] Ch 291 (CA).

[121] Chambers, 'Two Kinds of Enrichment' (2009) (n 12) 256, 262.

[122] Eg *Don King Productions Inc v Warren (No 1)* [2000] Ch 291 (CA); *Barbados Trust Co Ltd v Bank of Zambia* [2007] EWCA Civ 148, [2007] 1 Lloyd's Rep 495.

[123] See ch 5, s I.C.

[124] See ch 5, s II.

[125] Chambers, 'Two Kinds of Enrichment' (2009) (n 12) 262. See also Birks, *Unjust Enrichment* (2005) (n 1) 51.

[126] Chambers, 'Two Kinds of Enrichment' (2009) (n 12) 263.

[127] R Stevens, *Torts and Rights* (Oxford, Oxford University Press, 2007) 6.

in such a situation will be confined to a claim for restitution of the value of the right. It will be possible to obtain specific restitution of certain non-assignable rights, such as the right to immediate possession under a non-assignable lease, but not others, perhaps including an untransferable right to a market. Thus, while it is probably wrong to confine legal enrichment to assignable rights, in practice most enrichment by rights cases will involve the acquisition of an assignable right by the defendant such that the claimant can obtain specific restitution.

### *(ii) Enrichment by Release*

The corollary of the acquisition of a right is the release of an obligation owed by the defendant. Like the acquisition of a right, a release may be either factually or legally enriching. This book suggests that the release of any obligation is a legal enrichment as the defendant is no longer subject to the relevant duty or liability. As Laws LJ said in *Gibb v Maidstone*, there is 'no principled distinction between a benefit consisting in money paid and a benefit consisting in a claim foregone'.[128] However, while the release of an obligation regularly gives rise to monetary restitution on a factual enrichment basis,[129] the only reported cases recognising the reinstatement of specific obligations for unjust enrichment involve subrogation. These cases, which are examined in detail in chapter five,[130] involve the reinstatement of a liability where a security is released at the claimant's expense. As such, although the release of an obligation is a benefit that may be characterised factually or legally, the claimant is usually restricted to a factual enrichment claim for the value of the release, except in cases where the obligation released is a liability by way of security.

Although subrogation is the only instance of specific restitution of an enrichment by release recognised in the cases, claimants have sought specific restitution outside the context of subrogated securities. For instance, one interpretation of the enrichment of the Revenue pursued by the claimants in the *FII Group Litigation*[131] is that the Revenue was released from the obligation to allow certain tax reliefs when the claimants used those tax reliefs to offset invalidly exacted taxes. If the tax reliefs did not remain valid, the Revenue's legal enrichment was the release of the statutory tax reliefs. In addition to monetary restitution, the claimants sought to reinstate the reliefs for use in future years against valid tax obligations. The claim was unsuccessful in the Court of Appeal because 'Utilisation of the [tax] reliefs may have been a detriment to the Claimants, but did not represent a gain to the Revenue for the purpose of a restitutionary cause of action'.[132] Although there may have been other reasons to deny the claim, the

[128] *Gibb v Maidstone and Tunbridge Wells NHS Trust* [2010] EWCA Civ 678, [2010] IRLR 786 [30] (Laws LJ).
[129] See ch 4, s VI.
[130] See ch 5, s IV.A.
[131] *Test Claimants in the FII Group Litigation v IRC* [2010] EWCA Civ 103.
[132] Ibid [178]–[181] (Arden LJ).

finding on enrichment must be incorrect. The Revenue clearly received value by the exercise of the tax reliefs to offset *invalidly* exacted taxes that would otherwise been used to offset *validly* exacted taxes. The Revenue was released from a liability corresponding to the power of the claimants to elect to use the reliefs. In factual enrichment terms, the enrichment is the value received by the Revenue by the release of that liability, which is the present future value to the Revenue of receiving lawful taxes in subsequent years that would otherwise not have been received. This would have involved extremely complex questions of valuation,[133] but the Revenue undeniably received value. Assuming the tax reliefs did not remain available to the claimants, an alternative approach may have been to award specific restitution of the tax reliefs, which would have been to reinstate the tax reliefs and permit the claimants to use the tax reliefs in future years. Although this was not permitted by the Court of Appeal, the *FII Group Litigation* suggests a situation in which specific restitution of an enrichment by release may be appropriate in future cases.

### *(iii) Freedom of Choice*

Legal enrichment cases, unlike factual enrichment cases, do not require a secondary inquiry as to protection of the defendant's freedom of choice. It was shown in section II of this chapter that, for a defendant to be factually enriched, the defendant must have chosen the relevant benefit or the benefit must be incontrovertibly enriching. This requirement was explained as an instantiation of the principle of freedom of choice that arises in the enrichment inquiry where the defendant is held to be enriched by the value of a benefit in kind. It is suggested that the same considerations do not apply in legal enrichment cases for two reasons. First, establishing the defendant's legal enrichment depends simply on the defendant acquiring a right or being released from an obligation. The logic of a legal enrichment claim does not contemplate the defendant being ordered to make restitution in money for something that the defendant has not chosen or does not value. Second, the claim for specific restitution protects the defendant's freedom of choice by requiring that the defendant retain the right or remain amenable to the imposition of the obligation. The defendant cannot give specific restitution of a right that he does not hold or come under an obligation that cannot be imposed on him. Accordingly, in legal enrichment cases, the defendant's freedom of choice is not in issue, at least not at the enrichment stage. The possible application of the defence of change of position to legal enrichment claims is considered in chapter eight.[134]

133 Ibid [180] (Arden LJ).
134 See ch 8, s III.

## C. Specific Restitution

The only response to unjust enrichment is restitution. In the Birksian taxonomy applied in this book, this is usually taken to mean that unjust enrichment gives rise to a 'right' to restitution.[135] In the loose, undifferentiated sense of 'right' that extends to all four of the Hohfeldian meanings of 'right' outlined in chapter two, this statement is true. However, to be precise, causes of action in unjust enrichment give rise to two different kinds of restitution: claim-rights to monetary restitution or powers to obtain specific restitution. Where the defendant is enriched by the receipt of value, the right to monetary restitution reverses the transfer of value; where the defendant's enrichment is characterised legally as the acquisition of a right, specific restitution is the power to reverse the acquisition of the right; and where the defendant's enrichment is characterised legally as the release of an obligation, specific restitution is the reinstatement of the obligation, conferring a power on the claimant to obtain the right held as security. Consequently, the distinction between personal and 'proprietary' restitution is inaccurately drawn; the true distinction is between restitution of value and specific restitution of rights and obligations.

### *(i) Specific, Not 'Proprietary'*

This book prefers the terminology of 'specific restitution' to 'proprietary restitution'. 'Proprietary restitution' is an inaccurate label because the claimant does not obtain a property right; rather, the claimant obtains a persistent power, capable of binding third parties. Furthermore, the law permits another restitutionary response that is not captured by the distinction between 'personal' and 'proprietary' restitution: the reinstatement of an obligation. In restitutionary subrogation cases, the defendant comes under a liability that reverses the defendant's enrichment by release of an obligation and the claimant obtains a power to obtain a specific right on the same conditions as the original security. As it fails to capture the varieties of specific restitution, the distinction between personal and proprietary restitution is crude and misleading. This book prefers a distinction between 'monetary restitution'—a claim-right to restitution of value—and 'specific restitution'—a power to obtain a specific right or power.

### *(ii) Two Kinds of Restitution*

In section II on factual enrichment, we encountered the first kind of restitution: monetary restitution based on a transfer of value. Whenever the claimant seeks restitution of a factual enrichment, the response is always the same: a right to be paid the value of the enrichment received at the claimant's expense. By contrast, when the claimant seeks specific restitution of a legal enrichment, the structure of the claim is different. Neither at common law nor in equity does the defendant's

[135] See, eg Chambers, 'Resulting Trusts' (2006) (n 12) 256.

unjust enrichment give rise to a claim-right to restitution of a specific right. Rather, the claimant obtains a power to obtain a specific right or power through various mechanisms, namely the power to rescind, the power to rectify, the power to collapse a trust and a subrogated power to obtain a right or power held as security. The structure is the same in each case: to reverse the defendant's legal enrichment in circumstances that are unjust, the claimant has a power to obtain a specific right in order to reverse a legal enrichment. The power is restitutionary in purpose and effect.[136]

This approach to specific restitution is similar to the power model proposed by Häcker, who argues that 'proprietary restitution' takes 'the form of a power (which has to be exercised before any property right revests)'.[137] On Häcker's model, the exercise of a persistent power arising at common law will revest title (where this is possible) or give rise to a trust (where something else is required to revest title at law, such as registration). By contrast, where the power arises in equity, the exercise of the power will never revest legal title but will instead give rise to a trust over the right or power in question. In either case, Häcker regards the power as being 'literally "restitutionary"'.[138]

Although Häcker distinguishes an 'immediate trust' approach from the power model she advances,[139] nothing turns on the choice between these approaches for the purposes of this book. As explained in chapter two, a core aspect of a private trust is the beneficiary's power to obtain the rights or powers held on trust, which is a persistent power. Although the trust is more secure than other persistent powers,[140] often described as 'mere equities', which are defeated by subsequent bona fide purchasers of a purely equitable interest,[141] the restitutionary purpose and effect is identical. As such, the claimant will sometimes obtain a power under a trust and sometimes a power that is a 'mere equity', but what matters for the purposes of the enrichment model presented in this book is that, in every case, the claimant obtains a power to obtain a specific right or power that persists against third parties who acquire the right or power (subject to defences).

In chapter five, the four principal forms of a power to obtain specific restitution are examined: resulting trusts, rescission, rectification and subrogation. A detailed examination of each of these powers is postponed until chapter five, but it is useful now to set out the conclusion that each is a variety of specific restitution of a legal enrichment. First, the resulting trust is a common form of specific restitution. A resulting trust does not give rise to a *right* to restitution, but instead a *power* exercisable by the beneficiary to obtain restitution of the right or power

[136] B Häcker, 'Proprietary Restitution After Impaired Consent Transfers: A Generalised Power Model' (2009) 68 *CLJ* 324, 330.

[137] Ibid 325.

[138] Ibid 330.

[139] Ibid 328–29 *cf* McFarlane, *The Basic Structure of Property Law* (2008) (n 34) 299–322.

[140] *Qui prior est tempore, potior est iure* ('where the equities are equal, the first in time prevails').

[141] *Phillips v Phillips* (1861) 4 De GF&J 208, 218; 45 ER 1164, 1167 (Lord Westbury LC); *Cave v Cave* (1880) 15 Ch D 639 (Ch) 646–49 (Fry J).

held on trust. As such, where the defendant is enriched by the acquisition of a right, an immediate resulting trust gives the claimant a power to obtain restitution by collapsing the trust.

Second, rescission is more complex, but nonetheless restitutionary. As will be explained in chapter five, it is probably the case that rescission takes different forms at law and in equity. Where the power to rescind arises at law, the defendant's legal enrichment gives rise to a power to revest the legal title,[142] provided this is possible. Where it is not, for example because registration is required to revest title at law, the claimant will instead have a power to impose a trust by rescinding. Restitution where rescission gives rise to a trust involves the exercise of two separate powers, that is a power (to rescind) to obtain a power (under a trust) to obtain the right or power held on trust.[143] To complicate matters further, a power to rescind arising in equity may also take two forms.[144] Exercising the power to rescind will either give rise to: (i) an immediate trust; or (ii) a judicial order for specific restitution conditional upon counter-restitution. Until the operation of rescission at law and in equity is clarified by the courts, it is impossible to say with certainty which of these various forms specific restitution takes in rescission cases. However, it is concluded in chapter five that these differences are of process, not purpose. Both at law and in equity, the claimant has a power to obtain restitution by rescinding the transaction, which will effect restitution of specific rights or give rise to a second power to do so under a trust.

Finally, chapter five argues that subrogation may be restitutionary or prophylactic. Where it is restitutionary, subrogation involves the specific restitution of a legal enrichment: it reverses the release of a liability by reinstating that liability. The claimant does not have a claim-right to the right or power held as security, but rather a power exercisable under the conditions of the 'revived' liability. If the defendant fails to make restitution of value, the claimant may enforce the power by election and obtain the right or power held as security. Thus, although specific restitution takes a number of different forms, the claimant never obtains a claim-right to restitution of a specific right or power, but instead obtains a power to obtain specific restitution through various mechanisms.

### *(iii) The Availability of Specific Restitution*

Whether the unjust enrichment of the defendant will give rise to specific restitution is not a question of enrichment, and therefore strictly beyond the scope of this book. However, it can be readily admitted that specific restitution of a legal enrichment is more restricted than monetary restitution, and it is important to note that this book does not imply that specific restitution is available whenever the claimant establishes a legal enrichment. First, specific restitution is not available

[142] Eg *Car & Universal Finance Co Ltd v Caldwell* [1963] 1 QB 525 (CA).

[143] Häcker, 'Proprietary Restitution After Impaired Consent Transfers: A Generalised Power Model' (2009) (n 136) 330.

[144] See ch 5, fns 160–61 and accompanying text.

where the law does not recognise the existence of a claim for specific restitution of the right in question. For example, we will see in chapter five that the common law only recognises a claim to revest title of chattels, not intangibles.[145] Simply because a right to intangible property is a legal enrichment does not imply the existence of a claim for specific restitution of intangibles at law. Whether, and to what extent, specific restitution should be available is a question yet to be definitively answered by the courts and it is not answered in this work, although an outline of the way forward is suggested in chapter eight.[146]

Second, on the power model advocated here, specific restitution is made subject to the rules of contract, property and equity that determine the creation and acquisition of the relevant rights and obligations. For example, a particular right may attract registration requirements and restitution of that right may depend upon correction of the register. Instead of overriding the rules that apply to the creation and acquisition of the right in question, unjust enrichment gives the claimant a power to obtain restitution within the relevant rights regime. Where specific restitution is not possible or a defence protecting honest purchasers applies (such as bona fide purchaser, indefeasible title or an exception to *nemo dat quod non habet*), then the claimant is restricted to a claim for the value of the right or release. This is an aspect of what may be described as the 'subsidiary' nature of the law of unjust enrichment.

## IV. Conclusion

This chapter set out a superstructure for the enrichment inquiry in the law of unjust enrichment. It suggested that the enrichment inquiry is more complex than is commonly suggested in theoretical accounts applying a unitary definition of enrichment. Section I explained the purpose of the enrichment inquiry and outlined the content of, and justification for, the term 'enrichment'. The chapter then divided the enrichment inquiry into factual and legal enrichment.

In respect of factual enrichment cases, a two-stage model was presented, requiring the claimant to prove: (i) the receipt of value by the defendant; and (ii) the choice of the benefit by the defendant or its incontrovertibility. It was explained that monetary restitution raises difficult questions of freedom of choice as a defendant is required to make restitution in money for a benefit in kind. An objective approach to valuing the benefit conferred and identifying a transfer of value to the defendant was outlined as an alternative to the 'subjective devaluation' thesis favoured by some commentators. The intention here was only to outline a model for factual enrichment to be applied to the cases in chapter four. Further, the

[145] See ch 5, fns 156–59 and accompanying text.
[146] See ch 8, s III.

rejection of subjective devaluation and the elaboration of the 'choice of benefit' test are dealt with in detail in chapter six.

In relation to legal enrichment, it was contended that a defendant can be enriched by the acquisition of a right or release of an obligation *simpliciter*, without any recourse to the notion of value. In enrichment by rights cases, the claimant alleges that the defendant is enriched by the creation of a right held by the defendant and seeks specific restitution of the right that the defendant still holds. In enrichment by release cases, the claimant alleges that the defendant is enriched by the release of an obligation and seeks specific reinstatement of that obligation. Valuation is properly irrelevant to a finding of enrichment in either case. The application of the model of legal enrichment to the cases is postponed until chapter five.

# 4

# Factual Enrichment

Chapter three of this book explored the theoretical distinction between factual and legal enrichment. In chapter four and chapter five, the focus turns to justifying the model outlined in chapter three by reference to the cases. This chapter examines the factual characterisation of enrichment, where the claimant alleges that the defendant is enriched by the value of the benefit received and must make restitution of that value. Chapter five will then address legal enrichment cases, where the claimant relies on the acquisition of a right, or release of an obligation owed, by the defendant and claims that the defendant must make specific restitution.

The purpose of this chapter is to collect together the disparate common counts from which the modern law derives and show how these cases can be rationalised together within the principle of unjust enrichment. Historically, the common law differentiated between money and non-money claims for restitution:[1] the former traditionally under the labels of 'failure of consideration' or 'money had and received'; the latter disguised by labels such as quantum meruit and quantum valebat.[2] This chapter contends that there is no reason in principle for separating money and non-money awards. Rather, such a distinction falsely separates claims which ought to be considered together. It will be argued that the rationale for awarding restitution in unjust enrichment is the same whether the claim is for the value of money or the value of benefits in kind. A different analytic regime should not apply where the reason for restitution and the purpose of the legal response are the same.

This chapter argues that it is better to group money and non-money claims together in unjust enrichment and view the historical distinction between them as a question of proving enrichment:[3] whether a defendant has been enriched by the receipt of non-money benefits is an open question, whereas enrichment by the receipt of money (itself a measure of value) is incontrovertible.[4] The difficulty of establishing enrichment where the benefit is non-monetary has led claims involving non-money benefits to be artificially segregated from money claims

[1] Eg *Yeoman's Row Management Ltd v Cobbe* [2008] UKHL 55, [2008] 1 WLR 1752 [3], [42]–[43] (Lord Scott).

[2] *Cf Pearce v Brain* [1929] 2 KB 310 (KB) 312.

[3] A Burrows, 'Free Acceptance and the Law of Restitution' (1988) 104 *LQR* 576.

[4] *BP Exploration Co (Libya) Ltd v Hunt (No 2)* [1979] 1 WLR 783 (QB) 799 (Robert Goff J); P Birks, *Unjust Enrichment*, 2nd edn (Oxford, Clarendon Press, 2005) 49.

and has prevented claims with an identical rationale being considered together. Accordingly, the aim of this chapter is to recast the common counts in light of the enrichment model defended in this book.

Section I provides a brief introduction to the historical common counts in *indebitatus assumpsit* and argues that they were not separate causes of action but, rather, distinguished different types of enrichment that should be assimilated together in the enrichment inquiry. The remainder of the chapter then considers each category of case according to the type of enrichment asserted. Section II considers the most common enrichment by value: the receipt of money. It is argued that many cases of 'money had and received' are properly subsumed within the law of unjust enrichment as restitution of a factual enrichment. Section III then goes on to consider services, explaining how most—but not all—quantum meruit cases are better understood as unjust enrichment by the receipt of services. Section IV then makes the same argument in respect of quantum valebat claims for goods. Section V examines land and section VI considers the release of obligations as a valuable benefit in the law of unjust enrichment. It is shown that, in each case, the requirement to pay for the benefit received can be explained as the restitution of value for unjust enrichment. The discussion of freedom of choice and subjective devaluation is postponed until chapter six. For the purposes of the discussion in this chapter, it is assumed that the defendant chose the relevant benefit or it is incontrovertible.

## I. The Historical Position

To accept the proposed assimilation of the common counts in the enrichment model defended in this book, it is necessary to detour briefly into the history of 'quasi-contract', which is known to modern lawyers as 'unjust enrichment'. At the beginning of the seventeenth century, the common law did not explicitly have a concept of unjust enrichment or even 'quasi-contract'.[5] The forerunners of what we now know as unjust enrichment were scattered across the writs of debt, promise and account.[6] Due to the procedural impediments attaching to these writs, the popularity of the more flexible 'action on the case' swelled during the sixteenth century, as did the temptation to find a home for quasi-contractual claims in these more flexible actions.[7] This home was eventually to be found in the action on the

[5] JH Baker, 'The Use of Assumpsit for Restitutionary Money Claims' in E Schrage (ed), *Unjust Enrichment: The Comparative Legal History of the Law of Restitution* (Berlin, Duncker & Humblot, 1995) 31; JH Baker, 'The History of Quasi-Contract in English Law' in W Cornish and others (eds), *Restitution: Past, Present and Future* (Oxford, Hart, 1998) 39; D Ibbetson, *A Historical Introduction to the Law of Obligations* (Oxford, Oxford University Press, 1999) 264–65.

[6] RM Jackson, *The History of Quasi-Contract in English Law* (Cambridge, Cambridge University Press, 1936) 6; Baker, 'The Use of Assumpsit for Restitutionary Money Claims' (1995) (n 5) 31–32.

[7] Baker, 'The History of Quasi-Contract in English Law' (1998) (n 5) 39.

case upon *assumpsit*,[8] which alleged that the defendant breached an undertaking made to the claimant and must therefore compensate the defendant for the breach. It may have been this attempt to locate unjust enrichment in a form of action based upon a breach of an undertaking that for so long consigned unjust enrichment to the fringes of the law of contract.[9]

Until the seventeenth century, resting as it did upon the requirement of an undertaking,[10] the action on the case upon *assumpsit* was essentially contractual in nature. However, during the seventeenth century, the action of *assumpsit* began to depart from its origins in express promise to situations where no express promise or undertaking existed. The critical first step is usually traced to the extension of *indebitatus assumpsit*[11] approved in *Slade's Case*[12] in 1602.[13] The *indebitatus assumpsit* formula alleged that the claimant was owed a debt by the defendant, who had subsequently promised to pay it. *Slade's Case* found that every executory contract implied the necessary promise to perform, 'for when one agrees to pay money, or to deliver anything, thereby he assumes or promises to pay or deliver it'.[14] No longer required to point to a subsequent promise, claimants were able to plead in *assumpsit* and avoid recourse to the writ of debt (with its attendant procedural baggage). From the acceptance of this practice in *Slade's Case*, a promise inferred from all the circumstances came to suffice in *assumpsit*.

There is nothing necessarily fictional in finding an implied promise to perform obligations under a contract. In many cases, the circumstances can involve an actual, albeit implicit, promise to perform.[15] Nevertheless, during the course of the century, *Slade's Case* would broaden *assumpsit* from the confines of contractual liability to cases at the periphery of the law of contract. Where an undertaking was neither expressed nor implied from the circumstances, but was instead 'implied by law', the writ could extend beyond the confines of contractual liability.[16] And so it did: following the finding of an implied undertaking in *Slade's Case*, *assumpsit* gradually came to lie in numerous cases where the undertaking was entirely

[8] An *assumptio* is an undertaking, see M Woodley (ed), *Osborn's Concise Law Dictionary*, 10th edn (London, Sweet & Maxwell, 2005) 42; Baker, 'The Use of Assumpsit for Restitutionary Money Claims' (1995) (n 5) 33 fn 10.

[9] The history of the contractual and non-contractual theories of claims in *indebitatus assumpsit* in the 17th, 18th and 19th centuries is carefully traced in T Baloch, *Unjust Enrichment and Contract* (Oxford, Hart, 2009) 5–46.

[10] JB Ames, *Lectures on Legal History and Miscellaneous Legal Essays* (Cambridge, Harvard University Press, 1913) 149.

[11] *Indebitatus* means indebted. The 'plaintiff alleged that the defendant was indebted (*indebitatus*) to him in so much money, and that afterwards (on the same day), in consideration thereof, the defendant undertook (*assumpsit super se*) and faithfully promised to pay it; the action was brought for breach of this promise, rather than for the underlying debt': Baker, 'The Use of Assumpsit for Restitutionary Money Claims' (1995) (n 5) 33.

[12] *Slade's Case* (1602) 4 Co Rep 92b.

[13] See, eg C Fifoot, *History and Sources of the Common Law: Tort and Contract* (London, Stevens & Son, 1949) 359; A Denning, 'Quantum Meruit and the Statute of Frauds' (1925) 41 *LQR* 82.

[14] *Slade's Case* (1602) 4 Co Rep 92b, 94a.

[15] Ames, *Lectures on Legal History and Miscellaneous Legal Essays* (1913) (n 10) 152.

[16] Baker, 'The History of Quasi-Contract in English Law' (1998) (n 5) 41.

fictional, such as mistake, failure of consideration or where money had been given to the defendant to the use of another.[17] As Baloch convincingly establishes, these actions were distinct from contractual actions and understood to have an independent, non-contractual basis at least until the nineteenth century.[18]

The reason for the growth of *assumpsit* after *Slade's Case* was the writ's convenience for claimants. In particular, it was not necessary for the claimant in *indebitatus assumpsit* to set out all the details of how the debt arose.[19] It was sufficient for the claimant to plead the reason for the defendant's indebtedness in general terms, for example because of money had and received to the claimant's use or because the defendant had received services from the claimant and ought to be paid quantum meruit.[20] These common declarations became known as the common money counts: money had and received, money paid, account stated and quantum meruit and quantum valebat. It is from these counts that the corpus of the modern law of unjust enrichment evolved. The model of enrichment presented in this book treats these common counts as instances of the same principle applied to different factual circumstances. As such, it is contended that the common counts should, with some exceptions, be subsumed within the concept of enrichment.

Although modern cases still refer to 'claims for money had and received' or 'quantum meruit claims', the common counts are not causes of action. As Lord Esher MR explained in *Read v Brown*, the phrase 'cause of action' simply means 'every fact which it would be necessary for the plaintiff to prove, if traversed, in order to support his right to the judgment of the Court'.[21] 'Cause of action' thus refers to the material facts that give rise to the right asserted.[22] The common counts do not accurately disclose the facts that are necessary to establish modern restitutionary claims. Instead, they distinguish such claims based on the type of enrichment, that is money, services, goods, the discharge of obligations and so on. Under the modern law, we accept that the claimant must prove the facts necessary to show that the defendant is unjustly enriched at his expense, one of which is that the defendant is enriched. The abolition of the forms of action allows the courts to look beyond the form of the common counts to the underlying cause of action in unjust enrichment, such as mistake, duress, undue influence or failure of consideration.[23] By applying the factual enrichment model to each class of enrichment, the remainder of this chapter demonstrates how each of the common counts should be assimilated into the law of unjust enrichment.

[17] Ibbetson, *A Historical Introduction to the Law of Obligations* (1999) (n 5) 269.

[18] Baloch, *Unjust Enrichment and Contract* (2009) (n 9) 10–40.

[19] Ames, *Lectures on Legal History and Miscellaneous Legal Essays* (1913) (n 10) 153.

[20] Baker, 'The Use of Assumpsit for Restitutionary Money Claims' (1995) (n 5) 35.

[21] *Read v Brown* (1888) 22 QBD 128 (CA) 131 (Lord Esher MR); *Do Carmo v Ford Excavations Pty Ltd* (1984) 58 ALJR 287 (HCA) 292 (Wilson J).

[22] *Read v Brown* (1888) 22 QBD 128 (CA) 129 (Pollock B); *Cooke v Gill* (1873) 8 CP 107 (CCP) 116 (Lord Esher MR); *Buckley v Hann* (1850) 5 Ex 43, 155 ER 19.

[23] See *Moses v Macferlan* (1760) 2 Burr 1005, 1012; 97 ER 676, 681–82 (Lord Mansfield).

# II. Money

## A. Money Had and Received

Historically, the count in money had and received alleged that the defendant:[24]

> Not regarding his said several promises and undertakings, but conniving and fraudulently intending craftily and subtilly to deceive and defraud [the claimant] hath not yet paid the said several sums of money or any part thereof … [and] hath hitherto wholly refused and still refuses.

The language of the form of action was borrowed from the form of action of account against a receiver. As receivers are agents, there is a genuine, albeit sometimes implied, promise to account for the monies received and breach of this promise is the gist of the action. In this form, money had and received was contractual, based upon the breach of 'promises and undertakings' to pay. However, since at least the eighteenth century, the promise to pay was often fictional, a fiction which was repeated across the common counts. For example, in *Exall v Partridge*,[25] a case involving the non-money benefit of discharge of a legal obligation,[26] it was amply clear that the defendant had not promised to pay the claimant for the discharge of his rent. In fact, a claimant in money had and received needed to establish neither a promise to pay nor an intention to defraud, and the language of the form of action bears little resemblance to its modern usage.

In the modern law, money had and received is better understood, not as a cause of action, but as a response to various causes of action. First, as in its original incarnation, money had and received may refer to a claim under a genuine contract for the payment of money based on the agreement of the parties. For instance, the form was often used to compel agents to account on the basis of a genuine contractual agency.[27] Second, it is often, albeit not always, a description of a restitutionary response to unjust enrichment. For example, the seminal case of *Kelly v Solari*[28] was pleaded as money had and received, as was *Fibrosa Spolka Akcyjna v Fairbairn Lawson Combe Barbour Ltd*,[29] the first English decision to recognise unequivocally the principle of unjust enrichment. Third, 'money had and received' may also refer to restitution or disgorgement of money where the cause

[24] See H Stephen, *A Treatise on the Principles of Pleading in Civil Actions*, 2nd edn (London, Joseph Butterworth & Son, 1827) 312.

[25] *Exall v Partridge* (1799) 8 TR 308, 101 ER 1405. See also *Russell v Bell* (1842) 10 M&W 340, 352; 152 ER 500, 507 (Lord Abinger).

[26] For an explanation of why this is a non-money benefit, see P Birks, *An Introduction to the Law of Restitution*, revised edn (Oxford, Clarendon Press, 1989) 112.

[27] G Jones (ed), *Goff & Jones The Law of Restitution*, 7th edn (London, Sweet & Maxwell, 2007) §1-003.

[28] *Kelly v Solari* (1841) 9 M&W 54, 152 ER 24.

[29] *Fibrosa Spolka Akcyjna v Fairbairn Lawson Combe Barbour Ltd* [1943] AC 32 (HL).

of action is wrongs-based, as in *Reading v Attorney General*.[30] As 'money had and received' refers to a response to various different causes of action, it is not itself a cause of action.

### *Money had and Received as a Legal Response*

If 'money had and received' is not a cause of action, but rather a response to causes of action, what kind of response is it? While it often refers to the award of monetary restitution where the defendant has received money from the claimant,[31] the term is not limited to this meaning.[32] For example, it may refer to specific restitution of the right to money that the claimant can identify in the hands of the defendant[33] or to disgorgement of profits.[34] It is suggested in this book that it is simply outmoded terminology for either a money award or a proprietary claim to money. The term does not distinguish between restitution and disgorgement and it does not disclose a particular cause of action but rather straddles various causes of action. It does not provide any useful theoretical or taxonomical purpose; it is merely shorthand for an unspecified money award on some independent basis and use of the term should therefore generally be eschewed.

## B. Factual Enrichment in Money Cases

This book examined the conceptual nature of money in chapter two.[35] It was explained that money is a universal medium of exchange and functions as the standard numerical measure of relational value. This feature allows money to function as a store of value because anyone who values anything that can be purchased with money must likewise value money. On the enrichment model presented in this book, the receipt of 'money' thus *necessarily* qualifies as the receipt of value and a defendant who receives money is enriched by the value so received. In addition to the exchange value of the money received, the defendant may be enriched by the use value of money over time, as the Revenue was enriched in *Sempra Metals v IRC*. Furthermore, in certain cases that will be examined in chapter five, the defendant may be enriched by the right to money and the claimant may seek restitution of that right,[36] for example by way of a resulting trust.

[30] *Reading v Attorney General* [1951] AC 507 (HL). See also *Mahesan S/O Thambiah v Malaysian Government Officers Co-Operative Housing Society* [1979] AC 374 (PC) 376 (Lord Diplock); *Armagas Ltd v Mundogas SA* [1986] AC 717 (HL) 742–43 (Robert Goff LJ); *Petrotrade Inc v Smith* [2000] 1 Lloyd's Rep 486 (QB) 490 (David Steel J).

[31] Eg *Kelly v Solari* (1841) 9 M&W 54, 152 ER 24.

[32] *Cf* G Virgo, *The Principles of the Law of Restitution*, 2nd edn (Oxford, Oxford University Press, 2006) 21.

[33] Jones (ed), *Goff & Jones The Law of Restitution* (2007) (n 27) §1-002–§1-003. See also L Smith, 'Simplifying Claims to Traceable Proceeds' (2009) 125 *LQR* 338.

[34] Eg *Reading v Attorney General* [1951] AC 507 (HL).

[35] See ch 2, s I.B.

[36] *Cf Barros Mattos Junior v Macdaniels Ltd* [2004] EWHC 1188 (Ch), [2005] 1 WLR 247 [15] (Laddie J).

## (i) Exchange Value

As money is a store and measure of value, the receipt of money is the quintessential example of the receipt of value. There can thus be no doubt that the defendant is enriched where the defendant acquires the exchange value of money at the claimant's expense. The same is true in cases like *Goss v Chilcott*,[37] where, rather than receiving the money himself, the defendant requests that the money be paid to a third party.[38] In such cases, as the transfer to the third party is made at the defendant's request, the defendant has received the exchange value as much as if the money had been paid into the defendant's own bank account and then been credited to the third party thereafter.

Thus claims for the exchange value of money are straightforwardly explained in terms of factual enrichment. However, not much thought is given in the unjust enrichment literature to the definition of 'money'. It is important to note that the concept of money extends beyond simple physical currency, which is the narrowest economic definition: M0. The usual economic definition of money is M4, which includes deposits and other highly liquid assets that can readily be converted into currency.[39] This differs markedly from the layperson's idea of money as constituted by notes and coins, which is a conception of money as pieces of paper and metal that have a value, rather than money as an abstract measure of relational value.

With few exceptions, the law does not conceive of money in the simplistic lay fashion, instead adopting a more flexible and abstract approach to money consistent with its function as a measure of relational value. Depending on the context, the legal concept of money may include bank notes,[40] the right to be paid cash (for example a bank account),[41] and certain personalty.[42] Lord Mansfield recognised this point in 1758 in respect of negotiable instruments in *Miller v Race*, holding that bank notes 'are treated as money … by the general consent of mankind; which gives them the credit and currency of money, to all intents and purposes'.[43] Thus, the law adopts a functional approach to the definition of money, which extends the concept to rights and instruments that are equivalent

[37] *Goss v Chilcott* [1996] AC 788 (HL).

[38] See C Mitchell, P Mitchell and S Watterson, *Goff & Jones The Law of Unjust Enrichment*, 8th edn (London, Sweet & Maxwell, 2011) §5-04.

[39] M4 is defined by the Bank of England to include: sterling notes and coin; sterling deposits, including certificates of deposit; commercial paper, bonds, FRNs and other instruments of up to and including five years' original maturity issued by UK monetary financial institutions; claims on UK monetary financial institutions arising from repos (from December 2005); estimated holdings of sterling bank bills; and (from end-1986) 95% of the domestic sterling interbank (now inter-monetary financial institution) difference (allocated to wholesale deposits/other financial corporations, the remaining 5% being allocated to transits): Bank of England, 'Explanatory Notes—M4' (2008) www.bankofengland.co.uk/mfsd/iadb/notesiadb/M4.htm accessed 30 December 2011.

[40] *Wright v Reed* (1790) 3 TR 554, 100 ER 729; *Suffell v Bank of England* (1882) 9 QBD 555 (CA) 563 (Jessel MR).

[41] *Re Collings* [1933] Ch 920 (Ch).

[42] *Perrin v Morgan* [1943] AC 399 (HL) 407, 413 (Viscount Simon LC).

[43] *Miller v Race* (1758) 1 Burr 452, 457; 97 ER 398, 402 (Lord Mansfield).

to, or approximate, currency. This is consistent with the economic definition of money as M4 and references to 'money' as an enrichment in this book will, unless otherwise specified, refer to M4. The use of M4 is consistent with the relational conception of value adopted in chapter two and the theory of factual enrichment expounded in this book.

### *(ii) Use Value of Money*

In addition to a claim for the principal, the law recognises a separate, independent claim for the use value of money, as confirmed by the House of Lords in *Sempra Metals v IRC*[44] and *Deutsche Morgan Grenfell v IRC*.[45] In these cases, the House of Lords recognised the claimants' right to recover the interest on advanced corporation tax payments that they would not have made had they been entitled to make a group income election to pay those amounts later as mainstream corporation tax. The claims were not for the principal tax owing, which was due in any event, but for the interest on those sums in the interim. In effect, following the majority's reasoning in *Sempra*, if the payments were not due at the time they were made, the Revenue obtained an interest-free loan from the claimants until they became due. The benefit that is transferred is 'the opportunity to turn the money to account during the period of the enrichment',[46] a valuable benefit the receipt of which involves an objective transfer of value to the defendant. However, as we shall see in chapter six,[47] the use of money is not necessarily incontrovertibly enriching and it will be necessary to establish choice of the benefit or incontrovertibility to prove enrichment in use value cases.

The valuation of the use of money is often complex, but the purpose of the calculation is clear: to reverse the value transferred to the defendant by having the use of the money for a period of time. Lord Nicholls made it clear in *Sempra* that the valuation was objective, not subjective, holding that the question was 'the time value of money, measured objectively' and not 'the value of the benefits a defendant actually derived from the use of the money'.[48] While his Lordship went on to note that 'A benefit is not always worth its market value to a particular defendant',[49] his speech did not endorse idiosyncratic valuation and such an interpretation would be overbroad and inconsistent with authority. As explained in chapter three,[50] the question is the value of the use to a reasonable person *in the position of the defendant*, but not sharing the defendant's subjective preferences and priorities.[51] In *Sempra*, this test meant the interest rate for public sector

[44] *Sempra Metals Ltd v IRC* [2007] UKHL 34, [2008] 1 AC 561 [114] (Lord Nicholls).

[45] *Deutsche Morgan Grenfell plc v IRC* [2006] UKHL 49, [2007] 1 AC 558. See also *Westdeutsche Landesbank Girozentrale v Islington LBC* [1996] AC 669 (HL) 691 (Lord Goff) 719–20 (Lord Woolf); *Boake Allen Ltd v HMRC* [2006] EWCA Civ 25 [163]–[175] (Mummery LJ).

[46] *Sempra Metals Ltd v IRC* [2007] UKHL 34, [2008] 1 AC 561 [33] (Lord Hope).

[47] See ch 6, s III.B.

[48] *Sempra Metals Ltd v IRC* [2007] UKHL 34, [2008] 1 AC 561 [117] (Lord Nicholls).

[49] Ibid [119] (Lord Nicholls).

[50] See ch 3, s II.B.

[51] *Benedetti v Sawiris* [2010] EWCA Civ 1427 [145] (Etherton LJ).

borrowing rather than the prevailing rate in commercial markets;[52] it did not mean the subjective value attached to the use of the money by the Revenue. The courts below made no attempt to discern the value of the borrowing to the Revenue itself and, in the House of Lords, the majority held that it was not necessary to adduce evidence as to how the Revenue had actually used the money and it was clear that any profits made by the Revenue would not have been recoverable.[53] It was also not considered to be relevant whether the Government had any need to borrow the funds at the time. Plainly, this is inconsistent with a subjective devaluation approach. In use value cases, the calculation of the value transferred will be an objective valuation of the benefit to a reasonable person in the position of the defendant in the relevant market.

### *(iii) Combining Claims for the Principal and Use Value*

There is a further issue with use claims in respect of money, which is whether they can be combined with claims for the principal. This question had been complicated by the House of Lords decision in *Westdeutsche*,[54] where the majority had suggested that section 35A of the Supreme Court Act 1981 provided the sole jurisdiction to award interest in respect of restitutionary liabilities, thereby precluding the award of compound interest to achieve restitution of the full use value of the money obtained by the defendant. Subsequently, in *Sempra Metals*, the House of Lords held that section 35A does not provide an exclusive power to award interest, including in cases caught by the section.[55] However, the House of Lords equivocated on whether a claim for the principal sum and a claim for the use value could be combined. Lord Nicholls[56] and Lord Hope[57] declined to follow the majority in *Westdeutsche*, holding instead that the prohibition on compound interest awards in that decision did not apply where a use value claim was brought as the 'principal claim'. However, this produces indefensible distinctions, for example between cases where the principal sum has been paid back and cases where it has not. The defendant's enrichment by the value of the use of money does not turn on whether there is also a claim to the principal sum.[58]

The better view, adopted by Lord Walker[59] and Lord Mance,[60] is that the two claims can always be combined. In other words, a claimant can sue both for the money and interest on that sum. There is no double recovery in awarding interest

[52] See ch 2, fns 27–29 and accompanying text.

[53] *Sempra Metals Ltd v IRC* [2007] UKHL 34, [2008] 1 AC 561 [32] (Lord Hope) [117] (Lord Nicholls) [178], [180] (Lord Walker).

[54] *Westdeutsche Landesbank Girozentrale v Islington LBC* [1996] AC 669 (HL). See Mitchell, Mitchell and Watterson, *Goff & Jones The Law of Unjust Enrichment* (2011) (n 38) §§5-11–5-14.

[55] *Sempra Metals Ltd v IRC* [2007] UKHL 34, [2008] 1 AC 561 [114] (Lord Nicholls).

[56] Ibid [112] (Lord Nicholls).

[57] Ibid [36] (Lord Hope).

[58] Mitchell, Mitchell and Watterson, *Goff & Jones The Law of Unjust Enrichment* (2011) (n 38) §5-13.

[59] *Sempra Metals Ltd v IRC* [2007] UKHL 34, [2008] 1 AC 561 [183]–[184] (Lord Walker).

[60] Ibid [240] (Lord Mance).

at the relevant rate in addition to the principal sum as the face value is the same as at the time of receipt: the value of the money does not 'price in' the value of its use over time. Full restitution requires an award of both the principal value and the use value.[61]

# III. Services

## A. Quantum Meruit

### *(i) Quantum Meruit is Not a Cause of Action*

Quantum meruit simply means 'as much as he deserved'.[62] The historical form of action upon a quantum meruit required the satisfaction of four elements:[63]

1. That the claimant did certain work;
2. That the work was done at the 'special instance and request' of the defendant;
3. That the defendant 'faithfully promised' that he would pay the claimant what '[he] should reasonably deserve' for the work; and
4. An averment by the claimant as to what the work was reasonably worth.

Prior to the abolition of the forms of action with the passage of the Judicature Acts in 1873–75, quantum meruit undoubtedly referred to an action that required the satisfaction of these four elements. However, long after the abolition of the forms of action, the misconception that quantum meruit is a cause of action, rather than a response to a cause of action, casts a long shadow over the law. While some cases seem to take this view,[64] it is contended in this book that treating quantum meruit as a cause of action is misguided.

The form of action upon *assumpsit* for quantum meruit in fact extended to two kinds of cause of action: one in contract and one in 'quasi-contract', which we now describe as unjust enrichment. However, the effect of pleading fictions was that the same material facts could be demonstrated either by proof of the

[61] Mitchell, Mitchell and Watterson, *Goff & Jones The Law of Unjust Enrichment* (2011) (n 38) §4-05.

[62] HC Black, *Black's Law Dictionary*, 5th edn (St Paul, West Publishing Company, 1979) 1119. Strictly, the count is correctly expressed as '*quantum mereret*' as the promise necessarily relates to the future: Baker, 'The History of Quasi-Contract in English Law' (1998) (n 5) 41 fn 19.

[63] Adapted from the precedent in *R v W* (1670) in Baker and Milsom, *Sources of English Legal History: Private Law to 1750* (Butterworths, London 1986) 474–75. See also Fifoot, *History and Sources of the Common Law: Tort and Contract* (1949) (n 13) 379; Birks, *An Introduction to the Law of Restitution* (1989) (n 26) 269.

[64] *Yeoman's Row Management Ltd v Cobbe* [2008] UKHL 55, [2008] 1 WLR 1752 [3], [42] (Lord Scott); *Sopov v Kane Constructions Pty Ltd (No 2)* [2009] VSCA 141, (2009) 257 ALR 182 [13]; *Serck Controls Ltd v Drake & Scull Engineering Ltd* (2000) 73 Con LR 100 (QB) [33]–[34] (Judge Hicks QC).

relevant fact or by a fictional finding that removed the need to establish that fact. Consequently, the material facts that had to be proved to obtain a right to be paid quantum meruit depended on the cause of action. This means that there was no single quantum meruit 'cause of action'. As Robert Goff J explained in *British Steel Corporation v Cleveland Bridge & Engineering Co Ltd*,[65] 'the mere framing of a claim as a *quantum meruit* claim, or a claim for a reasonable sum, does not assist in classifying the claim as contractual or quasi–contractual'. Although the cause of action differed, the award was the same in either case: quantum meruit. Thus, quantum meruit is better understood as a response to a cause of action rather than a cause of action itself.[66]

The existence of differing underlying claims for quantum meruit is borne out by the modern rejection of the purported 'elements' of claims for quantum meruit in unjust enrichment. For example, in unjust enrichment cases, a 'request' is no longer necessary for a successful claim for quantum meruit. Following *BP Exploration v Hunt (No 2)*[67] and *Rowe v Vale of White Horse*,[68] it is now clear that a successful claim for quantum meruit requires the claimant to show that the defendant is 'enriched' rather than that the defendant requested, and agreed to pay for, the services in question. Far from being a modern invention, dispensing with the request requirement represents a formalisation of the fictions that historically achieved the same result in 'quasi-contract' cases.[69] The belated recognition that quantum meruit awards do not require a request or a promise to pay consigned these old fictions to history. Therefore, there is no single 'cause of action' that forms the basis for the award of a quantum meruit; quantum meruit is a response to different causes of action.

### *(ii) Quantum Meruit as a Legal Response*

The only uniting feature of the various kinds of claim for quantum meruit is that the measure of recovery is the same in each case: the claimant is entitled to be paid 'quantum meruit'. This formula describes two potential awards: compensation and restitution. In contractual quantum meruit cases, the award usually takes the form of making good the claimant's expected remuneration. For example, where

[65] *British Steel Corp v Cleveland Bridge and Engineering Co Ltd* [1984] 1 All ER 504 (QB) 509 (Robert Goff J).

[66] Quantum meruit is described as a remedy in *Peter v Beblow* [1993] 1 SCR 980 (SCC) 995–96 (McLachlin J).

[67] *BP Exploration Co (Libya) Ltd v Hunt (No 2)* [1979] 1 WLR 783 (QB) 805 (Robert Goff J).

[68] *Rowe v Vale of White Horse DC* [2003] EWHC 388 (Admin), [2003] 1 Lloyd's Rep 418 [12] (Lightman J). Free acceptance and choice of benefit are dealt with in detail in ch 6.

[69] The earliest reported decisions recognising a fictional request are: *Warbrook v Griffin* (1609) 2 Brownl 254, 123 ER 927; *Rogers v Head* (1610) Cro Jac 262, 79 ER 226 according to W Sheppard, *A Grand Abridgement of the Common and Statute Law of England* (London, Flesher, Streater and Twyford, 1675) Pt I, 86 but *cf* Baker, 'The Use of Assumpsit for Restitutionary Money Claims' (1995) 38 fn 34; *Vaux v Newman (The Six Carpenters' Case)* (1610) 8 Co Rep 146, fo 147, 77 ER 695; *Shepherd v Edwards* (1615) Cro Jac 370, 79 ER 317.

the parties agree upon payment of a 'reasonable sum'[70] or where the claimant is awarded a commission calculated on subsequent profits actually made.[71] This is a compensatory measure. However, where a quantum meruit is based on unjust enrichment, the courts nearly always award the claimant the market value of the benefit he has conferred on the defendant.[72] This kind of response is restitutionary: the reversal of the value received from the claimant.[73] In the House of Lords' most recent pronouncement on quantum meruit in *Yeoman's Row Management Ltd v Cobbe*, Lord Scott described quantum meruit as 'restitutionary in character, concentrating … on the value of [the] services'.[74] Accordingly, it is contended that, in unjust enrichment cases, the quantum meruit formula is simply restitution by another name where the benefit is a service: it reverses the receipt of value from the claimant.[75]

However, the case law is by no means uniform and a restitutionary analysis of quantum meruit must confront judicial equivocation regarding the proper calculation of the award. First, some judges seem to have taken the 'as much as he deserved' formula to import a broad discretion to award whatever the circumstances require.[76] It is typical to see comments such as 'there are no hard and fast rules for the assessment of a *quantum meruit*. All the factors have to be considered'.[77] Nonetheless, despite remarks such as this, an unprincipled discretionary approach has been eschewed by the courts in practice. As Lord Hope said in *Sempra Metals*, 'the recovery of money in restitution is not, as a general rule, a matter for the discretion of the court. A claim to recover money at common law is a matter of right'.[78] While adopting a pragmatic approach, the courts have attempted to calculate the value of the benefit conferred rather than simply selecting a 'fair' measure without constraints. The practical reality is that the available

[70] Eg *RTS Flexible Systems Ltd v Molkerei Alois Müller GmbH* [2010] UKSC 14, [2010] 1 WLR 753; *Steven v Bromley & Son* [1919] 2 KB 722 (CA).

[71] See discussion in A Lodder, 'Unjust Enrichment and the Assessment of *Quantum Meruit* Awards' (2010) 126 *LQR* 42, 44.

[72] See, eg *Pavey & Matthews v Paul* (1987) 162 CLR 221 (HCA) 227 (Mason and Wilson JJ) 263–64 (Deane J); *Costain Civil Engineering Ltd v Zanen Dredging and Contracting Co Ltd* (1996) 85 BLR 77 (QB) 94 (Wilcox J); *Lachhani v Destination Canada (UK) Ltd* (1996) 13 Const LJ 279 (QB) 283 (Colin Reese QC); *Hall & Tawse South Ltd v Ivory Gate Ltd* (1997) 62 Con LR 117 (QB) 135 (Judge Anthony Thornton QC); *ERDC Group Ltd v Brunel University* [2006] EWHC 687 (TCC), [2006] BLR 255 [42] (Judge Humphrey Lloyd QC); *Yeoman's Row Management Ltd v Cobbe* [2008] UKHL 55, [2008] 1 WLR 1752 [4] (Lord Scott); *Costello v MacDonald* [2011] EWCA Civ 930 [32] (Etherton LJ).

[73] See ch 1, fn 28.

[74] *Yeoman's Row Management Ltd v Cobbe* [2008] UKHL 55, [2008] 1 WLR 1752 [4] (Lord Scott). See also *Sopov v Kane Constructions Pty Ltd (No 2)* [2009] VSCA 141, (2009) 257 ALR 182 [35].

[75] This is implied by Robert Goff J in *BP Exploration Co (Libya) Ltd v Hunt (No 2)* [1979] 1 WLR 783 (QB) 805.

[76] See, eg *Lachhani v Destination Canada (UK) Ltd* (1996) 13 Const LJ 279 (QB) 283–84 (Colin Reese QC).

[77] *ERDC Group Ltd v Brunel University* [2006] EWHC 687 (TCC), [2006] BLR 255 [42] (Judge Humphrey Lloyd QC).

[78] *Sempra Metals Ltd v IRC* [2007] UKHL 34, [2008] 1 AC 561 [46] (Lord Hope) *cf* [184]–[187] (Lord Walker). See also *Lipkin Gorman v Karpnale Ltd* [1991] 2 AC 548 (HL) 578 (Lord Goff); *Kleinwort Benson Ltd v Lincoln CC* [1999] 2 AC 349 (HL) 385 (Lord Goff).

evidence of the market value will differ between cases and, further, that there will be different ways of ascertaining that value that may be appropriate in particular cases. What is important is that the courts are in agreement about the task: to calculate the value of the services conferred on the defendant.

Second, there are a number of decisions that focus on the cost to the claimant of performing the services in calculating the award.[79] This is part of a developing consensus, applied by Lord Scott in *Yeoman's Row Management v Cobbe*,[80] that the award is to be calculated on a 'cost-plus' basis,[81] that is the cost to the claimant of the work plus a reasonable profit margin. 'Cost-plus' should not be confused with a compensatory award. In most cases, the cost of the services plus the usual profit margin will provide an accurate objective measure of the value of the benefit conferred on the defendant.[82] Assuming the market to be competitive, cost-plus is a method of objectively ascertaining the market rate. Indeed, while discussing this cost-plus calculation for quantum meruit, Judge Bowsher QC said in *Laserbore Ltd v Morrison Biggs Wall Ltd*[83] that the best way to frame the question was that adopted by Saville J in *Greenmast Shipping Co v Jean Lion et Cie (The Saronikos)*: 'What would be a fair commercial rate for the services provided?'.[84] A quantum meruit is thus calculated, not by reference to the loss suffered by the claimant or the actual gain to the defendant,[85] but by reference to the reasonable market value of the benefit conferred on the defendant.

Finally, some confusion has resulted from cases where the work done is defective or deficient in some respect.[86] It is sometimes suggested that an award that is reduced to take into account deficient or defective performance is somehow

[79] See discussion in *Renard Constructions v Minister for Works* (1992) 26 NSWLR 234 (NSWCA) 276 (Meagher JA); *Kane Constructions Pty Ltd v Sopov* [2005] VSC 237; J Edelman and E Bant, *Unjust Enrichment in Australia* (Oxford, Oxford University Press, 2006) 118–19.

[80] *Yeoman's Row Management Ltd v Cobbe* [2008] UKHL 55, [2008] 1 WLR 1752 [42] (Lord Scott).

[81] See, eg *O'Sullivan v Management Agency and Music Ltd* [1985] QB 428 (CA) 459, 463, 468–69; *Laserbore Ltd v Morrison Biggs Wall Ltd* [1993] CILL 896 (QB); *Lachhani v Destination Canada (UK) Ltd* (1996) 13 Const LJ 279 (QB) 283 (Colin Reese QC); *Serck Controls Ltd v Drake & Scull Engineering Ltd* (2000) 73 Con LR 100 (QB) 113–15 (Judge Hicks QC); *A de Gruchy Holdings Ltd v House of Fraser (Stores) Ltd* [2001] All ER (D) 361 (QB) [12], [38] (Wilcox J); *ACT Construction Ltd v E Clarke & Sons (Coaches) Ltd* [2002] EWCA Civ 972; *ABB Engineering Construction Pty Ltd v Abigroup Contractors Pty Ltd* [2003] NSWSC 665 [195]–[198]; *ERDC Group Ltd v Brunel University* [2006] EWHC 687 (TCC), [2006] BLR 255 [37]–[39], [47] (Judge Humphrey Lloyd QC); *Sopov v Kane Constructions Pty Ltd (No 2)* [2009] VSCA 141, (2009) 257 ALR 182 [33]–[40].

[82] *Laserbore Ltd v Morrison Biggs Wall Ltd* [1993] CILL 896 (QB).

[83] Ibid.

[84] *Greenmast Shipping Co v Jean Lion et Cie (The Saronikos)* [1986] 2 Lloyds Rep 277 (QB) 279 (Saville J).

[85] *Cf* Ch 3, fn 89.

[86] See, eg *Basten v Butter* (1806) 7 East 479, 103 ER 185; *Crown House Engineering Ltd v Amec Projects Ltd* (1989) 48 BLR 32 (CA); *Laserbore Ltd v Morrison Biggs Wall Ltd* [1993] CILL 896 (QB); *Lachhani v Destination Canada (UK) Ltd* (1996) 13 Const LJ 279 (QB) 284 (Colin Reese QC); *Serck Controls Ltd v Drake & Scull Engineering Ltd* (2000) 73 Con LR 100 (QB); *ERDC Group Ltd v Brunel University* [2006] EWHC 687 (TCC), [2006] BLR 255 [123]–[128] (Judge Humphrey Lloyd QC).

different from an award of the market value of the benefit conferred.[87] This is not the case. Rather, making allowances for deficient performance is part and parcel of calculating the value received by the defendant. A restitutionary response does not mean the prevailing market rate for any work done by the claimant irrespective of the quality; likewise, 'cost-plus' does not mean any costs the claimant incurs, but rather 'all costs *reasonably* and *necessarily* incurred in *properly* carrying out the works' (emphasis in original).[88]

### *(iii) Quantum Meruit Awards for Unjust Enrichment*

As quantum meruit has often confusingly been regarded as a cause of action rather than a response, quantum meruit awards have not traditionally been conceived as restitution for unjust enrichment.[89] While quantum meruit has its origins in contract, at least some quantum meruit awards are not consent-based. In *William Lacey (Hounslow) Ltd v Davis*,[90] the defendant's argument that a quantum meruit award is necessarily contractual was rejected by the court.[91] The court held that, despite the contractual origins of quantum meruit awards, quantum meruit was also available in 'quasi-contract'.[92] The court went on to explain that this 'quasi-contract' was imposed by law, rather than arising from the objectively manifested intentions of the parties,[93] which entails that the underlying basis of the claim is not consent.[94] The theoretical basis of so-called 'quasi-contractual' claims for quantum meruit should be understood today as unjust enrichment.[95] As we have seen, in unjust enrichment cases quantum meruit is simply restitution by another name for the performance of a service.

It is contended here that unjust enrichment usually provides the explanatory basis for quantum meruit awards in the context of void, unenforceable, terminated, frustrated and anticipated contracts. In *Pavey & Matthews v Paul*, Deane J

[87] *Cf* Mitchell, Mitchell and Watterson, *Goff & Jones The Law of Unjust Enrichment* (2011) (n 38) §5-36.

[88] *Lachhani v Destination Canada (UK) Ltd* (1996) 13 Const LJ 279 (QB) 283 (Colin Reese QC). See also *Serck Controls Ltd v Drake & Scull Engineering Ltd* (2000) 73 Con LR 100 (QB) [55] (Judge Hicks QC); *Eddy Lau Constructions Pty Ltd v Transdevelopment Enterprises Pty Ltd* [2004] NSWSC 273 [75] (Barrett J).

[89] *Yeoman's Row Management Ltd v Cobbe* [2008] UKHL 55, [2008] 1 WLR 1752 [3] (Lord Scott) *cf* [42]; *Kleinwort Benson Ltd v Glasgow CC (No 2)* [1996] QB 678 (CA) 700 (Millett LJ); R Goff and G Jones, *The Law of Restitution*, 4th edn (London, Sweet & Maxwell, 1993) 413–14. There are some notable exceptions, eg *BP Exploration Co (Libya) Ltd v Hunt (No 2)* [1979] 1 WLR 783 (QB); *Pavey & Matthews v Paul* (1987) 162 CLR 221 (HCA); *Whittle Movers Ltd v Hollywood Express Ltd* [2009] EWCA Civ 1189 [46] (Waller LJ).

[90] *William Lacey (Hounslow) Ltd v Davis* [1957] 1 WLR 932 (QB).

[91] G Fridman, 'Quantum Meruit' (1999) 37 *Alberta Law Review* 38, 39.

[92] *William Lacey (Hounslow) Ltd v Davis* [1957] 1 WLR 932 (QB) 936 (Barry J).

[93] Ibid.

[94] See *Craven-Ellis v Canons Ltd* [1936] 2 KB 403 (CA) 410 (Greer LJ).

[95] *Whittle Movers Ltd v Hollywood Express Ltd* [2009] EWCA Civ 1189 [46] (Waller LJ); *Pavey & Matthews v Paul* (1987) 162 CLR 221 (HCA) 227 (Mason & Wilson JJ).

explained that the basis for the quantum meruit award in these cases was the defendant's unjust enrichment:[96]

> The *quasi-contractual obligation* to pay … for a benefit which has been accepted will arise in a case where there is no applicable genuine agreement or where such agreement is frustrated, avoided or unenforceable. … [I]t is the very fact that there is no genuine agreement or that the genuine agreement is frustrated, avoided or unenforceable that provides occasion for … *the imposition by the law* of the obligation to make *restitution*. (emphasis added)

Thus, where a contract is void, a quantum meruit for work performed under the purported contract is generally available for unjust enrichment.[97] Second, a quantum meruit for unjust enrichment is similarly available where the contract is unenforceable, as held in *Dimond v Lovell*,[98] *Wilson v First County Trust Ltd (No 2)*[99] and *Pavey & Matthews v Paul*.[100] Third, the weight of judicial opinion favours the view that a claim for quantum meruit consequent upon discharge for breach or frustration is based on unjust enrichment.[101] Finally, where a party undertakes work expecting that a contract will come into existence but no contract is formed,[102] a quantum meruit for the services performed in anticipation of the contract is based on unjust enrichment.[103]

## B. Factual Enrichment in Services Cases

The factual enrichment model proposed in chapter three divides the enrichment inquiry in value cases into two limbs. The first limb identifies the receipt of value by the conferral of benefits on the defendant. The second limb, whether the defendant chose the benefit, determines whether the defendant is enriched by the value received. In the cases and literature on services, the first question is highly contested, largely because the import of the second question is overlooked. Two main arguments are put forward in this section. First, it is explained that the

[96] *Pavey & Matthews v Paul* (1987) 162 CLR 221 (HCA) 256 (Deane J).

[97] Eg *Craven-Ellis v Canons Ltd* [1936] 2 KB 403 (CA); *Rover International v Cannon Film Sales (No 3)* [1989] 1 WLR 912 (CA).

[98] *Dimond v Lovell* [2002] 1 AC 384 (HL).

[99] *Wilson v First County Trust Ltd (No 2)* [2003] UKHL 40, [2004] 1 AC 816. See also *Scarisbrick v Parkinson* (1869) 20 LT 175 (Ex); *Horton v Jones (No 2)* (1939) 35 SR(NSW) 305 (NSWSC); *Scott v Pattison* [1923] 2 KB 723 (KB).

[100] *Pavey & Matthews v Paul* (1987) 162 CLR 221 (HCA) 227–28 (Mason & Wilson JJ) 235–36 (Brennan J) 255–57, 262–63 (Deane J) *cf* 269 (Dawson J).

[101] *Lodder v Slowey* [1904] AC 442 (PC) 453; *Chandler v Boswell* [1936] 3 All ER 179 (CA) 186 (Greer LJ); *Luxor (Eastbourne) Ltd v Cooper* [1941] AC 108 (HL) 126 (Lord Russell) 141 (Lord Wright).

[102] *Cf RTS Flexible Systems Ltd v Molkerei Alois Müller GmbH* [2010] UKSC 14, [2010] 1 WLR 753.

[103] Eg *Morrison Shipping Co Ltd (in liquidation) v R* (1924) 20 Lloyd's L Rep 283 (HL) 287 (Viscount Cave); *Yeoman's Row Management Ltd v Cobbe* [2008] UKHL 55, [2008] 1 WLR 1752; *Whittle Movers Ltd v Hollywood Express Ltd* [2009] EWCA Civ 1189. See also S Ball, 'Work Carried Out Pursuant to Letters of Intent—Contract or Restitution' (1983) 99 *LQR* 572; E McKendrick, 'The Battle of the Forms and the Law of Restitution' (1988) 8 *OJLS* 197, 212.

distinction between pure services and services designed to produce an end-product is a distraction; instead, this purported distinction is entirely subsumed by the second question in the enrichment inquiry as to what benefit(s) the defendant chose. Second, it is submitted that all services, whether 'pure services' or services designed to produce an end-product, transfer value to the defendant. The provision of services for the defendant therefore always involves the receipt of value *capable of enriching* the defendant; whether the defendant *is enriched* depends on what benefits the defendant chose.

### *(i) Pure Services and Services Designed to Produce an End-Product*

Much of the commentary on services relies upon the distinction between pure services and services designed to produce an end-product.[104] For example, Burrows argues that the identification of a benefit turns upon this distinction: 'pure services' are received when performance starts; services designed to produce an end-product are received when part of the end product is transferred to the recipient.[105] Grantham and Rickett and Beatson go further and argue, for differing reasons, that pure services can never constitute benefits in the law of unjust enrichment. This book challenges the distinction between pure services and services designed to produce an end-product. The distinction puts the cart before the horse, assuming the content of the defendant's choice from the nature of the services rather than inquiring into that choice. It is suggested here that the pure services/end-product distinction conflates the receipt of value and choice of benefit limbs of the enrichment inquiry and that, properly understood, the requirement of choice of benefit renders the distinction otiose.

The first problem with the distinction is that it is not supported by the cases. There is no suggestion in the cases that pure services are to be treated any differently from services designed to produce an end-product. Indeed, there are several examples in which courts have allowed a quantum meruit for pure services, even where the services did not save a necessary expense.[106] The most contentious decision supporting this conclusion is *Planché v Colburn*,[107] where the claimant recovered for researching and writing services despite tendering no part of the finished product. Many commentators think this case is wrongly decided because of the absence of any enrichment to the defendant and, as a result, explain the result as an award of contractual damages for reliance loss or as an example of unjust sacrifice.[108] However, Tindal CJ stressed that it was not a breach of contract

[104] Eg J Beatson, *The Use and Abuse of Unjust Enrichment* (Oxford, Clarendon Press, 1991) 23; A Skelton, *Restitution and Contract* (Oxford, Mansfield, 1998) 10–11; Virgo, *The Principles of the Law of Restitution* (2006) (n 32) 71–72; A Burrows, *The Law of Restitution*, 3rd edn (Oxford, Oxford University Press, 2010) 46–47.

[105] Burrows, *The Law of Restitution* (2010) (n 104) 46–47.

[106] See, eg *Planché v Colburn* (1831) 5 C&P 58, 172 ER 876.

[107] Ibid. For a more recent example involving similar facts, see *Myers v Macmillan Press Ltd* (Unreported QBD, 3 March 1998).

[108] For a discussion of these arguments, see Burrows, 'Free Acceptance and the Law of Restitution' (1988) (n 3) 588–89; M Garner, 'The Role of Subjective Benefit in the Law of Unjust Enrichment'

claim.[109] Further, this line of argument confuses the two stages of the enrichment inquiry, receipt of value and choice of benefit. As regards the receipt of value, Planché performed researching and writing services for Colburn & Bentley and they therefore received the valuable benefit of Planché's time and labour. As regards choice of the benefit, Colburn & Bentley may have requested: (i) the manuscript; (ii) the researching and writing services; or (iii) both. Whether the defendants *chose* the researching and writing services or 'the article when complete'[110] goes to the choice of benefit test, not the receipt of value. Bosanquet J explicitly rejected the submission that recovery on the quantum meruit count necessarily required 'the Plaintiff ... to have tendered or delivered the work'.[111] Of course, minds may legitimately differ over the effect of the evidence given by Jerdan, the editor of the *Literary Gazette*, and the parties themselves as to whether Colburn & Bentley had chosen the research work as well as the finished manuscript, but the result turned on a finding of fact: whether the defendants requested the researching and writing services or just the finished manuscript.

Burrows and Virgo challenge the suggestion that the contract in *Planché v Colburn* may be one that commissioned the research and the work of writing the book, as well as the completed manuscript, because the defendant cannot be regarded as having *received* the benefit of the work.[112] This argument does not appreciate the nature of a transfer of value. Enrichment does not necessarily depend on receipt of an end-product; it depends on identifying a transfer of value to the defendant through a benefit chosen by the defendant. A defendant who commissions certain work *in addition* to the delivery of a finished product receives value both by receipt of the product and by the claimant carrying out his undertaking to do what is requested. The law is familiar with this notion in the context of money claims for total failure of consideration.[113] In *Hyundai Heavy Industries Co Ltd v Papadopoulos*,[114] the House of Lords noted that contracts 'to build, launch, equip and complete' a ship and then 'to deliver and sell her' could not be equated with simple sale of goods contracts.[115] There is no reason for a less nuanced analysis in non-money claims. Why are requests for work to

(1990) 10 *OJLS* 42, 53–54; Beatson, *The Use and Abuse of Unjust Enrichment* (1991) (n 104) 35; C Mitchell and C Mitchell, 'Planché v Colburn' in C Mitchell and P Mitchell (eds), *Landmark Cases in the Law of Restitution* (Oxford, Hart, 2006) 92. The award is treated as restitutionary in *Slowey v Lodder* (1901) 20 NZLR 321 (NZCA).

[109] *Planché v Colburn* (1831) 5 C&P 58, 61 (Tindal CJ).

[110] Ibid 60.

[111] *Planché v Colburn* (1831) 8 Bing 14, 16; 131 ER 305, 307 (Bosanquet J).

[112] Virgo, *The Principles of the Law of Restitution* (2006) (n 32) 66 fn 20; Burrows, *The Law of Restitution* (2010) (n 104) 46.

[113] As explained in the most recent edition of Goff & Jones, another context where such an inquiry is common arises under the Sale of Goods Act 1979: Mitchell, Mitchell and Watterson, *Goff & Jones The Law of Unjust Enrichment* (2011) (n 38) §5-24 fn 60.

[114] *Hyundai Heavy Industries Co Ltd v Papadopoulos* [1980] 1 WLR 1129 (HL). See also *Stocznia Gdanska SA v Latvian Shipping Co* [1998] 1 WLR 574 (HL) 587–88 (Lord Goff).

[115] *Hyundai Heavy Industries Co Ltd v Papadopoulos* [1980] 1 WLR 1129 (HL) 1134 (Viscount Dilhorne) 1148 (Lord Fraser).

be divided simplistically into pure services and services designed to produce an end-product? The court in *Planché v Colburn* was entitled to find that it was not merely a request for the sale of a book, but a request for the research and writing of the book also. An analogy may be a request made of a scientist to discover a drug to cure a specific disease, where the request is for years of clinical research and testing as well as the finished drug. In such circumstances, if the research work is requested by the defendant as well as the drug, the defendant's freedom of choice is not infringed when the defendant is made to pay for the scientist's work and labour even though the scientist is unable to find a cure. The question turns on the scope of the request.

A second reason for rejecting the distinction is the identification of the enrichment in cases involving services designed to produce an end-product. The value that the defendant receives from the claimant is often treated as the value of the service itself, not the end-product.[116] So, in *BP Exploration v Hunt (No 2)*, the relevant value was the value of the exploration of the concession, not the enhanced value of the concession itself. Although the Act required the court to treat the end-product as a ceiling on recovery,[117] Robert Goff J was unequivocally concerned with the value of the exploration services. It will depend on the facts of the individual case whether the relevant transfer of value is the value of the services or the end-product or some combination of the two.

The third problem with the distinction between pure services and services designed to produce an end-product is that it entails a different approach to identifying value where a service yields an asset or money. This is not the law. This point can be easily demonstrated where the end-product is worth less than the market value of the service. Suppose a defendant requests the claimant to build an execrable addition to his house[118]—is the benefit the end-product or the building services? If it were simply the end-product, then the defendant could say that the objective value received is nil: the house has diminished in value and the addition is worthless. However, he has received value through the performance of a service he chose, and must therefore pay the market value of the work done, not the market value of the end-product. There is no difference in the value transferred between a service with a tangible but ultimately worthless end-product and a pure service. The law does not segregate services cases into services designed to produce an end-product and pure services.

[116] Eg *Angelopoulos v Sabatino* [1995] 65 SASR 1 (SASC); *Yeoman's Row Management Ltd v Cobbe* [2008] UKHL 55, [2008] 1 WLR 1752 [40]–[41] (Lord Scott); *Peet Ltd v Richmond* [2009] VSC 130 *cf Van Den Berg v Giles* [1979] 2 NZLR 111 (NZHC); *Lexane Pty Ltd v Highfern Pty Ltd* [1985] 1 Qd R 446; *Fensom v Cootamundra Racecourse Reserve Trust* [2000] NSWSC 1072; *Taylor v Streicher* [2007] NSWSC 1006. See Virgo, *The Principles of the Law of Restitution* (2006) (n 32) 71; Mitchell, Mitchell and Watterson, *Goff & Jones The Law of Unjust Enrichment* (2011) (n 38) §5-26.

[117] *BP Exploration Co (Libya) Ltd v Hunt (No 2)* [1979] 1 WLR 783 (QB) 802 (Robert Goff J); P Birks, 'In Defence of Free Acceptance' in A Burrows (ed), *Essays on the Law of Restitution* (Oxford, Clarendon Press, 1991); Mitchell, Mitchell and Watterson, *Goff & Jones The Law of Unjust Enrichment* (2011) (n 38) §§5-22–5-24.

[118] See *BP Exploration Co (Libya) Ltd v Hunt (No 2)* [1979] 1 WLR 783 (QB) 803 (Robert Goff J).

### (ii) *Transfer of Value in Services Cases*

On the factual enrichment approach adopted in this book, there can be no doubt that the performance of services involves a transfer of value recognised by the market. The performance of a valuable service attracts a fee, whether or not that service results in a tangible end-product. It is a trite observation that the market attaches value to the building of houses and the cutting of hair, the mowing of lawns and the performance of live music.[119] The same is true of the law. Defendants have been ordered to pay quantum meruit for services as diverse as the making and alteration of clothes,[120] the building of houses,[121] the provision of management and professional services,[122] the making of repairs to property[123] and the provision of research services.[124] Some of these services saved a necessary expense,[125] some did not;[126] some were designed to produce an end-product,[127] others were not.[128]

The picture that emerges from the cases is that the law follows the logic of the market: it treats services themselves as transferring value that may enrich a defendant. However, a quite different view emerges from the academic writing on enrichment, where numerous commentators qualify the way in which services may constitute benefits, including Beatson,[129] Grantham and Rickett,[130] Burrows[131] and Virgo.[132] While all these commentators agree that services that save a necessary expense are incontrovertibly enriching, there is considerable disagreement as to when 'pure services' are otherwise enriching. It is argued that, in this respect, the academic commentary has departed from the case law and that pure services constitute benefits in the law of unjust enrichment.

Perhaps the most renowned attack on pure services constituting benefits in the law of unjust enrichment is presented by Beatson. Beatson rejects the contention that 'pure services' can constitute a benefit, unless they save another's necessary

[119] Virgo, *The Principles of the Law of Restitution* (2006) (n 32) 64; Mitchell, Mitchell and Watterson, *Goff & Jones The Law of Unjust Enrichment* (2011) (n 38) §5-21. See also *BP Exploration Co (Libya) Ltd v Hunt (No 2)* [1979] 1 WLR 783 (QB) 801–02 (Robert Goff J).

[120] *Vaux v Newman (The Six Carpenters' Case)* (1610) 8 Co Rep 146; *Rolte v Sharp* (1626) Cro Car 77, 79 ER 668.

[121] *Sumpter v Hedges* [1898] 1 QB 673 (CA).

[122] *Craven-Ellis v Canons Ltd* [1936] 2 KB 403 (CA); *Brenner v First Artists' Management Pty Ltd* [1993] 2 VR 221 (VSC); *Independent Grocers Co-operative Ltd v Noble Lowndes Superannuation Consultants Ltd* (1993) 60 SASR 525 (SASC); *Damberg v Damberg* [2001] NSWCA 87, (2001) 52 NSWLR 492; *Andrew Shelton & Co v Alpha Healthcare* [2002] VSC 248, [2003] 5 VR 577.

[123] *Gray v Hill* (1826) Ry&M 420.

[124] *Planché v Colburn* (1831) 5 C&P 58, 172 ER 876.

[125] Eg *Rowe v Vale of White Horse DC* [2003] EWHC 388 (Admin), [2003] 1 Lloyd's Rep 418.

[126] Eg *Brenner v First Artists' Management Pty Ltd* [1993] 2 VR 221 (VSC).

[127] Eg *Sumpter v Hedges* [1898] 1 QB 673 (CA).

[128] Eg *Craven-Ellis v Canons Ltd* [1936] 2 KB 403 (CA).

[129] Beatson, *The Use and Abuse of Unjust Enrichment* (1991) (n 104) 31–33.

[130] R Grantham and C Rickett, *Enrichment and Restitution in New Zealand* (Oxford, Hart, 2000) 20–21, 60–61.

[131] Burrows, *The Law of Restitution* (2010) (n 104) 46–47.

[132] Virgo, *The Principles of the Law of Restitution* (2006) (n 32) 66.

expenditure.[133] Beatson's argument is based on the premise that 'exchange value, transferability or capacity to produce income'[134] are the necessary criteria for 'wealth' and a defendant who receives a pure service cannot exchange, transfer or derive income from it. Beatson's position has been disapproved in *Re Berkeley Applegate (Investment Consultants) Ltd*[135] and *Brenner v First Artists' Management*,[136] as well as being widely rejected in the literature.[137] The first reason to reject this approach is that it relies upon the distinction between pure services and services designed to produce an end-product rejected above, but it is useful to offer an additional reason: Beatson's requirement of a 'marketable residuum in the hands of the defendant'[138] confuses immediate and extant value. As contended in chapter seven, the proper inquiry is directed to the receipt of value at the moment of transfer, not whether the defendant retains anything that can later be given up. The benefit received by the defendant at the moment of transfer is having the claimant employ his labour, time and skill (and often his money, assets and materials) towards some end.[139] An approach that focuses exclusively on whether there is something left after the moment of transfer misunderstands value. Other than in respect of change of position, the law is concerned with the restitution of the value received rather than the value retained by the defendant.[140]

A different argument is proffered by Grantham and Rickett.[141] Grantham and Rickett suggest that the law of unjust enrichment depends on whether or not the benefit can be restored; if the benefit is not restorable then it is not an enrichment for the purpose of unjust enrichment. Their argument, which is explicitly premised on an extant enrichment approach, must fail for similar reasons to Beatson's. First, it cannot explain the various cases of recovery for pure services with no restorable benefit. Second, it is even more restrictive than Beatson's approach because many end-products may be non-restorable, such as perishables. Third, on this approach recovery would logically be limited to the portion of the benefit that is restorable, which confuses prima facie liability and change of position.[142] A defendant who is not entitled to change of position (eg due to bad faith) would still have no liability in restitution if part of the benefit were squandered and therefore not restorable.

133 Beatson, *The Use and Abuse of Unjust Enrichment* (1991) (n 104) 33.

134 Ibid 31.

135 *Berkeley Applegate (Investment Consultants) Ltd* [1989] Ch 32 (Ch) 50 (Edward Nugee QC).

136 *Brenner v First Artists' Management Pty Ltd* [1993] 2 VR 221 (VSC) 257 (Byrne J).

137 P Birks, 'In Defence of Free Acceptance' in A Burrows (ed), *Essays on the Law of Restitution* (Oxford, Clarendon Press, 1991) 132–35; K Mason and J Carter, *Restitution Law in Australia* (Sydney, Butterworths, 1996) [935]; Virgo, *The Principles of the Law of Restitution* (2006) (n 32) 71–72; Burrows, *The Law of Restitution* (2010) (n 104) 47.

138 Beatson, *The Use and Abuse of Unjust Enrichment* (1991) (n 104) 23.

139 Birks, *An Introduction to the Law of Restitution* (1989) (n 26) 126–29, 232; P Maddaugh and J McCamus, *The Law of Restitution* (Aurora, Canada Law Book, 1990) 39, 411, 429–30; Birks, 'In Defence of Free Acceptance' (1991) (n 117) 105, 140–41.

140 Burrows, *The Law of Restitution* (2010) (n 104) 47.

141 Grantham and Rickett, *Enrichment and Restitution in New Zealand* (2000) (n 130) 61.

142 See ch 8, s III.

The final academic position that must be addressed is that shared by Burrows[143] and Virgo.[144] They argue that, where the claimant provides a service designed to produce an end-product and no part of this product is received, the defendant is not enriched. In this way, whether services are 'received' by the defendant provides the bright line between restitution for unjust enrichment and reliance damages.[145] However, this book has argued that the distinction between pure services and end-product services is a red herring that distracts attention from identifying the benefit chosen by the defendant. It is not the case that a service that is designed to produce an end-product requires that end-product be tendered for the defendant to be enriched.[146] Nor does this mean, as Birks argues,[147] that all services are automatically enriching because the defendant has had the benefit of the claimant's time and labour, subject to the defendant's right subjectively to devalue that benefit. While the claimant's expending time and labour for the defendant objectively involves a transfer of value, this book contends that the defendant is only enriched by those benefits he chose; it may be the claimant's time and labour or the end-product or both or neither.

## IV. Goods

### A. Quantum Valebat

#### *(i) Quantum Valebat is Not a Cause of Action*

For precisely the same reasons as articulated in respect of quantum meruit, the count of quantum valebat is not a cause of action, but a legal response. Originally, the quantum meruit form was not restricted to the provision of services, and could be adapted to reach fact patterns including the supply of goods (quantum valebat), the hire of goods (*quantum habere meruit*), the provision of food or lodging and the use and occupation of real property.[148] According to most orthodox accounts of the period,[149] in the middle of the seventeenth century quantum meruit became confined to cases involving work done, while quantum valebat emerged around the same time as the correct form for cases involving the supply of goods.

143 Burrows, *The Law of Restitution* (2010) (n 104) 46–47.

144 Virgo, *The Principles of the Law of Restitution* (2006) (n 32) 66.

145 Skelton, *Restitution and Contract* (1998) (n 104) 11.

146 Birks, 'In Defence of Free Acceptance' (1991) (n 117) 137–41. See also G Palmer, *The Law of Restitution* (Boston, Little Brown, 1978) §4.2 *cf* Skelton, *Restitution and Contract* (1998) (n 104) 11; Burrows, *The Law of Restitution* (2010) (n 104) 46–47.

147 Birks, 'In Defence of Free Acceptance' (1991) (n 117) 137–41.

148 Baker, 'The History of Quasi-Contract in English Law' (1998) (n 5) 43.

149 See Fifoot, *History and Sources of the Common Law: Tort and Contract* (1949) (n 13) 361 fn 18; Fridman, 'Quantum Meruit' (1999) (n 91) fn 1 citing *Boult v Harris* (1676) 3 Keb 469 and *Webb v Moore* (1691) 2 Vent 279.

Baker has shown this timeline to be incorrect.[150] There are precedents for quantum valebat as early as *Turner v Nelethropp*[151] in 1531, and the form was approved in *Royle v Bagshaw*[152] in 1589. The better view is that quantum meruit and quantum valebat were concurrent developments of the same form of action that only came to be rigorously distinguished by the end of the seventeenth century.[153] There is nothing in the development of quantum valebat that is inconsistent with the suggestion that the quantum meruit form was generalised to cases other than those involving services. The differentiation of quantum meruit and quantum valebat was most likely a linguistic refinement of the quantum meruit form as it applied to different fact situations, not the development of a new form of action.

Consequently, there is no historical warrant for segregating awards involving non-money benefits into different causes of action, such as quantum meruit, quantum valebat or *quantum habere meruit*. On the contrary, the development of the various non-money awards suggests that these forms of action share an identical historical origin and are amenable to the same analysis. Like quantum meruit, then, quantum valebat may be a response to a genuine contract, unjust enrichment and potentially other causes of action and should be understood as a response to those causes of action rather than a cause of action itself.

### *(ii) Quantum Valebat as a Legal Response*

Quantum valebat is best understood as a restitutionary award for the value of goods delivered to the defendant. In the above discussion of services cases it was noted that there is some debate over the proper calculation of quantum meruit awards, although it was shown that the awards are virtually always restitutionary in character. There is less debate concerning the proper calculation of quantum valebat awards, which are typically quantified by reference to the value of the goods received by the defendant.[154] As Robert Goff J explained in *BP Exploration v Hunt (No 2)*:[155]

> [T]he basic measure of recovery in restitution is the reasonable value of the plaintiff's performance: in a case of services, a *quantum meruit* or reasonable remuneration, and in a case of goods, a quantum valebat or reasonable price.

Further, 'the cause of action arises when the goods are sold and delivered'.[156] Accordingly, Robert Goff J went on to assess a 'just sum' under the Law Reform (Frustrated Contracts) Act 1943 for the farm-in oil delivered to Hunt 'in the

[150] Baker, 'The Use of Assumpsit for Restitutionary Money Claims' (1995) (n 5) 37.

[151] *Turner v Nelethropp* (1531) KB 27/1078, m 66.

[152] *Royle v Bagshaw* (1589) Cro Eliz 149, 78 ER 407.

[153] This conclusion is borne out by precedents cited by Baker, which show a conflation of the two forms in the latter half of the 17th century: Baker, 'The Use of Assumpsit for Restitutionary Money Claims' (1995) (n 5) 37 fn 26.

[154] See, eg *Weatherby v Banham* (1832) 5 C&P 228, 172 ER 950; *BP Exploration Co (Libya) Ltd v Hunt (No 2)* [1979] 1 WLR 783 (QB) 839 (Robert Goff J).

[155] *BP Exploration Co (Libya) Ltd v Hunt (No 2)* [1979] 1 WLR 783 (QB) 805 (Robert Goff J).

[156] Ibid 836 (Robert Goff J).

nature of a *quantum valebat*' as the 'market value of the benefit itself' when received.[157] This approach is entirely consistent with the factual enrichment thesis advanced here as the purpose and effect of the award is to reverse the immediate transfer of value to the defendant at the claimant's expense.

### *(iii) Quantum Valebat Awards for Unjust Enrichment*

While it is undoubtedly the case that quantum valebat awards are available for unjust enrichment, in practice such claims are less common than claims for quantum meruit. This is because the common law protects goods in a number of ways in which it does not protect services. First, the tort of conversion is the typical cause of action where the defendant has received goods to which the claimant holds an immediate right to possession.[158] The award of compensation in conversion is generally assessed by reference to the full value of the goods at the time of the conversion[159] and the claimant is entitled to consequential losses,[160] which makes conversion an attractive basis for protecting property rights to chattels. Second, as per the model defended in this book, claims for legal enrichment are commonly available in respect of goods. These claims are considered in the next chapter, but it suffices for present purposes to note that the claimant may seek restitution of the right to goods through resulting trusts, rescission or rectification, provided the defendant retains the goods and the other requirements of such claims are satisfied. Nonetheless, there will be circumstances where these alternative claims are not available or desirable and the claimant will seek restitution of the value of the goods in unjust enrichment.

As with quantum meruit, quantum valebat is typically based either on a contractual obligation to pay a reasonable sum or on the principle of unjust enrichment. A contractual quantum valebat award is available where a contract for the sale of goods fails to fix the price but is sufficiently certain in other necessary respects.[161] The agreement will either explicitly or implicitly be for the payment of a reasonable sum. Additionally, prior to the Sale of Goods Act 1979, where the seller delivered a different quantity of goods from that specified in the contract, the buyer was obliged to pay quantum valebat, rather than at the contract price.[162] The 'reasonable sum' in these cases will almost always be the value of the goods

[157] Ibid 839 (Robert Goff J).

[158] See *Kuwait Airways Corp v Iraqi Airways Co (Nos 4 and 5)* [2002] UKHL 19, [2002] 2 AC 883 [39] (Lord Nicholls).

[159] *Pacific Acceptance Corp Ltd v Mirror Motors Pty Ltd* (1961) 61 SR(NSW) 548 (NSWSC); *BBMB v Eda Holdings Ltd* [1990] 1 WLR 409 (PC) 412 (Lord Templeman); *IBL Ltd v Coussens* [1991] 2 All ER 133 (CA) 143 (Nicholls J); M Bridge, *Personal Property Law*, 3rd edn (Oxford, Oxford University Press, 2002) 72.

[160] *Davis v Oswell* (1837) 7 C&P 804; *Bodley v Reynolds* (1846) 8 QB 779; *Chubb Cash Ltd v John Crilley & Son* [1983] 1 WLR 599 (CA) 604 (Bush J); *Gaba Formwork Contractors Pty Ltd v Turner Corp Ltd* (1991) 31 NSWLR 175 (NSWSC); Bridge, *Personal Property Law* (2002) (n 159) 72.

[161] Eg *Royle v Bagshaw* (1589) Cro Eliz 149, 78 ER 407.

[162] See, eg *Shipton v Casson* (1826) 5 B&C 378, 383; 108 ER 141, 144 (Bayley J); *Oxendale v Wetherell* (1829) 9 B&C 386, 387–88; 109 ER 143, 145; *Steven v Bromley & Son* [1919] 2 KB 722 (CA) 728.

and the award will therefore be restitutionary in effect. However, this position has been altered by the Sale of Goods Act 1979,[163] which obliges the buyer to pay the contract rate where the seller delivers a different quantity of goods from that stipulated in the contract.

More commonly, however, quantum valebat awards are a response to unjust enrichment. The well-known case of *Weatherby v Banham*[164] provides an early example of quantum valebat in the absence of a contract: the claimant was awarded the value of the magazines received by the defendant on a quantum valebat basis, despite the fact that the contract was with the deceased former occupant of the premises. *Boulton v Jones*[165] provides another nineteenth century example where the court considered, but rejected, a quantum valebat claim on the basis of unjust enrichment. Jones ordered pipe from a shop owned by Brocklehurst unaware that Brocklehurst had sold the shop on to Boulton. When Jones received an invoice from Boulton, he refused to pay it as he had intended to enter into a contract with Brocklehurst, against whom he held a right of set-off. There was obviously no contractual basis for Boulton's claim; instead, Boulton claimed on a quantum valebat basis. In the House of Lords' decision in *Shogun Finance Ltd v Hudson*, Lord Millett noted that 'We would classify the case today as an example of a claim in unjust enrichment'.[166] Consequently, it is clear that quantum valebat awards are often examples of restitution for unjust enrichment.

As explained above in relation to quantum meruit, unjust enrichment will provide the explanatory basis for quantum valebat awards where goods are delivered pursuant to a contract that is void, unenforceable, frustrated or terminated for breach. The availability of the claim in a contractual context was confirmed in *Bartholomew v Markwick*,[167] where the court accepted that a claimant could recover on a quantum valebat basis for goods delivered under a contract terminated for breach by the other party. The same result was reached in a frustrated contract context by Robert Goff J in *BP Exploration v Hunt (No 2)* on the quantum valebat claim for the farm-in oil.[168] An identical analysis applies where the contract is void or unenforceable: the avoided or unenforceable contract is not the basis for the award of a quantum valebat; the award is founded instead on the defendant's unjust enrichment by the receipt of goods at the claimant's expense.

[163] Sale of Goods Act 1979, s 30.

[164] *Weatherby v Banham* (1832) 5 C&P 228, 172 ER 950.

[165] *Boulton v Jones* (1857) 2 H&N 564, 157 ER 232.

[166] *Shogun Finance Ltd v Hudson* [2003] UKHL 62, [2004] 1 AC 919 [96] (Lord Millett). See also *Eastbourne BC v Foster* [2001] EWCA Civ 1091, [2001] All ER (D) 135 [32] (Rix LJ).

[167] *Bartholomew v Markwick* (1864) 15 CBR 711, 716; 143 ER 964, 967 (Erle CJ). See also *Appleby v Myers* (1866) 1 CP 615 (CCP) 622 (Montague Smith J) reversed on different grounds in *Appleby v Myers* (1867) 2 CP 651 (Ex).

[168] *BP Exploration Co (Libya) Ltd v Hunt (No 2)* [1979] 1 WLR 783 (QB) 839 (Robert Goff J).

## B. Factual Enrichment in Goods Cases

### *(i) Transfer of Value in Goods Cases*

It is clear that the receipt of a right to valuable goods involves a transfer of value to the defendant, but it is important to note that the transfer of value depends on the right acquired by the defendant, that is whether the defendant obtains title, or some lesser right, to the goods. Where the defendant receives both title and possession, the full market exchange value of the goods will be transferred to the defendant. This occurred in *McDonald v Coys of Kensington*,[169] where McDonald, pursuant to the statutory scheme, obtained title to the mark upon registration. McDonald was enriched by the value of that right, which was the market value of the TAC1 registration mark. Accordingly, the court found that he was under an obligation to make restitution of the market value: £15,000.[170] Where the defendant acquires title, but is not yet in possession of the goods, then the exchange value of the right may be lower, particularly where obtaining possession may require legal action.

Where the defendant acquires a lesser right, such as a right to possession of the goods, it is the *value* of that lesser right that has been transferred to the defendant, even though the defendant's right to possession is a new right to possession.[171] This point can be demonstrated by *Huyton SA v Peter Cremer GmbH & Co*,[172] where the existence of such a claim was recognised, although ultimately not successful. The case involved the sale and shipment of a large quantity of wheat to the Sudan by Cremer, the seller, to Huyton, the buyer. Mance J held that property in the wheat was only intended to pass on payment, not on delivery ex ship or by Huyton's acceptance of the delivery. As payment had not yet been made, 'possession had been given, although property had not yet passed'.[173] The dispute concerned the validity of a compromise agreement, which Cremer alleged had been obtained by illegitimate pressure. One of Cremer's claims was that Huyton was obliged to pay restitution of the value of the wheat and its failure to do so constituted illegitimate pressure. Mance J accepted the possibility of such a claim, holding:[174]

> Had Cremer shown that Huyton could not return the goods, Cremer could no doubt have acquired a restitutionary right .... [T]he measure of recovery might then have related to the value of the goods in the Sudan rather than the contract price

On the facts, Huyton refused to pay for the wheat (and thereby obtain title to the wheat) until Cremer presented the documentation required by the contract,

[169] *McDonald v Coys of Kensington* [2004] EWCA Civ 47, [2004] 1 WLR 2775.

[170] Ibid [42] (Mance LJ).

[171] See Edelman and Bant, *Unjust Enrichment in Australia* (2006) (n 79) 123–24, 130–31; Mitchell, Mitchell and Watterson, *Goff & Jones The Law of Unjust Enrichment* (2011) (n 38) §5-17.

[172] *Huyton SA v Peter Cremer GmbH & Co* [1999] 1 Lloyd's Rep 620 (QB).

[173] Ibid 634 (Mance J).

[174] Ibid.

which it did not do. Furthermore, Cremer failed to establish that Huyton could not return the wheat; Huyton argued that it held the wheat at all times at Cremer's disposal. The important point for present purposes is that Mance J accepted that, if Huyton had refused to make the wheat available to Cremer, it would have been enriched by the value of the wheat, even though legal title had not passed. As the wheat was now siloed in Port Sudan, the value of Huyton's possession of the wheat was reduced. Mance J rightly intimated that it is this lesser value that would have enriched Huyton if it had chosen to accept the wheat despite Cremer's failure to produce the documentation required for payment.

This position must confront the commonly held view that the defendant is not enriched unless title passes because enrichment is legal, not factual, and the defendant has received no legal right.[175] In response to this objection, Birks has suggested that this is merely a technical objection and that the recipient is factually enriched by the use of the thing[176] or, in his final work, that the claimant can electively relinquish title in order to say that the defendant is enriched.[177] However, this debate is unsatisfactory because the arguments get off on the wrong footing: the recipient of someone else's property usually does obtain a legal property right:[178] a right to possession.[179] The right to possession acquired by the recipient is a lesser interest than the true owner's right to possession or a prior right to possession,[180] but it is undoubtedly a property right recognised by the law as held in *Costello v Chief Constable of Derbyshire Constabulary*.[181] Provided the recipient has both factual possession and an intention to possess, he will acquire a right to possession.[182] The recipient's enrichment may thus be characterised either

[175] W Swadling, 'A Claim in Restitution?' [1996] *LMCLQ* 63, 65; R Grantham and C Rickett, 'Restitution, Property and Ignorance—A Reply to Mr Swadling' [1996] *LMCLQ* 463, 465; R Grantham and C Rickett, 'Restitution, Property and Mistaken Payments' [1997] *RLR* 83, 87.

[176] P Birks, 'Property and Unjust Enrichment: Categorical Truths' [1997] *New Zealand Law Review* 623, 654–56.

[177] Birks, *Unjust Enrichment* (2005) (n 4) 66–67.

[178] A similar analysis is advanced by Lionel Smith in L Smith, 'Unjust Enrichment, Property and the Structure of Trusts' (2000) 116 *LQR* 412, 426.

[179] *Armory v Delamirie* (1722) 1 Str 505, 93 ER 664; *Jeffries v Great Western Rail Co* (1856) 5 E&B 802, 805; 119 ER 680, 682 (Lord Campbell CJ); *The Winkfield* [1902] P 42 (CA); *Gollan v Nugent* (1988) 166 CLR 18 (HCA) 28 (Brennan J); *Perpetual Trustees v Perkins* (1989) Aust Torts Rep ¶80-295 (SCT) 69,201 (Green CJ). For the historical development and philosophy of the right of possession see: D Harris, 'The Concept of Possession in English Law' in A Guest (ed), *Oxford Essays in Jurisprudence* (Oxford, Clarendon Press, 1961) 69–106; F Von Savigny, *Von Savigny's Treatise on Possession*, 6th edn (London, Sweet & Maxwell, 1979).

[180] J Tarrant, 'Property Rights to Stolen Money' (2005) 32 *University of Western Australia Law Review* 234, 240–42. Tarrant uses the language of a right *of* possession as distinguished from a right *to* possession, see also A Honoré, 'Ownership' in A Guest (ed), *Oxford Essays in Jurisprudence* (Oxford, Clarendon Press, 1961) 114–15.

[181] *Costello v Chief Constable of Derbyshire Constabulary* [2001] EWCA Civ 381, [2001] 1 WLR 1437 [31].

[182] F Pollock and R Wright, *An Essay on Possession in the Common Law* (Oxford, Clarendon Press, 1888); Tarrant, 'Property Rights to Stolen Money' (2005) (n 180). For the Roman law origins of this dual requirement, see B Nicholas, *An Introduction to Roman Law* (Oxford, Clarendon Press, 1962) 112–14; J Thomas, *Textbook of Roman Law* (Oxford, North-Holland, 1976) 139–41.

factually or legally. This is not to say that Birks is incorrect to assert that the use of the thing constitutes enrichment—that is a different claim considered separately below—but Birks is wrong to assume the defendant has not also received a right with an exchange value. The defendant acquires a new right and has received value: where title does not pass, the defendant has a right of possession good against the world except the true owner; where title does pass, the defendant obtains a legal right. These rights are valuable and can be exchanged.

One further point that is sometimes made in this context is that the defendant's lesser right to possession does not come 'at the expense of the claimant' as the claimant retains legal title.[183] This argument misunderstands transfers of value. The claimant is not alleging that the defendant is enriched by the acquisition of a right that was previously held by the defendant or that the claimant's legal right is in any way extinguished.[184] Rather, the defendant is enriched by the creation of a new right to possession, the *value* of which comes at the expense of the claimant. Where the transfer of the goods to the defendant correspondingly reduces the value of the claimant's right to possession, there is a transfer of value at the claimant's expense. For instance, in *Huyton v Peter Cremer*, Cremer's right to possession of the wheat as the true owner had a market exchange value. When Cremer delivered the goods to Huyton in the Sudan, Mance J was of the opinion that, provided Cremer could not get the wheat back, Huyton would be enriched by the value of the wheat in the Sudan. This was so even though title had not passed to Huyton, who merely had a right to possession of the wheat. This did not matter: if Cremer could not get the wheat back from Huyton, then Cremer could not exchange the wheat and the value of Cremer's right to exchange the wheat was transferred to Huyton. The value of the wheat in Huyton's possession correspondingly came from Cremer.

### *(ii) Use Value of Goods*

Although the historical availability of a claim for the use value of chattels is sometimes disputed,[185] Baker notes that the quantum meruit form was adapted in the early common law as *quantum habere meruit* to reach the hire of chattels.[186] Whatever the historical position, the use of chattels now undoubtedly constitutes a benefit capable of enriching a defendant, as recognised by Robert Goff J in *BP Exploration v Hunt (No 2)*.[187] The authoritative modern example is the case of *Dimond v Lovell*,[188] where Dimond had the use of a motor vehicle under a hire purchase agreement that was unenforceable by reason of the Consumer Credit

[183] Swadling, 'A Claim in Restitution?' (1996) (n 175).

[184] See B McFarlane, *The Basic Structure of Property Law* (Oxford, Hart, 2008) 18.

[185] See, eg Ames, *Lectures on Legal History and Miscellaneous Legal Essays* (1913) (n 10) 164–65; Edelman and Bant, *Unjust Enrichment in Australia* (2006) (n 79) 103.

[186] Baker, 'The History of Quasi-Contract in English Law' (1998) (n 5) 43.

[187] *BP Exploration Co (Libya) Ltd v Hunt (No 2)* [1979] 1 WLR 783 (QB) 799 (Robert Goff J); *ABB Power Generation v Chapple* [2001] WASCA 412, (2001) 25 WAR 158.

[188] *Dimond v Lovell* [2002] 1 AC 384 (HL).

Act 1974. While there was no enforceable contract between the parties, the hire purchase company argued that Dimond had the use of the car and should pay on a quantum valebat basis. The hire purchase company was unsuccessful before the House of Lords as it was held that allowing restitution for the use value in these circumstances would stultify the legislative policy rendering the contract unenforceable. However, there was no doubt that Dimond was enriched by the use of the vehicle. Lord Hoffmann held that Dimond 'has had 8 days use of a Ford Mondeo for nothing. She has certainly been enriched'.[189] Therefore, but for the public policy objection, the House of Lords would undoubtedly have entertained an unjust enrichment claim based on the use value of goods.

As with money, the actual use to which the goods are put is irrelevant to quantifying restitutionary liability. For example, it would not have mattered in *Dimond v Lovell* whether Dimond had driven the Ford Mondeo or not. The opportunity to use the vehicle is the relevant benefit. Dimond had the opportunity to use a car for eight days at no cost; this is directly analogous to the interest-free loan to the Revenue in *Sempra Metals*.[190] The right to use a car for eight days is a valuable benefit, quantified by market rental rates for similar vehicles. Thus, Dimond's enrichment is the market value of the opportunity to use the vehicle. Provided the choice of benefit or incontrovertible enrichment test is satisfied, as explained in chapter six, she is enriched.

### *(iii) Combining Exchange Value and Use Value Claims*

Unlike money, a claim for use value cannot be combined with a claim for the restitution of the relevant asset as the use value is priced into the exchange value.[191] For example, the exchange value of a car in the market incorporates the value of driving that car. A claim for restitution of the value of the car as well as the reasonable rent for the period of use would permit the claimant double recovery. To put it another way, where a defendant is required to make restitution of the exchange value of a car to the claimant, the defendant's enrichment is the value of his right to the car in the market. Absent a specific restitution claim, the defendant gets to keep the car and continue using it. If the claimant were entitled to the use of the car in addition to the exchange value, then the claimant could sue for the reasonable rent for the entire period of use, even though the defendant has effectively 'bought' the car by paying its market exchange value.

However, a *legal* enrichment claim for the car could be combined with a claim for reasonable rent for the use of the car as the claimant is entitled to restitution of the two separate enrichments received by the defendant: the specific right to the car and the value of its use.[192] The combination of rescission and value claims

[189] Ibid 397 (Lord Hoffmann).

[190] *Sempra Metals Ltd v IRC* [2007] UKHL 34, [2008] 1 AC 561 [33] (Lord Hope).

[191] Mitchell, Mitchell and Watterson, *Goff & Jones The Law of Unjust Enrichment* (2011) (n 38) §4-05.

[192] See, eg *Erlanger v The New Sombrero Phosphate Co* (1878) 3 App Cas 1218 (HL).

is considered in chapter five,[193] but it suffices for present purposes to note that there is no double recovery. If the claimant were restricted to specific restitution of the title to the car, then the claimant would be restricted to a right to repossess an older, usually depreciated vehicle and the defendant would have obtained the use of the car in the interim for free. As the claimant is asking for the right to the car rather than the value of this right, full restitution is not achieved simply by revesting title. The value of the use transferred to the defendant is not reversed by specific restitution of title to the car.

# V. Land

## A. Unjust Enrichment Claims to Land

As with claims to chattels, the protection of rights to land is not usually achieved through the law of unjust enrichment. First, there are wrongs-based claims for the protection of rights in land that may be more advantageous, in particular the tort of trespass. For example, the availability of restitution for trespass to land was recognised in *Ministry of Defence v Ashman*[194] and *Inverugie v Hackett*.[195] Second, the defendant may be able to make a rights-based claim for the land, for example by way of rescission, rectification or resulting trust. These claims are legal enrichment claims, not factual enrichment claims, and they are considered separately in chapter five below.

### *(i) Claims to The Exchange Value of Land*

In addition to the protection afforded to real property in the law of torts and specific restitution of property rights, the model presented in this book suggests the availability of a value-based unjust enrichment claim where the benefit is land and the claimant seeks monetary restitution. However, due to the nature of land and the effectiveness of land registration regimes, the only claims in the reports concern the use and occupation of real property, as opposed to claims based on the exchange value of a right to land. Nonetheless, there is no existing precedent or theoretical obstacle to recognising a claim to the exchange value of a right to land acquired by the defendant. Accordingly, it remains open to a court to find that a defendant is enriched by the acquisition of a right to land and award restitution of the value of that right.

### *(ii) Claims to The Use Value of Land*

Claims to the use value of land have long been recognised in the common law: the claimant may recover restitution of the value of the use and occupation of land

[193] See ch 5, s II.C.
[194] *Ministry of Defence v Ashman* (1993) 66 P&CR 195 (CA).
[195] *Inverugie v Hackett* [1995] 1 WLR 713 (PC).

by the defendant with the claimant's permission in circumstances where there is no agreement as to payment of rent.[196] There are historical examples of restitution of the value of the use and occupation of land under the quantum valebat count. For example, in *Hamerton v Stead*,[197] a quantum valebat was allowed for the occupation of a premises by a tenant pending the execution of a lease between the landlord and tenant. Moreover, the quantum meruit form was also adapted to the use and occupation of real property.[198]

## B. Factual Enrichment in Land Cases

### *(i) Claims to The Exchange Value of Land*

Although there are no reported cases on point, the enrichment model would apply to rights in land in precisely the same way as it does to goods. The defendant may be enriched by the acquisition of title to land or some lesser right, such as possession, and the transfer of value to the defendant in such cases will depend on the nature of the right conferred and its exchange value.

### *(ii) Claims to The Use Value of Land*

In addition to the exchange value claim, it is clear that the use and occupation of land is a benefit that is capable of transferring value to the defendant. The defendant will be enriched by the market value of the opportunity to use or occupy the land. As with goods, the actual use to which the land is put is not the relevant measure for restitutionary relief. It does not matter, for example, if the defendant's use is not profitable.[199] In *Lewisham LBC v Masterson*,[200] Masterson had the use and occupation of a derelict former coal yard from 1987–91 in anticipation of entering into a 15-year lease over the yard that never materialised. Although Masterson did not make any profitable use of the derelict yard, Buxton LJ held that 'the benefit that the defendant has received will, in a use and occupation case, be exactly that—the ability to use and occupy the premises'.[201] Like the use of the Ford Mondeo in *Dimond v Lovell* or the Revenue's use of the Advanced Corporation Tax payments in *Sempra*, the defendant's benefit is the opportunity to use the land, usually measured by the market rental rates for the property.

[196] *Mason v Welland* (1728) Skin 238, 243; 90 ER 109, 111; *Beverley v Lincoln Gas Light and Coke Co* (1837) 6 Ad&E 829, 839; 112 ER 318, 322–23; *Mayor of Thetford v Tyler* (1845) 8 QB 95, 100; 115 ER 810, 812–13 (Lord Denman CJ); *Churchward v Ford* (1857) 2 H&N 446, 448–49; 157 ER 184, 185–86; *Turner v York Motors Pty Ltd* (1951) 85 CLR 55 (HCA) 65; *Graves v Graves* [2007] EWCA Civ 660, [2007] 3 FCR 26. See Mitchell, Mitchell and Watterson, *Goff & Jones The Law of Unjust Enrichment* (2011) (n 38) §5-18.

[197] *Hamerton v Stead* (1824) 3 B&C 478, 107 ER 811.

[198] Baker, 'The History of Quasi-Contract in English Law' (1998) (n 5) 43.

[199] *Lewisham LBC v Masterson* (2000) 80 P&CR 117 (CA) 123 (Buxton LJ).

[200] Ibid.

[201] Ibid 122 (Buxton LJ).

The award for the use value of land is restitutionary in nature, calculated to reverse the value transferred to the defendant by the use and occupation of the land. The use value of land 'accrues, like interest, de die in diem'.[202] It is clear from *Lewisham LBC v Masterson* that 'open market value would ordinarily be the appropriate test of valuation',[203] not the contractually stipulated rent. The remedy is thus restitutionary, quantifying the value transferred to the defendant, rather than compensating the claimant for expectation losses at the contractually agreed rate.

# VI. Release of Obligations

## A. Money Paid

### *(i) Money Paid is Not a Cause of Action*

Actions for money paid to the defendant's use lay where the claimant paid money to a third party in circumstances that discharged the defendant's obligation to the third party.[204] A famous example is the case of *Exall v Partridge*,[205] where the claimant paid the defendant's rent in order to obtain release of his carriage from the defendant's landlord. It was held that the defendant's legal obligation to pay rent to the landlord was discharged by the claimant under circumstances of compulsion and the claimant was therefore entitled to restitution from the defendant. While money paid may at first glance seem better classified as the receipt of money, the benefit the defendant receives is not money but the discharge of a legal obligation, which is a non-money benefit.[206] This is made clear by the application of the count to circumstances other than the discharge of a debt. For instance, money paid lay in certain necessitous intervention cases. In *Jenkins v Tucker*,[207] the claimant, who was the father of the deceased, succeeded in an action in money paid against the defendant, who was the deceased's husband, to recover the expenses of her funeral where the husband was obliged by law to bury the body. The money paid count therefore extended to the performance of a legal liability of the defendant by a third party.

As with the other forms of action examined above, the form covered various different causes of action. First, it embraced contractual claims, such as a contractual right of indemnity by a surety against the principal debtor.[208] Second,

[202] *Slack v Sharpe* (1838) 8 Ad&E 366, 373; 112 ER 876, 879 (Patteson J).

[203] *Lewisham LBC v Masterson* (2000) 80 P&CR 117 (CA) 123 (Buxton LJ).

[204] See, eg *Osborne v Rogers* (1669) 1 Wms Saund 264, 85 ER 318; *Exall v Partridge* (1799) 8 TR 308, 101 ER 1405; *Moule v Garrett* (1872) 7 Ex 101 (Ex).

[205] *Exall v Partridge* (1799) 8 TR 308, 101 ER 1405.

[206] See Birks, *An Introduction to the Law of Restitution* (1989) (n 26) 112.

[207] *Jenkins v Tucker* (1788) 1 H Bl 90, 126 ER 55.

[208] Jones (ed), *Goff & Jones The Law of Restitution* (2007) (n 27) §1-003.

it lay in circumstances of unjust enrichment, such as *Exall v Partridge*, where the claimant is not requested to make the payment and no genuine contractual relationship arises, but an unjust factor is present. In *Exall v Partridge*,[209] the court found that the claimant had paid the defendant's rent at his 'special instance and request',[210] when it was quite clear that no such request had been made. *Exall v Partridge* turned, not upon a request by the defendant, but on the unquestionably enriching nature of the benefit that the defendant received by the discharge of his legal obligation. Consistently with the approach adopted in relation to the other common counts, it is therefore preferable to treat money paid as a response to different causes of action.

### *(ii) Money Paid as a Legal Response*

The response to claims for money paid is invariably restitutionary: the defendant is obliged to make restitution to the claimant for the value of the discharge of the defendant's liability. For example, in *Exall v Partridge*, the defendant was required to pay the claimant the value of the rental arrears discharged by the claimant. Likewise, in *Jenkins v Tucker*, the benefit conferred on the defendant was the defraying of the necessary expense of a funeral to bury his deceased wife. The defendant was obliged to pay the reasonable cost of a funeral 'in a manner suitable to his degree and situation in life',[211] not to compensate the claimant for his losses. The court suggests that the defendant would not have been liable for the claimant's losses if the claimant had paid for an extravagant funeral that was more expensive than the funeral the defendant would have had to provide. On the facts, the claimant had paid for a reasonable funeral 'on account of the wife … suitable to the degree of the husband' and was entitled to restitution of the value transferred.

## B. Factual Enrichment by the Release of Obligations

### *(i) Unjust Enrichment and the Release of Obligations*

On the basis of the claims falling within the count of money paid, it is clear that the release of a legal obligation owed to a third party is a recognised benefit capable of underpinning a factual enrichment claim.[212] However, as recognised by Laws LJ in *Gibb v Maidstone and Tunbridge Wells NHS Trust*,[213] the release of legal obligations to third parties is logically part of a broader recognition of the release

[209] *Exall v Partridge* (1799) 8 TR 308, 101 ER 1405.

[210] See Stephen, *A Treatise on the Principles of Pleading in Civil Actions* (1827) 212; Birks, *Unjust Enrichment* (2005) (n 4) 54–55.

[211] *Jenkins v Tucker* (1788) 1 H Bl 90, 94; 126 ER 55, 57 (Gould J).

[212] See Mitchell, Mitchell and Watterson, *Goff & Jones The Law of Unjust Enrichment* (2011) (n 38) §4-18.

[213] *Gibb v Maidstone and Tunbridge Wells NHS Trust* [2010] EWCA Civ 678, [2010] IRLR 786 [24]–[37] (Laws LJ).

of obligations as a valuable benefit in the law of unjust enrichment. It is argued here that, where the defendant's obligations are released at the claimant's expense, there is a transfer of value capable of enriching the defendant. Alternatively, in addition to monetary restitution, the claimant may be entitled to specific restitution by restitutionary subrogation, a claim considered in chapter five.[214]

It is now understood that contribution and recoupment cases are instances of unjust enrichment by the discharge of the defendant's obligation at the claimant's expense.[215] Contribution arises where the claimant and defendant are subject to the same obligation and the claimant discharges that obligation to the benefit of the defendant.[216] In *Moule v Garrett*, it was held that, where the claimant and defendant 'must divide the burden' of performance and one party discharges all or part of the other's share, the other party must make restitution of the difference.[217] For example, the defendant's obligation to pay contribution to a joint tortfeasor reverses the defendant's unjust enrichment by the release of his obligation to compensate the victim of the tort. The circumstances when payment by the claimant will release the defendant's liability are beyond the scope of this book but, provided the liability is released, there is a transfer of value factually enriching the defendant.[218]

The same is true in recoupment cases, where the claimant's liability is secondary to the defendant's rather than joint, but the claimant's discharge of the obligation releases the defendant from liability.[219] As Cockburn CJ put it in *Moule v Garrett*, the defendant will have an obligation in recoupment 'where the claimant has been compelled by law to pay ... money which the defendant was ultimately liable to pay, so that the latter obtains ... the discharge of his liability'.[220] That recoupment is a response to unjust enrichment was recognised by Lord Wright MR in *Brook's*

214 See ch 5, s IV.

215 *Brook's Wharf and Bull Wharf Ltd v Goodman Bros* [1937] 1 KB 534 (CA) 544–45 (Lord Wright MR); *Esso Petroleum Co Ltd v Hall Russell & Co Ltd (The Esso Bernicia)* [1989] AC 643 (HL) 662–63 (Lord Goff); *Kleinwort Benson Ltd v Vaughan* [1996] CLC 620 (CA) 624 (Nourse LJ); *James Hardie & Co Pty Ltd v Wyong Shire Council* (2000) 48 NSWLR 679 (NSWCA) 687 (Handley JA); *AMP Workers' Compensation Services (NSW) Ltd v QBE Insurance Ltd* [2001] NSWCA 267, (2001) 53 NSWLR 35 [22]–[24] (Handley JA); *Dubai Aluminium v Salaam* [2002] UKHL 48, [2003] 2 AC 366 [76] (Lord Hobhouse). See discussion in Mason and Carter, *Restitution Law in Australia* (1996) (n 137) 190; Edelman and Bant, *Unjust Enrichment in Australia* (2006) (n 79) 283–88; Mitchell, Mitchell and Watterson, *Goff & Jones The Law of Unjust Enrichment* (2011) (n 38) Ch 20.

216 *Brook's Wharf and Bull Wharf Ltd v Goodman Bros* [1937] 1 KB 534 (CA) 544 (Lord Wright MR); Edelman and Bant, *Unjust Enrichment in Australia* (2006) (n 79) 286–88.

217 *Moule v Garrett* (1872) 7 Ex 101 (Ex) 103 (Willes J).

218 See Mitchell, Mitchell and Watterson, *Goff & Jones The Law of Unjust Enrichment* (2011) (n 38) §§5-38–5-57 for a discussion of the rules on discharge of obligations.

219 Eg *Exall v Partridge* (1799) 8 TR 308, 101 ER 1405; *Johnson v Royal Mail Steam Packet Co* (1866) 3 CP 38 (CCP); *Moule v Garrett* (1872) 7 Ex 101 (Ex); *Kleinwort Benson Ltd v Vaughan* [1996] CLC 620 (CA); *AMP Workers' Compensation Services (NSW) Ltd v QBE Insurance Ltd* [2001] NSWCA 267, (2001) 53 NSWLR 35; *Cockburn v GIO Finance Ltd (No 2)* [2001] NSWCA 177, (2001) 51 NSWLR 624.

220 *Moule v Garrett* (1872) 7 Ex 101 (Ex) 104 (Cockburn CJ).

*Wharf*[221] and Nourse LJ in *Kleinwort Benson v Vaughan*.[222] Recoupment commonly arises in surety and indemnity arrangements, where the claimant agrees to be liable for the defendant's obligation and is called upon to perform, thereby releasing the defendant from the obligation to perform. The defendant's liability will also arise where the claimant discharges the defendant's liability under compulsion of law, as occurred in *Exall v Partridge*.[223] Where the claimant's payment is effective to discharge the defendant's liability,[224] the defendant is factually enriched by the value transferred.

Finally, the release of contractual obligations is similarly a valuable benefit capable of enriching the defendant. For example, where the claimant mistakenly pays money into the defendant's overdrawn bank account, the benefit the defendant obtains is not 'money', but release from the obligation to pay the bank to the extent of the mistaken payment. By extension, release from, or performance of, contractual obligations besides the obligation to pay money will also transfer value to the defendant. However, the factual enrichment claim for monetary restitution should not be confused with rescission of the contractual obligations, which is a legal enrichment claim considered in chapter five.[225]

### *(ii) Transfer of Value in Release of Obligation Cases*

As explained above, the discharge of the defendant's obligations is a non-money benefit. The defendant does not receive money from the claimant, but rather a service: the performance or release by the claimant of an obligation owed by the defendant. This point is highlighted by cases where the obligation discharged is non-monetary in nature, such as the obligation to clear a blocked drain in *Gebhardt v Saunders*[226] and the obligation to repair a damaged bridge in *Macclesfield Corp v Great Central Railway*.[227] Whether the defendant owes a debt or is under a duty to perform an act, the benefit to the defendant is the same: release from the obligation to perform. The release cases are therefore a particular subset of services cases where the service provided by the claimant is the release of an obligation. These cases should therefore be amenable to the same analysis as any other form of service: the performance of the service transfers value to the defendant and, provided the incontrovertible enrichment or choice of benefit test is satisfied, the release will enrich the defendant.

However, it is critical to understand that the transfer of value does not occur unless the obligation is released.[228] The rules on when a debt or obligation is

[221] *Brook's Wharf and Bull Wharf Ltd v Goodman Bros* [1937] 1 KB 534 (CA) 544–45 (Lord Wright MR).

[222] *Kleinwort Benson Ltd v Vaughan* [1996] CLC 620 (CA) 624 (Nourse LJ).

[223] *Exall v Partridge* (1799) 8 TR 308, 101 ER 1405.

[224] See discussion in Burrows, *The Law of Restitution* (2010) (n 104) 460–68; Mitchell, Mitchell and Watterson, *Goff & Jones The Law of Unjust Enrichment* (2011) (n 38) §§5-38–5-57.

[225] See ch 5, s II.

[226] *Gebhardt v Saunders* [1892] 2 QB 452 (QB).

[227] *Macclesfield Corp v Great Central Railway* [1911] 2 KB 528 (CA).

[228] Eg *Esso Petroleum Co Ltd v Hall Russell & Co Ltd (The Esso Bernicia)* discussed in ch 6, s III.A.

effectively discharged or released are not part of the law of unjust enrichment, although the law's concern to protect freedom of choice is apparent in the strict rules that govern when payment of another's debt will discharge that debt. The mere fact that the claimant has attempted to discharge an obligation of the defendant will not usually transfer value to the defendant unless the law considers the obligation to be released under the circumstances. If the claimant has effectively released the defendant's legal obligation, then a service has been provided that transfers value to the defendant.

The voluntary or mistaken discharge of a debt by another illustrates this point. It is difficult under English law to discharge the debt of another; the mere fact that a third party has paid the creditor does not ordinarily suffice to discharge the debt in the absence of authorisation or ratification by the debtor. Without authorisation or ratification, a voluntary payment to discharge the debt of another will never discharge the debt.[229] In cases where the third party pays the debt by mistake, it seems to have been settled in England that the payment will also not discharge the debt.[230] According to the Court of Appeal in *Crantrave Ltd v Lloyd's Bank plc*, the 'payment to the creditor will not of itself discharge the [liability] … [in] the absence of authorisation or ratification of the payment'.[231] In such a case, the third party may recover from the creditor in unjust enrichment on account of the mistake (and may even be subrogated to the creditor's rights),[232] but will have no action against the debtor because no value has been transferred to the debtor. The debt is still owing.

However, it is important to note that the requirement for authorisation or ratification in many debt discharge cases is a question of whether there has been a transfer of value, not a proxy for the choice of benefit test (discussed in chapter six). The requirement of authorisation or ratification in debt discharge cases is a condition of the effective discharge of the debt by a third party on the defendant's behalf. The relevant benefit to the defendant is not the payment or performance by the claimant, but the release of the defendant's obligation to pay or perform. Thus, where authorisation or ratification is required for discharge of a debt to be effective, that is generally necessary for a transfer of value to the defendant. In such a case, the authorisation or ratification by the defendant will then also establish that the defendant chose the benefit and is enriched, but the converse is not also true: where there is evidence that the choice of benefit test is satisfied, this does not imply that the debt is effectively discharged. The requirements for

[229] *James v Isaacs* (1852) 12 CB 791, 138 ER 1115; *Re Rowe* [1904] 2 KB 483 (CA); *Smith v Cox* [1940] 2 KB 558 (KB); *Guardian Ocean Cargoes Ltd v Banco do Brasil SA (No 1)* [1991] 2 Lloyd's Rep 68 (QB) 88 (Hirst J); *Electricity Supply Nominees Ltd v Thorn EMI Retail Ltd* (1991) 63 P&CR 143 (CA) 148 (Fox LJ).

[230] *Re Cleadon Trust Ltd* [1939] Ch 286 (CA); *Barclays Bank Ltd v W J Simms & Cooke (Southern) Ltd* [1980] QB 677 (QB) 700 (Robert Goff J); *Crantrave Ltd v Lloyds Bank plc* [2000] QB 917 (CA) 923 (Pill LJ) *cf B Liggett (Liverpool) Ltd v Barclays Bank* [1928] 1 KB 48 (KB).

[231] *Crantrave Ltd v Lloyds Bank plc* [2000] QB 917 (CA) 923 (Pill LJ).

[232] See ch 5, s IV.A.

the effective discharge of a debt are anterior to, and separate from, the question of whether that discharge enriches the defendant.

## VII. Conclusion

This chapter has applied the factual enrichment model to the different categories of benefit, demonstrating how the theory developed in chapter three of this book fits and explains the case law. First, it was shown that the treatment of the common money counts as separate causes of action is inaccurate and potentially misleading. Instead, the common counts are responses to different causes of action, including various causes of action in unjust enrichment. The response in unjust enrichment cases—although usually expressed as money had and received, quantum meruit, quantum valebat or money paid—is restitutionary and the only point of differentiation between these awards is the type of enrichment involved. Furthermore, it was shown that these awards are instantiations of the same principles of liability and there is no reason of principle for segregating money and non-money cases or justifying the differentiation of non-money benefits by type. The factual enrichment model proposed in this book both fits and explains the award of monetary restitution in all these cases.

Accordingly, it was shown that where the claimant seeks monetary restitution, whether the benefit is money, services, goods, land or release from an obligation, the enrichment inquiry is the same. As explained in chapter two, value is by definition an abstraction from the particular benefit to a standard for the comparison and exchange of qualitatively heterogeneous things in quantitatively comparable and equivalent terms. In factual enrichment cases, the liability is premised upon an abstract transfer of value and this chapter has shown that the defendant's enrichment can sensibly and consistently be explained by the receipt of value understood relationally. In this way, the factual enrichment model provides a coherent theoretical account of the restitution of value in the common law that permits the assimilation of the various common counts in *indebitatus assumpsit* in the modern law of restitution for unjust enrichment. However, as explained in chapter six, the choice of benefit or incontrovertible enrichment tests must also be satisfied to prove that the particular defendant is enriched.

# 5

# Legal Enrichment

This chapter addresses the other kind of enrichment in the law of unjust enrichment: legal enrichment. A defendant may be legally enriched by the acquisition of a right ('enrichment by rights') or the extinguishment of an obligation ('enrichment by release'). In either case, the enrichment can be conceived factually (as the *economic value* transferred to the defendant) or legally (by the change in the rights and obligations of the defendant). For instance, the acquisition of a right in circumstances giving rise to a claim in unjust enrichment may be considered enriching either as the unjust receipt of the *value of the right* or the unjust acquisition of *the right itself*. Likewise, the release of an obligation can be conceived either in terms of value (as in the cases examined in chapter four) or legal effect. However, unlike factual enrichment cases, the remedy in cases involving legal enrichment has rarely been recognised by the courts as a response to unjust enrichment. So, while a defendant who receives value as a result of a mistake, duress or failure of consideration is now commonly recognised as having an obligation to make restitution for unjust enrichment, the same analysis has not traditionally been applied to a defendant who, on identical grounds, obtains a right or release of an obligation that is reversed in law, rather than by an award of money.

This chapter seeks to introduce consistency of approach to the treatment of legal enrichment cases to align like cases with like. It will be explained that resulting trusts, rescission, rectification and subrogation cases are examples of specific restitution of a right or reinstatement of an obligation. Although the role of unjust enrichment in these areas is controversial, the courts have recognised the role of unjust enrichment in explaining rescission[1] and subrogation,[2] and there is some judicial support for an unjust enrichment explanation of resulting

[1] *Whittaker v Campbell* [1984] QB 318 (DC) 327 (Robert Goff LJ).

[2] See *Hewitt v Court* (1983) 149 CLR 639 (HCA); *Boscawen v Bajwa* [1996] 1 WLR 328 (CA) 335 (Millett LJ); *Banque Financiere de la Cité v Parc (Battersea) Ltd* [1999] 1 AC 221 (HL) 231 (Lord Hoffmann); *Birmingham Midshires Mortgage Services Ltd v Sabherwal* (1999) 80 P&CR 256 (CA) 264 (Robert Walker LJ); *Khan v Permayer* [2001] BPIR 95 (CA) [36] (Morritt LJ); *Liberty Mutual Insurance Co (UK) Ltd v HSBC Bank plc* [2002] EWCA Civ 691; *Cheltenham and Gloucester plc v Appleyard* [2004] EWCA Civ 291; *Niru Battery Manufacturing Co v Milestone Trading Ltd (No 2)* [2004] EWCA Civ 487, [2004] 2 Lloyd's Rep 319 [27], [56] (Clarke LJ); *Filby v Mortgage Express (No 2) Ltd* [2004] EWCA Civ 759, [2004] 2 P&CR DG 16 [62] (May LJ); *Primlake Ltd (in liquidation) v Matthews Associates* [2006] EWHC 1227 (Ch), [2007] 1 BCLC 666 [339]–[340] (Lawrence Collins J); *Anfield (UK) Ltd v Bank of Scotland* [2010] EWHC 2374 (Ch) [10] (Proudman J).

trusts.[3] However, this book suggests that the ambit of unjust enrichment may be somewhat broader. In relation to executory contracts, it is suggested here that the traditional treatment of the cancellation of a defendant's rights by rescission is not simply an incident of 'contract', but rather a restitutionary response. Further, it is contended that rectification also involves specific restitution of a legal enrichment: the claimant's power to rectify, usually as the result of a mistake, is not a passive correction of an error in an instrument, but a doctrine that has substantive effect as restitution of rights.

A detailed consideration of the operation of each of these doctrines would be a separate book in itself. This chapter does not attempt a comprehensive examination of resulting trusts, rescission, rectification or subrogation. Rather, the purpose of this chapter is to demonstrate that these doctrines should all be understood as restitutionary responses. In each case, the claimant asserts that the defendant is enriched by a change in legal relations and demands specific restitution. The defendant is enriched by the acquisition of a right or the release of an obligation, not by economic value, and the claimant demands specific restitution of that right or reinstatement of that duty. The remedy in all these cases is restitutionary in purpose and effect: the reversal of the defendant's enrichment at the claimant's expense.

In the first category of legal enrichment, 'enrichment by rights', restitution may be achieved through the power to collapse a resulting trust, the power to rescind and the power to rectify. These remedies give the claimant the power to reverse the acquisition of a right. In the second category, 'enrichment by release', restitution is achieved by reinstating the released obligation and giving the claimant the correlative power to enforce it, as occurs in some subrogation cases. It will be shown that rationalising legal enrichment claims in this way is not merely a labour of reclassification. Rather, it correctly identifies the defendant's enrichment and differentiates the restitutionary response from value cases, as well as having numerous other substantive implications.

Section I addresses resulting trusts, which are the core case of specific restitution of an enrichment by rights. At least some resulting trusts are a response to unjust enrichment and all resulting trusts are best understood as effecting specific restitution of a right. In section II, the same analysis is applied to explain rescission. The power of rescission is a power to obtain specific restitution of contractual rights, as well as property rights and value transferred by performance under the contract. Section III then explains how rectification should be understood in the same terms, not as a passive correction of a written instrument, but as a response that achieves specific restitution of a right wrongly recorded in a written instrument. Finally, section IV considers rights of subrogation, which are recognised in English law as involving a response to unjust enrichment. It is explained

[3] See *Air Jamaica Ltd v Charlton* [1999] 1 WLR 1399 (PC) 1412 (Lord Millett); *Twinsectra v Yardley* [2002] UKHL 12, [2002] 2 AC 164 [92]–[100] (Lord Millett). See also extra-judicially: P Millett, 'Restitution and Constructive Trusts' (1998) 114 *LQR* 399.

that subrogation cases involve enrichment by the release of an obligation and restitution takes the form of reinstating that obligation, thereby giving the claimant a power to obtain specific restitution of a right.

# I. Resulting Trusts

The first example of specific restitution of a legal enrichment is the resulting trust. Where the defendant acquires a right at the expense of the claimant, the defendant is enriched by that right and, provided an unjust factor is proved, the claimant may seek specific restitution of that right in the form of a resulting trust. However, resulting trusts are not always a response to unjust enrichment. A trust that is declared by, and in favour of, the transferor may be described as 'resulting',[4] but such a trust arises by consent. It suffices for present purposes to show that *some* resulting trusts definitively do respond to unjust enrichment. Where this is the case, it will be contended that the best explanation is that the resulting trust effects specific restitution of an enrichment by rights. It is suggested that alternative explanations for the resulting trust in these cases are unsatisfactory. The view that resulting trusts are never a response to unjust enrichment is firmly rejected.

## A. What is a Resulting Trust?

### *(i) 'Two Types' of Resulting Trust*

Since Megarry J's decision in *Re Vandervell's Trust (No 2)*,[5] resulting trusts have typically been divided into two broad categories: (i) presumed intention resulting trusts or 'gratuitous transfer' resulting trusts; and (ii) automatic resulting trusts or 'failed trust resulting trusts'. In the first category of case, a gratuitous *inter vivos* transfer from A to B raises a presumption that B will hold the right acquired on trust for A. This presumption will not arise in circumstances of 'advancement',[6] such as where A is the father or husband of B. If the presumption is not rebutted by evidence to the contrary, then B will hold the rights on resulting trust for A.[7] The same presumption will arise in the case of a 'purchase money resulting trust'.

[4] In Birks's language, 'pro-sulting': P Birks, 'Retrieving Tied Money' in W Swadling (ed), *The Quistclose Trust: Critical Essays* (Oxford, Hart, 2004) 122 fn 5.

[5] *Re Vandervell's Trust (No 2)* [1974] Ch 269 (CA) 288–89, 294 (Megarry J). See P Millett, 'Pension Schemes and the Law of Trusts' (2000) 14 *Trusts Law International* 66, 73; R Chambers, 'Resulting Trusts' in A Burrows and A Rodger (eds), *Mapping the Law: Essays in Memory of Peter Birks* (Oxford, Oxford University Press, 2006) 249; W Swadling, 'Explaining Resulting Trusts' (2008) 124 *LQR* 72, 73.

[6] *Martin v Martin* (1959) 110 CLR 297 (HCA) 303 (Dixon CJ, McTiernan, Fullager & Windeyer JJ). It is not a 'presumption' of advancement: Swadling, 'Explaining Resulting Trusts' (2008) (n 5) 73.

[7] See *Dyer v Dyer* (1788) 2 Cox 92, 30 ER 42; *Fowkes v Pascoe* (1875) 10 Ch App 343 (CA) 352–53 (Sir George Mellish LJ); *The Venture* (1908) P 218 (CA) 229–30; *Stack v Dowden* [2007] UKHL 17, [2007] 2 AC 243 [123] (Lord Neuberger).

Where A contributes to the purchase price or the repayment of a mortgage over land, B will hold the right to the land on resulting trust in proportion to the respective contributions, except in relation to claims between cohabitants involving 'matrimonial or quasi-matrimonial homes' where a constructive trust analysis is preferred.[8]

In the second category of case, the 'failed trust' resulting trust, a transfer that fails to create an intended trust (for example due to the rule against perpetuities) results in the right acquired being held on resulting trust for the settlor. The right held on resulting trust 'results back' to the donor or settlor, giving him a power to collapse the trust and obtain restitution of the right held on trust. For instance, a resulting trust arose due to the failure of an intended express trust in *Vandervell v IRC*,[9] where the settlor failed to identify a beneficiary, and *Re Gillingham Bus Disaster Fund*,[10] where the trust failed for uncertainty from the outset.

However, there is no reason of principle for confining the resulting trust to these two instances and the two categories are not exhaustive.[11] There are various other examples where a resulting trust arises. In section II, which examines rescission, it will be seen that the courts have described the trust that arises following rescission in equity as a 'resulting trust'.[12] It is also argued that the trust that arises when a contract is disaffirmed in equity for fraud is best understood as a resulting trust.[13] In addition, a resulting trust may arise where money is misused by the executor of a deceased estate,[14] which involves neither a gratuitous transfer nor an attempt to create a trust that fails.[15] In *Twinsectra v Yardley*,[16] Lord Millett held that a resulting trust arises in favour of the lender where a loan of money is made for an exclusive purpose and ring-fenced from the recipient's other assets. Although the so-called '*Quistclose* trust' that arises on these facts has excited much controversy,[17] Lord Millett's approach confirms that the categories of resulting trust are not closed.

[8] *Stack v Dowden* [2007] UKHL 17, [2007] 2 AC 243 [31] (Lord Walker) [60] (Baroness Hale) *cf* [110]–[122] (Lord Neuberger).

[9] *Vandervell v IRC* [1967] 2 AC 291 (HL).

[10] *Re Gillingham Bus Disaster Fund* [1958] Ch 300 (Ch).

[11] Chambers, 'Resulting Trusts' (2006) (n 5) 249.

[12] *El Ajou v Dollar Land Holdings plc* [1993] 3 All ER 717 (Ch) 734 (Millett J); *Twinsectra v Yardley* [1999] Lloyd's Rep Bank 438 (CA) [99].

[13] See ch 5, s I.B.

[14] *Ryall v Ryall* (1739) 1 Atk 59, 26 ER 39. See also *Merchants Express Co v Morton* (1868) 15 Gr 274 (Ont Ch); *El Ajou v Dollar Land Holdings plc* [1993] 3 All ER 717 (Ch) 734 (Millett J).

[15] Chambers, 'Resulting Trusts' (2006) (n 5) 249.

[16] *Twinsectra v Yardley* [2002] UKHL 12, [2002] 2 AC 164.

[17] See P Millett, 'The Quistclose Trust: Who Can Enforce It?' (1985) 101 *LQR* 269; C Rickett, 'Different Views on the Scope of the Quistclose Analysis' (1991) 107 *LQR* 608; C Mitchell, 'Subrogation, Tracing and the *Quistclose* Principle' [1995] *LMCLQ* 451; R Chambers, *Resulting Trusts* (Oxford, Clarendon Press, 1997) 68–89; L Ho and P Smart, 'Reinterpreting the Quistclose Trust: a Critique of Chambers' Analysis' (2001) 21 *OJLS* 267; W Swadling (ed), *The Quistclose Trust: Critical Essays* (Oxford, Hart, 2004).

### *(ii) Resulting Trusts as Restitutionary Trusts*

The recognition of resulting trusts outside the two traditional categories is consistent with the view defended here: resulting trusts are simply restitutionary trusts, not a sub-category of trusts limited to the two instances specified by Megarry J. The feature that unites all these trusts is that they 'result back' to the transferor, that is the rights held on trust were acquired from (or at the expense of) the original transferor.[18] In effect, the acquisition of a right is 'reversed' by a power held by the claimant in respect of the right held by the defendant. In this way, resulting trusts are simply restitutionary trusts.

This is a broader definition than that adopted by Chambers, who argues that resulting trusts are defined by the event that gives rise to them: resulting trusts are those trusts that respond to unjust enrichment.[19] For Chambers, resulting trusts are thus mono-causal: the resulting trust responds to unjust enrichment 'outside its traditional categories as it does within them'.[20] This book takes a different view. It is argued that resulting trusts are an instance of specific restitution of rights, alongside rescission and rectification. Like all other forms of restitution, resulting trusts are multi-causal, arising in cases of consent, unjust enrichment and wrongdoing. The view defended here is that the resulting trust is defined by its restitutionary purpose and effect rather than by the event creating it.

There are three reasons for rejecting a mono-causal approach. First, 'resulting trusts' are defined by their structure and effect, not the event that generates the trust: the right held on trust 'results back' to the transferor. If resulting trusts are defined by the fact that the right acquired by the trustee is held on trust for the transferor, a resulting trust can arise on the basis of consent. It is clearly possible for the transferor of a right to declare a trust in favour of herself: such a trust would be both 'express' and 'resulting'.[21] Likewise, Swadling is correct to say that some resulting trusts may arise by way of a presumption of a declaration of trust.[22] These resulting trusts arise on the basis of consent, not unjust enrichment.

Second, some resulting trusts respond to wrongdoing. We will see in section II below that the trust arising following rescission in equity is described as 'resulting' and 'restitutionary'. This description of the trust is explicitly preferred by Millett J in *El Ajou*[23] and the Court of Appeal in *Twinsectra*.[24] The cases make no distinction between a power to rescind arising in unjust enrichment and a power to rescind arising from wrongdoing: irrespective of the ground for rescission, a 'resulting' trust arises

[18] P Birks, *Unjust Enrichment*, 2nd edn (Oxford, Clarendon Press, 2005) 304; Chambers, 'Resulting Trusts' (2006) (n 5) 251; Swadling, 'Explaining Resulting Trusts' (2008) (n 5) 72.

[19] See Chambers, 'Resulting Trusts' (2006) (n 5) 252–55.

[20] Ibid 253.

[21] See above n 4.

[22] W Swadling, 'A New Role for Resulting Trusts' (1996) 16 *LS* 110; W Swadling, 'A Hard Look at *Hodgson v Marks*' in P Birks and F Rose (eds), *Restitution and Equity* (London, Mansfield Press, 2000); Swadling, 'Explaining Resulting Trusts' (2008) (n 5).

[23] *El Ajou v Dollar Land Holdings plc* [1993] 3 All ER 717 (Ch) 734 (Millett J).

[24] *Twinsectra v Yardley* [1999] Lloyd's Rep Bank 438 (CA) [99].

over rights conferred pursuant to the contract. The same is also true in those cases where disaffirmation of the contract for fraud will give rise to an immediate resulting trust. Thus, resulting trusts respond to wrongdoing, as well as unjust enrichment.

Third, Chambers's mono-causal approach is inconsistent with the multi-causal approach to restitution outlined in chapter one.[25] If monetary restitution is available for wrongs and other events, there is no reason in principle that specific restitution should not similarly be available. Indeed, concurrent analyses may exist on the same facts, with the claimant able to claim restitution either based on unjust enrichment or a wrong. The case of *Ryall v Ryall*,[26] where an executor misappropriated trust assets to purchase land for himself, provides an example. The executor held the land on resulting trust for the estate, but this could be based either on the breach of fiduciary duty or fraud, or on the fact that the deceased had 'no intention to benefit' the executor. In either case, the remedy is restitutionary: the claimant has a power to obtain specific restitution of the land through the imposition of a resulting trust. However, concurrent causes of action will not always be possible. For example, where a right is conferred under a contract procured by a wrong, the claimant will need to rely on the wrong because 'no intention to benefit' is not a ground for rescinding a contract. Nevertheless, the trust that arises is no less a 'resulting' trust simply because the reason the trust arises is a wrong. It is therefore better to view resulting trusts as being multi-causal in precisely the same way as other forms of specific restitution, and indeed the remedy of restitution generally.

## B. Resulting Trusts and Unjust Enrichment

The theoretical basis of resulting trusts has excited considerable academic controversy and it is not necessary or desirable to attempt to resolve this debate in this book. The purpose of this section is more modest: to demonstrate that at least some resulting trusts are a response to unjust enrichment. After a brief introduction to the broader debate about the role of unjust enrichment in explaining resulting trusts, it is contended that at least some resulting trusts, including the so-called 'automatic' resulting trust that arises on failure of an express trust, are a response to unjust enrichment.

### *(i) The Scope of the Book and the Broader Debate*

The unjust enrichment explanation of resulting trusts was first proposed by Birks[27] and Chambers[28] and it has engendered considerable controversy ever

[25] See ch 1, s II.

[26] *Ryall v Ryall* (1739) 1 Atk 59, 26 ER 39.

[27] P Birks, 'Restitution and Resulting Trusts' in S Goldstein (ed) *Equity and Contemporary Legal Developments* (Jerusalem, Harry and Michael Sacher Institute for Legislative Research and Comparative Law, 1992) 335–73; P Birks, 'Trusts Raised to Reverse Unjust Enrichments: The *Westdeutsche* Case' [1996] *RLR* 3; Birks, *Unjust Enrichment* (2005) (n 18) 187–88.

[28] See Chambers, *Resulting Trusts* (1997) (n 17); R Chambers, 'Resulting Trusts in Canada' (2000) 38 *Alberta Law Review* 378; R Chambers, 'Resulting Trusts and Equitable Compensation' (2001) 15 *Trusts Law International* 2; Chambers, 'Resulting Trusts' (2006) (n 5).

since.[29] According to Birks and Chambers, resulting trusts are *always* an instance of 'proprietary restitution' for unjust enrichment where the claimant had 'no intention to benefit' the defendant.[30] They argue that, in the category of 'gratuitous transfer' resulting trusts, the presumption to be rebutted is that the transferor did not intend to benefit the transferee. In the category of 'failed trust' resulting trusts, the evidence positively establishes that the settlor did not intend to benefit the trustee as the settlor intended to create an equitable right in favour of someone else. Thus, in both categories of resulting trust the transferee is enriched by a right at the transferor's expense in circumstances where the transferor had 'no intention to benefit' the transferee.

The 'Birks–Chambers theory' has garnered judicial support from Lord Millett in *Air Jamaica v Charlton* and *Twinsectra v Yardley*,[31] and, in the past, implicit support from the High Court of Australia in *Nelson v Nelson*,[32] but it cannot be taken to state English law at present. In *Westdeutsche Landesbank Girozentrale v Islington LBC*, Lord Goff said:[33]

> Professor Birks has argued for a wider role for the resulting trust in the field of restitution .... [H]is thesis is avowedly experimental, written to test the temperature of the water. I feel bound to respond that the temperature of the water must be regarded as decidedly cold.

In the same case, Lord Browne-Wilkinson's leading speech favoured a presumed intention explanation, holding that all resulting trusts arise in response to 'the common intention of the parties'.[34] Furthermore, the Birks–Chambers theory is disputed in academic circles. Swadling is the theory's most trenchant critic, arguing that there is no reason for the law to respond to unjust enrichment with a resulting trust when a personal claim for the value of the enrichment will suffice.[35] Swadling prefers to explain the 'gratuitous transfer' cases by reference to a presumption of a declaration of trust by the transferor and dismisses any explicable basis for a resulting trust in the 'failed trust' cases.

### *(ii) Unjust Enrichment Resulting Trusts*

It is contended here that *some* resulting trusts cannot be explained by the prevailing 'presumed intention' explanation favoured by Lord Browne-Wilkinson in *Westdeutsche* and should instead be understood to arise in unjust enrichment. In

29 See Swadling, 'A New Role for Resulting Trusts' (1996) (n 22); Swadling, 'A Hard Look at *Hodgson v Marks*' (2000) (n 22); R Grantham and C Rickett, 'Resulting Trusts—A Rather Limited Doctrine' in P Birks and F Rose (eds), *Restitution and Equity, Volume 1: Resulting Trusts and Equitable Compensation* (London, Mansfield Press, 2000); Swadling, 'Explaining Resulting Trusts' (2008) (n 5); E O'Dell, 'The Resulting Trust' in R Grantham and C Rickett (eds), *Structure and Justification in Private Law* (Oxford, Hart, 2008).

30 Chambers, *Resulting Trusts* (1997) (n 17) 21; Chambers, 'Resulting Trusts' (2006) (n 5).

31 See above n 3.

32 *Nelson v Nelson* (1995) 184 CLR 538 (HCA) 549 (Deane & Gummow JJ) 586–87 (Toohey J).

33 *Westdeutsche Landesbank Girozentrale v Islington LBC* [1996] AC 669 (HL) 689 (Lord Goff).

34 Ibid 708 (Lord Browne-Wilkinson).

35 Swadling, 'A New Role for Resulting Trusts' (1996) (n 22); Swadling, 'A Hard Look at *Hodgson v Marks*' (2000) (n 22) 61; Swadling, 'Explaining Resulting Trusts' (2008) (n 5).

*Westdeutsche*, Lord Browne-Wilkinson held that all resulting trusts are a response to 'the common intention of the parties'.[36] Accordingly, it is presumed that the *transferee's* intention is to hold the right on resulting trust for the transferor. However, his Lordship's approach cannot withstand scrutiny. First, the *transferee's* intentions are properly irrelevant as it is the *transferor's* intent that is presumed or proved. Second, the House of Lords made it clear in *Vandervell* that 'failed trust' resulting trusts, unlike 'gratuitous transfer' resulting trusts, do not involve any presumption.[37] Rejecting Lord Browne-Wilkinson's approach, Swadling takes the view that the resulting trust is (or should be) a response to the presumed or proved intentions of the *transferor*.[38] While this may provide a reasonable explanation of the gratuitous transfer resulting trust, it leaves the failed trust resulting trust unexplained and, in Swadling's view, it is simply inexplicable: it 'defies legal analysis'.[39]

Swadling's conclusion regarding failed trust resulting trusts is unsatisfactory and must be rejected. Unlike the presumed intention explanation, the unjust enrichment explanation outlined above shows that failed trust resulting trusts are indeed susceptible of legal analysis. The Birks–Chambers thesis provides the outlines of a coherent and unified explanation of the failed trust resulting trust as a response to the unjust enrichment of the transferee in circumstances in which the transferor has 'no intention to benefit' the transferee. In cases such as *Re Gillingham Bus Disaster Fund*[40] and *Vandervell v IRC*,[41] the evidence establishes that the claimant had 'no intention to benefit' the transferee as the claimant instead intended to benefit the purported beneficiary or purpose of the failed trust. If the intended trustee acquired the rights free of the trust, he would be unjustly enriched at the expense of the claimant. The resulting trust reverses that enrichment.

However, as this book favours an unjust enrichment explanation of these resulting trusts, two of Swadling's arguments to the contrary merit detailed attention. First, Swadling argues that the 'no intention to benefit' theory cannot reach cases where the right is transferred by vitiated intention (eg by mistake), as the transferor *did intend* the transferee to take outright. This is a terminological point. Birks and Chambers argue that resulting trusts are a response to unjust enrichment, which means the resulting trust may respond to various unjust factors, including those involving vitiated, as opposed to absent, intent. The Birks–Chambers thesis is that a resulting trust arises where there is no *unvitiated* intention to benefit the

[36] *Westdeutsche Landesbank Girozentrale v Islington LBC* [1996] AC 669 (HL) 708 (Lord Browne-Wilkinson).

[37] See *Vandervell v IRC* [1967] 2 AC 291 (HL) 308–09 (Lord Reid) 315 (Lord Pearce) 321–23 (Lord Donovan) 329 (Lord Wilberforce); *Re Vandervell's Trust (No 2)* [1974] Ch 269 (CA) 294 (Megarry J).

[38] Swadling, 'Explaining Resulting Trusts' (2008) (n 5) 77–80. See also *Rathwell v Rathwell* (1978) 83 DLR (3d) 289 (SCC) 303 (Dickson J).

[39] Swadling, 'Explaining Resulting Trusts' (2008) (n 5) 102.

[40] *Re Gillingham Bus Disaster Fund* [1958] Ch 300 (Ch).

[41] *Vandervell v IRC* [1967] 2 AC 291 (HL).

transferee. But, taking account of Swadling's criticism, 'no intention to benefit' can be better expressed as 'absent or vitiated intention to benefit'.

Second, Swadling argues that, even if it is proved (by actual or presumed facts) that the transferor's intention to benefit was absent or vitiated, this is not enough to found a trust. Swadling here assumes his conclusion. By arguing that the long line of 'failed trust' resulting trust cases 'defy legal analysis', Swadling *assumes* that the transferor's having an absent or vitiated intention to benefit the transferee is not enough to create a trust. It may be readily conceded that proof that the transferor has an absent or vitiated intention is not enough to found an *express declaration of trust*, explicit or implied, but this does not mean it is incapable of providing the basis for a *non-express trust*. That the transferor has an absent or vitiated intention to benefit the transferee is precisely what seems to suffice in the 'failed trust' resulting trust cases, including *Vandervell*,[42] *Re Gillingham Bus Disaster Fund*[43] and *Re Vinogradoff*.[44] The resulting trust that arises is not express, thus it need not depend on proof of a declaration of trust. It should not simply be assumed that the automatic resulting trust cases are indefensible and cannot be generalised to explain other resulting trusts.

## C. Resulting Trusts as Specific Restitution of an Enrichment by Rights

Although this book takes the position that unjust enrichment provides the best explanation of the theoretical basis of failed trust resulting trusts, existing unjust enrichment accounts are unsatisfactory because they fail to capture an essential distinction between resulting trusts, which are an example of reversing a legal enrichment, and the factual enrichment cases that comprise much of the corpus of unjust enrichment. In particular, applying the orthodox generalisation of 'enrichment' as the receipt of value or an accretion to wealth misidentifies the defendant's enrichment in resulting trusts cases and potentially introduces irrelevant considerations that should be excluded. It is contended here that the legal enrichment model provides a more accurate account because it correctly identifies the enrichment as the right acquired by the defendant and not the receipt of value, which is irrelevant in resulting trusts cases.

The traditional approaches to the enrichment inquiry rejected in chapter three impose a uniform definition of enrichment in all cases of unjust enrichment, such as the receipt of 'value' or an 'accretion to wealth'. These undifferentiated definitions of enrichment have persisted in unjust enrichment explanations of resulting trusts, eliding the defendant's enrichment in resulting trusts cases and the defendant's enrichment in value cases. However, unlike the factual enrichment

[42] Ibid.

[43] *Re Gillingham Bus Disaster Fund* [1958] Ch 300 (Ch).

[44] *Re Vinogradoff* [1935] WN 68 (Ch). See also *Goodfellow v Robertson* (1871) 18 Gr 572 (Ont Ch); *Brown v Brown* (1993) 31 NSWLR 582 (NSWCA).

cases examined in chapter four, the value received at the moment of the defective transaction is *not* the relevant enrichment in resulting trusts cases. Value is not a thing, but a characteristic of things, and it cannot be held on trust. In resulting trust cases, it is the right acquired, not its value at the moment of receipt, that constitutes the defendant's enrichment.

This can be illustrated by the resulting trust that arose in *Vandervell v IRC*.[45] As part of an arrangement to minimise his tax exposure, Tony Vandervell funded a chair at the Royal College of Surgeons (RCS) through dividends declared on shares transferred to RCS. The Vandervell Trustee Company (VTC) was granted an option to repurchase the shares for £5,000, which option was to be held on undeclared trusts. The express trust of the option to repurchase the shares failed for want of a beneficiary and a resulting trust arose immediately in favour of Tony Vandervell. Crucially, it was the option-right, not its value, that was held on resulting trust in *Vandervell*. As Lord Upjohn said, 'We are, of course, only concerned with the option, and not with its ultimate exercise'.[46] While the value of the option-right fluctuated according to the value of the shares, the value is simply irrelevant to the conclusion that VTC is enriched. For instance, there can be no doubt a resulting trust of the option would have arisen even if the shares were worth less than the £5,000 option price.

Although the option in *Vandervell* was undoubtedly valuable and there was consequently also a transfer of value to VTC, this was of no importance to the creation of a resulting trust. Instead, what is *essential* for a resulting trust to arise is that the transferee acquired a right. Where the defendant has received value, but the claimant is unable to point to a specific right acquired by the defendant that is capable of being the subject matter of a trust, there can be no resulting trust. For example, a resulting trust cannot arise where the enrichment is the improvement of an existing right rather than the acquisition of a right.[47] Thus, it is important that the generalisation 'enrichment' identifies the enrichment in resulting trusts cases as the right acquired, rather than its value.

Moreover, this is a difference of substance, not simply a question of theoretical elegance and taxonomy. In addition to identifying the subject matter of the resulting trust correctly, there are at least three other substantive implications that follow from the legal enrichment approach. First, as highlighted by *Vandervell*, there is no valuation exercise in resulting trusts cases. It is not relevant that the acquisition of the right increases the net wealth of the defendant or makes the defendant factually better off. A resulting trust will arise *irrespective* of the value of the right. Thus, defining enrichment as value or wealth erroneously incorporates questions of valuation into a determination of whether the defendant is enriched when it is simply not relevant.

45 *Vandervell v IRC* [1967] 2 AC 291 (HL).
46 Ibid 314 (Lord Upjohn).
47 Chambers, 'Resulting Trusts' (2006) (n 5) 258.

Second, as will be examined in chapter six, the fact that the right itself is held on trust, not its value, means that freedom of choice concerns do not pertain to resulting trusts as they do in factual enrichment claims. It does not matter for the imposition of a resulting trust whether the defendant chose to acquire the right or was even aware of the transfer of the right at the claimant's expense. For instance, in *Re Vinogradoff*,[48] a grandmother transferred £800 of war loan stock into the joint names of her and her granddaughter, who was four years old. The stock was held on resulting trust, despite the fact that the granddaughter did not know of the transfer and could not be an express trustee of the stock under the Law of Property Act 1925.

Third, as explained in chapter three, a different restitutionary response follows from the identification of the enrichment as a right, rather than value. The imposition of a resulting trust does not reverse the defendant's enrichment as the defendant still holds the right acquired at the claimant's expense. The resulting trust does not revest the right held by the defendant, nor does the defendant come under a duty to make restitution of that right; rather, the claimant obtains a *power* in relation to the right held by the defendant and the defendant comes under a corresponding *liability* to the claimant. The resulting trust is thus a quite distinct remedy from the restitutionary response in factual enrichment cases, although it is one of the kinds of remedy described as 'restitution' in chapter one.

The resulting trust is better understood within the wider framework of restitution of a legal enrichment. On the model defended here, the existing approach asks the wrong question: it is not a question of proving unjust enrichment and then asking whether personal or proprietary restitution is available; rather, the claim for specific restitution differs in substance. To obtain specific restitution of a right, the claimant must prove a legal enrichment by rights and the question is whether specific restitution of that right is available or not. Like all other cases of specific restitution of rights, the remedy is a power to obtain a specific right. This approach highlights certain differences between factual and legal enrichment cases, while also drawing attention to similarities between resulting trusts and other legal enrichment cases. Moreover, this provides the framework for the future development of the law of resulting trusts. As Lord Millett has argued extra-judicially,[49] the expansion of resulting trusts should depend on whether a novel claim is sufficiently analogous to a recognised claim that specific restitution should be available as a matter of principle. Although the precise ambit of the resulting trust is not yet fixed in English law, the model presented here provides the principles within which future cases should be decided.

[48] *Re Vinogradoff* [1935] WN 68 (Ch).

[49] Millett, 'Restitution and Constructive Trusts' (1998) (n 3) 410.

## II. Rescission

In *Whittaker v Campbell*, Robert Goff LJ said 'The remedy of rescission, by which the unjust enrichment of the [defendant] is prevented … is a straightforward remedy in restitution'.[50] A party to a contract may be enriched by both: (i) the contractual rights obtained; and (ii) benefits received through performance of the contract. It is contended here that the power of rescission is a power to reverse the enrichments received by the counterparty, subject to counter-restitution of enrichments received by the rescinding party. Where the contract is purely executory, the defendant is legally enriched by the contractual rights created and the power to rescind is a power to obtain specific restitution of those contractual rights by reversing the creation of rights in a defective contract. However, where the contract has been executed, performance under the contract may confer additional benefits that may be characterised either factually or legally. Thus, the power to rescind an executed contract is a power to obtain specific restitution of the contractual rights *as well as* restitution of value or specific restitution of rights conferred and obligations released by performance.

Rescission has traditionally been understood as being an aspect of the law of contract (or gifts or trusts), with the effect that the theoretical basis of the power was not rigorously explored until relatively recently. Commentators and judges were content to describe rescission as incidental to the requirements for formation of contracts. This view has been defended by Lionel Smith and is explored in detail below.[51] However, a body of scholarship has suggested that the power to rescind is restitutionary in nature. For instance, Birks and Nahan influentially argued that rescission of contracts is always restitutionary because rescission revests the contractual rights conferred.[52] Virgo[53] and Janet O'Sullivan[54] agree that rescission is restitutionary, although only where a tangible benefit has been conferred under the contract that can be returned. Burrows formerly took the narrower view preferred by Virgo and Janet O'Sullivan,[55] but treats both views as defensible in the most recent edition of *The Law of Restitution*.[56] Although these academics have rightly recognised the restitutionary purpose and effect of rescission, their analyses are unsatisfactory insofar as they fail to distinguish

[50] *Whittaker v Campbell* [1984] QB 318 (DC) 327 (Robert Goff LJ).

[51] See below nn 75–82 and accompanying text.

[52] P Birks, *An Introduction to the Law of Restitution*, revised edn (Oxford, Clarendon Press, 1989) 163; N Nahan, 'Rescission: A Case for Rejecting the Classical Model?' (1997) 27 *University of Western Australia Law Review* 66, 72–73. See also J Edelman and E Bant, *Unjust Enrichment in Australia* (Oxford, Oxford University Press, 2006) 102.

[53] G Virgo, *The Principles of the Law of Restitution*, 2nd edn (Oxford, Oxford University Press, 2006) 29.

[54] J O'Sullivan, 'Rescission as a Self-help Remedy: A Critical Analysis' (2000) 59 *CLJ* 509, 525–28. Janet O'Sullivan is not to be confused with Dominic O'Sullivan, who is the O'Sullivan in D O'Sullivan, S Elliott and R Zakrzewski, *The Law of Rescission* (Oxford, Oxford University Press, 2008).

[55] A Burrows, *The Law of Restitution*, 2nd edn (London, Butterworths, 2002) 57–58.

[56] A Burrows, *The Law of Restitution*, 3rd edn (Oxford, Oxford University Press, 2010) 17–20.

between factual and legal enrichment, which is critical to a fuller understanding of rescission.

This book suggests a fundamentally different approach: a model of rescission that separately considers the factual and legal characterisation of enrichments conferred by the act of contracting and the performance of the contract. It is argued that contractual rights are an enrichment within the definition in chapter three of 'rights which by their nature are capable of assignment' and that rescission of contractual rights is a form of specific restitution. In addition, this model unpacks '*restitutio in integrum*' as a process of restitution and counter-restitution between the parties to reverse enrichments received by both parties to the contract. In sub-section A, the operation of the power of rescission is briefly explained. Sub-section B then argues that rescission is restitutionary in purpose and effect. Finally, sub-section C applies the legal enrichment model to rescission of: (i) purely executory contracts; (ii) partly and fully-executed contracts; and (iii) contracts that confer property rights (ie 'proprietary rescission').

## A. The Power of Rescission

Rescission is a power—in the Hohfeldian sense identified in chapter two—to set aside the rights and obligations created by a transaction, including a contract, conveyance, gift or declaration of trust. Although the discussion in this book will centre on rescission of contracts, the model developed below is generally applicable to other voidable transactions, including gifts, deeds or trust instruments.[57] The critical difference is that the donee need not know of the ground for rescission in order for a gift or trust to be rescinded.[58] It is clear that a claimant can rescind a transaction at common law by reason of fraudulent misrepresentation,[59] duress,[60] and non-disclosure in particular contexts.[61] In equity, in addition to these grounds, the claimant may rescind by reason of innocent misrepresentation,[62] undue influence,[63] breach of fiduciary fair-dealing rules, certain unilateral mistakes and unconscionable bargain.[64] Depending on the ground for rescission,

57 O'Sullivan, Elliott and Zakrzewski, *The Law of Rescission* (2008) (n 54) Ch 29.

58 Ibid §§29.17–29.23.

59 See, eg *Load v Green* (1846) 15 M&W 216, 153 ER 828; *Clough v London and North Western Railway Co* (1871) 7 Ex 26 (Ex); *Newbigging v Adam* (1886) 34 ChD 582 (CA); *Mahesan S/O Thambiah v Malaysian Government Officers Co-Operative Housing Society* [1979] AC 374 (PC) 383; *Hunter BNZ Finance Ltd v CG Maloney Pty Ltd* (1988) 18 NSWLR 420 (NSWSC).

60 See, eg *Whelpdale's Case* (1605) 5 Co Rep 119a, 77 ER 239; *Enimont Overseas AG v RO Jugotanker Zadar (The Olib)* [1991] 2 Lloyd's Rep 108 (QB) 118; *Dimskal Shipping Co SA v International Transport Workers Federation (The Evia Luck)* [1992] 2 AC 152 (HL) 165; *Halpern v Halpern (No 2)* [2007] EWCA Civ 291, [2008] QB 195.

61 See, eg *Brotherton v Aseguradora Cobeguros (No 2)* [2003] EWCA Civ 705, [2003] 2 All ER (Comm) 298; *Drake Insurance plc v Provident Insurance plc* [2003] EWCA Civ 1834, [2004] QB 601; *Ionides v Pender* (1874) 9 QB 531 (QB).

62 *Lamare v Dixon* (1873) 6 HL 414 (HL).

63 *Dunbar Bank plc v Nadeem* [1998] 3 All ER 876 (CA).

64 See O'Sullivan, Elliott and Zakrzewski, *The Law of Rescission* (2008) (n 54) §10.25.

rescission may be a response to a wrong (eg fraud or breach of fiduciary duty) or unjust enrichment (eg undue influence or duress).

It should be noted that 'rescission' may have two relevant 'aspects' in this context.[65] First, it refers to the *power* to set aside (ie cancel with retrospective effect)[66] obligations under a contract, gift or trust by reason of mistake, misrepresentation, duress or undue influence.[67] Second, 'rescission' refers to the *effect* of exercising this power, that is the setting aside of the obligation itself. While the term is often used in both senses, it should be understood as having only one meaning. Where a transaction is entered into in circumstances that generate a power of rescission, the claimant obtains a 'power to rescind' and the exercise of that power effects 'rescission'. However, this singular meaning should be differentiated from the use of 'rescission' in circumstances of termination where a contract is 'rescinded' *de futuro*, that is to the extent that it remains executory.[68] This book is not concerned with rescission *de futuro* upon termination for breach.

### *Self-help or Judicial Remedy?*

There is considerable dispute as to whether rescission is a self-help remedy or a judicial order.[69] This debate is not central to the conclusions reached in this book as the theory of enrichment defended here is capable of explaining both self-help and judicial order theories of rescission. However, one powerful view[70] is that common law rescission is a self-help remedy,[71] whereas equitable rescission requires a court order.[72] This is consistent with the leading speech of Lord

[65] Ibid §1.28; E Bant, *The Change of Position Defence* (Oxford, Hart, 2009) 89–90.

[66] *Mackender v Feldia AG* [1967] 2 QB 590 (CA) 603 (Diplock LJ); *Johnson v Agnew* [1980] AC 367 (HL) 393; *FAI General Insurance Co Ltd v Ocean Marine Mutual Protection and Indemnity Association Ltd* (1997) 41 NSWLR 559 (NSWSC) 563; O'Sullivan, Elliott and Zakrzewski, *The Law of Rescission* (2008) (n 54) §1.10.

[67] *Dunbar Bank plc v Nadeem* [1998] 3 All ER 876 (CA).

[68] *McDonald v Dennys Lascelles Ltd* (1933) 48 CLR 457 (HCA) 476–77 (Sir Owen Dixon); *Johnson v Agnew* [1980] AC 367 (HL) 397; *Hurst v Bryk* [2002] 1 AC 185 (HL) 194 (Lord Millett); O'Sullivan, 'Rescission as a Self-help Remedy: A Critical Analysis' (2000) (n 54) 509–10; O'Sullivan, Elliott and Zakrzewski, *The Law of Rescission* (2008) (n 54) §§1.02–1.03, 1.06–1.09, 1.26–1.29; Burrows, *The Law of Restitution* (2010) (n 56) 16.

[69] See O'Sullivan, 'Rescission as a Self-help Remedy: A Critical Analysis' (2000) (n 54); O'Sullivan, Elliott and Zakrzewski, *The Law of Rescission* (2008) (n 54) Ch 3, §§10.03–10.14, 10.34–10.38.

[70] O'Sullivan, Elliott and Zakrzewski, *The Law of Rescission* (2008) (n 54) §§3.01–3.15, 3.34–3.54, 10.03–10.14. See also Virgo, *The Principles of the Law of Restitution* (2006) (n 53) 29–30.

[71] *Car & Universal Finance Co Ltd v Caldwell* [1963] 1 QB 525 (CA). See also *Reese River Silver Mining Co v Smith* (1869) 4 HL 64 (HL) 74 (Lord Hatherley); *Abram Steamship Co Ltd Westville Shipping Co Ltd* [1923] AC 773 (HL) 781 (Lord Atkinson); *Brotherton v Aseguradora Cobeguros (No 2)* [2003] EWCA Civ 705, [2003] 2 All ER (Comm) 298 [27] (Mance LJ) [44]–[48] (Buxton LJ).

[72] *Cooper v Phibbs* (1867) 2 HL 149 (HL); *Allcard v Skinner* (1887) 36 ChD 145 (CA) 186–87; *Spence v Crawford* [1939] 3 All ER 271 (HL) 288 (Lord Wright); *O'Sullivan v Management Agency and Music Ltd* [1985] QB 428 (CA); *Cheese v Thomas* [1994] 1 WLR 129 (CA); *Maguire v Makaronis* (1998) 188 CLR 449 (HCA); *Johnson v EBS Pensioner Trustees Ltd* [2002] EWCA Civ 164, [2002] Lloyd's Rep PN 309 *cf Reese River Silver Mining Co v Smith* (1869) 4 HL 64 (HL) 73; *Abram Steamship Co Ltd Westville Shipping Co Ltd* [1923] AC 773 (HL) 781, 785; *Horsler v Zorro* [1975] Ch 302 (Ch) 310; *Brotherton v Aseguradora Cobeguros (No 2)* [2003] EWCA Civ 705, [2003] 2 All ER (Comm) 298 [27], [44]–[48]; *Drake Insurance plc v Provident Insurance plc* [2003] EWCA Civ 1834, [2004] QB 601

Blackburn in *Erlanger v The New Sombrero Phosphate Co*,[73] which recognised the different approaches to rescission at law and in equity, although the distinction is not clear-cut. In this book, the differences between the jurisdictional approaches will only be examined to the extent necessary to show that rescission is restitutionary both at law and in equity.

## B. Rescission and Restitution

Traditionally, rescission has not always been understood as a restitutionary response, even though the grounds for rescission are recognised unjust factors and wrongs and the effect of rescission is to reverse benefits conferred on the defendant at the claimant's expense. This book suggests that, as recognised in *Whittaker v Campbell*,[74] rescission is restitutionary. However, this argument must overcome three entrenched views of the power of rescission: first, the view, defended by Lionel Smith, that rescission is simply an inherent aspect of the creation of the contractual right; second, the view adopted by Burrows, Virgo and Janet O'Sullivan, that cancellation of contractual rights is not restitutionary; and third, the idea that *restitutio in integrum* is a different process from restitution and counter-restitution.

### *(i) Rescission as an Inherent Aspect of the Right*

That rescission is simply an inherent aspect of the contractual right is usually assumed rather than defended. However, Lionel Smith has made a case for this view of rescission:[75]

> [A]n analysis in unjust enrichment is not needed to explain why a consensually created obligation may be voidable at the instance of the obliged person. That person's obligation was, from the moment of its formation, voidable, and it was voidable because the conditions of its formation did not fully satisfy the requirements for [its] creation

Further, Smith takes the view that property rights transferred pursuant to a voidable obligation are also recoverable as an aspect of the law of contract: the power to 'avoid that contract is also a power to revest that legal title in the claimant'.[76] Thus, for Smith, the power to obtain specific restitution of property transferred pursuant to a voidable obligation is an inherent qualification of the underlying obligation.

[31]–[32]. See O'Sullivan, Elliott and Zakrzewski, *The Law of Rescission* (2008) (n 54) §§11.55–11.91, 11.100–11.105.

[73] *Erlanger v The New Sombrero Phosphate Co* (1878) 3 App Cas 1218 (HL) 1278 (Lord Blackburn). See also *Spence v Crawford* [1939] 3 All ER 271 (HL) 290 (Lord Wright); *O'Sullivan v Management Agency and Music Ltd* [1985] QB 428 (CA) 457.

[74] *Whittaker v Campbell* [1984] QB 318 (DC) 327 (Robert Goff LJ).

[75] L Smith, 'Unjust Enrichment: Big or Small?' in S Degeling and J Edelman (eds), *Unjust Enrichment in Commercial Law* (Sydney, Lawbook Co, 2008) 43.

[76] Ibid 44.

The first reason Smith's view is rejected in this book is that it is flatly inconsistent with the existence of specific restitution for unjust enrichment. Smith's approach explicitly limits the scope of unjust enrichment to cases where a *duty* to make restitution arises. It therefore excludes all cases of specific restitution because, as articulated in chapter three, specific restitution is always a power to obtain restitution, not an immediate right to it. As we saw in section I, in resulting trusts cases, the claimant obtains a power to obtain restitution of the rights held on trust; the defendant does not come under a duty to transfer those rights to the claimant unless the power is exercised. The same structure holds in rescission, rectification and subrogation cases, where the defendant likewise comes under a liability to make restitution of a right still held when the power is exercised.

The second reason for rejecting Smith's approach is that it is fictional to transpose an inherent qualification of the contractual right into an inherent qualification of a property right acquired under the contract. Where C is fraudulently induced to sell a car to D, D has both a *contractual* right to obtain the car from C and, when title passes, a *property* right to the car enforceable against the world. Smith's view is that because 'the original transfer of the title took place through, and by virtue of, the contract', D's property right to the car should be viewed, like the contractual right to the car, as a 'kind of flawed asset'.[77] However, in the common law, the property right is not always transferred by the contract, but may be transferred by delivery, registration or some other act independent of the contract. Although the contract is the reason why delivery, registration or other acts transferring title are taken, those acts create a property right that is distinct from the contractual right and does not share its inherent qualifications. It is difficult to see why a qualification 'inherent' in D's *contractual* rights also qualifies D's *property* right to the car, which is not part of the contract and is exigible against the world, not just C.

The better view is that, as rescission of a contract refers to setting aside contractual rights and obligations *inter se*, rescission is not what restores title to property rights transferred under the contract. Rescission merely sets aside the personal rights and obligations between the parties. In the above example of the fraudulently induced sale of a car: the contract comprises a series of personal rights and obligations between the parties *inter se*, but this does not include the property right to the car. Setting aside the personal rights under the contract partly reverses D's enrichment by cancelling contractual rights unjustly obtained, but something beyond setting aside the contract is required to revest the property right to the car in C. This is clear in equity, where a long line of cases have held that rescission of a contract under which property rights are transferred does not, of itself, effect restitution of the property rights obtained under the contract.[78] At least since

[77] Ibid.

[78] *Leech v Leech* (1674) 2 Ch Rep 100, 21 ER 623; *Lady Hudson's Case* (1704) 2 Eq Cas Abr 52, 22 ER 45; *Clavering v Clavering* (1704) Prec Chan 235, 24 ER 114; *Harrison v Owen* (1738) 1 Atk 520, 26 ER 328; *Bolton v Bishop of Carlisle* (1793) 2 H Bl 259, 263; 126 ER 540, 542; *Perrott v Perrott* (1811) 14 East 423, 431; 104 ER 665, 668; *Re Way's Trust* (1864) 2 De GJ&S 365, 46 ER 416. See O'Sullivan, Elliott and Zakrzewski, *The Law of Rescission* (2008) (n 54) §§1.21–1.23, 3.52 *cf* W Swadling, 'Rescission, Property and the Common Law' (2005) 121 *LQR* 123.

1862 it has been recognised that an order for reconveyance of the property right is necessary *in addition to* an order that the contract be rescinded.[79] Although common law rescission takes place by election, it is likewise not the cancellation of the contract that effects restitution of rights conferred by performance. Rescission of the contract, as outlined in detail below, is only one part of a *power to obtain restitution*. Specific restitution of contractual rights is but one aspect of the claimant's entitlement to restitution because the contractual rights are only one aspect of the defendant's enrichment.

Third, Smith's approach insufficiently appreciates the similarity between rescission and restitution. In *Shogun Finance Ltd v Hudson*,[80] a fraudster procured finance from Shogun Finance for the purchase of a car by deceiving Shogun as to his identity, and then sold the car to Hudson. As the House of Lords elaborated, fraud can make a contractual obligation void or voidable.[81] A contract that is 'valid until rescinded is called a voidable contract, and is to be distinguished from a void contract, which is an apparent contract that never comes into being'.[82] Where the obligation is void—on the majority approach, no contract was formed due to Shogun's intention to contract with someone else—there is no legal enrichment because no right is ever created. There is therefore no acquisition of a legal right to be reversed. However, where a vitiation of consent renders an obligation merely voidable—as it was on the approach of Lord Nicholls and Lord Millett—the right to the car is valid unless and until the power to rescind is exercised. In this case, there is an enrichment to be reversed, there is a need to justify reversing that enrichment and there is the possibility of changes in position or third-party intervention that may prevent restitution. This is the logic and structure of a claim for restitution in unjust enrichment or wrongs. Thus, while Smith is quite right to say that the 'vitiation of consent' qualifies the right and explains its voidability, this is precisely the reason for regarding rescission as a response to the unjust factor or wrong rendering the contract voidable.

Finally, the approach adopted in this book is preferable because it identifies the same basis for the power to rescind in every case, rather than segregating rescission of purely executory contracts from rescission generally. As argued above, Smith's explanation cannot adequately account for restitution of property rights and value transferred under the contract, so it can only effectively explain rescission of purely executory contracts. However, the power to rescind a contract on identical grounds—mistake, undue influence, duress and so on—must have the same theoretical basis, regardless of when that power is exercised. The fact that a power is exercised before or after performance of the contract cannot determine its theoretical basis.

[79] *Clark v Malpas* (1862) 4 De GF&J 401, 405; 45 ER 1238, 1240. See O'Sullivan, Elliott and Zakrzewski, *The Law of Rescission* (2008) (n 54) §3.52.

[80] *Shogun Finance Ltd v Hudson* [2003] UKHL 62, [2004] 1 AC 919.

[81] Ibid 932–33 (Lord Nicholls) 947–48 (Lord Millett).

[82] O'Sullivan, Elliott and Zakrzewski, *The Law of Rescission* (2008) (n 54) §1.04. See also §§1.31–1.32.

### *(ii) Cancellation of Rights is Restitutionary*

This book has shown that existing definitions of 'restitution' inadequately account for the varieties of specific restitution. Once factual and legal enrichment are distinguished, it is easier to see that specific restitution takes different forms. In the case of legal enrichment by the creation of a right, specific restitution may take the form of the cancellation of rights. Rescission, whether at law or in equity, will cancel all obligations, including those intended to survive the termination of the contract, such as liquidated damages clauses (unless they are both severable and untainted by the unjust factor generating the power to rescind).[83] Accordingly, only certain severable clauses, most commonly arbitration clauses, may survive rescission.[84] As Lord Wilberforce said in *Johnson v Agnew*, 'the contract is treated in law as never having come into existence'.[85]

Although the contract is avoided *ab initio*, the law recognises that there was formerly a contract in existence that conferred valid contractual rights and imposed valid contractual obligations.[86] So, if the power of rescission is not exercised, the contract remains on foot and the rights remain valid and the obligations binding. The power of rescission is a power to cancel a *valid* contract with retrospective effect. As established in chapter three,[87] contractual rights are within the category of rights which by their nature are assignable and are undoubtedly capable of constituting a legal enrichment. Since the parties obtained rights against each other prior to rescission, the exercise of the power of rescission *reverses the creation* of contractual rights. In this way, rescission reverses the rights arising from the transaction and is restitutionary in purpose and effect.

### *(iii)* Restitutio in Integrum *as Restitution and Counter-restitution*

The classification of rescission as a restitutionary remedy is complicated by the idea that rescission involves *restitutio in integrum*,[88] that is rescission both cancels the rights and obligations under the contract *and* returns the parties to their original positions as regards value transferred and rights acquired under the

[83] Ibid §1.12.

[84] See, eg *Harbour Assurance Co (UK) v Kansa Ltd* [1993] QB 701 (CA) *cf Heyman v Darwins Ltd* [1942] AC 356 (HL). The survival of these clauses is explicable on the grounds that, while the defendant is enriched by the rights acquired, that enrichment is not unjust because these clauses are not affected by the unjust factor, see, eg *Vee Networks v Econet Wireless International Ltd* [2004] EWHC 2909 (Comm), [2005] 1 Lloyd's Rep 192 [19]–[22]; *Fiona Trust & Holding Corp v Privalov* [2007] EWCA Civ 20, [2007] 2 Lloyd's Rep 267 [23]–[29]; *Premium Nafta Product Ltd v Fili Shipping Co Ltd* [2007] UKHL 40, [2007] 4 All ER 951 [35].

[85] *Johnson v Agnew* [1980] AC 367 (HL) 393 (Lord Wilberforce).

[86] *Mackender v Feldia AG* [1967] 2 QB 590 (CA) 603 (Diplock LJ); *FAI General Insurance Co Ltd v Ocean Marine Mutual Protection and Indemnity Association Ltd* (1997) 41 NSWLR 559 (NSWSC) 563.

[87] See ch 3, fns 118–20 and accompanying text.

[88] *Erlanger v The New Sombrero Phosphate Co* (1878) 3 App Cas 1218 (HL) 1278; *Newbigging v Adam* (1886) 34 ChD 582 (CA) 588, 592–94; *Brown v Smitt* (1924) 34 CLR 160 (HCA) 166; *Johnson v Agnew* [1980] AC 367 (HL) 392–93 (Lord Wilberforce); *Cheese v Thomas* [1994] 1 WLR 129 (CA) 135 (Sir Donald Nicholls VC).

contract. There are two competing views of '*restitutio in integrum*'. The first view is that the contract cannot be rescinded unless the *status quo ante* can be restored and the court's objective is to put the parties in the position they occupied prior to the contract. The second view, and that favoured here, is that rescission of the contract (ie cancelling the contractual rights) is simply part of achieving restitution and counter-restitution, subject to defences including change of position. On this view, the wrong or unjust factor that justifies rescinding the contract entitles the claimant to restitution of other enrichments conferred by performance of the contract.[89] Restitution by the defendant begets counter-restitution of enrichments received by the claimant, with each claim potentially subject to the defence of change of position. It is contended here that *restitutio in integrum* is best understood under the second model.

The difficulty with the first view, that *restitutio in integrum* means to 'restore the *status quo ante*',[90] is that it wrongly confuses *restitutio in integrum* with damages in contract and tort.[91] In contract and tort, the aim of damages is to restore the claimant to a position equivalent to the financial position she would have occupied had the contract been performed or the tort not been committed. The approach is counter-factual, aiming not to reverse a defective transaction, but to achieve a particular financial outcome. For this reason, consequential losses are compensated. However, rescission is different, as illustrated by *Redgrave v Hurd*.[92] The purchaser of a solicitor's practice, labouring under an innocent misrepresentation from the defendant, incurred various expenses in preparing to take over the practice, including relocating to Birmingham. When the purchaser discovered the misrepresentation and rescinded, these expenses were not reimbursed as part of *restitutio in integrum*. The court does not attempt to put the claimant and defendant in the position as if the transaction had not been made; instead, the court is attempting *to reverse the transfer of benefits in a defective transaction*. For this reason, transaction costs and expenses not required by the contract are not incorporated in *restitutio in integrum*.[93] Consequently, rescission may leave a party better or worse off than if the contract had never been entered into: it is a process of reversing enrichments conferred and received in the defective transaction, not achieving a financial adjustment as if the transaction had never existed.

The better view is that *restitutio in integrum* simply refers to the process of restitution and counter-restitution,[94] subject to change of position.[95] In unjust

[89] See *Spence v Crawford* [1939] 3 All ER 271 (HL) 288–89 (Lord Wright).

[90] *Johnson v Agnew* [1980] AC 367 (HL) 392–93 (Lord Wilberforce).

[91] *Cheese v Thomas* [1994] 1 WLR 129 (CA) 135 (Sir Donald Nicholls VC); Nahan, 'Rescission: A Case for Rejecting the Classical Model?' (1997) (n 52) 68.

[92] *Redgrave v Hurd* (1881) 20 ChD 1 (CA).

[93] Eg *Newbigging v Adam* (1886) 34 ChD 582 (CA); *Sibley v Grosvenor* (1916) 21 CLR 469 (HCA); *Hayes v Ross (No 3)* [1919] NZLR 786 (NZHC); *McAllister v Richmond Brewing Co (NSW) Pty Ltd* (1942) 42 SR(NSW) 187 (NSWSC).

[94] *Dunbar Bank plc v Nadeem* [1998] 3 All ER 876 (CA) 884–85 (Millett LJ).

[95] Regarding the application of change of position to the two opposing claims, see Bant, *The Change of Position Defence* (2009) (n 65) Ch 4.

enrichment, both at law[96] and in equity,[97] the claimant's power to obtain restitution is subject to counter-restitution of enrichments received from the defendant. As Lord Wright made clear in *Spence v Crawford*, the claimant must not 'be unjustly enriched, as he would be if he both got back what he had parted with and kept what he had received in return'.[98] If the claimant obtains restitution of the *defendant's* enrichment, this gives rise to a failure of consideration for the *claimant's* enrichment.[99] Once the claimant elects to exercise the power, therefore, each party has the right to restitution against the other.[100] If this analysis is correct, Robert Goff LJ is right in *Whittaker*[101] to regard rescission as restitutionary in purpose and effect.

However, due to the historical development of rescission at law and in equity, the requirement to make counter-restitution may differ between the jurisdictions.[102] At law, the claimant has an independent obligation to make counter-restitution upon electing to rescind; the defendant thus has an independent claim to restitution against the claimant.[103] By contrast, it is arguable that, in equity, rescission is either conditional upon counter-restitution or counter-restitution is achieved through the process of equitable accounting.[104] If counter-restitution in equity is achieved pursuant to the judicial order, the defendant does not have an independent claim to restitution against the claimant. Nonetheless, regardless of the jurisdictional differences as to process, the same principle is common to law and equity: to obtain restitution, the claimant is required to give up the contractual rights received, as well as the value of part-performance by the defendant and any rights acquired pursuant to the contract. Thus, *restitutio in integrum* should be understood as the reversal of the transaction by restitution and counter-restitution of enrichments conferred by each party.

In addition, the requirement of '*restitutio in integrum*' is relevant at the defences stage. It remains the case that, where counter-restitution is impossible, rescission will be refused.[105] Although there is considerable overlap with change of position,

[96] *Clough v London and North Western Railway Co* (1871) 7 Ex 26 (Ex) 37; *Halpern v Halpern (No 2)* [2007] EWCA Civ 291, [2008] QB 195, 218 (Carnwath LJ).

[97] *Lindsay Petroleum v Hurd* (1874) 5 PC 221 (PC) 245–46; *Brown v Smitt* (1924) 34 CLR 160 (HCA) 172 (Isaacs and Rich JJ); *Cheese v Thomas* [1994] 1 WLR 129 (CA) 136 (Sir Donald Nicholls VC); *Greater Pacific Investments Pty Ltd v Australian National Industries Ltd* (1996) 39 NSWLR 143 (NSWCA) 151; *Maguire v Makaronis* (1998) 188 CLR 449 (HCA) 477–78.

[98] *Spence v Crawford* [1939] 3 All ER 271 (HL) 288–89 (Lord Wright).

[99] Burrows, *The Law of Restitution* (2010) (n 56) 569–71.

[100] *David Securities Pty Ltd v Commonwealth Bank of Australia* (1992) 127 CLR 353 (HCA).

[101] *Whittaker v Campbell* [1984] QB 318 (DC) 327 (Robert Goff LJ).

[102] O'Sullivan, Elliott and Zakrzewski, *The Law of Rescission* (2008) (n 54) §15.60.

[103] Ibid §§14.45, 15.60.

[104] Ibid §§15.57–15.60.

[105] *Clarke v Dickson* (1858) El B&E 148, 120 ER 463; *Western Bank of Scotland v Addie* (1866–69) 1 Sc 145 (HL Sc); *Halpern v Halpern (No 2)* [2007] EWCA Civ 291, [2008] QB 195, 217–222 (Carnwath LJ). The position at common law is more strict than equity, see *Erlanger v The New Sombrero Phosphate Co* (1878) 3 App Cas 1218 (HL) 1278 (Lord Blackburn); *Spence v Crawford* [1939] 3 All ER 271 (HL) 279 (Lord Thankerton); *Alati v Kruger* (1955) 94 CLR 216 (HCA) 224 (Dixon CJ, Webb, Kitto and Taylor JJ); Nahan, 'Rescission: A Case for Rejecting the Classical Model?' (1997) (n 52) 68–69.

the defence that counter-restitution is impossible differs in certain respects from a *pro tanto* change of position defence.[106] Although the defence that counter-restitution is impossible is beyond the scope of this book, it is important to note that it may prevent restitution of value or specific restitution even though the defendant is enriched.[107] Moreover, although the value of the right is not relevant to establishing a legal enrichment, a change in the value of the right may render counter-restitution impossible. Consequently, that the defendant is legally enriched does not entail that specific restitution is available: where counter-restitution is impossible, for example because the subject matter of the right has changed irrevocably,[108] specific restitution may be denied.

## C. Rescission as Specific Restitution of an Enrichment by Rights

There are two competing views of the way the power of rescission effects restitution. The first view is that, if the power to rescind is exercised, the 'contract is treated in law as never having come into existence'[109] and any performance by either party is performance on a basis that has failed and a right to restitution of the value transferred follows. As Millett LJ put it in *Portman Building Society v Hamlyn Taylor Neck*:[110]

> The obligation to make restitution must flow from the ineffectiveness of the transaction under which the money was paid and not from a mistake or misrepresentation which induced it.

On this understanding, the right to restitution arises from the failure of basis occasioned by rescission of the contract. There are thus two separate events: first, the power to rescind is a response to either unjust enrichment or a wrong, that is the misrepresentation, duress, undue influence or other ground rendering the contract voidable; and, second, once the contract is rescinded, there is a failure of basis and restitution of the value of performance or property rights obtained by performance is thus always a response to unjust enrichment.

The difficulty with Lord Millett's view is revealed by conceptualising contractual rights as a legal enrichment. Lord Millett artificially segregates the defendant's contractual rights from other enrichments received. The benefits conferred under the contract are not the sum total of the enrichment: the defendant is enriched by the contractual rights *and* benefits conferred by performance of it. The claimant is entitled to reverse the whole of the defendant's enrichment, not merely to set the

[106] Bant, *The Change of Position Defence* (2009) (n 65) 234–36.

[107] See *Halpern v Halpern (No 2)* [2007] EWCA Civ 291, [2008] QB 195.

[108] Eg *Clarke v Dickson* (1858) El B&E 148, 120 ER 463; *Western Bank of Scotland v Addie* (1866–69) 1 Sc 145 (HL Sc).

[109] *Johnson v Agnew* [1980] AC 367 (HL) 393. This is subject to certain limited exceptions for clauses that may survive rescission, see O'Sullivan, Elliott and Zakrzewski, *The Law of Rescission* (2008) (n 54) §§1.12, 1.14.

[110] *Portman Building Society v Hamlyn Taylor Neck* [1998] 4 All ER 202 (CA) 208 (Millett LJ).

contract aside. This is why the cases describe the power to rescind not simply as the power to avoid the contract, but to effect *restitutio in integrum.*[111] To reverse the defective transaction, the claimant must be entitled to reverse the acquisition of rights and the transfer of value gained by the defendant at the claimant's expense, while also making counter-restitution of enrichments received. Hence, the preferable approach is that taken in this chapter: the power to rescind should be understood as one aspect of a broader power to obtain restitution for the wrong or unjust factor rendering the contract voidable.

To illustrate the operation of this model of rescission in the cases, it is useful to group the case law into three categories: (i) rescission of purely executory contracts by cancellation of the contractual rights created by the contract; (ii) rescission of partly or fully-executed contracts by cancellation of contractual rights and restitution of the value of performance; and (iii) rescission of contracts that confer rights by the cancellation of contractual rights and restitution of those specific rights. In each case, the power to rescind the contract is restitutionary, but in the latter two cases rescission of the contractual rights is not sufficient, of itself, to achieve restitution and is therefore only one aspect of effecting restitution in full.

### *(i) Rescission of Purely Executory Contracts*

The restitutionary effect of rescission of purely executory contracts has generated significant academic debate. Where C promises to pay D £100 as a result of a misrepresentation by D, but has not yet paid, C can rescind the contract. For Birks and Nahan, rescission of this purely executory contract is restitutionary because rescission revests the contractual rights conferred.[112] They take the view that D's contractual right to payment of £100 is a benefit that enriches D; rescission revests C's contractual rights. On the other hand, Virgo[113] and Janet O'Sullivan[114] argue that rescission is restitutionary except where the contract is purely executory. They take the view that rescission of an executory contract will simply extinguish D's contractual right to payment without restitutionary consequences.[115] Stevens defends a third view: he agrees with Birks and Nahan that the source of the power to rescind is unjust enrichment, but contends that it is not restitutionary, for the reasons articulated by Virgo and O'Sullivan.[116]

[111] See above n 88.

[112] Birks, *An Introduction to the Law of Restitution* (1989) (n 52) 163; Nahan, 'Rescission: A Case for Rejecting the Classical Model?' (1997) (n 52) 72–73. See also Edelman and Bant, *Unjust Enrichment in Australia* (2006) (n 52) 102.

[113] Virgo, *The Principles of the Law of Restitution* (2006) (n 53) 29.

[114] O'Sullivan, 'Rescission as a Self-help Remedy: A Critical Analysis' (2000) (n 54) 525–28.

[115] See in a different context *Criterion Properties plc v Stratford UK Properties LLC* [2004] UKHL 28, [2004] 1 WLR 1846 [27] (Lord Scott) *cf Johnson v Agnew* [1980] AC 367 (HL) 392–93 (Lord Wilberforce).

[116] R Stevens, 'Is There a Law of Unjust Enrichment?' in S Degeling and J Edelman (eds), *Unjust Enrichment in Commercial Law* (Sydney, Lawbook Co, 2008) 14.

The distinction between factual and legal enrichment reveals the error that undermines both sides of this debate. There is no need to identify a transfer of value to the defendant in cases of legal enrichment and therefore the objection from Virgo and O'Sullivan—that no benefit can be conferred without performance—is wrongly made. D's right to payment of £100 from C is an enrichment, both factually (for example, D can immediately assign the debt for value) and legally (D has a contractual right against C). The defendant has received a benefit, not by performance of the contract, but by the contractual right to performance. Virgo and O'Sullivan's position limits the definition of restitution to the restoration of value and *non-contractual* rights, but oddly excludes *contractual* rights. As explained in chapter three,[117] there is no warrant for treating every other right capable of assignment as a legal enrichment, but arbitrarily excluding contractual rights.

Conversely, Birks and Nahan mischaracterise rescission as 'revesting'[118] contractual rights because they also fail to distinguish between the creation of rights and the transfer of value. The contractual right is not 'given back' or revested; the contractual right is cancelled, which was argued above to be a restitutionary response to a legal enrichment: it reverses the creation of the right that enriched the defendant. Likewise, by classifying rescission of contractual rights as a non-restitutionary response to unjust enrichment, Stevens takes too narrow a view of restitution: restitution refers to the reversal of the defendant's enrichment, not simply the restoration of benefits to the claimant.

The view adopted here is that, where a contract is purely executory, restitution is achieved by rescission without more: there is no additional factual enrichment to be reversed (there has been no performance) and no restitution of property rights (the contract is executory and no property rights were ever created pursuant to it). The defendant is enriched by the contractual rights acquired and any secondary right to sue for damages for repudiatory breach of the executory contract. Rescission reverses the acquisition of these rights and is therefore restitutionary. As explained above, while they are different forms of restitution, reversing the creation of rights (for example, rescission) and reversing the transfer of value (for example, monetary restitution) share the same purpose and effect.[119] As O'Sullivan, Elliott and Zakrzewski make clear, 'In the case of a purely executory contract complete *restitutio in integrum* is achieved simply by extinguishing the contract *ab initio*'.[120]

## (ii) Rescission of Partly or Fully-executed Contracts

In cases of part or full performance of a defective contract, the claimant's power to obtain restitution entails both a power to cancel the contractual rights (rescission)

[117] See ch 3, fns 118–20 and accompanying text.

[118] Nahan also uses 'reclaiming': Nahan, 'Rescission: A Case for Rejecting the Classical Model?' (1997) (n 52) 74 fn 26.

[119] Bant, *The Change of Position Defence* (2009) (n 65) 91.

[120] O'Sullivan, Elliott and Zakrzewski, *The Law of Rescission* (2008) (n 54) §12.17.

and to reverse any transfer of value under the rescinded contract. In other words, each party is enriched by the contractual rights created and, to the extent that the contract has been executed, by the value of that performance. In the language of this book, these cases involve restitution of both legal and factual enrichments. This is an instance where rescission of both value and rights does not involve double recovery.

### Value Claims and Rescission at Common Law

The common law has historically taken a more limited approach to claims for the restitution of the value of performance under a rescinded contract than that supported above. It is clear that the claimant will be entitled to 'money had and received', that is restitution of the sums paid under the contract.[121] Furthermore, it is clear that a claimant would be entitled at common law to the use value of money paid under a rescinded contract by application of the House of Lords' decision in *Sempra Metals Ltd v IRC*.[122]

Aside from money and the use of money, however, the availability of a value claim following rescission at common law is equivocal. *Selway v Fogg*[123] is authority against restitution of the value of goods and services performed under a contract rescinded at law.[124] The claimant was induced to enter into a contract to carry away rubbish for the defendant for £15 following a fraudulent misrepresentation as to the amount of rubbish. The claimant performed and was paid the contract price, but he sued for the difference between the contract price and the market value of the service provided (£20). The court held that, even if the claimant had not affirmed the contract by performing after discovering the fraud, he was not entitled to rescind and sue in *assumpsit* for the value of the service provided. In reaching this conclusion, Parke B relied on two earlier cases denying *assumpsit* for the value of goods following rescission.[125] Despite early authority permitting restitution in goods cases,[126] the preponderance of authority suggests that restitution of the value of goods sold under the rescinded contract is not available at common law.[127]

[121] Eg *Flight v Booth* (1834) 1 Bing NC 370, 376; 131 ER 1160, 1162; *Clarke v Dickson* (1858) El B&E 148, 120 ER 463; *Coastal Estates v Melevende* [1965] VR 433 (VSC) 434, 439, 454–55; *Enimont Overseas AG v RO Jugotanker Zadar (The Olib)* [1991] 2 Lloyd's Rep 108 (QB) 118; *Dimskal Shipping Co SA v International Transport Workers Federation (The Evia Luck)* [1992] 2 AC 152 (HL) 165.

[122] *Sempra Metals Ltd v IRC* [2007] UKHL 34, [2008] 1 AC 561 [48]–[49] (Lord Hope) [118]–[119] (Lord Nicholls). See also *Maguire v Makaronis* (1998) 188 CLR 449 (HCA).

[123] *Selway v Fogg* (1839) 5 M&W 83, 151 ER 36.

[124] Eg O'Sullivan, Elliott and Zakrzewski, *The Law of Rescission* (2008) (n 54) §§14.42–14.44.

[125] *Read v Hutchinson* (1813) 3 Camp 352, 170 ER 1408; *Ferguson v Carrington* (1829) 9 B&C 59, 109 ER 22.

[126] *De Symonds v Minchwich* (1796) 1 Esp 430, 170 ER 409.

[127] *Read v Hutchinson* (1813) 3 Camp 352, 170 ER 1408; *Ferguson v Carrington* (1829) 9 B&C 59, 109 ER 22; *Strutt v Smith* (1834) 1 CM&R 312, 149 ER 1099. See O'Sullivan, Elliott and Zakrzewski, *The Law of Rescission* (2008) (n 54) §§14.34–14.35.

This nineteenth-century line of authority is inconsistent with the approach in this book, which suggests that the claimant has a power to obtain restitution of both the contractual rights and the value of performance rendered. There seems to be no good reason why the value claim is denied in these cases and the denial of such a claim is the subject of sustained modern criticism.[128] It is also, as we shall see below, inconsistent with the position in equity and there is no justification for the different approach at law. Moreover, this rule is difficult to reconcile with the availability of a value-based claim where the contract is terminated.[129] The approach defended in this book highlights the unsoundness of the nineteenth-century position and provides a principled case for permitting the restitution of the value of performance at common law.

### Value Claims and Rescission in Equity

As at common law, restitution of money paid is available following rescission in equity.[130] Unlike at common law, the claim is not described as being for 'money had and received'.[131] However, as argued in chapter four, the language of 'money had and received' is unhelpful and the language of restitution should be preferred: both at law and in equity, there is a right to the restitution of value of money paid under a rescinded contract. Rescission in equity also extends to restitution of the use value of money,[132] and again this would seem to be required by the House of Lords' decision in *Sempra Metals*.

In cases besides money, however, the authority on value claims following rescission in equity is uneven. It is clear that claims for the use value of land or chattels are generally allowed as an ancillary to restitution of the specific right,[133] typically measured by the prevailing market value of renting or using the asset in question.[134] However, there is some historical hostility to awarding claims to the

[128] G Palmer, *The Law of Restitution* (Boston, Little Brown, 1978) vol I, §3.16; C Mitchell, P Mitchell and S Watterson, *Goff & Jones The Law of Unjust Enrichment*, 8th edn (London, Sweet & Maxwell, 2011) §36-07; O'Sullivan, Elliott and Zakrzewski, *The Law of Rescission* (2008) (n 54) §§14.34–14.35, 14.41–14.44.

[129] Eg *Planché v Colburn* (1831) 5 C&P 58, 172 ER 876; *De Bernady v Harding* (1853) 8 Ex 822, 155 ER 1586; *Prickett v Badger* (1856) 1 CBNS 296, 140 ER 123; *Bartholomew v Markwick* (1864) 15 CBR 711, 143 ER 964.

[130] *Redgrave v Hurd* (1881) 20 ChD 1 (CA); *Newbigging v Adam* (1886) 34 ChD 582 (CA); *Daly v Sydney Stock Exchange Ltd* (1985) 160 CLR 371 (HCA); *Re Goldcorp Exchange* [1995] 1 AC 74 (PC) 102.

[131] *With v O'Flanagan* [1936] ChD 575 (CA) 585–86; *Senanayake v Cheng* [1966] AC 63 (PC) 76–77; *Mihaljevic v Eiffel Tower Motors Pty Ltd and General Credits Ltd* [1973] VR 545 (VSC) 565. See O'Sullivan, Elliott and Zakrzewski, *The Law of Rescission* (2008) (n 54) §15.36.

[132] See in particular *Sempra Metals Ltd v IRC* [2007] UKHL 34, [2008] 1 AC 561 [239] (Lord Mance).

[133] See *York Buildings Co v Mackenzie* (1795) 8 Bro PC 42, 3 ER 432; *Small v Atwood* (1832) You 407; *Gibson v D'Este* (1843) 2 Y&CCC 542, 63 ER 243; *Cooper v Phibbs* (1867) 2 HL 149 (HL); *Allcard v Skinner* (1887) 36 ChD 145 (CA); *Lagunas Nitrate Co v Lagunas Syndicate* [1899] 2 Ch 392 (CA) 461; *Spence v Crawford* [1939] 3 All ER 271 (HL) 284; *McCarthy v Kenny* [1939] 3 DLR 556 (ONHC); *Alati v Kruger* (1955) 94 CLR 216 (HCA); *Atlantic Lines and Navigation Co Inc v Hallam Ltd (The Lucy)* [1983] 1 Lloyd's Rep 188 (QB) 202; *Cheese v Thomas* [1994] 1 WLR 129 (CA).

[134] *Cf* O'Sullivan, Elliott and Zakrzewski, *The Law of Rescission* (2008) (n 54) §§17.07–17.12.

value of rights as an alternative to specific restitution. This appears to have been settled by *Mahoney v Purnell*.[135] That case involved the sale of a hotel business in breach of fiduciary duty. The defendant then sold the hotel and left the company insolvent, with the proceeds of sale dissipated. May J awarded the claimant the difference between the value of the hotel when sold by the claimant and the value the claimant received from the defendant 'as an adjunct to setting aside the agreement'.[136] Under the model presented above, this award is the difference between restitution of the value of the hotel and counter-restitution of the sale price.[137] Importantly, the value of the asset when transferred was the relevant measure in *Mahoney v Purnell*,[138] and this is consistent with the immediate enrichment thesis advanced in chapter seven.

Birks and Burrows both support the availability of 'pecuniary rescission' (ie a claim for the value of a right transferred) consequent upon rescission.[139] The model presented in this book shows why a value claim should be available. As the claimant has a power to obtain restitution of the enrichment received by the defendant, the exercise of that power should reverse the defendant's enrichment in full: the contractual rights must be cancelled, property rights given up and the value of performance repaid, subject to counter-restitution by the claimant and other bars to rescission. Moreover, where the ground for rescission arises in unjust enrichment, the value claim would be subject to the defence of change of position, ensuring that innocent defendants are not worse off than if the contract had never been entered into to the extent of any change of position.[140]

Although there is no authority directly on point, the same award should in principle be permitted where the claimant has provided services. It is clear that a contract can be rescinded in equity where the claimant has received services from the defendant,[141] and vice versa.[142] Following rescission, the party providing the services has been awarded compensation for expenses incurred in providing the service in *Ormes v Beadel*,[143] and disgorgement of profits in *O'Sullivan v*

[135] *Mahoney v Purnell* [1996] 3 All ER 61 (QB). See also *McKenzie v McDonald* [1927] VLR 134 (VSC); *McCarthy v Kenny* [1939] 3 DLR 556 (ONHC); *Kupchak v Dayson Holdings Co Ltd* (1965) 53 DLR (2d) 482 (BCCA).

[136] *Mahoney v Purnell* [1996] 3 All ER 61 (QB) 89 (May J).

[137] This occurs through the process of counter-restitution by accounting in equity: O'Sullivan, Elliott and Zakrzewski, *The Law of Rescission* (2008) (n 54) §§15.55–15.57, 15.63. See, eg *Lagunas Nitrate Co v Lagunas Syndicate* [1899] 2 Ch 392 (CA) 461 (Rigby LJ); *Sibley v Grosvenor* (1916) 21 CLR 469 (HCA) 476.

[138] See also *McKenzie v McDonald* [1927] VLR 134 (VSC); *Kupchak v Dayson Holdings Co Ltd* (1965) 53 DLR (2d) 482 (BCCA) *cf McCarthy v Kenny* [1939] 3 DLR 556 (ONHC).

[139] P Birks, 'Unjust Factors and Wrongs: Pecuniary Rescission for Undue Influence' [1997] *RLR* 72; Birks, *Unjust Enrichment* (2005) (n 18) 226–28; Burrows, *The Law of Restitution* (2010) (n 56) 18–19.

[140] See O'Sullivan, Elliott and Zakrzewski, *The Law of Rescission* (2008) (n 54) §15.31.

[141] *Atlantic Lines and Navigation Co Inc v Hallam Ltd (The Lucy)* [1983] 1 Lloyd's Rep 188 (QB); *O'Sullivan v Management Agency and Music Ltd* [1985] QB 428 (CA).

[142] *Ormes v Beadel* (1860) 2 Giff 166, 176; 66 ER 70, 76; *Rees v De Bernardy* [1896] 2 Ch 427 (Ch) 450.

[143] *Ormes v Beadle* (1860) 2 Giff 166, 176; 66 ER 70, 76.

*Management Agency*.[144] These awards suggest that there is no reason in principle to deny a restitutionary claim for the value of services. Further support for this conclusion is derived from the availability of use value claims discussed above, where restitution takes the form of a reasonable user or reasonable rent award,[145] typically at the prevailing market value.[146] The use of money or an asset was shown to be closely analogous to the provision of a service in chapter four.

### *(iii) Proprietary Rescission*

'Proprietary rescission' refers to the situation where rescission effects specific restitution of a right acquired through performance of the contract. Since Parke B's decision in *Load v Green*,[147] it has been recognised that title passes under a voidable contract at law. The same was true in equity from the time of Lord Westbury's decision in *Phillips v Phillips*.[148] Both at law and in equity, it is now orthodox that a defendant can acquire rights under a voidable contract.[149] It is also true of both jurisdictions that rescission of the voidable contract will sometimes give rise to specific restitution of rights conferred under it.[150] Although Swadling has cast doubt on the historical correctness of the line of cases awarding proprietary rescission,[151] there can be no doubt that English law recognises specific restitution of rights through rescission.[152] It is contended here that, in proprietary rescission cases, the claimant has a power to obtain restitution, the exercise of which effects specific restitution of both contractual rights and rights acquired by the defendant under the contract.

[144] *O'Sullivan v Management Agency and Music Ltd* [1985] QB 428 (CA). See O'Sullivan, Elliott and Zakrzewski, *The Law of Rescission* (2008) (n 54) §§15.39–15.43.

[145] See, eg *Sibley v Grosvenor* (1916) 21 CLR 469 (HCA); *Brown v Smitt* (1924) 34 CLR 160 (HCA); *Alati v Kruger* (1955) 94 CLR 216 (HCA); *Atlantic Lines and Navigation Co Inc v Hallam Ltd (The Lucy)* [1983] 1 Lloyd's Rep 188 (QB) 202; *Cheese v Thomas* [1994] 1 WLR 129 (CA).

[146] O'Sullivan, Elliott and Zakrzewski, *The Law of Rescission* (2008) (n 54) §17.07 *cf* §§17.04–17.06 and the cases cited there, which suggest an account of actual income or profits is available as an alternative remedy. This measure is rejected in ch 7.

[147] *Load v Green* (1846) 15 M&W 216, 221; 153 ER 828, 830 (Parke B). See also *Clough v London and North Western Railway Co* (1871) 7 Ex 26 (Ex) 32.

[148] *Phillips v Phillips* (1861) 4 De GF&J 208, 45 ER 1164. See also *Tottenham v Green* (1863) 32 LJ Ch(NS) 201; *Cave v Cave* (1880) 15 ChD 639 (Ch) 649.

[149] *Latec Investments Ltd v Hotel Terrigal Pty Ltd* (1965) 113 CLR 265 (HCA) 277–78, 282, 284, 291; *National Provincial Bank v Ainsworth* [1965] AC 1175 (HL) 1254; *Greater Pacific Investments Pty Ltd v Australian National Industries Ltd* (1996) 39 NSWLR 143 (NSWCA) 152–53; *Bristol and West Building Society v Mothew* [1998] Ch 1 (CA) 22–23; *Twinsectra v Yardley* [1999] Lloyd's Rep Bank 438 (CA) 461–62.

[150] Common law: *Load v Green* (1846) 15 M&W 216, 221; 153 ER 828, 830 (Parke B); *Clough v London and North Western Railway Co* (1871) 7 Ex 26 (Ex) 32; *Re Eastgate* [1905] 1 KB 465 (KB); *Tilley v Bowman* [1910] 1 KB 745 (KB); *Car & Universal Finance Co Ltd v Caldwell* [1963] 1 QB 525 (CA); *Hunter BNZ Finance Ltd v CG Maloney Pty Ltd* (1988) 18 NSWLR 420 (NSWSC) 432–33; *Irons v Wang* [2004] DCR 830 (NZDC). Equity: *Allcard v Skinner* (1887) 36 ChD 145 (CA); *El Ajou v Dollar Land Holdings plc* [1993] 3 All ER 717 (Ch).

[151] See Swadling, 'Rescission, Property and the Common Law' (2005) (n 78) 125, 135–36.

[152] See above n 150.

Under the enrichment model presented in this book, the power to rescind contractual rights is but a part of the claimant's power to obtain restitution; the claimant's power to obtain restitution extends to the defendant's enrichments by performance under the voidable contract. As a result of the unjust factor or wrong, the defendant is enriched by *both* the contractual rights and any additional rights acquired by performance of the contract; the claimant is entitled, on the basis of that unjust factor or wrong, to restitution of both the contractual rights and other rights acquired by the defendant. For this reason, the fraud, undue influence or other factor rendering the contract voidable also renders property rights transferred pursuant to the contract liable to restitution upon rescission.[153] Accordingly, the reason for restitution of the specific right is precisely the same reason that entitled the claimant to rescind.

Arguably, specific restitution differs between law and equity. At common law, the property right is revested upon the exercise of the power to obtain restitution at the claimant's election. As rescission is exercised by self-help, title at law is regained immediately upon valid exercise of the power to obtain restitution of enrichments conferred under the voidable contract. Proprietary rescission at common law is exemplified by *Car & Universal Finance v Caldwell*,[154] where the contract was rescinded immediately upon Caldwell's reporting the fraud to the police and Automobile Association. However, specific restitution of rights at common law will not be available where it is not possible for the right to be revested at law. This is consistent with the approach outlined in chapter three,[155] which noted that the power to obtain specific restitution for unjust enrichment is subject to the regime governing the creation and transfer of the relevant right. So, while the common law will revest title to tangible personal property and permit the claimant to sue for interference with his or her right to possession, as occurred in *Caldwell*, it will not revest legal rights in intangible property because there is no common law mechanism for revesting such rights.[156] For this reason, a chose in action against a bank cannot be the subject of proprietary rescission at common law.[157] Following *Feret v Hill*,[158] the same is true of land, which may not be revested by election at law.[159] In practice, the requirement that the right be capable

[153] O'Sullivan, Elliott and Zakrzewski, *The Law of Rescission* (2008) (n 54) §1.23.

[154] *Car & Universal Finance Co Ltd v Caldwell* [1963] 1 QB 525 (CA). See also *Load v Green* (1846) 15 M&W 216, 221; 153 ER 828, 830 (Parke B); *Clough v London and North Western Railway Co* (1871) 7 Ex 26 (Ex) 32; *Universe Tankships Inc of Monrovia v International Transport Workers Federation (The Universe Sentinel)* [1983] 1 AC 366 (HL) 385 (Lord Diplock); *Hunter BNZ Finance Ltd v CG Maloney Pty Ltd* (1988) 18 NSWLR 420 (NSWSC) 432–33; *Irons v Wang* [2004] DCR 830 (NZDC); O'Sullivan, Elliott and Zakrzewski, *The Law of Rescission* (2008) (n 54) §§14.03–14.06.

[155] See ch 3, s III.C.

[156] O'Sullivan, Elliott and Zakrzewski, *The Law of Rescission* (2008) (n 54) §14.21.

[157] *Cf Jones & Sons (a firm) (Trustee) v Jones* [1997] Ch 159 (CA).

[158] *Feret v Hill* (1854) 15 CB 207, 223–27;139 ER 400, 406–08.

[159] *Canham v Barry* (1855) 15 CB 597, 611–12; 139 ER 558, 565–66; *R v Saddlers' Co* (1863) 10 HLC 303, 422; 11 ER 217, 228; *Taylor v Chester* (1869) 4 QB 309 (QB) 311–12 *cf Gordon v Chief Commissioner of Metropolitan Police* [1910] 2 KB 1080 (CA) 1089. See discussion in O'Sullivan, Elliott and Zakrzewski, *The Law of Rescission* (2008) (n 54) §§14.23–14.28.

of being revested at law precludes proprietary rescission by the act of election at common law in many cases. The claimant will instead need to rescind by judicial order in equity.

In equity, by contrast, it is arguable that legal title is not revested by the election to disaffirm the contract. Instead, it seems legal title is revested by one of two mechanisms: (i) by an act ordered by the court as part of the judicial order effecting rescission;[160] or (ii) by the exercise of a power as beneficiary under a resulting trust to revest the legal title.[161] While it is clear that the claimant obtains a proprietary right upon the judicial order effecting rescission in equity,[162] the cases are not clear as to what kind of trust or other equitable interest arises.[163] Consistently with the understanding of resulting trusts in section I above, the equitable right that arises following rescission is restitutionary and, therefore, a resulting trust. This view is supported by Millett J's decision in *El Ajou v Dollar Land Holdings*, where his Lordship called it 'an old-fashioned institutional resulting trust',[164] and the Court of Appeal decision in *Twinsectra v Yardley*,[165] which described the trust as a 'restitutionary resulting trust', although it has elsewhere been described as 'constructive'.[166] Although the claimant's power to obtain restitution is exercised through the court in equitable rescission cases, the claimant nonetheless has the power to reverse the defendant's enrichment by cancelling the contractual rights and obtaining restitution of value and rights transferred by performance.

Thus, the difference between common law and equitable rescission is one of process, not purpose and effect. In both cases, the defendant is unjustly enriched by rights and the claimant has a power to obtain restitution or affirm the contract. The consequence of exercising that power to obtain restitution is to effect specific restitution of rights (although restitution occurs at the moment of election at law and at the date of the order in equity). The way in which specific restitution is effected also differs, but the outcome is the same: at law, the power is exercised by election and immediately revests legal title, provided this is possible at common law and third-party rights have not supervened; in equity, the power is exercised

[160] *Clark v Malpas* (1862) 4 De GF&J 401, 45 ER 1238; *Alati v Kruger* (1955) 94 CLR 216 (HCA) 229; *O'Sullivan v Management Agency and Music Ltd* [1985] QB 428 (CA) 459, 469, 473; *Norwich Peterborough BS v Steed* [1993] Ch 116 (CA) 132–33; *Maguire v Makaronis* (1998) 188 CLR 449 (HCA) 459, 478, 500. See O'Sullivan, Elliott and Zakrzewski, *The Law of Rescission* (2008) (n 54) §§15.04–15.06.

[161] *Alati v Kruger* (1955) 94 CLR 216 (HCA) 223–24; *Lonrho plc v Fayed (No 2)* [1992] 1 WLR 1 (Ch) 11–12 (Millett J); *Shalson v Russo* [2003] EWHC 1637 (Ch), [2005] Ch 281 [116]–[127] (Rimer J) *cf Latec Investments Ltd v Hotel Terrigal Pty Ltd* (1965) 113 CLR 265 (HCA) 278, 290–91. See O'Sullivan, Elliott and Zakrzewski, *The Law of Rescission* (2008) (n 54) §16.23.

[162] See *Lonrho plc v Fayed (No 2)* [1992] 1 WLR 1 (Ch) 11–12; *El Ajou v Dollar Land Holdings plc* [1993] 3 All ER 717 (Ch) 735; *Bristol and West Building Society v Mothew* [1998] Ch 1 (CA) 22–23; *Twinsectra v Yardley* [1999] Lloyd's Rep Bank 438 (CA) 461–62; *Shalson v Russo* [2003] EWHC 1637 (Ch), [2005] Ch 281 [116]–[124] (Rimer J).

[163] O'Sullivan, Elliott and Zakrzewski, *The Law of Rescission* (2008) (n 54) §16.56.

[164] *El Ajou v Dollar Land Holdings plc* [1993] 3 All ER 717 (Ch) 734 (Millett J).

[165] *Twinsectra v Yardley* [1999] Lloyd's Rep Bank 438 (CA).

[166] *Daly v Sydney Stock Exchange Ltd* (1985) 160 CLR 371 (HCA) 387–90; *Greater Pacific Investments Pty Ltd v Australian National Industries Ltd* (1996) 39 NSWLR 143 (NSWCA) 153.

through the judicial order and legal title is revested either pursuant to judicial orders or through a resulting trust. The restitutionary purpose of the remedy is identical in both cases, but the difference in structure is mandated by the regime governing the right in question or the nature of equitable intervention. Proprietary rescission, in both forms, is specific restitution of an enrichment by rights.

### *(iv) Rescission on Terms*

Understanding rescission as a restitutionary remedy is complicated by the availability of rescission on terms. Conditional relief is a general equitable doctrine comprising orders for the transaction to be set aside on condition that the party seeking rescission makes counter-restitution and takes other necessary steps to effect *restitutio in integrum*.[167] This is a limited power to be exercised in accordance with settled principles of law rather than an untempered judicial discretion to remake the contract. The terms must be 'necessary to procure *restitutio in integrum*'.[168] As Ferris J held in *Allied Irish Bank v Byrne*:[169]

> [T]he court seeks to put that party into the position in which he would have been if the representation had not been made. This involves ascertaining what the position would have been if the transaction had not taken place. It does not involve reforming the transaction to accord with the representation.

While there are a number of statements in the cases that appear to depart from the requirement that rescission on terms is limited to what is necessary to achieve restitution and counter-restitution,[170] those cases are inconsistent with more recent authority in *De Molestina v Ponton*.[171] O'Sullivan, Elliott and Zakrewzski rightly describe the unfettered discretion to achieve 'practical justice' through rescission on terms as 'heretical' and historically unjustified.[172] This book takes the same view: rescission 'on terms' should properly be understood as allowing the imposition of conditions on rescission intended to achieve *restitutio in integrum* under the circumstances, not carte blanche to mould discretionary relief to achieve some other purpose.

[167] O'Sullivan, Elliott and Zakrzewski, *The Law of Rescission* (2008) (n 54) §15.46. See *Brown v Smitt* (1924) 34 CLR 160 (HCA) 172 (Isaacs v Rich JJ); *Cheese v Thomas* [1994] 1 WLR 129 (CA) 136 (Sir Donald Nicholls VC); *Greater Pacific Investments Pty Ltd v Australian National Industries Ltd* (1996) 39 NSWLR 143 (NSWCA) 151; *Maguire v Makaronis* (1998) 188 CLR 449 (HCA) 477–78.

[168] *TSB Bank plc v Camfield* [1995] 1 WLR 430 (CA) 434 (Nourse LJ).

[169] *Allied Irish Bank plc v Byrne* [1995] 1 FCR 430 (Ch).

[170] See, eg *O'Sullivan v Management Agency and Music Ltd* [1985] QB 428 (CA) 458 (Dunn LJ) 466–67 (Fox LJ) 471 (Waller LJ); *Vadasz v Pioneer Concete (SA) Pty Ltd* (1995) 184 CLR 102 (HCA) 112–15.

[171] *De Molestina v Ponton* [2002] 1 Lloyd's Rep 271 (QB). See also *TSB Bank plc v Camfield* [1995] 1 WLR 430 (CA) 434–37 (Nourse LJ); *Kirwan v Cresvale Far East Ltd* [2002] NSWCA 395, (2002) 44 ACSR 21 [140]–[142].

[172] O'Sullivan, Elliott and Zakrzewski, *The Law of Rescission* (2008) (n 54) §§13.13–13.24.

# III. Rectification

The third example of specific restitution of rights is rectification, which has a similar structure and restitutionary effect to rescission. Rectification is a remedy to amend a written legal instrument (such as a contract document, conveyance, trust deed or instrument of registration) to reflect the agreement of the parties or, in unilateral rectification cases,[173] the understanding of one of the parties.[174] It usually takes the form of a court order altering the wording of the instrument and thereby changing its effect,[175] although a court may treat an instrument as having been 'rectified' without a formal order.[176] It will be shown that, where rectification is court-ordered, it is a form of specific restitution of a legal enrichment; but, where there is no formal order for rectification, the question should be understood as one of construction.[177] As with rescission, the discussion here will focus on rectification of instruments in the context of contract, but it is also applicable to rectification of instruments in other contexts.

## A. The Availability of Rectification

Rectification is available on the basis of unjust enrichment, including mistake[178] and undue influence,[179] and wrongdoing, including fraud,[180] misrepresentation[181] and breach of fiduciary duty.[182] It may also be available where the non-mistaken party is estopped from relying on the instrument.[183] However, mistake is the most common basis for rectification. In contract, the availability of rectification of the written document for mistake depends upon whether the mistake is made by both parties to the contract ('common mistake') or only one party ('unilateral mistake').[184] The basis for rectification and the rules that apply in each situation are distinct and are examined separately below.

[173] Eg *A Roberts & Co Ltd v Leicestershire CC* [1961] Ch 555 (Ch).

[174] See A Burrows, 'Construction and Rectification' in A Burrows and E Peel (eds), *Contract Terms* (Oxford, Oxford University Press, 2007) 84–85.

[175] *Murray v Parker* (1854) 19 Beav 305, 52 ER 367; *Crane v Hegeman-Harris Co Inc* [1939] 1 All ER 662 (ChD); *The Rhodian River* [1984] 1 Lloyd's Rep 373 (QB). See E Peel, *Treitel on The Law of Contract*, 12th edn (London, Sweet & Maxwell, 2007) §8-059.

[176] *The Nile Rhapsody* [1994] 1 Lloyd's Rep 382 (CA); *OTV Birwelco Ltd v Technical & General Guarantee Co Ltd* [2002] EWHC 2240 (TCC), [2002] 4 All ER 668 [39].

[177] Burrows, 'Construction and Rectification' (2007) (n 174) 90–99.

[178] Eg *Murray v Parker* (1854) 19 Beav 305, 52 ER 367; *Faraday v Tamworth Union* [1917] 86 LJ Ch 436 (Ch); *W Higgins Ltd v Northampton Corp* [1927] 1 Ch 128 (Ch).

[179] *The Nai Genova* [1984] 1 Lloyd's Rep 353 (CA) 365.

[180] *Blay v Pollard & Morris* [1930] 1 KB 628 (CA).

[181] *Wimpey (UK) Ltd v VI Construction Ltd* [2005] EWCA Civ 77, [2005] BLR 135 [56].

[182] *The Nai Genova* [1984] 1 Lloyd's Rep 353 (CA) 365.

[183] *A Roberts & Co Ltd v Leicestershire CC* [1961] Ch 555 (Ch); *The Nai Genova* [1984] 1 Lloyd's Rep 353 (CA) 363.

[184] Peel, *Treitel on The Law of Contract* (2007) (n 175) §8-059.

### *(i) Common Mistake*

Rectification of a written contract for mistake will generally only be permitted where the document *erroneously records* the intention of both parties.[185] So, in *Murray v Parker*,[186] John and David Parker agreed to a sublease from Murray at a rent of £340 and agreed to pay 'all taxes, land tax and insurance' that applied. The lease was executed, recording the rent of £340, but stating that the rent figure 'included' the land tax. The land tax was redeemed by the head lessor and the Parkers then refused to pay the land tax. On these facts, Murray was entitled to rectify the lease to require the Parkers to pay the redeemed land tax. Sir John Romilly MR held that:[187]

> [T]o justify the Court in reforming an executed deed, it must appear that there has been a mistake common to both the contracting parties, and that the agreement has been carried into effect by the deed in a manner contrary to the intention of both.

Thus, rectification was permissible because the written document failed to record accurately the intention of *both* parties.

Peter Gibson LJ has identified four requirements for common mistake rectification,[188] which were confirmed by Lord Hoffmann in the leading decision in the House of Lords in *Chartbrook Ltd v Persimmon Homes Ltd*.[189] First, there must be a prior and 'continuing common intention' between the parties, although there is no need for this to amount to a binding contract.[190] Second, that common intention must have been objectively manifested.[191] Third, that intention must continue at the moment of execution of the instrument to be rectified. Fourth, there has been a common mistake in the drawing up of the written instrument of contract such that the written document does not accurately record the parties' common intention. In addition, there must be no bar to rectification, such as lapse of time or the intervention of third-party rights.[192]

### *(ii) Unilateral Mistake*

Unilateral mistake rectification arises in circumstances where one party has either laboured under a mistake in the lead up to the contract or is mistaken as to what is recorded in the document and the other party is not so mistaken.[193] Where the

[185] *Faraday v Tamworth Union* [1917] 86 LJ Ch 436 (Ch); *W Higgins Ltd v Northampton Corp* [1927] 1 Ch 128 (Ch).

[186] *Murray v Parker* (1854) 19 Beav 305, 52 ER 367.

[187] Ibid 308–09 (Sir John Romilly MR).

[188] *Swainland Builders Ltd v Freehold Properties Ltd* [2002] EWCA Civ 560, [2002] 2 EGLR 71 [33] (Peter Gibson LJ). See also Burrows, 'Construction and Rectification' (2007) (n 174) 85–87.

[189] *Chartbrook Ltd v Persimmon Homes Ltd* [2009] UKHL 38, [2009] 1 AC 1101 [48] (Lord Hoffmann).

[190] *Joscelyne v Nissen* [1970] 2 QB 86 (CA) 98 (Russell LJ).

[191] Ibid.

[192] *Smith v Jones* [1954] 1 WLR 1089 (Ch).

[193] Burrows, 'Construction and Rectification' (2007) (n 174) 87–90. Eg *A Roberts & Co Ltd v Leicestershire CC* [1961] Ch 555 (Ch); *Commission for the New Towns v Cooper (Great Britain) Ltd* [1995] Ch 259 (CA).

document is a voluntary settlement on trust, a unilateral mistake of the settlor will be sufficient to found a power to rectify the settlement.[194] There is no need to show wrongdoing on the part of the defendant. However, where the written document records a contract, unilateral mistake rectification will only be permitted where there is proof of the defendant's wrongdoing.

Accordingly, in a contractual context, a unilateral mistake will only give rise to a power to rectify the written document where: (i) the non-mistaken party procures the mistake by wrongdoing; or (ii) the non-mistaken party knew of the mistake by the other party and failed to correct it.[195] Burrows explains that the requirements therefore differ from common mistake rectification in three respects:[196] first, there is evidently no requirement for a common intention; second, there is correspondingly no requirement that such a common intention be outwardly manifested; and, third, there is no requirement of a mistake in the *drawing up* of the contract, so a mistake in the negotiations prior to contracting will suffice.[197]

The requirement of fraud or knowledge of the mistake on the part of *the defendant* in unilateral mistake cases involving rectification of a contract demonstrates that the basis of the claim is wrongdoing.[198] In *Blay v Pollard & Morris*,[199] Scrutton LJ said the claimant need prove 'unilateral mistake in one party, fraud or conduct equivalent to fraud in the other party'.[200] The basis of the claim is thus the wrongdoing of the party procuring the mistake. Rectification will also be allowed for a unilateral mistake where the non-mistaken party has knowledge[201] or constructive knowledge[202] of the mistake. In these circumstances, although the non-mistaken party did not procure the mistake, knowledge of the innocent party's mistake is sufficient to constitute 'wrongdoing' and the document may be rectified at the election of the innocent party. Thus, where the document records a contract, the basis of the claim for unilateral mistake rectification should be understood as a wrong.

### *(iii) Who May bring the Claim?*

Where a unilateral mistake entitles a party to rectify, the claim is brought by the mistaken party to reverse the enrichment of the other party. For instance, in *Commissioner for the New Towns v Cooper*,[203] the claimant could sue to rectify

194 *Re Butlin's Settlement Trusts* [1976] Ch 251 (Ch).

195 See Peel, *Treitel on The Law of Contract* (2007) (n 175) §8-067.

196 Burrows, 'Construction and Rectification' (2007) (n 174) 90.

197 See *A Roberts & Co Ltd v Leicestershire CC* [1961] Ch 555 (Ch); *Commission for the New Towns v Cooper (Great Britain) Ltd* [1995] Ch 259 (CA).

198 See *Commission for the New Towns v Cooper (Great Britain) Ltd* [1995] Ch 259 (CA).

199 *Blay v Pollard & Morris* [1930] 1 KB 628 (CA).

200 Ibid 633 (Scrutton LJ). See also *May v Platt* [1900] 1 Ch 616 (Ch).

201 *A Roberts & Co Ltd v Leicestershire CC* [1961] Ch 555 (Ch); *Thomas Bates & Son Ltd v Wyndham's (Lingerie) Ltd* [1981] 1 WLR 505 (CA); *Commission for the New Towns v Cooper (Great Britain) Ltd* [1995] Ch 259 (CA); *Wimpey (UK) Ltd v VI Construction Ltd* [2005] EWCA Civ 77, [2005] BLR 135. See Peel, *Treitel on The Law of Contract* (2007) (n 175) §8-067.

202 *Thomas Bates & Son Ltd v Wyndham's (Lingerie) Ltd* [1981] 1 WLR 505 (CA); *Wimpey (UK) Ltd v VI Construction Ltd* [2005] EWCA Civ 77, [2005] BLR 135.

203 *Commission for the New Towns v Cooper (Great Britain) Ltd* [1995] Ch 259 (CA).

the terms of an agreement conferring a put option on the defendant, which had deliberately obtained the put option in such a way as to ensure the claimant did not realise what it was granting. Similarly, where the claim is on the basis of undue influence or relates to a voluntary settlement, the claim is brought by one party to reverse the enrichment of the other.

However, common mistake cases involving the erroneous recording of a contract may potentially be different. In common mistake cases, either one or both parties obtains contractual rights that were not intended to be recorded in the document and either one or both parties may thus be legally enriched. The claim may therefore be brought by any party that has mistakenly conferred contractual rights on another party and rectification will achieve both restitution and counter-restitution of rights by restoring the intended bargain. Alternatively, rectification can be sought by consent of both parties.[204]

## B. Rectification as Specific Restitution of Rights

This book takes the view that, like rescission, rectification should be understood as an example of specific restitution of rights. In contract cases, rectification will reverse the creation of contractual rights by reason of a wrong or unjust factor. So, in *Murray v Parker*,[205] rectification reversed John and David Parker's legal enrichment by the acquisition of a contractual right to rent the premises from Murray without paying the land tax, which enrichment was unjust because of common mistake. Rectification differs from rescission in that the enrichment is only those rights wrongly recorded in the written document rather than all the contractual rights unjustly acquired in a voidable contract. As a result, specific restitution is more narrowly tailored in rectification cases: the claimant may reverse the legal enrichment by electing to rectify only those rights unjustly or wrongly obtained. In addition to restitution of the contractual rights, it will be shown that rectification may also revest property rights or reverse a transfer of value that occurred pursuant to the unrectified contract.

### *(i) Rectification and Construction*

Burrows has argued that contextual construction of contract terms has usurped rectification in many circumstances. Instead of a formal order to rectify an instrument, in some cases courts may interpret the term 'contextually' to obviate the need for rectification. For example, Burrows cites *Prenn v Simmonds*,[206] where 'profits of RTT Ltd' was read to mean 'consolidated profits of the RTT Group', and *Investors Compensation Scheme v West Bromwich BS*,[207] where 'any claim (whether sounding in rescission for undue influence or otherwise)' was read as 'any claim

[204] *Burford (Fareham) Ltd v Christian Vision* [2005] EWHC 2533 (Ch).
[205] *Murray v Parker* (1854) 19 Beav 305, 52 ER 367.
[206] *Prenn v Simmonds* [1971] 1 WLR 1381 (HL).
[207] *Investors Compensation Scheme Ltd v West Bromwich BS* [1998] 1 WLR 896 (HL).

sounding in rescission (whether for undue influence or otherwise)'. Following the leading House of Lords decision in *Chartbrook Ltd v Persimmon Homes Ltd*,[208] it is clear that a more liberal approach to construction will obviate the need for rectification in certain circumstances formerly the province of rectification. Thus, where rectification is not claimed and the case can be resolved following the approach to construction adopted in *Chartbrook*, the question is properly one of contractual interpretation and beyond the scope of the book.

However, where there is a formal order for rectification, it is clear that this is not simply a question of construction of the contract. There is still scope for rectification where, for instance, an entire agreed clause is omitted from a contract or an entire contractual clause is mistakenly inserted into a contract, and it would not be possible to resolve the problem by construction.[209] Likewise, construction could not cure mistakes as to the legal effect of the written document, as opposed to mistakes of fact.[210] Moreover, where the claimant successfully seeks an order for rectification, it is clear that the court is not merely construing the contract: it is ordering a substantive change to the language of the written instrument. It is submitted below that this is best understood as restitution of a legal enrichment.

### *(ii) Rectification as Restitution*

Chambers rightly notes that rectification of a transaction mirrors the rescission of an equivalent transaction.[211] In the case of a purely executory contract, rectification effects restitution of the contractual rights created by the erroneous recording of the terms of the agreement. The rights so obtained are a legal enrichment and the enrichment is unjust by reason of the mistake or other factor giving rise to rectification. Rectification achieves restitution of mistakenly recorded rights by amending or supplementing the document to restore the prior agreement (in common mistake cases) or restitution of mistakenly conferred rights by restoring the agreement intended by the mistaken party (in unilateral mistake cases). The value of the unrectified rights is properly irrelevant; the enrichment is the legal rights obtained by the defendant and the remedy reverses the defendant's enrichment by amending the written document to restore the agreement.

The distinction between factual and legal enrichment explains rectification of executed contracts. Although some older authorities suggest that rectification of executed contracts is barred,[212] it is clear that, if this ever was the case, it no longer represents English law.[213] So, where property rights are acquired pursuant to

[208] *Chartbrook Ltd v Persimmon Homes Ltd* [2009] UKHL 38, [2009] 1 AC 1101.

[209] See L Nicholls, 'My Kingdom for a Horse: The Meaning of Words' (2005) 121 *LQR* 577, 586; Burrows, 'Construction and Rectification' (2007) (n 174) 96.

[210] Burrows, 'Construction and Rectification' (2007) (n 174) 94 fn 66.

[211] R Chambers, 'Two Kinds of Enrichment' in R Chambers, C Mitchell and J Penner (eds), *Philosophical Foundations of the Law of Unjust Enrichment* (Oxford, Oxford University Press, 2009) 253.

[212] *May v Platt* [1900] 1 Ch 616 (Ch).

[213] *Murray v Parker* (1854) 19 Beav 305, 52 ER 367; *Thompson v Hickman* [1907] 1 Ch 550 (Ch).

a contract that is subsequently rectified, the power of rectification is part of the restitutionary remedy afforded to reverse the acquisition of those property rights under the unrectified contract. For example, following execution of a contract in a formal deed of conveyance or lease, the formal instrument may be rectified.[214] In these cases, rectification may restore legal title, reversing the creation of a property right by the unrectified instrument.

Where rectification of the instrument does not restore legal title, rectification will create an equitable 'right' to the property right transferred in the defective contract. While Chambers calls the interest that arises 'an equitable interest … the nature of [which] is not entirely clear'[215] and notes that it has been described variously as a 'constructive trust'[216] or 'beneficial ownership',[217] it is best understood as equivalent to the resulting trust that arises following rescission. Indeed, the power to rectify a transaction is structurally identical to the power to rescind it: the claimant has a power to obtain restitution to reverse an enrichment by rights. Like other proprietary powers in respect of rights, the power to rectify binds third parties,[218] except for bona fide purchasers for value without notice.[219]

The legal enrichment approach to rectification can be demonstrated by reference to *Blacklocks v JB Developments (Godalming) Ltd*.[220] The defendants purchased land which, due to a mistake in a previous conveyance, included a disputed portion that was occupied by the claimants. The claimants were entitled to rectification of the register to restore title to the disputed portion. On these facts, the defendants were legally enriched by acquiring title to the disputed portion. The claimants did not seek restitution of the value of the disputed portion and, indeed, the value was entirely irrelevant to the claim as framed. Instead, the claimants sought to reverse the defendant's acquisition of title to the disputed portion *in law*. Specific restitution in this case was achieved by rectification of the register, which reversed the enrichment by restoring title to the disputed portion to the claimants. Although the claimant's power to rectify arose against the prior owners, it persisted against the defendants as their inquiries prior to the purchase had revealed to them the true boundary of the land.

In this way, rectification is analogous to rescission and this book applies the same model to both remedies. The power of rectification should be understood, like the power to rescind, as an aspect of the power to obtain restitution for an unjust factor or wrong. This power to obtain restitution includes restitution

[214] *Murray v Parker* (1854) 19 Beav 305, 52 ER 367; *Cowen v Truefitt Ltd* [1899] 2 Ch 309 (CA); *Stait v Fenner* [1912] 2 Ch 504 (Ch). See Peel, *Treitel on The Law of Contract* (2007) (n 175) §8-070.

[215] Chambers, 'Two Kinds of Enrichment' (2009) (n 211) 253.

[216] *Taitapu Gold Estates Ltd v Prouse* [1916] NZLR 825 (NZHC); *Blacklocks v JB Developments (Godalming) Ltd* [1982] Ch 183 (Ch).

[217] *Malory Enterprises Ltd v Cheshire Homes (UK) Ltd* [2002] EWCA Civ 151, [2002] Ch 216.

[218] *Craddock Bros v Hunt* [1923] 2 Ch 136 (CA); *Blacklocks v JB Developments (Godalming) Ltd* [1982] Ch 183 (Ch).

[219] Eg *Smith v Jones* [1954] 1 WLR 1089 (Ch).

[220] *Blacklocks v JB Developments (Godalming) Ltd* [1982] Ch 183 (Ch).

of value transferred or rights acquired pursuant to the mistaken term of the unrectified document. Although there appear to be no cases where a value claim is made as part of a claim for rectification, in principle such a claim should be available. More commonly, the claimant will be entitled to restitution of rights acquired pursuant to the mistaken term, which is clearly available through rectification as demonstrated by *Blacklocks v JB Developments*. Thus, rectification may restore property rights acquired pursuant to a defective transaction.

## IV. Enrichment by Release of Obligations

This book subdivides legal enrichment into 'enrichment by rights' and 'enrichment by release'; this section examines cases of 'enrichment by release'. In these situations, the defendant's legal enrichment is the *release of a duty or liability*. As explained in chapter four,[221] the discharge or release of an obligation often involves a transfer of value that may found a factual enrichment claim. However, the award of security interests and rights of subrogation in unjust enrichment shows that *specific* restitution is sometimes awarded to reinstate the obligation. This situation is the corollary of the three examples of enrichment by rights identified above: if a defendant can be enriched by the acquisition of rights, the defendant can be enriched by the release of obligations. Whereas specific restitution of rights involves reversing the acquisition of the right, specific restitution in enrichment by release cases involves reinstating the obligation.

Courts have often awarded equitable liens or subrogated the claimant to the rights of the defendant or a third party,[222] but the justification and theoretical basis for this response is contested. One important consequence of the division between factual and legal enrichment in this book is that it clarifies when the award of a security interest in these cases is restitutionary and when it is not. It is argued here that a power to enforce a security will be restitutionary where it reverses the release of an obligation of the defendant at the claimant's expense by granting the claimant a power formerly held by the defendant or a third party; in all other cases, the award of a security interest involves granting a power to the claimant for prophylactic purposes, including: (i) to protect a value-based enrichment claim by way of security; and (ii) to prevent the unjust enrichment of the defendant or third parties. Security interests are thus sometimes, but not always, restitutionary.

[221] See ch 4, s VI.

[222] Chambers, 'Resulting Trusts' (2006) (n 5) 256–57; Chambers, 'Two Kinds of Enrichment' (2009) (n 211) 269. See, eg *Hewitt v Court* (1983) 149 CLR 639 (HCA); *Banque Financiere de la Cité v Parc (Battersea) Ltd* [1999] 1 AC 221 (HL).

## A. Subrogation

Subrogation involves granting the claimant rights or powers held (or formerly held) by the defendant against a third party or by a third party against the defendant.[223] Mitchell and Watterson distinguish two situations: 'subrogation to subsisting rights', which involves the claimant assuming still existing rights of the defendant or a third party, from 'subrogation to extinguished rights', which involves the claimant assuming reinstated rights *formerly held* by the defendant or a third party.[224] The latter is often called 'reviving subrogation', but it does not actually involve reviving the discharged rights of the defendant or third party in the name of the claimant.[225] Rather, as Lord Hoffmann made clear in *Banque Financière de la Cité v Parc (Battersea) Ltd*,[226] the claimant obtains a new right.

### *(i) Distinguishing Contractual Subrogation from Subrogation in Unjust Enrichment*

Subrogation may be a response to various causes of action, most commonly contract and unjust enrichment.[227] Contractual subrogation arises where the parties have agreed that the claimant may be subrogated to the position of the defendant or a third party in the circumstances. This regularly arises in the context of insurance contracts where insurers are subrogated to the rights of the insured party against the party causing the loss. As a response to the intentions of the contracting parties, contractual subrogation arises in the category of consent, not unjust enrichment.[228] Accordingly, contractual subrogation is beyond the scope of this book.

Subrogation is also available in unjust enrichment.[229] In *Parc (Battersea)*,[230] Lord Hoffmann explained that there were two roles for subrogation in the law of unjust enrichment: (i) reversing the defendant's unjust enrichment; or (ii) preventing the defendant's unjust enrichment from arising.[231] These two

[223] *Orakpo v Manson Investments Ltd* [1978] AC 95 (HL) 104 (Lord Diplock).

[224] See C Mitchell and S Watterson, *Subrogation Law and Practice*, revised edn (Oxford, Oxford University Press, 2007) §§1.05–1.08. See also C Mitchell, 'Subrogation: Persistent Misunderstandings' in A Burrows and A Rodger (eds), *Mapping the Law: Essays in Memory of Peter Birks* (Oxford, Oxford University Press, 2006) 106.

[225] Mitchell, 'Subrogation: Persistent Misunderstandings' (2006) (n 224) 109; Mitchell and Watterson, *Subrogation Law and Practice* (2007) (n 224) §§3.10–3.18.

[226] *Banque Financiere de la Cité v Parc (Battersea) Ltd* [1999] 1 AC 221 (HL) 236 (Lord Hoffmann) *cf Boscawen v Bajwa* [1996] 1 WLR 328 (CA) 341 (Millett LJ).

[227] *Banque Financiere de la Cité v Parc (Battersea) Ltd* [1999] 1 AC 221 (HL) 231–32 (Lord Hoffmann); Mitchell, 'Subrogation: Persistent Misunderstandings' (2006) (n 224) 106; Mitchell and Watterson, *Subrogation Law and Practice* (2007) (n 224) §1.02.

[228] *Hobbs v Marlowe* [1978] AC 16 (HL) 39 (Lord Diplock); *Banque Financiere de la Cité v Parc (Battersea) Ltd* [1999] 1 AC 221 (HL) 231–32 (Lord Hoffmann). See Virgo, *The Principles of the Law of Restitution* (2006) (n 53) 24.

[229] See above n 2.

[230] *Banque Financiere de la Cité v Parc (Battersea) Ltd* [1999] 1 AC 221 (HL).

[231] Ibid 231 (Lord Hoffmann). See also *Orakpo v Manson Investments Ltd* [1978] AC 95 (HL) 104 (Lord Diplock).

categories correspond to the division outlined below between restitutionary and prophylactic subrogation. In the former category, the claimant's payment releases the defendant from a liability and subrogation is a form of specific restitution *reversing* a legal enrichment. However, in the latter category, subrogation is not restitutionary. Instead, subrogation to subsisting rights *prevents* the unjust enrichment of the defendant or third parties at the claimant's expense.

### *(ii) Restitutionary Subrogation*

A common scenario for restitutionary subrogation in unjust enrichment is where the claimant discharges a secured debt of the defendant. The claimant may then be subrogated to the secured creditor's charge. *Butler v Rice* is a typical case.[232] Mr Rice asked Butler to lend him £450 to pay off a bank mortgage over a property in his wife's name. Mr Rice did not inform Butler that the property was not in his name. Butler advanced the loan on a £300 mortgage over the wife's property and a guarantee for the remainder; the bank's mortgage was thereby discharged. However, Mrs Rice refused to execute a mortgage over the land in favour of Butler. She had known nothing of the transaction until the bank's mortgage was discharged. On these facts, Warrington J held that Butler was entitled to be subrogated to the bank's mortgage over the property to secure his right to repayment of the £450 he had advanced.

In this situation, Mrs Rice was enriched by the payment of the £450 debt *and* the discharge of the mortgage over her property: she obtained the 'property discharged from the debt of £450, not one penny of which she has paid off herself'.[233] In addition to the payment of the debt, Mrs Rice is enriched by the removal of a *liability* in respect of her right to the property: she was under a Hohfeldian liability to give up the land should the lender exercise the power to repossess following default. As a result of Butler's payment, she had obtained the release of this liability and held the property free from any encumbrance. To reverse this legal enrichment, Butler was entitled to be subrogated to the bank's charge against Mrs Rice's land, which reinstated the liability and provided Butler with a conditional power to obtain the land if his claim for monetary restitution was not satisfied. The restitutionary character of the subrogation is revealed by the reinstatement of Mrs Rice's liability under the *bank's* charge, rather than the £300 mortgage and guarantee that had been agreed by Butler and Mr Rice. Butler's payment had enriched Mrs Rice by the removal of a conditional liability upon the land and subrogating Butler to the mortgage reversed that enrichment.

The decision in *Boscawen v Bajwa*[234] is to the same effect. Bajwa was selling his house. The Abbey National lent money to the purchasers of the house, intending to take a first charge over the property to secure the loan. The funds were paid

[232] *Butler v Rice* [1910] 2 Ch 277 (Ch). See also *Ghana Commercial Bank v Chandiram* [1960] AC 732 (PC).

[233] *Butler v Rice* [1910] 2 Ch 277 (Ch) 282 (Warrington J).

[234] *Boscawen v Bajwa* [1996] 1 WLR 328 (CA).

to the purchasers' solicitors and then to the vendor's solicitors, who discharged Bajwa's mortgage over the property with Halifax Building Society. The sale never took place. Bajwa's judgment creditors obtained a charging order against the property and sold the house. In a suit by the judgment creditors to enforce the charging order, Abbey National counter-claimed that it was entitled to priority over the proceeds of sale by right of subrogation to Halifax's charge over the property. The Court of Appeal held that Abbey National was entitled to be subrogated to the charge. As Abbey National had an equitable right traceable into the funds that discharged Bajwa's mortgage, Bajwa was legally enriched at the expense of Abbey National: the money discharged Bajwa's liability and the claimant paid the money on a failure of consideration.[235] Consequently, the Abbey National was entitled to specific restitution of that enrichment: the Court of Appeal held that they were entitled to be subrogated to the Halifax charge over the property. The right of subrogation secured the claimant's right to restitution of the value of its payment, ensuring that it could enforce the mortgage to obtain restitution and thereby preventing the unjust enrichment of Mr Bajwa's other creditors at the claimant's expense.

### *(iii) Prophylactic Subrogation*

Subrogation is not always restitutionary. Subrogation to subsisting rights is not an example of specific restitution of a legal enrichment. By definition, the claimant's payment to the defendant's creditor does not release the defendant from a liability; instead, the defendant's existing liability is transferred to the claimant for twin prophylactic purposes identified by Mitchell as being:[236]

> [T]o prevent the creditor from recovering twice over by enforcing his rights once he has been paid by the claimant, or to prevent the defendant from escaping liability in the event that the creditor does not sue him.

As the payment to the creditor does not release the defendant's obligation, he is not enriched by the payment. The subrogation does not involve the reinstatement of a released liability and it is not a form of specific restitution of a legal enrichment.

Subrogation to subsisting rights may prevent the unjust enrichment of the defendant or third parties. First, it may prevent the unjust enrichment of the defendant in two ways: first, where the claimant has no direct claim in unjust enrichment against the defendant, subrogation ensures the defendant does not escape liability if the creditor were to forbear from suing; second, where the claimant has an independent factual enrichment claim against the defendant, subrogation to existing rights may provide ancillary protection to the direct right to restitution of value, because it ensures that the claimant is either paid or has recourse to the security. Second, it may prevent the unjust enrichment of third parties who would otherwise benefit from the claimant's payment, including a

235 See Mitchell, 'Subrogation, Tracing and the Quistclose Principle' (1995) (n 17) 455–56.
236 Mitchell, 'Subrogation: Persistent Misunderstandings' (2006) (n 224) 106.

creditor who may otherwise recover twice or third parties who might share in the payment in circumstances of insolvency. As we shall see, subrogation served both of these purposes in *Parc (Battersea)*. In accordance with these prophylactic purposes, the claimant may seek subrogation against either: (i) the unjust enrichment defendant; or (ii) a third party that would be unjustly enriched in the absence of subrogation.

Contrary to the approach taken by Mitchell and Watterson,[237] the House of Lords decision in *Parc (Battersea)*[238] is an example of prophylactic, not restitutionary, subrogation.[239] The claimant (BFC) lent money to the debtor company (Parc) to refinance a debt owed to a third party (RTB). BFC advanced the money on the strength of a letter purporting to prioritise BFC's debt over all companies in the Omni Group, which included Parc. The letter did not, as a matter of law, have this effect. RTB held a first charge over the property and the defendant (OOL), which was also a company in the Omni Group, held a second charge. Parc became insolvent. The claimant argued that, having mistakenly discharged part of the debt owed to RTB, it should be subrogated to RTB's first charge in order to prevent OOL's unjust enrichment at its expense. The House of Lords held that OOL would be enriched by the repayments to RTB if BFC were not subrogated to the rights held by RTB. Importantly, the House of Lords stressed that the claimant was only entitled to be subrogated to RTB's rights vis-à-vis OOL and did not take priority over any other creditors of the debtor company.[240] The subrogation was thus designed to prevent OOL's unjust enrichment only.

Although regarding subrogation as a response to unjust enrichment and describing it as 'restitutionary', the majority of the House of Lords did not understand the remedy to reverse an *existing* enrichment of OOL. Lord Hoffmann described subrogation as 'an equitable remedy to reverse *or prevent* unjust enrichment' (emphasis added)[241] but went on to decide the case on the basis that subrogating BFC to RTB's charge would *prevent* OOL's unjust enrichment:[242]

> In this case, I think that *in the absence of subrogation*, O.O.L. would be enriched at B.F.C.'s expense and that prima facie such enrichment would be unjust. ... [S]ubrogation is not a right or a cause of action but an equitable remedy against a party *who would otherwise* be unjustly enriched. It is a means by which the court regulates the legal relationships between a plaintiff and a defendant ... in order to *prevent* unjust enrichment (emphasis added).

Accordingly, the consequence of subrogating BFC to the first charge as against OOL is that 'O.O.L. would be prevented from being able to enrich itself to the extent that B.F.C.'s money paid off the R.T.B. charge'.[243]

[237] Mitchell and Watterson, *Subrogation Law and Practice* (2007) (n 224) §§4.30–4.32.
[238] *Banque Financiere de la Cité v Parc (Battersea) Ltd* [1999] 1 AC 221 (HL).
[239] See also *Chetwynd v Allen* [1899] 1 Ch 353 (Ch).
[240] *Banque Financiere de la Cité v Parc (Battersea) Ltd* [1999] 1 AC 221 (HL) 228 (Lord Steyn) 237 (Lord Clyde).
[241] Ibid 231 (Lord Hoffmann).
[242] Ibid 234–36 (Lord Hoffmann).
[243] Ibid 237 (Lord Hoffmann).

On the model of enrichment presented in this book, Lord Hoffmann is right to treat this claim as preventing, rather than reversing, unjust enrichment. In the first instance, it was Parc, not OOL, that was enriched as a result of BFC's mistaken payment. Parc was factually enriched, not legally enriched. RTB's charge was not discharged by BFC's payment: while Parc's debts were partially discharged, the charge was not released. There is thus no enrichment by release and this is not an instance of specific restitution by subrogation to extinguished rights. Rather, to the extent that the payment diminished Parc's liability to RTB, there was a transfer of value to Parc at BFC's expense. Accordingly, BFC only had a claim for monetary restitution against Parc. If BFC had sought to be subrogated to RTB's charge in a direct claim against Parc, such subrogation would not reverse any legal enrichment, but could arguably have been justified on a prophylactic basis as protecting BFC's monetary restitution claim and preventing the unjust enrichment of a third party, namely OOL. However, on the exceptional facts of *Parc (Battersea)*, such subrogation would have been contrary to the contractual arrangements between BFC and Parc, which is why it was not sought in the House of Lords.

Although BFC had a direct claim against Parc for the value of the mistaken payment, it brought suit against OOL, the second chargee, because Parc was insolvent. As a result of BFC's payment, OOL was benefitted by the improved position of its charge. The consequence of prioritisation is that OOL's rights were potentially more valuable,[244] depending on the extent to which Parc could not repay its debt obligations. The hopeless insolvency of Parc meant that OOL's charge had a higher value following the repayments to RTB.[245] Therefore, provided the other requirements of an unjust enrichment claim are met, BFC would have a claim for monetary restitution against OOL. Arguably, however, the increased value of OOL's charge would not be *at the expense of* BFC until OOL's debt was satisfied and BFC's was not, and then only to the extent that BFC remained unpaid. The initial transfer of value from BFC to Parc would become a transfer of value from BFC to OOL when, and to the extent that, OOL was repaid and BFC was not. Otherwise, BFC's payment to Parc would simultaneously have enriched both Parc and OOL at the moment it was made, which ignores the possibility that OOL and BFC could both have been paid in full. The better view is that there is no transfer of value *from* BFC to OOL unless and until BFC is unpaid. Nor does OOL obtain a right or release from an obligation at BFC's expense: OOL has the same security interest it held before BFC's mistaken payment. There is thus no enrichment for subrogation to reverse.

Lord Steyn took a different approach, understanding the defendants to have conceded enrichment by admitting that the repayments towards RTB's charge

[244] See P Watts, 'Subrogation: A Step Too Far?' (1998) 114 *LQR* 341, 344; S Worthington, 'Restitution and Insolvency' in F Rose (ed) *Restitution and Insolvency* (London, Mansfield Press, 2000) 72–74; Mitchell, 'Subrogation: Persistent Misunderstandings' (2006) (n 224) 117; Mitchell and Watterson, *Subrogation Law and Practice* (2007) (n 224) §§4.14–4.22.

[245] *Cf Banque Financiere de la Cité v Parc (Battersea) Ltd* [1999] 1 AC 221 (HL) 239 (Lord Hutton).

improved their position *pro tanto* as chargee.[246] Finding that this enrichment was at BFC's expense and by reason of a mistake on BFC's part, his Lordship took the view that there was thus a claim for monetary restitution against OOL without any need for subrogation.[247] This approach is consistent with the enrichment model in this book, but differs on the 'at the expense of' question. This book takes the view, as Lord Hoffmann did, that the subrogation did not reverse OOL's unjust enrichment at BFC's expense, but instead prevented it.

However, even if Lord Steyn's approach to the 'at the expense of' question is adopted, his Lordship's analysis of enrichment is consistent with the model presented in this book. If OOL were enriched at BFC's expense by the increased value of the charge, Lord Steyn held that OOL had an obligation to make restitution of the value to BFC *irrespective of a right of subrogation*. Following the approach to factual enrichment in this book, that must be right. If OOL had received value at BFC's expense, the right to restitution of the value transferred would arise irrespective of any right to subrogation. Moreover, Lord Steyn's conclusion that there is a claim in unjust enrichment for the value would be inconsistent with awarding a right of subrogation. If BFC were subrogated to RTB's first charge as against OOL, then BFC would be paid in priority to OOL and OOL would not be enriched. There would be no transfer of value to OOL from BFC to reverse. Therefore, Lord Steyn is right to see the unjust enrichment claim and the right to subrogation as alternatives on the facts of *Parc (Battersea)*: either OOL is enriched by value, BFC is entitled to restitution of that value and subrogation is not required, or, alternatively, OOL is not enriched and BFC may be subrogated to prevent OOL's unjust enrichment from arising.

### *(iv) Conclusion*

Although subrogation is not always a restitutionary response to an enrichment by release, it is often restitutionary in nature. In restitutionary subrogation cases, the claimant asserts that the defendant is enriched by the release of a liability at the claimant's expense and seeks reinstatement of that liability. In prophylactic subrogation cases, subrogation is either ancillary to the principal claim against the defendant, which is a factual enrichment claim, or it is prophylactic. The prophylactic purpose is two-fold: (i) to secure a monetary restitution award against the defendant; and (ii) to prevent the unjust enrichment of the defendant or a third party.

## B. Equitable Liens

In certain circumstances, the courts have been prepared to award an equitable lien to secure a monetary restitution award.[248] In these cases, it is the award of

[246] Ibid 227 (Lord Steyn).
[247] Ibid 228 (Lord Steyn).
[248] Eg *Cooper v Phibbs* (1867) 2 HL 149 (HL).

monetary restitution that reverses the transfer of value to the defendant, not the lien. The grant of a lien performs the same prophylactic purposes as non-restitutionary subrogation: a security interest to ensure that monetary restitution is an effective remedy and to prevent the unjust enrichment of the defendant or third parties. The lien operates to ensure that the claimant gets paid by the defendant and to afford the claimant priority over third parties if the defendant becomes insolvent. In this way, it prevents the unjust enrichment of third-party creditors who might benefit from the enrichment conferred by the claimant on the defendant in an insolvency. However, the reason for the award of a security interest in addition to monetary restitution in some cases and not others is not clear and is beyond the scope of this book. For present purposes, it suffices to conclude that the security interest is not restitutionary in nature: it does not reverse the defendant's enrichment. A lien does not provide an equitable right or power to obtain a specific right or reinstate a specific obligation; rather, it secures a claim to monetary restitution.[249]

For example, one situation where the common law imposes an equitable lien was recognised by Millett LJ in *Boscawen v Bajwa*:[250]

> If the plaintiff's money has been applied by the defendant ... not in the acquisition of a landed property but in its improvement, then the court may treat the land as charged with the payment to the plaintiff of a sum representing the amount by which the value of the defendant's land has been enhanced by the use of the plaintiff's money.

The lien is prophylactic, not restitutionary. It is not an instance of specific restitution of rights; the defendant is not enriched by a right or the release of a liability. Rather, the defendant is enriched by the value received at the claimant's expense and the lien secures the right to monetary restitution. Accordingly, the claimant is entitled to claim the value received by the defendant but is not entitled to restitution of the property right or a proportionate share in the asset.[251] The lien is granted to prevent a third party from sharing in the increased value of the asset in the event of the defendant's insolvency by ensuring that the claimant is paid first. The basis for granting an equitable lien in such cases (and not granting a security interest in others) is therefore not a question of enrichment and is beyond the scope of this book.

## V. Conclusion

This chapter applies the legal enrichment model to the cases, dividing legal enrichment into 'enrichment by rights' and 'enrichment by release'. In relation to

[249] *Giumelli v Giumelli* (1999) 196 CLR 101 (HCA) 120 (Gleeson CJ, McHugh, Gummow and Callinan JJ).
[250] *Boscawen v Bajwa* [1996] 1 WLR 328 (CA) 335 (Millett LJ).
[251] Virgo, *The Principles of the Law of Restitution* (2006) (n 53) 640.

enrichment by rights, the claim is that the defendant acquired and holds a right at the claimant's expense. The law's response is to award the claimant specific restitution: a power to reverse the acquisition of a specific right by the defendant, either by imposing a resulting trust, rescinding the transaction, or rectifying a legal instrument. In addition, the chapter also identified subrogation as an example of specific restitution of an enrichment by release, while distinguishing prophylactic subrogation and equitable liens.

With respect to resulting trusts, it was shown that at least some, and perhaps many, resulting trusts are an example of specific restitution of an enrichment by rights. The view that resulting trusts are only a response to unjust enrichment was rejected in favour of the recognition that resulting trusts respond to unjust enrichment as well as other events. Where the defendant unjustly acquires a right capable of being held on trust, the resulting trust 'reverses' that enrichment by conferring a power on the claimant to obtain restitution of the right held on trust. Although the law of resulting trusts is yet to be definitively settled in English law, it was submitted that the analysis of resulting trusts within the legal enrichment model provides the broad outlines for the incremental recognition of resulting trusts by analogy from the recognised instances.

In relation to rescission, it was argued that the power to rescind is simply an aspect of a power to obtain restitution for the unjust factor rendering the transaction voidable. The model of rescission defended in this chapter identified the unjust factor or wrong as the source of both the power to rescind the transaction and obtain restitution of value and rights conferred by performance of the transaction. This analysis applies equally to executed and executory obligations. Where value or rights are conferred pursuant to a voidable transaction, the claimant has a choice either to affirm the transaction or to rescind and obtain restitution of the rights conferred in the contract, deed or instrument, *as well as* value transferred and rights conferred by performance. In return, the claimant must make counter-restitution of the rights acquired in the instrument, as well as other enrichments received from the defendant.

Rectification follows a similar structure to rescission, but relates only to the acquisition of particular rights in a transaction rather than a power to avoid the transaction in its entirety. Rectification allows a party to reverse the enrichment of the other party by the acquisition of a right mistakenly recorded in an instrument. As the ground for rectification relates only to certain rights obtained in the instrument, restitution is narrowly tailored: the claimant may reverse the enrichment by rights by electing to rectify those rights unjustly or wrongly obtained. In addition, rectification of an instrument may also have the effect of revesting rights erroneously transferred under the unrectified instrument and, in principle, should give rise to a right to restitution of value transferred by reason of the erroneous recording. It was shown that rectification is not simply a passive correction of a document, but a substantive doctrine effecting restitution of rights unjustly obtained.

Finally, this chapter examined the relationship between legal enrichment and the award of security interests and subrogation. Subrogation has now been widely recognised as a response to unjust enrichment in English law, but the distinction between subrogation reversing unjust enrichment and subrogation preventing unjust enrichment in Lord Hoffmann's speech in *Parc (Battersea)* is yet to be fully developed in the courts. It was argued here that restitutionary subrogation is a form of specific restitution of a legal enrichment, reversing an enrichment by release of an obligation. By contrast, in prophylactic subrogation cases, subrogation either secures personal rights to monetary restitution or prevents the unjust enrichment of third parties (or serves both of these purposes). Likewise, equitable liens are not restitutionary in nature, but instead perform a prophylactic function similar to prophylactic subrogation.

# 6

# Freedom of Choice

Freedom of choice is relevant to unjust enrichment in several different ways, one of which is in determining whether or not the particular defendant is enriched. However, although protection of freedom of choice has been rightly identified as part of the enrichment inquiry in both the cases and academic commentary, the precise role of freedom of choice is unclear because of the failure to distinguish factual and legal enrichment. This chapter contends that one important consequence of this book is that it clarifies the proper role of freedom of choice in the enrichment inquiry by distinguishing the freedom of choice concerns that pertain to each kind of claim. It will be contended that only factual enrichment cases incorporate a requirement of choice of the benefit to establish enrichment. It is suggested that the test for a 'choice' is objective, requiring: (i) that the defendant has the choice to accept or reject the benefit and chooses to accept it; and (ii) that a reasonable person would understand the defendant's choice as involving an assumption of responsibility to pay for the benefit.

There is a preliminary, philosophical question as to why freedom of choice has anything to do with enrichment. As explained in chapter three, the same freedom of choice issues are not present in legal enrichment cases as in factual enrichment cases because the claim only requires the defendant to give up precisely the benefit received. However, in factual enrichment cases, the defendant is often required to make restitution in money for a benefit in kind. A system that did not protect the defendant's freedom of choice would force purchases upon defendants, requiring recipients of benefits to pay for them in money irrespective of their choices. This is not the approach adopted by English law. The enrichment inquiry is understood in English law as imposing a requirement that the claimant establish that the particular defendant is enriched, a requirement that grew out of the need to show a 'request' in several of the old forms of action in *indebitatus assumpsit*. The request avoided the objection that the defendant had not chosen the benefit and thus should not be forced to pay for it. As will be demonstrated below, the need to show a request has given way to a more nuanced protection of freedom of choice, but the underlying principle remains the same: the law of unjust enrichment protects the defendant's freedom of choice as part of the enrichment inquiry.

There are two dominant theories concerning the way in which the law of unjust enrichment takes freedom of choice into account at the enrichment stage: 'subjective devaluation' theories, which permit the defendant to deny that the benefit received was worth its market value to him; and 'choice of benefit' theories, which hold that the question is whether or not the defendant chose the benefit, not whether the particular defendant valued it.[1] Both types of theory attempt to respond to the concern that making a defendant pay money's worth for a benefit in kind may infringe his freedom of choice or autonomy. The critical philosophical question for choosing between the two theories is therefore to what extent the law's concern for freedom of choice requires the enrichment inquiry to protect the defendant. Fundamentally, this is a question about whether defendants' subjective valuations, personal preferences and spending priorities are relevant or whether it is enough to establish that the defendant objectively manifested a choice for the benefit and assumed the responsibility to pay for it. As we shall see, this question has been settled in favour of an objective valuation approach by the Court of Appeal in *Benedetti v Sawiris*.[2]

Section I rejects subjective devaluation. It is shown that: (i) the 'request requirement' in the forms of action does not provide support for subjective devaluation; (ii) the modern cases do not apply a subjective devaluation approach; (iii) subjective devaluation is inconsistent with the law's adoption of relational value; and (iv) protection of the defendant's freedom of choice does not require subjective devaluation. Section II then proposes a choice of benefit test and examines what constitutes a choice of benefit by the defendant. It is contended that a valid 'choice' requires acceptance of a benefit objectively manifesting an assumption of responsibility to pay for that benefit. Finally, section III outlines the circumstances in which a benefit will be incontrovertibly enriching without proof of choice of the benefit. It is contended that the 'incontrovertible enrichment' test allows proof of enrichment in the absence of choice whenever the nature of the benefit is such that the defendant's freedom of choice is not infringed by making him pay money's worth for a benefit in kind.

## I. Rejecting Subjective Devaluation

Subjective devaluation theories insist that the defendant's freedom of choice can only be properly protected by allowing the defendant to value the benefit at the price the defendant would have paid. The defendant can say that he would not have bought the benefit at all or would not have bought it at market price. Conversely, if the defendant values the benefit higher than the market price, some subjective devaluation theories accept that the benefit can be 'subjectively revalued' at the higher price.[3] This section rejects subjective devaluation theory

[1] See McGhee, 'The Nature of the Enrichment Enquiry' in J Edelman and S Degeling (eds), *Unjust Enrichment in Commercial Law* (Pyrmont, Lawbook Co, 2009).

[2] *Benedetti v Sawiris* [2010] EWCA Civ 1427.

[3] See, eg M Garner, 'The Role of Subjective Benefit in the Law of Unjust Enrichment' (1990) 10 *OJLS* 42, 43; G Virgo, *The Principles of the Law of Restitution*, 2nd edn (Oxford, Oxford University Press, 2006) 88–89; C Mitchell, P Mitchell and S Watterson, *Goff & Jones The Law of Unjust Enrichment*,

as a matter of law and principle. It is argued that the cases generally do not support a subjective devaluation approach and that protection of freedom of choice does not require the law to take into account the defendant's subjective valuation, personal preferences and spending priorities, as explained by Etherton LJ in *Benedetti v Sawiris*.[4]

Proponents of subjective devaluation rely on three main arguments. First, that the request requirement in the forms of action provides an historical basis for subjective devaluation. Second, that the modern cases allow a defendant subjectively to devalue non-money benefits. Third, that the law's protection of freedom of choice requires this concession to subjective valuation. These arguments are considered below and each is rejected in turn. Sub-section A shows that the request requirement in the forms of action had nothing to do with subjective valuation, while sub-section B demonstrates that the cases generally do not allow subjective devaluation. Rather, as McLachlin J held in *Peter v Beblow*, the law of unjust enrichment is committed to a 'straightforward economic approach' to value.[5] Sub-section C then explains that subjective devaluation theories involve either a strong or weak commitment to idiosyncratic valuation, either of which is inconsistent with the law's commitment to relational value. Finally, in sub-section D, it is shown that the protection of freedom of choice does not require subjective devaluation. It is argued that objective facts and conduct showing that the defendant manifested a choice of the benefit in circumstances that objectively demonstrate an assumption of responsibility to pay for it provides a sufficient normative basis for liability. Accordingly, proving a particular defendant is enriched is not subjective; nor is it concerned with value: the question is an objective one qualified by protection of the defendant's freedom of choice.

## A. The Request Requirement

As we saw in chapter four, in non-money cases, the common counts of quantum meruit, quantum valebat and money paid all required that the work be done at the defendant's 'special instance and request'. Birks suggested in *An Introduction to the Law of Restitution* that the request requirement was an historical basis for 'subjective devaluation'.[6] Virgo makes the same point in *The Principles of the Law of Restitution*, arguing that 'The principle of subjective devaluation originates from

8th edn (London, Sweet & Maxwell, 2011) §4-11. For a possible example of subjective revaluation, see *Benedetti v Sawiris* [2009] EWHC 1330 (Ch), which was reversed on this point in *Benedetti v Sawiris* [2010] EWCA Civ 1427 and criticised in A Lodder, 'Unjust Enrichment and the Assessment of Quantum Meruit Awards' (2010) 126 *LQR* 42, 46–47.

[4] *Benedetti v Sawiris* [2010] EWCA Civ 1427 [145] (Etherton LJ).

[5] *Peter v Beblow* [1993] 1 SCR 980 (SCC) 990 (McLachlin J). See also *Garland v Consumers' Gas Co* [2004] SCC 25, [2004] 1 SCR 629 (SCC) [31]; *Pacific National Investments Ltd v City of Victoria* [2004] SCC 75, [2004] 3 SCR 545 (SCC) [15].

[6] P Birks, *An Introduction to the Law of Restitution*, revised edn (Oxford, Clarendon Press, 1989) 109. See also Virgo, *The Principles of the Law of Restitution* (2006) 68.

the forms of action which required the defendant to have requested a particular benefit before a restitutionary remedy could be awarded'.[7] However, this misapprehends the request requirement.[8] The request requirement was not concerned with value, nor was it concerned with identifying whether a benefit had been conferred on the defendant. The identification and valuation of the benefit were separate elements of the form of action that had nothing to do with the existence of a request. Rather, the request, whether explicit or implicit, was evidence that the defendant *chose* the benefit conferred by the claimant.

This is most clearly demonstrated by the historical form of action upon a quantum meruit. Two of the 'elements' of the form of action, which were enumerated in chapter four,[9] are inconsistent with a subjective devaluation approach. First, the form of action upon a quantum meruit involved an exclusively objective approach to identifying benefits in services cases. The first 'element' required the claimant to state in his declaration the service that had been performed for the defendant and the court would then determine the work done on an objective basis.[10] In *Planché v Colburn*,[11] Planché outlined in his declaration the 'work and labour, care and diligence, in and about the composing and writing'[12] of a considerable portion of the work on costume and ancient armour commissioned by the defendants. The court referred to the evidence of Jerdan, the editor of the *Literary Gazette*, to establish the terms of engagement and the work done by Planché.[13] The identification of the benefit was thus an objective exercise relying on the evidence of a third party as to the work Planché had done. Although the defendants argued that they were benefitted only by 'the article when complete',[14] the court did not treat that subjective view as relevant to the existence of a benefit for the quantum meruit count. Rather, it was relevant to a different element of the action: what the defendants had *requested* from Planché. As such, *Planché v Colburn* exemplifies an objective approach to the identification of the benefit received by the defendant.

Second, the historical form of action for quantum meruit required an averment by the *claimant*, not the defendant, as to how much the work was *reasonably* worth, not how much it was worth to the defendant.[15] The court would then decide what the work was reasonably worth. In other words, just as the existence of a benefit was established objectively, so to was the *valuation* of that benefit. For this reason, Planché was able to recover a reasonable sum for work and labour on a quantum meruit basis, even though the publishers did not consider

[7] Virgo, *The Principles of the Law of Restitution* (2006) (n 3) 68.

[8] See also S Scott, 'Restitution and the Argument of Subjective Devaluation' (1993) 15 *New Zealand Universities Law Review* 246, 259.

[9] See ch 4, s III.A.

[10] See *R v W* (1670) in Baker and Milsom, *Sources of English Legal History: Private Law to 1750* (London, Butterworths, 1986) 474–75; *Basten v Butter* (1806) 7 East 479, 103 ER 185.

[11] *Planché v Colburn* (1831) 5 C&P 58, 172 ER 876.

[12] Ibid 59.

[13] Ibid 59.

[14] Ibid 60.

[15] See ch 4, fn 63 and accompanying text.

themselves benefitted by the research work Planché had completed. Clearly, the court awarded an objectively determined reasonable sum, not the value the publishers subjectively attached to the work after the fact. There is no suggestion in any of the pre-Judicature Act cases examined in chapter four that the value should be other than an objectively ascertained value.

The same is true of the request requirement in the other common counts. Having emerged from the quantum meruit count,[16] the quantum valebat count replicated the structure of quantum meruit, including the objective identification of the benefit and the averment by the claimant, not the defendant, as to what the goods were reasonably worth. The money paid count was similar, requiring that the liability be discharged at the defendant's 'special instance and request', although no actual request was necessary and the value of the liability released was objectively ascertained. In *Jenkins v Tucker*, for example, the defendant was obliged to pay the reasonable cost of a funeral for his wife defrayed by the claimant at his 'special instance and request'. The subjective value of the payment to the defendant was irrelevant, with the court finding that the defendant was liable for the costs of a reasonable funeral for a person in the defendant's position.[17]

## B. Subjective Devaluation in the Cases

It is suggested here that the cases supporters of subjective devaluation rely upon in support of a principle of subjective devaluation are better understood by the choice of benefit analysis. The cases demonstrate, not that the law takes a subjective approach to value, but that it takes freedom of choice seriously, which is the principle that underpins the oft-quoted dictum of Pollock CB in *Taylor v Laird*: 'One cleans another's shoes; what can the other do but put them on?'[18] Indeed, Birks's own explanation of *Taylor v Laird* is that the court was concerned to emphasise the need for a choice of the benefit.[19] Birks's error was to take freedom of choice to entail a concession to idiosyncratic valuation, arguing that 'benefits in kind have value to a particular individual only so far as he chooses to give them value'.[20] The object of this section is to address and reject the assumption that protection of the defendant's freedom of choice is achieved by subjective devaluation.

[16] See ch 4, s IV.A.

[17] *Jenkins v Tucker* (1788) 1 H Bl 90, 94; 126 ER 55, 57 (Gould J).

[18] *Taylor v Laird* (1856) 25 LJ Ex 329 (Ex) 332 (Pollock CB). Indeed, many other judicial statements that are regularly cited in support of subjective devaluation are better understood as relating to choice of the benefit rather than subjectivity of value, see, eg *Falcke v Scottish Imperial Insurance Co* (1886) 34 ChD 234 (CA) 248 (Bowen LJ); *Magical Waters Fountains Ltd v City of Sarnia* (1990) 74 OR (2d) 682 (ONCJ) 690–91 (Gatreau J); *Peel (Regional Municipality) v Canada* [1992] 3 SCR 762 (SCC) [25] (McLachlin J); *Sharwood & Co v Municipal Financial Corp* (2001) 197 DLR (4th) 477 (ONCA) [26] (Laskin JA).

[19] Birks, *An Introduction to the Law of Restitution* (1989) (n 6) 111–12.

[20] Ibid 109. See also Virgo, *The Principles of the Law of Restitution* (2006) (n 3) 68.

### (i) Services Cases

As we have already seen, the objective approach historically adopted by the courts in quantum meruit is an obstacle to a subjective approach to value. Modern services cases have also generally adopted an objective approach to the question of enrichment. Two recent examples are the Privy Council advice in *Blue Haven Enterprises Ltd v Tully*[21] and the High Court decision in *JS Bloor Ltd v Pavillion Developments Ltd*,[22] neither of which is consistent with subjective devaluation. In *Blue Haven*, the claimant, White, set up the infrastructure for a coffee plantation on land purchased from Tully. A prior purchaser, Robinson, subsequently obtained the land by an order for specific performance, including the fruits of White's work in developing the plantation. White then claimed against Robinson for the value of the work done. Although White's claim was unsuccessful because Robinson had informed White of his prior interest, it is important for present purposes that Robinson was enriched by the work White had done.[23] Although the enrichment point was not argued, the Privy Council found that Robinson had been saved the cost of developing the coffee plantation. Critically, the approach of the Privy Council to the benefit that Robinson had obtained was entirely objective. The Privy Council did not ask whether Robinson would have developed the plantation differently or whether he would have made the same expenditures. Indeed, he may well have developed the plantation differently and, if he were entitled subjectively to devalue the improvements to the property, he could deny that he wanted the coffee plantation set up as White had done. However, Robinson intended to set up a coffee plantation and did not seek to argue that he had not chosen the improvements in question. As what he had received was objectively valuable, he was enriched.

By contrast, *Bloor v Pavillion* is a case where the freedom of choice point was taken by the defendant, who successfully argued that it did not choose the service provided by the claimant. The claimant, JS Bloor Ltd, mistakenly built a road that, under the contract, was supposed to be built by the defendant, Pavillion Developments. While Pavillion did want a road to be built, it successfully argued that it did not choose the building services provided by Bloor because, under the contract, it had chosen to build the road itself and it did not have 'the opportunity to design and procure the work to [its] specification'.[24] The evidence was that Pavillion would have built a cheaper road without foul drainage or service ducts or the same storm drains and gullies as the £93,072.73 road built by Bloor. As the benefit was not incontrovertible and the defendant did not choose the benefit, the claimant could not prove that the defendant was enriched. Importantly, the case cannot be explained by subjective devaluation: Pavillion clearly subjectively valued

[21] *Blue Haven Enterprises Ltd v Tully* [2006] UKPC 17 *cf Cooper v Phibbs* (1867) 2 HL 149 (HL).
[22] *JS Bloor Ltd v Pavillion Developments Ltd* [2008] EWHC 724 (TCC).
[23] *Blue Haven Enterprises Ltd v Tully* [2006] UKPC 17 [19]–[20] (Lord Scott).
[24] *JS Bloor Ltd v Pavillion Developments Ltd* [2008] EWHC 724 (TCC) [45] (Kirkham J).

the road, it just would have built a different, cheaper version.[25] Yet, Pavillion was not required to pay Bloor the value of the cheaper road. The case was not decided on the basis that Pavillion could subjectively devalue the £93,072.73 value of the road and pay the subjective value that it attached to it; rather, it was decided on the basis that Bloor did not choose the road provided by Pavillion and 'had no real alternative but to accept it … Pavillion could not in reality reject the road'.[26] The focus on choice of the benefit in *Bloor v Pavillion* makes it clear that the different outcomes in *Blue Haven* and *Pavillion* turn on the choice of the relevant benefit, not subjective devaluation.

### *(ii) Goods Cases*

Virgo suggests that *Boulton v Jones*[27] provides 'one of the best examples of subjective devaluation'.[28] In that case, the defendant, Jones, ordered pipe from a shop owned by Brocklehurst. Unbeknown to the defendant, Brocklehurst had sold the shop on to Boulton. When Jones received an invoice from Boulton, he refused to pay it as he had intended to enter into a contract with Brocklehurst, against whom he held a right of set-off. There was evidently no contract between Boulton and Jones, but the interesting point for present purposes is that Jones was not required to pay for the goods on a quantum valebat. Virgo argues that this is because the right of set-off entitled Jones subjectively to devalue the pipe he had ordered; he would not have ordered the pipe if he had had to pay for it. However, *Boulton v Jones* is flatly inconsistent with subjective devaluation. In the absence of any other evidence of his subjective valuation, the evidence is that Jones subjectively valued the pipe at the value of the right of set-off he held against Brocklehurst. Jones was not indifferent to the pipe; he ordered it intending to use his set-off because he desired the pipe and valued it at the same value as the right of set-off. The reason Jones did not have to pay for the pipe is, as will be explained below,[29] that Jones could objectively show that he did not expect to pay for the pipe because of the right of set-off. He did not assume financial responsibility for the benefit.[30]

### *(iii) Explicit Judicial Endorsement of Subjective Devaluation*

Even the explicit endorsements of 'subjective devaluation' in *Ministry of Defence v Ashman*[31]—followed in identical circumstances in *Ministry of Defence v Thompson*[32]—and *McDonald v Coys of Kensington*[33] do not provide strong

[25] *Cf* Mitchell, Mitchell and Watterson, *Goff & Jones The Law of Unjust Enrichment* (2011) (n 3) §4-07.

[26] *JS Bloor Ltd v Pavillion Developments Ltd* [2008] EWHC 724 (TCC) [47]–[49] (Kirkham J).

[27] *Boulton v Jones* (1857) 2 H&N 564, 157 ER 232.

[28] Virgo, *The Principles of the Law of Restitution* (2006) (n 3) 67.

[29] See below n 116 and accompanying text.

[30] *Cf* P Millett, *On Villainy* (Brisbane, University of Queensland Press, 2007) 108–09, who argues that the case should be understood as an instance of change of position.

[31] *Ministry of Defence v Ashman* (1993) 66 P&CR 195 (CA) 201 (Hoffmann LJ).

[32] *Ministry of Defence v Thompson* (1993) 25 HLR 552 (CA).

[33] *McDonald v Coys of Kensington* [2004] EWCA Civ 47, [2004] 1 WLR 2775 [28] (Mance LJ).

support for a subjective approach to enrichment.[34] First, in *Ashman*, the Ministry of Defence sought a market rate of £108.93 per month from Ashman for staying in married quarters after she had separated from her husband, a flight sergeant in the Royal Air Force. The couple had previously been entitled to a concessionary rate of £95.41. Hoffmann LJ held that Ashman should only pay the rate for alternative local authority housing because she could rely on 'subjective devaluation'.[35] Kennedy LJ also endorsed subjective devaluation, explicitly focussing on the 'value to Mrs Ashman of the use of the property'.[36] However, instead of an award reflecting the subjective value of the housing to Ashman, the majority awarded the reasonable objective value of alternative, low-cost housing that a person in Ashman's economic position might have chosen.

The decision of the majority is inconsistent with subjective devaluation. The court did not attempt to ascertain what the accommodation was subjectively worth to Ashman. It is perfectly possible that she may have subjectively valued the housing *above* the concessionary rate; she might have thought the concessionary rate a great deal, even though she was unable to afford more. For instance, although a student receives concessionary rates for college accommodation, he may personally value the accommodation at the market rate and decide to stay in residence at the market rate once he graduates. However, if he finds he cannot afford to remain in residence, the subjective value of the college accommodation to him is not the value of the low-cost housing he is able to afford. He subjectively values the college accommodation at the market rate, but chooses to live elsewhere for less. Ashman's economic situation, and the value of low-cost housing she may have chosen had the circumstances been different, is not a proxy for the value to her of the housing she actually received. It is a measure of what she could afford, not her subjective valuation of what she in fact received.

Nor is the result explicable on a choice of benefit approach. Hoffmann LJ focussed repeatedly on Ashman's lack of choice of the benefit, noting that 'the open market value will ordinarily be appropriate because the defendant has *chosen* to stay in the premises' and that 'Mrs. Ashman would certainly not have stayed in the premises at the market rate if she had any *choice* in the matter' (emphasis added).[37] While Hoffmann LJ's focus on the choice of benefit is consistent with authority, it is not consistent with the award. If, as the court held, Ashman was not in a position to accept or reject the housing, then she did not choose the benefit and she was not enriched. If Ashman did have a choice to accept or reject the

[34] Subjective devaluation was mentioned in obiter, but not applied, in the following additional cases: *McFarlane v Tayside Health Board* [2000] 2 AC 59 (HL) 112 (Lord Millett); *Kuwait Airways Corp v Iraqi Airways Co (No 6)* [2004] EWHC 2603 (Comm) [447] (Cresswell J); *Sempra Metals Ltd v IRC* [2007] UKHL 34, [2008] 1 AC 561 [119] (Lord Nicholls) [184], [187] (Lord Walker) [232]–[233] (Lord Mance); *Shi v Jiangsu Native Produce Import & Export Corp* [2010] EWCA Civ 1582 [21]–[26] (Dyson LJ).

[35] *Ministry of Defence v Ashman* (1993) 66 P&CR 195 (CA) 201 (Hoffmann LJ).

[36] Ibid 200 (Kennedy LJ).

[37] Ibid 201 (Hoffmann LJ). See Virgo, *The Principles of the Law of Restitution* (2006) (n 3) 68 where he notes that choice of the benefit is the rationale for the decision in *Ministry of Defence v Ashman*.

housing and chose to remain in possession, then she should have had to pay the market rate for the housing in question, not the market rate for entirely different housing. The approach in *Ashman* and *Thompson* is not an approach that has been followed in other cases and it is not supported in this book.

Second, *McDonald v Coys of Kensington* was a case that involved objective evidence that the defendant valued the benefit in question. Following the auction of a car at which McDonald was the highest bidder, Coys, the auctioneers, failed to retain the personalised registration mark TAC 1 in accordance with the seller's instructions. McDonald knew that he was not entitled to the mark. However, under the relevant statutory scheme, the right to register title in a mark passed to the purchaser if the seller failed to apply to retain the mark. Mance LJ's comments supporting subjective devaluation were entirely obiter.[38] It was clear on the evidence that McDonald had chosen the mark.[39] As is discussed in relation to the 'readily returnable' test in section III, the mark was readily returnable at any time and the defendant's refusal to return the mark evinced an objectively ascertainable choice of the benefit. This was not a case in which subjective devaluation played any role.

### *(iv) The Rejection of Subjective Devaluation in* Benedetti v Sawiris

The fate of the subjective devaluation thesis in English law appears to have been settled by the Court of Appeal decision in *Benedetti v Sawiris*, which concerned a claim for quantum meruit for brokerage services rendered by Benedetti to the defendants in a large acquisition. It was common ground that Benedetti was entitled to be remunerated on a quantum meruit basis. In valuing the benefit received by Sawiris, Patten J at first instance rightly took the view that 'The valuation has to be carried out as at the date when the services were rendered and should, as a general rule, approximate to market value'.[40] However, Patten J then went on to rely on the valuation Sawiris placed on Benedetti's services in settlement negotiations (€75.1 million) in preference to the 'market value' of the services assessed by the industry standard commission of 0.3 per cent of the transaction value (€36.3 million).[41] Patten J held that post-contractual evidence of the value Sawiris placed on Benedetti's work was admissible 'if and so far as that evidence does show the value which the paying party (albeit with the benefit of hindsight) considered that the services were actually worth'.[42] Although this may be interpreted as an attempt to rely on post-contractual evidence to ascertain the market value of the services at the time they were provided, the €75.1 million figure was, at best, an attempt by Sawiris to value Benedetti's services 'with the benefit of hindsight' after the successful conclusion of the transaction.[43]

[38] *McDonald v Coys of Kensington* [2004] EWCA Civ 47, [2004] 1 WLR 2775 [28] (Mance LJ).

[39] Ibid [38]–[40] (Mance LJ).

[40] *Benedetti v Sawiris* [2009] EWHC 1330 (Ch) [528] (Patten J).

[41] Ibid [567]–[571] (Patten J).

[42] Ibid [568] (Patten J).

[43] For a critical view of the first instance judgment see Lodder, 'Unjust Enrichment and the Assessment of Quantum Meruit Awards' (2010) (n 3).

In overturning the decision of Patten J on the question of valuation, both Arden[44] and Etherton[45] LJJ rejected subjective devaluation and Rimer LJ[46] agreed with both judgments on this point. The clearest rejection of the subjective devaluation thesis is in the judgment of Etherton LJ, who held that Sawiris's 'gain is to be measured objectively, that is to say, what a reasonable person would pay for the benefit in question', citing *BP (Exploration) v Hunt* and *Sempra Metals* in support of this conclusion. His Lordship was unequivocal in his view that the idiosyncratic valuation to the defendant is irrelevant:[47]

> While the application of the principle of subjective devaluation involves taking into account the actual characteristics of the defendant and circumstances to show that the actual benefit in a particular case is less than the ordinary market value ... what is relevant is not the degree of personal emotional joy or misery of the defendant for what the claimant has done, or the defendant's generous or parsimonious personality. What is relevant is the existence of conditions increasing or decreasing the objective value of the benefit to any reasonable person in the same (unusual) position as the defendant.

Hence, Etherton LJ's judgment rejects idiosyncratic valuation and rightly holds that the subjective preferences and priorities of the individual defendant are irrelevant to the valuation of the defendant's enrichment. On the approach adopted by Etherton LJ, the factual enrichment is, as advocated in this book, the 'objective value' of the benefit to a reasonable person in the position of the defendant.

Although Arden LJ's judgment is less robust in its rejection of subjective valuation, Arden LJ found that 'Mr Sawiris' perception as to a higher value of Mr Benedetti's services casts little, if any, light on the *objective* value of Mr Benedetti's services' (emphasis added)[48] and that there was no reason to depart from such objective valuation on the facts. However, in an admittedly difficult passage, Arden LJ's judgment appears to reject subjective devaluation in all cases:[49]

> I would accept that in some circumstances it is appropriate to take the value of the benefit to the particular defendant. But it would not be appropriate to do so in all circumstances. For example, it would not be appropriate to do so where the value to the defendant was less than market value. But the value to Mr Sawiris was clearly higher than market value: should the judge have taken the offer of €75.1m into account?

If it is never appropriate 'to take the value of the benefit to the particular defendant ... where the value to the defendant [is] less than market value', that leaves only the situation where the value to the defendant is greater than market value. It appears that Arden LJ is rejecting subjective *devaluation* but accepting the possibility that subjective *revaluation* may be appropriate 'in some circumstances'.

44 *Benedetti v Sawiris* [2010] EWCA Civ 1427 [84], [101] (Arden LJ).
45 Ibid [140]–[145] (Etherton LJ).
46 Ibid [172] (Rimer LJ).
47 Ibid [145] (Etherton LJ).
48 Ibid [101] (Arden LJ).
49 Ibid [84] (Arden LJ).

While Arden LJ was, like Etherton LJ, quite right to reject subjective devaluation, it is unfortunate that Arden LJ entertained the possibility of subjective revaluation in certain cases. On the argument advanced in this chapter, subjective valuations, whether higher or lower, are irrelevant, and for the reasons outlined in chapter seven, subjective revaluation has no place in English law.[50]

While both Etherton LJ and Arden LJ employ the language of 'subjective devaluation' to describe the objective valuation of a benefit to a reasonable person in the position of the defendant, this language should be eschewed for the reasons articulated in this chapter. Once it is understood that the defendant's freedom of choice is protected by requiring a choice of the benefit by the defendant, it is clear that so-called 'subjective devaluation' is neither subjective, nor about value. The choice of benefit language adopted in this book more accurately describes the process of valuation undertaken by the Court of Appeal in *Benedetti v Sawiris.*

## C. Subjective Devaluation and Relational Value

Subjective devaluation is a concept that, if taken literally, relies on an idiosyncratic conception of value. Burrows's approach relies explicitly on the 'individuality of value'[51] and Virgo contends that 'if the defendant does not value the enrichment as much as the reasonable person would, this should be taken into account when valuing the benefit'.[52] A robustly idiosyncratic approach to value is favoured by the editors of Goff & Jones, who say that courts may 'assess the value of the benefit by reference to the defendant's personal value system rather than the market'.[53] Thus, subjective devaluation suggests that the defendant's own valuation of the benefit received is relevant to the award of monetary restitution. In this strong form, subjective devaluation is incompatible with a relational theory of value. Value, conceived relationally, is an abstraction from the particular individual and particular thing being valued to a quantitatively comparable standard for exchange. Weinrib explains the point in this way:[54]

> [B]ecause value abstracts from the parties' particularity, neither value nor its transfer is determined subjectively. Whether a person … received … value is an objective question, the answer to which is systematically determined by exchanges within a competitive market. Value, therefore, cannot be subjectively devalued.

As explained in chapter two, Weinrib fails to account for objective valuation methods other than exchange in a competitive market, but his broader point is correct.

[50] See ch 7, fns 77–78 and accompanying text.

[51] A Burrows, *The Law of Restitution*, 3rd edn (Oxford, Oxford University Press, 2010) 47.

[52] Virgo, *The Principles of the Law of Restitution* (2006) (n 3) 98.

[53] Mitchell, Mitchell and Watterson, *Goff & Jones The Law of Unjust Enrichment* (2011) (n 3) §4-06.

[54] E Weinrib, 'Correctively Unjust Enrichment' in R Chambers, C Mitchell and J Penner (eds), *Philosophical Foundations of the Law of Unjust Enrichment* (Oxford, Oxford University Press, 2009) 38.

Subjective devaluation is simply incompatible with the concept of relational value because value, understood relationally, is the result of aggregated subjective value judgments about all things of value that can be exchanged for anything else of value. If an individual either holds or expresses her own idiosyncratic valuation of a good or service ('I would only pay £5 for that'), she is using 'value' in a way that is inconsistent with the law's adoption of relational value.

However, it may rightly be objected that this is not what the leading theories of subjective devaluation propound, despite the awkward use of both 'subjective' and 'devaluation'. What Birks, Burrows and Virgo appear to mean by 'subjective devaluation' is really an objective valuation to a reasonable person in the defendant's position with the defendant's characteristics, preferences and priorities. For example, subjective devaluation theories accept that the defendant's idiosyncratic valuation can be overcome by the incontrovertible benefit test.[55] So, in the most recent edition of *The Law of Restitution*, Burrows clarifies that by 'subjective devaluation' he means an 'objective [test] but qualified by some subjectivity depending on the characteristics of the defendant'.[56] In this weaker form, subjective devaluation is not concerned with the unexpressed state of mind of the defendant and some idiosyncratic valuation that the defendant has not manifested outwardly, but rather discerning the parties' subjective intentions as objectively manifested.[57] Subjective devaluation is then the application of a highly stylised reasonable person test that takes into account almost all of the characteristics of the defendant. This is why, even in the seminal case for subjective devaluation theories, Ashman's personal valuation of the married quarters in *Ministry of Defence v Ashman* was irrelevant. Hoffmann and Kennedy LJJ instead settled upon an objectively reasonable value for alternative housing for a person in Ashman's economic position and circumstances.[58]

Nevertheless, even the weaker form of subjective devaluation is inconsistent with a relational concept of value. Value, understood relationally, is an *objective* standard for the comparison and exchange of qualitatively different things in quantitatively comparable terms; it abstracts from the subjective preferences and priorities of individual defendants. While Birks, Burrows and Virgo are not committed to the strong form of subjective devaluation that would allow a defendant to plead his or her un-manifested idiosyncratic value of a good or service, the objective value to a reasonable person in the defendant's position with all the defendant's characteristics, preferences and priorities is simply a proxy for the idiosyncratic value of a person a lot like the defendant.

Moreover, if there were uncontroverted objective evidence that the defendant honestly and reasonably regarded the good or service to be worth a particular amount and had expressed this view to reliable witnesses before the litigation,

[55] Eg Virgo, *The Principles of the Law of Restitution* (2006) (n 3) 98; Burrows, *The Law of Restitution* (2010) (n 51) 47–51.

[56] Burrows, *The Law of Restitution* (2010) (n 51) 44 fn 6.

[57] See ibid 44 fn 6; Mitchell, Mitchell and Watterson, *Goff & Jones The Law of Unjust Enrichment* (2011) (n 3) §4-09.

[58] *Ministry of Defence v Ashman* (1993) 66 P&CR 195 (CA).

unless that idiosyncratic valuation could not be held by a reasonable person in the defendant's position, Birks, Burrows and Virgo seem to be committed to allowing the defendant to devalue the good or service to that extent. This is idiosyncratic valuation, albeit within certain limits of reasonableness and admissibility. Any objective reasonable person test that incorporates the particular preferences, priorities and valuations of the individual defendant only pretends to be relational. The law of unjust enrichment is committed to relational value; the question is the appropriate method of valuation taking account of the market for the good or service, not when to permit an idiosyncratic valuation to trump a market valuation.

That the defendant's subjective valuation should properly be irrelevant can be illustrated by the possible subjective valuations where the claimant has sold a car that the defendant has agreed to pay for under a void contract. Assuming that the car has a competitive market and the contract price is evidence of the defendant's idiosyncratic valuation, there are four possibilities for idiosyncratic and relational value to diverge: first, D may have contracted *knowingly* at a price *above* the market value; second, D may have contracted *unknowingly* at a price *above* the market value; third, D may have contracted *knowingly* at a price *below* the market value and, fourth, D may have contracted *unknowingly* at a price *below* the market value.

In the first situation, D knows the contract price, £6,000, to be higher than the market price, £5,000. The higher idiosyncratic value represents his 'consumer surplus': the subjective utility to D above the market value.[59] D may pay more for a variety of reasons, but where the contract is void and C seeks restitution on a quantum valebat basis, D's higher subjective valuation does not change the value D received. D could not exchange the car for £6,000 just because he subjectively valued it more highly than the market; he is not 'more enriched' than an identical defendant who subjectively values it at the market rate. On a quantum valebat, the court would award what the car is actually worth.

The second situation is the converse of the first: D may unknowingly have contracted above market (£6,000), in which case he incorrectly believed the car to be worth more than the market price (£5,000). Holding D to his idiosyncratic valuation in assessing a quantum valebat is to hold him to a mistaken valuation. Outside of a binding contract, it makes no sense to make a restitutionary award at the higher amount simply because D mistakenly overvalued the benefit. The contract price necessarily provides poor evidence of the market value where the defendant mistakenly overvalues the car. The law of unjust enrichment should not hold defendants to mistaken valuations.

Third, D may have contracted at £4,000, knowing that figure to be less than the market value of £5,000. This is a no doubt common situation, and occurred

[59] See J Edelman, 'The Meaning of Loss and Enrichment' in R Chambers, C Mitchell and J Penner (eds), *Philosophical Foundations of the Law of Unjust Enrichment* (Oxford, Oxford University Press, 2009) 221–23.

in *Ministry of Defence v Ashman*[60] and *Ministry of Defence v Thompson*.[61] The claimant may not realise he can charge more or he may have agreed to contract below market for a variety of reasons, such as gaining market share, building an ongoing relationship with the defendant or reducing inventory for internal business reasons. Although D's idiosyncratic valuation is lower than the market value, it only makes sense to award the lower agreed price in contract. Where the contract is void, D's idiosyncratic value can no more alter the value of the benefit transferred than the converse situation where D's idiosyncratic valuation is higher than the market.

Finally, the same situation must obtain where D unknowingly agreed to pay less (£4,000) than the market value (£5,000). If a defendant who incorrectly over-values the good or service is not bound to pay the higher idiosyncratic valuation in assessing a quantum valebat, then a defendant who mistakenly undervalues the good cannot logically be entitled to rely on that lower idiosyncratic valuation. In all four situations, the idiosyncratic valuation is properly irrelevant. Outside of a binding contract, it only makes sense to view the value transferred in relational terms; the alternative is to commit to idiosyncratic valuations, whether they are too high or too low, intentional or mistaken, and this is not the law.

## D. Subjective Devaluation and Freedom of Choice

Freedom of choice plays a distinctly different role in contractual obligation from the obligation to make restitution for unjust enrichment. The institution of contract provides for and protects the practice of undertaking voluntary obligations.[62] A distinguishing feature of contractual obligation is the role of voluntariness in incurring the obligations.[63] For this reason, freedom of choice is strongly protected in contract, which permits the parties free reign to determine and shape the content of most (although not all) contractual obligations. By contrast, freedom of choice plays no *necessary* role in incurring an obligation to make restitution in unjust enrichment. For example, in *Kelly v Solari*,[64] Solari's obligation to make restitution arose because the insurance company paid her by mistake, not because she voluntarily incurred the obligation. Rather than justifying the imposition of the primary obligation in the first place, the defendant's free choice is a reason why Solari could object to the obligation to make restitution. The obligation to make restitution for unjust enrichment is underpinned by corrective justice, not the fact that in some sense the obligation is voluntarily incurred. Freedom of choice is thus only relevant to a restitutionary obligation

[60] *Ministry of Defence v Ashman* (1993) 66 P&CR 195 (CA).

[61] *Ministry of Defence v Thompson* (1993) 25 HLR 552 (CA).

[62] See discussion in J Raz, 'Promises in Morality and Law' (1982) 95 *Harvard Law Review* 916; Sheinman, 'Contractual Liability and Voluntary Undertaking' (2000) 20 *OJLS* 205; D Kimel, *From Promise to Contract: Towards a Liberal Theory of Contract* (Oxford, Hart, 2003).

[63] Raz, 'Promises in Morality and Law' (1982) (n 62).

[64] *Kelly v Solari* (1841) 9 M&W 54, 152 ER 24.

because the defendant can object to the obligation to make restitution where her freedom of choice is infringed. Consequently, restitutionary obligations are not voluntarily determined and shaped by the parties: the objective of restitution is not to (re)make a contract for the parties at the price and on the terms that they might have agreed for the benefit conferred.[65]

Of course, subjective devaluation theories do not suggest that protection of the defendant's freedom of choice entails that restitutionary obligations are voluntarily determined by the parties. However, subjective devaluation theories claim a role for freedom of choice in determining the content of the obligation to make restitution. Although restitution is not awarded on all the terms and conditions that the defendant would voluntarily have agreed, these theories hold that restitution is restricted to the price the defendant would have paid for the benefit. If subjective devaluation is the law, why is the price the only aspect of the obligation determined by the free choice of the defendant? Why, for example, is it not relevant that the defendant would only have paid for the benefit in instalments or by a particular date? Subjective devaluation theory depends on the assertion that price is special and that the protection of the defendant's freedom of choice requires the obligation to make restitution be limited to the defendant's subjective valuation of the benefit received. As will be shown below, the defendant's freedom of choice can be adequately protected without resorting to subjective valuation by a requirement that the defendant's choice freely manifest an assumption of responsibility to pay for the benefit. It is not necessary for the protection of the defendant's freedom of choice that the obligation to make restitution in money be limited to subjective valuation of the benefit.

Choice of benefit theories hold that defendants can reasonably be held to the market value of benefits they have chosen, subject to defences. If the underlying principle is respect for the defendant's autonomy, then it is acceptable to hold the defendant responsible for choices autonomously made. As McInnes explains, the question is 'not the defendant's personal *valuation* of a benefit, but rather this personal *choice* to accept financial responsibility for it'.[66] On McInnes's approach, the 'second limb' of the unjust enrichment inquiry requires the claimant to establish either that the defendant 'chose to assume financial responsibility for his benefit, or had no choice to make given the very nature of that gain'.[67] On the choice of benefit approach, the enrichment inquiry is explicitly premised upon freedom of choice, rather than subjective valuation.

As a matter of principle, this must be right. The obligation to make restitution of an enrichment does not arise because of the defendant's freedom of choice; rather, the defendant can object to the obligation to make restitution if his freedom

[65] See *Benedetti v Sawiris* [2010] EWCA Civ 1427 [54] (Arden LJ).

[66] M McInnes, 'Enrichment Revisited' in J Neyers, M McInnes and S Pitel (eds), *Understanding Unjust Enrichment* (Oxford, Hart, 2004) 175 fn 44. See also J Edelman and E Bant, *Unjust Enrichment in Australia* (Oxford, Oxford University Press, 2006) 107–08.

[67] McInnes, 'Enrichment Revisited' (2004) (n 66) 207.

of choice is not respected. However, a defendant who voluntarily assumes the responsibility to pay for a benefit cannot make this objection. If the defendant's choice of a benefit constitutes an assumption of responsibility to pay for that benefit, the defendant cannot refuse to pay market value on the basis that her subjective valuation differs from the market valuation. If the defendant did not conclude a valid contract to pay less but accepted the benefit in circumstances in which she objectively assumed financial responsibility to pay for the benefit, there is a sufficient normative basis for imposing liability to pay market value, subject to defences. For example, if a defendant requests services knowing that they are to be paid for but does not agree on, or even contemplate, a particular price, then the defendant has assumed responsibility to pay for those services through her request for performance, even if no contract arises. If the defendant intended to pay a different price or subjectively anticipated certain conditions upon that payment, then the defendant should have contracted to that effect.

It is not the purpose of the law of unjust enrichment to make the 'next best' contract for the parties when they have failed to conclude a valid contract. As Arden LJ held in *Benedetti v Sawiris*, 'The court is specifically not concerned to ascertain what kind of agreement the parties would have come to'.[68] This is clear from the fact that restitution for unjust enrichment ignores the other terms and conditions of the contract the parties would have concluded. For example, if the parties' contract is void or unenforceable and the claimant seeks restitution on a quantum meruit for his performance, the various terms and conditions of the contract do not govern the award of restitution. As is explained below in section III, the price is merely evidence of the market value and there is no suggestion that the other terms of the contract affect the restitutionary remedy. The contract price is not special. Analogously, the resulting trust arising on failure of an express trust, which is examined in chapter five, does not incorporate the terms and conditions of the intended express trust. For example, the trustee of the resulting trust has no obligation to invest the trust property, even if the express trust included such an obligation. The obligation to make restitution arises independently due to the defendant's unjust enrichment; it is not a surrogate for the contract that the parties (would have) reached at the price the parties (would have) agreed and subject to the conditions that the parties (would have) incorporated. The difficulty comes in identifying what constitutes a sufficient expression of choice and what circumstances will vitiate that choice. This is considered in detail in section II, which outlines the requirements for proof of choice of the benefit.

### *Conclusion*

The concept of 'subjective devaluation' was a misstep in the original model of unjust enrichment presented in Birks's *An Introduction to the Law of Restitution*. Since Birks enunciated the principle, only *Ministry of Defence v Ashman* and

[68] *Benedetti v Sawiris* [2010] EWCA Civ 1427 [54] (Arden LJ).

*Ministry of Defence v Thompson*, both wrongs cases, provide any ratio decidendi in support of an approach grounded in subjective valuation, and even these cases did not attempt to measure restitution by the defendant's subjective valuation of the RAF housing. By contrast, the Court of Appeal decision in *Benedetti v Sawiris* rejected the relevance of the defendant's subjective valuation of the benefit in the enrichment inquiry and, in so doing, rejected the subjective devaluation thesis. As will be shown in sections II and III, the case law can be better explained in terms of an objectively ascertained choice to accept or reject the benefit.

## II. Proof of Choice of Benefit

As detailed in section I, the substance behind the request requirement in the old forms of action was not subjective devaluation, but the choice of the benefit by the defendant. This is reflected in the protection of the defendant's freedom of choice in the modern law of unjust enrichment. The individual has a right to choose how to dispose of his resources that is violated by requiring a defendant to pay for a benefit that is conferred on him without his choice.[69] However, as a result of misunderstanding freedom of choice to require 'subjective devaluation', the content of a valid 'choice' and the application of the choice of benefit test in different contexts has been under-examined. This section attempts to remedy this lacuna by detailing an objective choice of the benefit theory that is consistent with the cases and ensures the protection of the defendant's freedom of choice.

### A. Choice of the Benefit

What does it mean to say that a defendant has 'chosen' the benefit? In *Brenner v First Artists' Management*, Byrne J held that an obligation to pay restitution arises where:[70]

> [T]he recipient of the services, as a reasonable person, should have realised that a person in the position of the provider of the services would expect to be paid for them and did not take a reasonable opportunity to reject those services.

Although Byrne J was discussing free acceptance, which is examined below, this statement correctly encapsulates the two elements of a valid 'choice': (i) the defendant must have a choice to accept or reject the benefit and objectively manifest acceptance of the benefit; and (ii) the choice must be made in circumstances that constitute an assumption of responsibility to pay for the benefit. Factual enrichment requires that there be a genuine choice of the benefit accepting the financial consequences of that choice.

[69] See above n 18.
[70] *Brenner v First Artists' Management Pty Ltd* [1993] 2 VR 221 (VSC) 260 (Byrne J).

### (i) Acceptance of the Benefit

Regarding the first element, the case law typically expresses the question in terms of whether the defendant could 'accept or reject' the benefit in question.[71] In *Sumpter v Hedges*,[72] the defendant had the choice to accept or reject the building materials and tools, but no choice to accept or reject the unfinished house on his land. Collins LJ held that a quantum meruit for the building services should be refused because 'the circumstances must be such as to give an option to the defendant to take or not to take the benefit of the work done'.[73] Similarly, in *JS Bloor v Pavillion Developments* it was dispositive that the defendant 'had no real alternative but to accept' and 'could not in reality reject the road',[74] while in *Benedetti v Sawiris* the investors 'were unable to refuse' Benedetti's services and had not 'had an opportunity to reject the benefit'.[75] The same position was adopted by the House of Lords in *Miles v Wakefield MDC*,[76] where Lord Templeman and Lord Brightman explicitly based liability on the choice to 'accept' or 'reject' the non-conforming work. Unlike the language of subjective devaluation, the explicit language of 'choice' and 'acceptance' is prevalent throughout the case law, even long after the rejection of quasi-contractual theories of liability that premised liability on the inference of a new contract. Rather than relying on subjective valuation to protect the defendant's freedom of choice, the law has repeatedly and explicitly applied a choice or acceptance-based test.

Taking a similarly objective approach to the question, Edelman suggests that the test is whether the defendant 'desired' the benefit.[77] However, this is not the language adopted by the judges and it leads to results that are not supported by the cases. For example, where the claimant mistakenly builds an addition to the defendant's house while the defendant is away, provided the defendant is not incontrovertibly enriched by the work (for example, the defendant has not realised the work in money by selling the property) and none of the other tests of choice of the benefit is met, the defendant is not enriched. The defendant may return home and be delighted by the addition to her house and proclaim to the claimant that it is precisely the improvement that she always wanted and desired. Nonetheless, the defendant has no choice to accept or reject the benefit and the cases are unequivocal: unless the benefit is incontrovertible, the defendant must

[71] Eg *Taylor v Laird* (1856) 25 LJ Ex 329 (Ex); *Sumpter v Hedges* [1898] 1 QB 673 (CA); *Forman Co Pty Ltd v The Liddesdale* [1900] AC 190 (PC); *Miles v Wakefield MDC* [1987] AC 539 (HL); *Bookmakers' Afternoon Greyhound Services Ltd v Gilbert* [1994] FSR 723 (Ch); *JS Bloor Ltd v Pavillion Developments Ltd* [2008] EWHC 724 (TCC).

[72] *Sumpter v Hedges* [1898] 1 QB 673 (CA).

[73] Ibid 676 (Collins LJ). See also *Munro v Butt* (1858) 7 E&B 739, 753; 120 ER 275, 281 (Lord Campbell CJ); *Leigh v Dickeson* (1884) 15 QBD 60 (CA) 64 (Brett MR); *Oliver v Lakeside Property Trust Pty Ltd* [2005] NSWSC 1040 [88].

[74] *JS Bloor Ltd v Pavillion Developments Ltd* [2008] EWHC 724 (TCC) [47]–[49] (Kirkham J).

[75] *Benedetti v Sawiris* [2010] EWCA Civ 1427 [115], [118] (Arden LJ).

[76] *Miles v Wakefield MDC* [1987] AC 539 (HL) 552–53 (Lord Brightman) 561 (Lord Templeman).

[77] Edelman, 'The Meaning of Loss and Enrichment' (2009) (n 59). See also Edelman and Bant, *Unjust Enrichment in Australia* (2006) (n 66) 108.

have the opportunity to accept or reject the benefit. By contrast, on Edelman's approach, objective proof that the defendant desired the benefit (for instance, evidence that she had contacted builders and made plans for an identical addition before going away on holiday) would suffice to establish enrichment, which is inconsistent with the explicit approach in cases such as *JS Bloor v Pavillion Developments*,[78] where it was clear Pavillion 'desired' the road.

### *(ii) Assumption of Responsibility*

The second element for establishing a 'choice' is that the acceptance of the benefit by the defendant must objectively manifest an assumption of responsibility to pay for it. English law protects defendants who choose a benefit where the objective circumstances involve no acceptance by the defendant of an obligation to pay. The law requires the choice to be, in this sense, a 'real' one. In *Brenner v First Artists' Management*, Byrne J identifies the underlying principle as being 'the expectation of the parties that the work would be paid for';[79] in *Mohamed v Alaga & Co*, Lord Bingham accepted the claimant could recover on a quantum meruit where 'the surrounding circumstances [were] such as to show that such services were not rendered gratuitously'.[80] For instance, the requirement for the choice of the benefit to manifest a responsibility to pay was determinative in *Gilbert v Knight*.[81] The defendant requested and received surveying services in circumstances where it was objectively reasonable to understand that those services were provided for by a £30 fee for 'possible extras' contained in the contract between the parties. The claimant did not say anything about a fee until after the work was finished and Davies LJ held that, for the quantum meruit to succeed, there must be an 'implication that the person liable is agreeing to pay'.[82]

Thus, the assumption of responsibility requirement is usually, but not always, satisfied where the defendant accepts the benefit in circumstances that show it is non-gratuitously given. However, there is some controversy as to the relevant test: must the defendant subjectively accept that the benefit is not offered gratuitously or is it enough that a reasonable person would understand that the benefit is not gratuitous? In *Brenner*, Byrne J suggested that the test was whether the defendant 'as a reasonable person, should have realised that a person in the position of the [claimant] would expect to be paid for them'.[83] This is consistent with the objective test applied by Lord Bingham in *Mohamed v Alaga*,[84] and the objective approach to enrichment favoured in this book. It provides adequate protection for the defendant's freedom of choice because reasonable defendants will not be required

[78] *JS Bloor Ltd v Pavillion Developments Ltd* [2008] EWHC 724 (TCC).
[79] *Brenner v First Artists' Management Pty Ltd* [1993] 2 VR 221 (VSC) 258 (Byrne J).
[80] *Mohamed v Alaga & Co* [2000] 1 WLR 1815 (CA) 1825 (Lord Bingham).
[81] *Gilbert v Knight* [1968] 2 All ER 248 (CA).
[82] Ibid 251 (Davies LJ).
[83] *Brenner v First Artists' Management Pty Ltd* [1993] 2 VR 221 (VSC) 260 (Byrne J). See also *Angelopoulos v Sabatino* [1995] 65 SASR 1 (SASC).
[84] *Mohamed v Alaga & Co* [2000] 1 WLR 1815 (CA) 1825 (Lord Bingham).

to pay. As with the defence of change of position, the unreasonable defendant is not protected from financial responsibility for their choices and actions.

A defendant who accepts a benefit will not have assumed responsibility to pay for that benefit in two common situations. First, acceptance is not enough to establish enrichment if the objective surrounding circumstances show that the defendant reasonably understood he would not have to pay for the benefit.[85] This principle is illustrated by *Rowe v Vale of White Horse*.[86] The defendant could have accepted or rejected the proffered sewerage services and chose to accept them, but the circumstances were such that the defendant reasonably believed the sewerage services to be offered free of charge. Rather, the defendant's enrichment in *Rowe* was conceded because it was incontrovertibly enriching: the defendant was saved a necessary expense. A similar issue arose in *Boulton v Jones*,[87] where Jones undoubtedly chose and valued the pipe he ordered, but reasonably believed he had obtained it from Brocklehurst against whom he held a right of set-off, rather than the claimant, Boulton. Although Boulton clearly did not offer the pipe gratuitously, Jones had not been informed that the vendor had changed and he reasonably believed he could exercise a right of set-off. Thus, he did not accept financial responsibility to pay for the benefit. Likewise, if the objective circumstances show that the claimant and the defendant understood a third party would alone be liable to pay, then the choice of the benefit does not give rise to liability on the part of the defendant.[88]

However, *Upton-on-Severn RDC v Powell*[89] runs contrary to this line of authority. In response to a call from the defendant requesting a fire brigade, the claimant council sent its fire brigade to put out a fire on the defendant's farm. Although all the parties were under the mistaken impression that the farm was in the Upton fire district, it was actually in the Pershore fire district. The defendant was entitled to the services of the Pershore brigade free of charge, but the Upton brigade could contract out its services outside of the district. Upton claimed a quantum meruit for the reasonable value of the fire services and succeeded, even though the objective evidence was that all the parties reasonably believed the claimant was providing the services free of charge. The result can only be justified if the references to an 'implied contract' between the parties in *Upton-on-Severn v Powell* are read to mean that the request led to the formation of a genuine contract between the parties to pay a reasonable fee. Indeed, Lord Green MR seems to have taken the 'implied contract' reasoning to mean that there was a 'contractual relationship' because 'the appellant wanted the services of Upton; he

[85] *Gilbert v Knight* [1968] 2 All ER 248 (CA); *Rowe v Vale of White Horse DC* [2003] EWHC 388 (Admin), [2003] 1 Lloyd's Rep 418.

[86] *Rowe v Vale of White Horse DC* [2003] EWHC 388 (Admin), [2003] 1 Lloyd's Rep 418.

[87] *Boulton v Jones* (1857) 2 H&N 564, 157 ER 232.

[88] *Bridgewater v Griffiths* [2000] 1 WLR 524 (QB) 532. See also *Rowe v Vale of White Horse DC* [2003] EWHC 388 (Admin), [2003] 1 Lloyd's Rep 418 [14] (Lightman J); *Benedetti v Sawiris* [2010] EWCA Civ 1427 [112] (Arden LJ).

[89] *Upton-on-Severn RDC v Powell* [1942] 1 All ER 220 (CA).

asked for the services of Upton—that is the request that he made—and Upton, in response to that request, provided those services'.[90] Nonetheless, the existence of a contract is highly unlikely on the facts given that both parties did not think there was any obligation to pay until after the work was done. As such, *Upton-on-Severn RDC v Powell* cannot be reconciled with the other authorities on point and should be considered wrongly decided.

The second common situation where there will be no assumption of responsibility to pay is where the claimant offers the benefit in circumstances that objectively involve no condition of payment,[91] such as a busker hoping to be paid for street performances. Even if the defendant understands that the benefit is offered with the hope of payment, the choice of the benefit, for example by listening to the busker's performance, will not amount to an assumption of the responsibility to pay. For the same reason, if the defendant makes it clear to the claimant that he is not willing to pay for the goods or services and the claimant provides them anyway, the circumstances will not objectively involve an acceptance by the defendant of responsibility to pay for the benefit.[92] This occurred in *Bookmakers' Afternoon Greyhound Services Ltd v Gilbert*.[93] The claimants provided material incorporated in racing commentaries displayed by the defendant in its shops. The claimants made it clear that they wished to be paid for this information, but the defendant was equally clear that it did not intend to pay. The claimants continued to provide the information despite the defendant's clear unwillingness to pay and, accordingly, Aldous J held that the defendant was not liable. Even though the claimants clearly expected to be paid, there was no assumption of responsibility to pay for the benefits by the defendant. The same principle was applied by the majority in *Chief Constable of Greater Manchester Police v Wigan Athletic FC*,[94] where additional policing was provided over Wigan's steadfast objections and the police, aware of Wigan's objections, performed in the knowledge that Wigan did not accept responsibility to pay for the extra police provided.

This principle will also cover the situation where the defendant reprehensibly seeks out a benefit for which he has no intention of paying. McGhee criticises the choice of benefit test on the basis that it does not adequately explain liability in circumstances where the defendant's reprehensible conduct is the basis for a

[90] Ibid 221 (Lord Greene MR). See J Beatson, *The Use and Abuse of Unjust Enrichment* (Oxford, Clarendon Press, 1991) 37 fn 83.

[91] Eg *Whittle Movers Ltd v Hollywood Express Ltd* [2009] EWCA Civ 1189 [22] (Waller LJ); *MSM Consulting Ltd v Tanzania* [2009] EWHC 121 (QB). Although this is often expressed in terms of risk-taking, it is better understood as a question of the conditionality of the transfer, see F Wilmot-Smith, 'Replacing Risk Taking Reasoning' (2011) 27 *LQR* 61.

[92] *Brenner v First Artists' Management Pty Ltd* [1993] 2 VR 221 (VSC) 259 (Byrne J); *Bookmakers' Afternoon Greyhound Services Ltd v Gilbert* [1994] FSR 723 (Ch); *Chief Constable of Greater Manchester Police v Wigan Athletic FC* [2008] EWCA Civ 1449, [2009] 1 WLR 1580 [47]–[50] (Sir Andrew Morritt C). See also *Rowe v Vale of White Horse DC* [2003] EWHC 388 (Admin), [2003] 1 Lloyd's Rep 418 [14] (Lightman J).

[93] *Bookmakers' Afternoon Greyhound Services Ltd v Gilbert* [1994] FSR 723 (Ch).

[94] *Chief Constable of Greater Manchester Police v Wigan Athletic FC* [2008] EWCA Civ 1449, [2009] 1 WLR 1580.

finding of enrichment.[95] In his view, such defendants have 'no intention of assuming financial responsibility for the benefit' and therefore do not satisfy the second element of an effective choice of the benefit. However, McGhee's criticism wrongly assumes a subjective approach to the determination of choice. The view taken in this book is that, applying Lord Bingham's test in *Mohamed v Alaga*, an assumption of responsibility will exist where 'the surrounding circumstances [were] such as to show that such services were not rendered gratuitously'.[96] Where, for example, a benefit is procured by the defendant exercising duress over the claimant, the defendant has chosen the benefit but, on any reasonable objective test, the claimant did not offer the benefit gratuitously. Irrespective of the defendant's subjective intention to take the benefit without paying for it, the choice of the benefit coupled with objective evidence that the benefit was not offered gratuitously is sufficient to amount to a choice of the benefit accepting the financial consequences of that choice. Consequently, if an objective choice of benefit test is applied, there is no need to explain these cases by way of an estoppel or a bar that prevents the defendant from denying that he chose the benefit on the basis of his conduct.[97]

### *(iii) Onus of Proof*

It is clear that the law of enrichment is sensitive to the defendant's freedom of choice. However, must the claimant prove that the defendant chose the benefit or is the onus on the defendant to show that he did not choose it? Although the question of onus is sometimes confused by subjective devaluation, the position seems to be that the defendant must adduce evidence showing that he did not choose the benefit.[98] If the defendant does not satisfy this evidential burden, proof of an objective transfer of value is sufficient to establish enrichment; if the defendant does raise evidence that he did not choose the benefit, the onus is on the claimant to prove the defendant's choice of the benefit on the balance of probabilities. This approach is consistent with treating the defendant's enrichment as an element of the cause of action that, ultimately, the claimant must prove.

This approach to the evidential burden and onus of proof explains the different outcomes in *Blue Haven v Tully*[99] and *JS Bloor v Pavillion Developments*,[100] both cases in which the defendant objectively received value from improvements to land carried out by the claimant. As discussed above, in *Blue Haven*, the defendant did not attempt to argue that he did not choose the work done by the claimant, whereas, in *Pavillion Developments*, the point was taken by the defendant. The

[95] McGhee, 'The Nature of the Enrichment Enquiry' (2009) (n 1) 83–84.

[96] *Mohamed v Alaga & Co* [2000] 1 WLR 1815 (CA) 1825 (Lord Bingham).

[97] *Cf* McInnes, 'Enrichment Revisited' (2004) (n 66) 177.

[98] This is one interpretation of the majority approach in *Sempra Metals Ltd v IRC* [2007] UKHL 34, [2008] 1 AC 561 [48] (Lord Hope) [116]–[117] (Lord Nicholls) [186] (Lord Walker). See Mitchell, Mitchell and Watterson, *Goff & Jones The Law of Unjust Enrichment* (2011) (n 3) §4-08.

[99] *Blue Haven Enterprises Ltd v Tully* [2006] UKPC 17.

[100] *JS Bloor Ltd v Pavillion Developments Ltd* [2008] EWHC 724 (TCC).

claimant, Bloor, attempted to argue that Pavillion had accepted the road by its conduct but was unable to discharge its onus to prove that the defendant had chosen the benefit. Accordingly, an objective benefit enriches the defendant unless the defendant argues that he did not choose the benefit, in which case the onus is on the claimant to establish that the defendant did choose it.

### *(iv) Tests for Choice*

The following sections consider a number of categories of case in which the defendant will be proved to have chosen the benefit, including: (i) where the defendant requests the benefit; (ii) where the benefit is readily returnable but the defendant refuses to return it; and (iii) where the defendant freely accepts the benefit. However, these categories do not exhaust the scenarios in which proof of choice by the defendant may be established. Rather, it is argued above that any objective evidence showing that, on the balance of probabilities, the defendant chose the benefit in circumstances in which she objectively assumed responsibility for payment will suffice. For example, in *Angelopoulos v Sabatino*,[101] the owner of a hotel licence bent over backwards to encourage prospective tenants to spend considerable amounts of money on the hotel in the near future. There was no explicit request for the work to be done by the prospective tenants, but there was sufficient evidence through the statements and conduct of the defendant to establish a choice of the benefit. It is clear from this approach that evidence proving choice of the benefit by the defendant is the essential requirement for enrichment and the three categories of case considered in the following sections are merely common situations in which enrichment will be established on this basis.

## B. Request

As noted previously,[102] English law historically required a request to show choice of the benefit by the defendant. The request was part of the forms of action upon a quantum meruit, quantum valebat, and money paid. In many circumstances, a request will lead to the formation of an oral contract,[103] but this is not always the case. For instance, the contract may be void,[104] unenforceable[105] or terminated for breach,[106] or there may have been performance in anticipation of a contract

[101] *Angelopoulos v Sabatino* [1995] 65 SASR 1 (SASC).

[102] Ch 6, s I.A.

[103] See Mitchell, Mitchell and Watterson, *Goff & Jones The Law of Unjust Enrichment* (2011) (n 3) §4-27.

[104] Eg *Craven-Ellis v Canons Ltd* [1936] 2 KB 403 (CA); *Rover International v Cannon Film Sales (No 3)* [1989] 1 WLR 912 (CA).

[105] Eg *Deglman v Guaranty Trust Co of Canada and Constantineau* [1954] SCR 725 (SCC); *Pavey & Matthews v Paul* (1987) 162 CLR 221 (HCA).

[106] Eg *Planché v Colburn* (1831) 5 C&P 58, 172 ER 876.

that was never concluded.[107] An example is *Brenner v First Artists' Management*,[108] which concerned claims for restitution by two managers for the value of services conferred on the singer, Daryl Braithwaite, as part of a campaign to revive his career. The services were provided under what the parties understood to be a contractual relationship, but no binding contract came into existence due to uncertainty in key aspects of the agreement. Although there was no contract, there was no doubt that the management services had been requested and that the managers 'would expect to be paid for them' and the defendant 'did not take a reasonable opportunity to reject those services'.[109] In these circumstances, the reason for a finding of enrichment is the request of the benefit by the defendant. Where that request objectively manifests an assumption of responsibility to pay for the benefit, as it did in Brenner, the defendant's enrichment will be established.

The operation of request as proof of the choice of the benefit was explained by Robert Goff J in *British Steel Corp v Cleveland Bridge and Engineering Co Ltd*.[110] The parties expected a contract to be concluded and, on that basis, the defendant requested the claimant commence production of the cast steel nodes to expedite performance 'pending the preparation and issuing to you of the official form of sub-contract'. Robert Goff J held that:[111]

> If thereafter, as anticipated, a contract was entered into, the work done as requested will be treated as having been performed under that contract; if, contrary to their expectation, no contract was entered into, then the performance of the work is not referable to any contract … and the law simply imposes an obligation on the party who made the request to pay a reasonable sum for such work as has been done pursuant to that request, such an obligation sounding in quasi contract or, as we now say, in restitution.

Importantly, the request is taken by Robert Goff J to show choice of the benefits provided, even if the party did not expect to pay for that work under the concluded contract. As such, the defendant may 'find himself liable to pay for work which he would not have had to pay for … if the anticipated contract had come into existence'.[112] According to Robert Goff J, this included preparatory work that would not otherwise have been separately recoverable under the anticipated contract, irrespective of whether the defendant valued the preparatory work separately from the full performance. This approach is clearly inconsistent with

[107] Eg *British Steel Corp v Cleveland Bridge and Engineering Co Ltd* [1984] 1 All ER 504 (QB).

[108] *Brenner v First Artists' Management Pty Ltd* [1993] 2 VR 221 (VSC). See also *Pavey & Matthews v Paul* (1987) 162 CLR 221 (HCA); *Vedatech Corp v Crystal Decisions (UK) Ltd* [2002] EWHC 818 (Ch); *Pacific National Investments Ltd v City of Victoria* [2004] SCC 75, [2004] 3 SCR 545 (SCC).

[109] *Brenner v First Artists' Management Pty Ltd* [1993] 2 VR 221 (VSC) 260 (Byrne J).

[110] *British Steel Corp v Cleveland Bridge and Engineering Co Ltd* [1984] 1 All ER 504 (QB). See also *William Lacey (Hounslow) Ltd v Davis* [1957] 1 WLR 932 (QB); *Pavey & Matthews v Paul* (1987) 162 CLR 221 (HCA); *ABB Power Generation v Chapple* [2001] WASCA 412, (2001) 25 WAR 158; *Vedatech Corp v Crystal Decisions (UK) Ltd* [2002] EWHC 818 (Ch); *Pacific National Investments Ltd v City of Victoria* [2004] SCC 75, [2004] 3 SCR 545 (SCC).

[111] *British Steel Corp v Cleveland Bridge and Engineering Co Ltd* [1984] 1 All ER 504 (QB) 511 (Robert Goff J).

[112] Ibid 511 (Robert Goff J).

subjective devaluation. Instead, the request is the exercise of a choice that assumes responsibility to pay for the work done pursuant to the request.

However, the obligation to make restitution for work that is requested is limited in scope by the request. This point is clear from the majority in *Chief Constable of Greater Manchester Police v Wigan Athletic FC*.[113] In that case, the issue was whether the defendant football club had requested 'special police services' under section 25 of the Police Act 1996 and thereby incurred an obligation to make restitution of the value of those services. In the 2003–04 and 2004–05 seasons, over Wigan's objections, higher levels of policing were provided at home games and the police claimed restitution of the value of the additional policing. The majority held that the police services provided had to 'match' the request and, since Wigan had objected to the additional policing, no request could be implied under section 25. The Chancellor, Sir Andrew Morritt, held that:[114]

> '[T]he request' must match the special police services supplied. The match need not be exact because it is for the Chief Constable to determine the level of policing required. So, if a person asks the police authority to provide special police services at a private event and the services are provided at the level the police authority considers to be necessary it is no answer … that the request had not specified the level of policing actually supplied. Conversely, if a promoter asks for onsite policing and the police authority concludes that only offsite policing is required it cannot, without more, charge the promoter for the offsite policing for which he did not ask.

Leaving to one side the question of the correctness of the majority's interpretation of the Police Act, *Wigan* demonstrates that the court will construe the request and ascertain the scope of the defendant's choice of the benefit. Only those benefits within the scope of the request enrich the defendant unless some other basis for enrichment, such as incontrovertible enrichment, is established.

Further, not every request objectively involves an assumption of responsibility to pay for the work.[115] As discussed, this was the case in *Boulton v Jones*,[116] where there was clearly a request of the pipe by the defendant. However, there was objective evidence that the defendant did not expect to pay for the benefit other than by way of set-off and the choice did not therefore manifest an assumption of responsibility to pay for the benefit. The defendant's entirely reasonable assumption as to the identity of the vendor and the existence of a right of set-off undermined any assumption of responsibility to pay for it. *Boulton v Jones* is analogous to a customer with store credit requesting an item in order to use up that credit before it expires, receiving and using the item, and then being told he must pay for it because the store had changed owners.

[113] *Chief Constable of Greater Manchester Police v Wigan Athletic FC* [2008] EWCA Civ 1449, [2009] 1 WLR 1580. See also *Ellis v Hamlen* (1810) 3 Taunt 52, 53; 128 ER 21, 23 (Mansfield CJ).

[114] *Chief Constable of Greater Manchester Police v Wigan Athletic FC* [2008] EWCA Civ 1449, [2009] 1 WLR 1580 [32] (Sir Andrew Morritt C).

[115] See McInnes, 'Enrichment Revisited' (2004) (n 66) 176–77.

[116] *Boulton v Jones* (1857) 2 H&N 564, 157 ER 232.

*Incomplete Contractual Performance*

Part performance of contractual obligations presents a special difficulty for establishing enrichment on the basis of a request because, although the defendant requested the performance, the claimant has only delivered part of the requested benefit. In such a case, the defendant will often have received value,[117] but can the claimant establish that the defendant has chosen the part performance and is therefore enriched? Burrows has argued that enrichment should be presumed for part performance of obligations under a contract.[118] This argument implies a choice of the part performance from the defendant's request for the whole, but, as Virgo points out, the request only shows that the defendant chose 'the whole and not necessarily the part performance'.[119] The cases do not support a presumption of choice in these circumstances. However, enrichment can often be established in cases of part performance on the basis of the other tests considered in this chapter. For example, the claimant may be able to establish that the defendant is enriched by part performance where the defendant completes the performance and thereby saves a necessary expenditure, as occurred in *Lodder v Slowey*,[120] or where the part performance has been realised in money or is readily returnable.

Moreover, there is a further and controversial question about the role of the contract price in cases of incomplete contractual performance: is the defendant's enrichment pro rated or limited by the contractual price?[121] There is deep disagreement, both within and between common law jurisdictions, as to whether the price for the services agreed in the contract has any relevant bearing on the unjust enrichment claim. For example, Cooke J in *Taylor v Motability Finance Ltd*[122] and Colin Reese QC in *Lachhani v Destination Canada (UK) Ltd*[123] both favoured a contractual ceiling for recovery in the unjust enrichment claim, and the High Court of Australia treated the contract price as a ceiling on recovery in *Pavey & Matthews v Paul*.[124] On the other hand, the dominant view that has emerged from *Boomer v Muir*,[125] *Renard Constructions v Minister for Works*,[126] and *Rover*

[117] Virgo, *The Principles of the Law of Restitution* (2006) (n 3) 94.

[118] A Burrows, 'Free Acceptance and the Law of Restitution' (1988) 104 *LQR* 576 *cf* Burrows, *The Law of Restitution* (2010) (n 51) 52–53.

[119] Virgo, *The Principles of the Law of Restitution* (2006) (n 3) 95. See Garner, 'The Role of Subjective Benefit in the Law of Unjust Enrichment' (1990) (n 3) 53; R Stevens, 'Three Enrichment Issues' in A Burrows and A Rodger (eds), *Mapping the Law: Essays in Memory of Peter Birks* (Oxford, Oxford University Press, 2006) 55.

[120] *Lodder v Slowey* [1904] AC 442 (PC).

[121] See discussion in A Skelton, *Restitution and Contract* (Oxford, Mansfield, 1998) 53–62, 66–67, 75–77.

[122] *Taylor v Motability Finance Ltd* [2004] EWHC 2619 (Comm) [26] (Cooke J). See also Stevens, 'Three Enrichment Issues' (2006) (n 119) 60.

[123] *Lachhani v Destination Canada (UK) Ltd* (1996) 13 Const LJ 279 (QB) 284 (Colin Reese QC).

[124] *Pavey & Matthews v Paul* (1987) 162 CLR 221 (HCA).

[125] *Boomer v Muir* 24 P (2d) 570 (1933) (DCAC).

[126] *Renard Constructions v Minister for Works* (1992) 26 NSWLR 234 (NSWCA).

*International v Cannon Film Sales (No 3)*[127] is that the contract price is no more than evidence of the market value.[128] The contract price will tend to be more persuasive where there is no other readily available evidence of the market price,[129] but the contract price will provide weak evidence of the market price where the parties have mutually abandoned the agreement or the benefit actually conferred is very different from that contemplated by the agreement.[130]

In relation to identifying the defendant's enrichment, this book follows the dominant view: the contract price is merely evidence of market value because the basis of the claim is unjust enrichment, not contract. Why should a claim that does not rely on the contract be affected by the valuation in the contract? The reason usually proffered for a contractual ceiling is 'subjective devaluation':[131] the contract price represents the subjective value that the defendant attached to full performance and therefore part performance cannot subjectively be worth more than the contract price to the defendant. However, this book has shown that subjective devaluation is not part of English law; the contract price merely illustrates the defendant's subjective valuation of the benefit, which is not relevant to whether the defendant chose the benefit.

McInnes suggests a different reason for a contractual ceiling to the restitutionary claim based on a choice of benefit analysis. McInnes argues that the defendant should 'be considered enriched only to the *extent* indicated by his request'.[132] While there is a choice of the benefit, there is only an assumption of responsibility to pay for it up to the amount of the request. However, this analysis confuses the scope of the request (ie what benefit was chosen) with the valuation question. As established above, the defendant's choice of the benefit in circumstances that assume responsibility to pay for it is sufficient to overcome the objection from freedom of choice. The defendant's subjective valuation is irrelevant. Moreover, the cases do not support a contractual ceiling. As McInnes concedes, the defendant's enrichment is not limited to the amount of the request, as otherwise claims exceeding the contract price would never be successful.

A preferable explanation that is consistent with the cases is that, while the contract price is not determinative of the defendant's enrichment, in many cases recovery will be limited to the contract price because any benefit the defendant

[127] *Rover International v Cannon Film Sales (No 3)* [1989] 1 WLR 912 (CA) 927–28 (Kerr LJ) 934 (Dillon LJ).

[128] See also *BP Exploration Co (Libya) Ltd v Hunt (No 2)* [1979] 1 WLR 783 (QB); *Mohamed v Alaga and Co* [1998] 2 All ER 720 (Ch) 726 (Lightman J); *Lewisham LBC v Masterson* (2000) 80 P&CR 117 (CA) 123 (Buxton LJ); *Sopov v Kane Constructions Pty Ltd (No 2)* [2009] VSCA 141, (2009) 257 ALR 182 [26]; Virgo, *The Principles of the Law of Restitution* (2006) (n 3) 101; Stevens, 'Three Enrichment Issues' (2006) (n 119) 61–62.

[129] Mitchell, Mitchell and Watterson, *Goff & Jones The Law of Unjust Enrichment* (2011) (n 3) §4-49.

[130] *Benedetti v Sawiris* [2009] EWHC 1330 (Ch) [534] (Patten J) affirmed on this point by *Benedetti v Sawiris* [2010] EWCA Civ 1427 [63]–[70] (Arden LJ). See Mitchell, Mitchell and Watterson, *Goff & Jones The Law of Unjust Enrichment* (2011) (n 3) §4-49.

[131] See, eg Virgo, *The Principles of the Law of Restitution* (2006) (n 3) 94–96, 100–04.

[132] McInnes, 'Enrichment Revisited' (2004) (n 66) 177.

receives in excess of the contract price will not be unjust.[133] If the claimant is paid the full contract price for only part performance of his contractual obligations, the claimant has received everything that he expected to receive under the contract.[134] As such, where the claimant has made a bad bargain, the fact that the defendant's enrichment exceeds the contract price does not mean the claimant can escape the contract and claim market value. This is not because the defendant is not enriched; it is because the enrichment in excess of the contract price is not unjust. This may be what Cooke J intended in *Taylor v Motability* when he held that, although the contract price is merely evidence of the market value, recovery in excess of the contract price 'would be unjust since it would put the innocent party in a better position than he would have been if the contract had been fulfilled'.[135]

However, the contract price will not always provide a ceiling. For example, it may be that the reason why the contract is avoided undermines the claimant's acceptance of the contract price, such as where the claimant lacked the mental capacity to enter the contract or laboured under undue influence.[136] In such circumstances, recovery in excess of the contract price may be justified. This solution is preferable to that expounded by McInnes because it does not necessarily limit the enrichment to the amount of the defendant's request, which is inconsistent with the cases. Rather, it prevents the claimant from recovering more than he or she bargained for when the contract price can be taken to have been validly accepted by the claimant. The defendant is enriched by the market value of the benefit, but the excess over the contract price is not unjust. For present purposes, the important point is that the contractual ceiling is not an enrichment question, but may be part of establishing that the enrichment is unjust.

## C. Readily Returnable Benefits

The second group of choice of benefit cases was recognised by Mance LJ in *McDonald v Coys of Kensington*: where the benefit 'is readily returnable without substantial difficulty or detriment and [the defendant] chooses to retain it ... rather than to retransfer it on request'.[137] Although Mance LJ considered the 'readily returnable' test to be a test of incontrovertible benefit rather than proof of

[133] Stevens, 'Three Enrichment Issues' (2006) (n 119) 60.

[134] See the analogous approach in subrogation cases where, even if the defendant is enriched by the release of a liability, the enrichment is not unjust if the claimant obtained the security for which he bargained: *Filby v Mortgage Express (No 2) Ltd* [2004] EWCA Civ 759, [2004] 2 P&CR DG16 [62] (May LJ).

[135] *Taylor v Motability Finance Ltd* [2004] EWHC 2619 (Comm) [26] (Cooke J).

[136] This is the flipside of Virgo's argument in circumstances in which the reason for invalidity undermines the contract price as evidence of the defendant's subjective valuation of the benefit: Virgo, *The Principles of the Law of Restitution* (2006) (n 3) 103. See also *Perpetual Trustees Victoria Ltd v Ford* [2008] NSWSC 29, (2008) 70 NSWLR 611 [124]–[125] (Harrison J).

[137] *McDonald v Coys of Kensington* [2004] EWCA Civ 47, [2004] 1 WLR 2775 [37] (Mance LJ). See also *Benedetti v Sawiris* [2010] EWCA Civ 1427 [116] (Arden LJ).

choice of the benefit,[138] it is difficult to accept his reasoning on this point.[139] The significant factor for Mance LJ was not that the incontrovertibly enriching nature of the benefit, but rather that the defendant '*chooses* to retain it … rather than to retransfer it on request' (emphasis added).[140] Indeed, Mance LJ goes on to consider the evidence that showed that McDonald 'attached real value to the mark'[141] and 'regarded himself as subjectively benefitted by the mark'.[142] McDonald's decision to retain the mark showed that he chose the benefit, not that the benefit was objectively incontrovertible. Thus, it is preferable to view the refusal to restore a retained benefit to the claimant as an exercise of freedom of choice by the defendant: a defendant who refuses to make a readily returnable benefit available has chosen that benefit and is therefore enriched by it.

Further, while Mance LJ's judgment refers to 'retransferring' the benefit to the defendant and couches the test in terms of whether the benefit is 'readily returnable without substantial difficulty or detriment',[143] it is important to understand that the relevant test should not be whether or not the defendant has refused to *return* the benefit to the claimant, but whether the defendant has refused to *make it available* to the claimant. As Mance LJ made clear in the earlier decision in *Huyton SA v Peter Cremer GmbH & Co*,[144] the obligation to make 'specific restitution' of a thing does not require the defendant to return the thing or seek out its rightful possessor, but simply to make the thing available. While the defendant's indifference to *returning* the thing does not necessarily amount to a choice of the benefit in question, a refusal to *make it available* to the claimant is not mere indifference: it is a choice to retain it. Reformulating Mance LJ's test in this way is important for two reasons: first, it correctly pinpoints the relevant choice by the defendant; second, it avoids the objection by the defendant that, although he did not want the benefit, it was too onerous or difficult a burden for him to return it. A defendant will not be taken to value a benefit under the 'readily returnable' test provided he makes the benefit available to the claimant where this can be done 'without substantial difficulty or detriment'.

[138] *McDonald v Coys of Kensington* [2004] EWCA Civ 47, [2004] 1 WLR 2775 [40] (Mance LJ). Virgo interprets the test in this way also: Virgo, *The Principles of the Law of Restitution* (2006) (n 3) 77–78.

[139] See Stevens, 'Three Enrichment Issues' (2006) (n 119) 50.

[140] *McDonald v Coys of Kensington* [2004] EWCA Civ 47, [2004] 1 WLR 2775 [37] (Mance LJ) *cf Weatherby v Banham* (1832) 5 C&P 228, 172 ER 950; *Read v Rann* (1830) 10 B&C 438, 441; 109 ER 513, 515 (Parke J).

[141] *McDonald v Coys of Kensington* [2004] EWCA Civ 47, [2004] 1 WLR 2775 [39] (Mance LJ).

[142] Ibid [40] (Mance LJ).

[143] Ibid [37] (Mance LJ).

[144] *Huyton SA v Peter Cremer GmbH & Co* [1999] 1 Lloyd's Rep 620 (QB) 633–34 (Mance J). See also *Capital Finance Co Ltd v Bray* [1964] 1 WLR 323 (CA); *Metals & Ropes Co v Tattersall* [1966] 2 Lloyd's Rep 166 (CA) where the defendant was obliged to inform the claimant of the location of the chattels and facilitate their collection. See generally A Dugdale, *Clerk & Lindsell on Torts*, 18th edn (London, Sweet & Maxwell, 2000) 769–70; M Bridge, *Personal Property Law*, 3rd edn (Oxford, Oxford University Press, 2002) 57.

Although it is sometimes cited for the same proposition, *Weatherby v Banham*[145] is not explicable on the same grounds. The claimants published the *Racing Calendar* and delivered it to Westbrook until his death in 1820. After this, the defendant, who had succeeded to the property of Westbrook and moved into the house, continued to receive the *Racing Calendar*. In an action in *assumpsit* for the value of the *Racing Calendars* received, Lord Tenterden CJ held that 'If the defendant receive the books, and *use them*, I think that the action is maintainable' (emphasis added).[146] It was critical that the defendant 'use' or 'keep' the goods, as the defendant had the choice to accept or reject the magazines and use may evince a choice to accept them. However, the case cannot be explained on the basis that the calendars were readily returnable, as there is no evidence that the defendant refused to make the calendars available to the claimant. The decision may be explained on the grounds that acceptance of the calendars by the defendant indicates a choice of the benefit manifesting an assumption of responsibility to pay. As the delivery was clearly marked to Westbrook and the defendant had succeeded to his estate, the claimant objectively expected payment for the goods and the acceptance and use of the goods by the defendant may amount to an assumption of responsibility to pay for them. Unfortunately, the report is not clear as to whether the evidence could sustain such a finding.

## D. Free Acceptance

The third situation that will commonly constitute a choice of benefit is where the claimant has freely accepted further benefits conferred on him when he had a reasonable opportunity to reject or prevent his further enrichment.[147] Birks[148] suggested that, when a defendant 'freely accepted' a benefit in circumstances where there was objectively an expectation of payment, the defendant could not assert that he did not value that benefit. In rejecting Birks's approach, Burrows rightly pointed out that free acceptance may show nothing more than 'indifference to the objective benefit being rendered'.[149] Instead, Burrows proposed a test of his own:

[145] *Weatherby v Banham* (1832) 5 C&P 228, 172 ER 950.

[146] Ibid 228 (Lord Tenterden CJ).

[147] See, eg *Van Den Berg v Giles* [1979] 2 NZLR 111 (NZHC); *Brenner v First Artists' Management Pty Ltd* [1993] 2 VR 221 (VSC) 259–60; *Angelopoulos v Sabatino* [1995] 65 SASR 1 (SASC) [49]–[51]; *Bridgewater v Griffiths* [2000] 1 WLR 524 (QB); *Andrew Shelton & Co v Alpha Healthcare* [2002] VSC 248, [2003] 5 VR 577 [128]; *Rowe v Vale of White Horse DC* [2003] EWHC 388 (Admin), [2003] 1 Lloyd's Rep 418; *McDonald v Coys of Kensington* [2004] EWCA Civ 47, [2004] 1 WLR 2775; *W Cook Builders Pty Ltd (in liquidation) v Lumbers* [2007] SASC 20, (2007) 96 SASR 406 [77]–[85] reversed on other grounds in [2008] HCA 27; *Chief Constable of Greater Manchester Police v Wigan Athletic FC* [2008] EWCA Civ 1449, [2009] 1 WLR 1580 [47]; *Benedetti v Sawiris* [2010] EWCA Civ 1427 [106]–[121] (Arden LJ).

[148] Birks, *An Introduction to the Law of Restitution* (1989) (n 6) 266. See also Virgo, *The Principles of the Law of Restitution* (2006) (n 3) 82–88; Mitchell, Mitchell and Watterson, *Goff & Jones The Law of Unjust Enrichment* (2011) (n 3) §§4-29–4-23.

[149] Burrows, *The Law of Restitution* (2010) (n 51) 57. See also Burrows, 'Free Acceptance and the Law of Restitution' (1988) (n 118); Garner, 'The Role of Subjective Benefit in the Law of Unjust Enrichment' (1990) (n 3).

'reprehensible seeking-out', where the defendant's conduct demonstrates that he values the benefit but is unwilling to pay for it.[150] While this 'reprehensible seeking-out' test avoids the problem posed by the indifferent defendant, it is unnecessarily circumscribed. In his most recent edition, Burrows points out that 'There is no need for the seeking-out to be reprehensible in order to overcome subjective devaluation. It is the positive 'choice' that is crucial'.[151] Accordingly, he now favours a test of 'demanding or taking'. The decisive requirement, it is contended here, should be proof that the defendant has chosen the benefit, and 'seeking-out' a benefit (including demanding or taking it) in circumstances that objectively involve an expectation of payment is generally sufficient to demonstrate that the defendant has chosen it and assumed responsibility to pay for it.

There is a further difficulty with a test based on 'seeking-out' the benefit, which is most easily illustrated by Birks's famous example of the defendant who stands by and watches a window-cleaner wash his windows labouring under the mistaken impression that this is the house of the client who engaged his services.[152] The defendant has not sought the benefit, but merely remained silent and marvelled at his good fortune. This kind of conduct was undoubtedly caught by Birks's test of 'free acceptance', as the defendant had an opportunity to reject the window-cleaning and failed to do so. However, this conduct would not be caught either by Burrows's 'demanding or taking' test as the defendant may simply be indifferent to the washing of his windows. Thus, it would seem that accepting Burrows's test precludes recovery where a defendant stands by and receives a benefit, knowing it is being offered non-gratuitously, despite having a reasonable opportunity to reject it.

In order to catch this kind of conduct and overcome the objections posed by Burrows, Birks subsequently defended free acceptance by arguing that it was never intended to show that the defendant valued the benefit, but rather functioned as a bar to the defendant's asserting subjective devaluation.[153] Birks's revised argument was accepted in a dictum of Mance LJ in *McDonald v Coys of Kensington*.[154] However, there is a difficulty with Birks's reasoning. The claimant has the onus of proving that the defendant chose the benefit and barring the defendant from 'subjectively devaluing' the benefit does not prove the positive claim that the defendant chose the benefit. Due to the defendant's 'unconscionability', Birks bars the defendant from raising evidence that he did not choose the benefit; but this cannot relieve the claimant of the need to establish enrichment, a necessary element of the cause of action. Unconscionability is a blunt instrument: it demands

[150] A Burrows, *The Law of Restitution*, 2nd edn (London, Butterworths, 2002) 24–25.

[151] Burrows, *The Law of Restitution* (2010) (n 51) 56; *McDonald v Coys of Kensington* [2004] EWCA Civ 47, [2004] 1 WLR 2775 [32] (Mance LJ).

[152] Birks, *An Introduction to the Law of Restitution* (1989) (n 6) 266.

[153] P Birks, 'In Defence of Free Acceptance' in A Burrows (ed) *Essays on the Law of Restitution* (Oxford, Clarendon Press, 1991); P Birks, *Unjust Enrichment*, 2nd edn (Oxford, Clarendon Press, 2005) 56. See also Virgo, *The Principles of the Law of Restitution* (2006) (n 3) 87.

[154] *McDonald v Coys of Kensington* [2004] EWCA Civ 47, [2004] 1 WLR 2775 [28]–[32] (Mance LJ).

every 'freely accepting' defendant pay the market value of the benefit received, even if he is indifferent to the benefit and there is no positive evidence that he chose it.

The better way to view the argument from 'free acceptance' is that it establishes choice of the benefit, rather than proof of subjective valuation. The defendant is under no duty to prevent the mistaken window-cleaner from washing his windows, but if he fails to take a reasonable opportunity to prevent the window-cleaner from washing his windows, then he has exercised a free choice to continue to receive the service. It is not claimed that free acceptance establishes that the defendant valued the benefit: he may value it or be entirely indifferent to it. By failing to prevent the window-cleaner from expending valuable time and effort cleaning his windows when it was reasonable for the defendant to reject those window-cleaning services, the defendant has made a choice knowingly to receive the benefit from that point onwards. Indeed, where the services conferred after the opportunity to reject are part of a whole, like the cleaning of a window, a choice to receive the rest of the service may even constitute a choice of the work done before the opportunity to reject. It is a question of construing the benefit the defendant chose. The important point is that, even if the defendant is indifferent to the value of the services, a decision to allow the conferral of further benefits by the claimant rather than to reject those benefits is a choice freely made. The law need not protect the defendant's freedom of choice when he has exercised a free choice to accept a benefit in circumstances where a reasonable person would understand that the benefit is offered on condition of payment. The fact that the choice comes with consequences does not prevent it from being a free one and a defendant who does not reject a benefit that is non-gratuitously given may thereby assume the responsibility to pay for it.

Moreover, unlike the unconscionability bar favoured by Birks and Virgo, the choice of benefit approach does not impose an obligation on the defendant to reject or prevent the window-cleaner from washing his windows, and therefore involves less interference with freedom of choice. As with mitigation of damage in tort, the defendant in unjust enrichment is under no obligation to stop the window-cleaner from washing his windows,[155] but if he chooses to stand by and let him continue then he has failed to take a reasonable opportunity to prevent his enrichment and is liable to the extent of this failure to 'mitigate'.

While the emphasis clearly differs, it may be questioned whether the approach proposed here differs from Birks and Virgo's approach to free acceptance in practice. Their approach relies on the unconscientious conduct of the defendant and bars any appeal to subjective devaluation; the choice of benefit approach focuses on choice—whether or not it was reasonable for the defendant to reject or prevent the receipt of further benefits—and holds the defendant liable only to the extent that he has exercised a choice by not preventing his enrichment. The window-cleaning example is illustrative. If the defendant comes upon the window-cleaner

[155] Kimel, *From Promise to Contract: Towards a Liberal Theory of Contract* (2003) (n 62) 109–10.

after he has washed the second-floor windows but before he has washed the first-floor windows, the question is whether letting the window-cleaner continue amounts to a choice of the service in respect of the first-floor windows or a choice of the entire service. The defendant could only reasonably have rejected the cleaning of the first-floor windows and is thus only liable for the market value of this part of the work, unless his choice is construed as a choice of all the work. An approach based on an 'unconscionability' bar is simply not as sensitive to questions of choice: an unconscionable defendant is prevented from raising evidence that he did not choose (or value) the benefit received and the claimant is therefore relieved of the onus of proving that the defendant chose (or valued) the window-cleaning services. Of course, Birks and Virgo could reach a different conclusion by arguing that the defendant's conduct was only unconscientious once he discovered the window-cleaner and failed to stop him from washing the first-floor windows. On this argument, although the defendant acted unconscionably, he can subjectively devalue the window cleaning prior to his free acceptance, but not afterwards. However, if this is what is meant by 'unconscientious', then the unconscionability approach is ultimately concerned with the choice to accept or reject the proffered benefit. The real reason for the defendant's liability is that it was reasonable for him to reject the benefit and he did not do so: he made the choice to accept further benefits and cannot therefore appeal to freedom of choice when required to pay for those benefits.

## III. Incontrovertible Enrichment

Generally, if the defendant argues that he is not enriched by the benefit received at the claimant's expense, the claimant will need to establish that the defendant chose the benefit in order to satisfy the enrichment requirement. However, in certain circumstances, the claimant can prove enrichment without proving a choice of the benefit. These circumstances are traditionally understood as 'incontrovertible benefit' or, in the language of this book,[156] 'incontrovertible enrichment' cases. The incontrovertible enrichment test has been generally accepted by the courts.[157] As the Supreme Court of Canada articulated in *Peel (Regional Municipality) v Canada*, a defendant will be incontrovertibly enriched by 'an unquestionable benefit, a benefit which is demonstrably apparent and not subject

[156] Benefit was defined in ch 2, s IV.C.

[157] *BP Exploration Co (Libya) Ltd v Hunt (No 2)* [1979] 1 WLR 783 (QB); *Proctor & Gamble Philippine Manufacturing Corp v Peter Cremer GmbH (The Manila)* [1988] 3 All ER 843 (QB); *Peel (Regional Municipality) v Canada* [1992] 3 SCR 762 (SCC); *Rowe v Vale of White Horse DC* [2003] EWHC 388 (Admin), [2003] 1 Lloyd's Rep 418; *McDonald v Coys of Kensington* [2004] EWCA Civ 47, [2004] 1 WLR 2775 [33] (Mance LJ).

to debate and conjecture'.[158] Such incontrovertibly enriching benefits fall into two categories: (i) where the defendant is saved a necessary expense; and (ii) where the defendant has received a benefit that is money or money-like. While the underlying principle is also freedom of choice, the 'incontrovertible enrichment' test is separate from the choice of benefit test. The basis of the 'incontrovertibility' is that no reasonable defendant in the defendant's circumstances could deny that the benefit is enriching, not that the defendant chose the benefit. As such, it will apply in circumstances where there is clear evidence that the defendant has not chosen the benefit but the defendant nevertheless cannot appeal to freedom of choice to refuse to make restitution.

## A. Saved Necessary Expense

The first category of incontrovertible enrichment arises where the claimant has saved the defendant a necessary expenditure. An obvious example is the discharge of a defendant's legal liability where there can be no doubt that the defendant would have otherwise had to discharge the liability.[159] The payment of another's debt or the satisfaction of another's legal liability is incontrovertibly enriching because it is equivalent to the receipt of the same value that would have been necessary to satisfy the liability. It is as if the defendant received the amount of the liability in money: spared the expense of satisfying the debt or legal liability, the defendant may now use the equivalent sum for any purpose she desires. However, it is not suggested that the defendant would inevitably have chosen to satisfy the legal liability; rather, the expenditure is necessary because the defendant could have been compelled by law and the liability could have been enforced in money terms against the defendant. The corollary of this point is that, where the defendant can show that the creditor had no right to enforce the debt,[160] or that the defendant would have had a defence to the claim,[161] or (arguably) that the debt would have been compromised or not called in, then the discharge will

[158] *Peel (Regional Municipality) v Canada* [1992] 3 SCR 762 (SCC) [43] (McLachlin J). See also Birks, *An Introduction to the Law of Restitution* (1989) (n 6) 116.

[159] See, eg *Exall v Partridge* (1799) 8 TR 308, 101 ER 1405; *Moule v Garrett* (1872) 7 Ex 101 (Ex) 104; *Brook's Wharf and Bull Wharf Ltd v Goodman Bros* [1937] 1 KB 534 (CA) 544; *County of Carleton v City of Ottawa* [1965] SCR 663 (SCC); *Peel (Regional Municipality) v Canada* [1992] 3 SCR 762 (SCC); *AMP Workers' Compensation Services (NSW) Ltd v QBE Insurance Ltd* [2001] NSWCA 267, (2001) 53 NSWLR 35, 40; *Amertek Inc v Canadian Commercial Corp* (2003) 229 DLR (4th) 419 (ONSC) 419; *Littlewoods Retail Ltd v HMRC* [2010] EWHC 1071 (Ch), [2010] STC 2072 [121].

[160] See, eg *Bonner v Tottenham & Edmonton Permanent Investment BS* [1899] 1 QB 161 (CA); *Peel (Regional Municipality) v Canada* [1992] 3 SCR 762 (SCC); *Wessex Regional HA v John Laing Construction Ltd* (1994) 39 Con LR 56 (QB); *OLL Ltd v Secretary of State for the Home Department* [1997] 3 All ER 897 (QB); *Cockburn v GIO Finance Ltd (No 2)* [2001] NSWCA 177, (2001) 51 NSWLR 624.

[161] See, eg *West of England Fire Insurance Co v Isaacs* [1897] 1 QB 226 (CA); *Coupar Transport (London) Ltd v Smith's (Acton) Ltd* [1959] 1 Lloyd's Rep 369 (QB) 380–81; *Euro-Diam Ltd v Bathurst* [1990] 1 QB 1 (CA) 38–39 (Kerr LJ).

not be incontrovertible and the claimant will need to establish the defendant's enrichment on another basis.

Enrichment may also be established, in the absence of a legal liability, 'where it is clear on the facts (on a balance of probabilities) that had the plaintiff not paid, the defendant would have done so'.[162] The reasoning behind the incontrovertibility is identical to legal necessity cases, as the defendant is no more able to controvert a factually necessary expenditure than a legally necessary expenditure. If the court finds that the expenditure was inevitable, then the defendant would have paid the equivalent sum of money as he is saved by the claimant's satisfying that liability. Factual necessity can explain the finding of enrichment in *Craven-Ellis v Canons Ltd*,[163] where the defendant company would necessarily have employed a managing director, and *Rowe v Vale of White Horse*,[164] where the defendant would necessarily have had to obtain sewerage services. Although there was no unjust factor,[165] the incontrovertible nature of Rowe's enrichment was common ground.[166]

The same reasoning underpins cases where the claimant discharges a liability that would otherwise inevitably have been owed by the defendant, even though the effect of the claimant's discharging the liability is that the defendant never comes under the obligation.[167] Unfortunately, the English cases on point suggest that there is no enrichment in such circumstances.[168] A preferable approach is taken in Australia. Contribution was awarded on the basis of unjust enrichment in *AMP Workers' Compensation Services (NSW) Ltd v QBE Insurance Ltd*,[169] where the claimant insurance company, QBE, paid out to settle a workplace accident claim against a negligent employee that was also covered by the employer's workplace compensation insurance policy with AMP. The employer was never sued for vicarious liability for the accident and its liability to the employee was discharged by QBE's payout under the settlement. The effect of QBE's payment was that AMP never became liable to pay out under its contract with the employer, although

[162] *Peel (Regional Municipality) v Canada* [1992] 3 SCR 762 (SCC) [46] (McLachlin J). See also Mitchell, Mitchell and Watterson, *Goff & Jones The Law of Unjust Enrichment* (2011) (n 3) §4-19.

[163] *Craven-Ellis v Canons Ltd* [1936] 2 KB 403 (CA).

[164] *Rowe v Vale of White Horse DC* [2003] EWHC 388 (Admin), [2003] 1 Lloyd's Rep 418. See also *Great Northern Railway Co v Swaffield* (1874) 9 Ex 132 (Ex); *Re Rhodes* (1890) 44 ChD 94 (CA); *Upton-on-Severn RDC v Powell* [1942] 1 All ER 220 (CA); *Monks v Poynice* (1987) 8 NSWLR 662 (NSWSC); *Berkeley Applegate (Investment Consultants) Ltd* [1989] Ch 32 (Ch) 50; Virgo, *The Principles of the Law of Restitution* (2006) (n 3) 76; Birks, *Unjust Enrichment* (2005) (n 153) 60.

[165] *Rowe v Vale of White Horse DC* [2003] EWHC 388 (Admin), [2003] 1 Lloyd's Rep 418 [13]–[14] (Lightman J).

[166] Ibid [12] (Lightman J).

[167] Mitchell, Mitchell and Watterson, *Goff & Jones The Law of Unjust Enrichment* (2011) (n 3) §§4-22–4-26.

[168] See especially *Receiver for Metropolitan Police District v Croydon Corp* [1956] 1 WLR 1113 (QB).

[169] *AMP Workers' Compensation Services (NSW) Ltd v QBE Insurance Ltd* [2001] NSWCA 267, (2001) 53 NSWLR 35.

otherwise it would inevitably have been liable.[170] Accordingly, AMP was enriched by QBE's payment as it discharged an otherwise inevitable liability.

By contrast, if the claimant's payment is not effective to discharge the liability, then there is no enrichment. This is what distinguishes *The Esso Bernicia*[171] from the *AMP Workers' Compensation Services* case. Esso voluntarily agreed to make payments in respect of oil pollution damage under the Tanker Owners Voluntary Agreement Concerning Liability for Oil Pollution (TOVALOP). It then claimed against Hall Russell, the shipbuilders responsible for the spill, for the sums paid under TOVALOP as Hall Russell would inevitably have had to pay these claims if Esso had not done so. Lord Goff rejected this claim for restitution 'because Esso has not by its payment discharged the liability of Hall Russell, and so has not enriched Hall Russell'.[172] Esso's payments were voluntary and the recipients 'continue to have vested in them rights of action against Hall Russell in respect of the loss or damage which was the subject matter of Esso's payment to them'.[173]

## B. Money-Like Benefits

The second category of incontrovertible enrichment cases involve money and benefits that are essentially money-like. As explained in chapter four,[174] the definition of money extends beyond simple physical currency, which is the narrowest economic definition of money: M0. Deposits and other highly liquid assets that can readily be converted into currency, which fall within the definition of M4,[175] will also typically be incontrovertible.[176] Further, certain commodities, shares and inventory may be sufficiently money-like to be regarded as incontrovertibly enriching. Although economic definitions of money and liquidity offer some guidance, it is impossible on the current state of the law to offer a comprehensive definition or bright line to delimit when benefits will be so unquestionable that the defendant's freedom of choice is not at issue. However, the test should be whether the benefit is sufficiently money-like that the defendant's freedom of choice is not infringed by a conclusive finding of enrichment.

### *(i) Realisation in Money*

The realisation of a benefit in money is a more difficult case. In *Greenwood v Bennett*,[177] Bennett entrusted a car to Searle to make certain repairs. Instead of

[170] Ibid 39 (Handley JA). The liability thus pre-empted must have inevitably arisen, which is why there is no enrichment in *Peel (Regional Municipality) v Canada* [1992] 3 SCR 762 (SCC), see Mitchell, Mitchell and Watterson, *Goff & Jones The Law of Unjust Enrichment* (2011) (n 3) §4-26.

[171] *Esso Petroleum Co Ltd v Hall Russell & Co Ltd (The Esso Bernicia)* [1989] AC 643 (HL).

[172] Ibid 663 (Lord Goff).

[173] Ibid.

[174] Ch 4, s II.B.

[175] See ch 4, fn 39.

[176] Edelman and Bant, *Unjust Enrichment in Australia* (2006) (n 66) 109.

[177] *Greenwood v Bennett* [1973] QB 195 (CA). See also *Munro v Willmott* [1949] 1 KB 295 (KB); *McKeown v Cavalier Yachts Pty Ltd* (1998) 13 NSWLR 303 (NSWSC); *Conrad v Feldbar Construction Co Ltd* (2004) 70 OR (3d) 298 (ONSC); *Cox v Young* (2005) 6 NZ Conv & Prop Rep 761 (NZHC).

making the repairs, Searle crashed the vehicle and then, representing himself as the owner, sold it to Harper for £75. Harper, mistakenly believing he was now the owner, then carried out £226 worth of labour and materials to repair the car. When Searle's deception was discovered, Bennett recovered the car at trial and sold it for £400. Thus, the increase in the value of the car as a result of Harper's repairs was £325. In interpleader proceedings contested (in effect) between Bennett and Harper, Bennett prevailed before the Court of Appeal, but Harper was awarded £226 on a quantum meruit basis for the repairs. It is clear that Bennett did not choose the repairs carried out by Harper (he was not even aware the vehicle had been involved in an accident) and it is arguable that the repairs were not a necessary expense as Bennett may have decided to sell the car in its unrepaired state. As such, Bennett would not necessarily have incurred the expense. However, as Bennett realised the service in money, he could not deny that he was enriched.[178] If money is incontrovertible, then something that is realised as money is likewise incontrovertible. Accordingly, Bennett's freedom of choice is not infringed by finding that he is enriched by the value of Harper's services: £226.

But what about a benefit that can be, but has not yet been, realised in money? Hirst J in *Proctor & Gamble Philippine Manufacturing Corp v Peter Cremer GmbH*,[179] Judge Bowsher QC in *Marston Construction Co Ltd v Kigass Ltd*[180] and Mance LJ in *McDonald v Coys of Kensington*[181] all held that, in these circumstances, it is sufficient that the benefit be 'realisable'.[182] However, Burrows and Virgo rightly point out that the 'realisable benefit' test is too broad: it goes beyond the class of money-like benefits and sanctions an objective determination of whether a benefit can be realised, which may infringe the freedom of choice of the individual defendant.[183] Instead, Burrows suggests that the test is whether it is 'reasonably certain that [the defendant] will realise the positive benefit'[184] and Virgo suggests a test of 'where it is inevitable that the defendant will realize the benefit'.[185] However, these more restrictive tests have not found favour with the courts. In *McDonald v Coys of Kensington*, Mance LJ thought that Burrows's approach was 'too restrictive ... [as] a requirement of proof of intention might itself also encourage tactical stances or manoeuvring'[186] by the defendant to avoid the court's finding that the benefit would be realised.

[178] See Birks, *An Introduction to the Law of Restitution* (1989) (n 6) 116ff.

[179] *Proctor & Gamble Philippine Manufacturing Corp v Peter Cremer GmbH (The Manila)* [1988] 3 All ER 843 (QB) 855 (Hirst J).

[180] *Marston Construction Co Ltd v Kigass Ltd* (1989) 46 BLR 109 (QB).

[181] *McDonald v Coys of Kensington* [2004] EWCA Civ 47, [2004] 1 WLR 2775 [34]–[36] (Mance LJ).

[182] See Mitchell, Mitchell and Watterson, *Goff & Jones The Law of Unjust Enrichment* (2011) (n 3) §4-16–4-17.

[183] Virgo, *The Principles of the Law of Restitution* (2006) (n 3) 81; Burrows, *The Law of Restitution* (2010) (n 51) 49.

[184] Burrows, *The Law of Restitution* (2010) (n 51) 49.

[185] Virgo, *The Principles of the Law of Restitution* (2006) (n 3) 81.

[186] *McDonald v Coys of Kensington* [2004] EWCA Civ 47, [2004] 1 WLR 2775 [35] (Mance LJ).

This book accepts the criticism that Burrows and Virgo level at the 'realisable benefit test'. It dilutes the concept of 'incontrovertibility' by admitting benefits that can be controverted and do not necessarily enrich the defendant. Beyond the class of money-like benefits identified above, the law requires stricter protection of the defendant's freedom of choice. Further, as Virgo points out, the courts do not engage in an assessment of whether the benefit is likely, or is reasonably certain, to be realised.[187] A benefit is only incontrovertible when it is truly unquestionable and therefore a defendant will only be enriched where the benefit is money-like or has been *realised* in money, not merely where it has the potential to be so realised.

Superficially, adopting the 'realised benefit' approach appears to focus on the defendant's extant enrichment, whereas the 'realisable benefit' approach is consistent with the focus on immediate enrichment advocated in chapter seven. This is because, even where the benefit is subsequently realised, at the moment of receipt the defendant only had a realisable benefit. In this way, the realised benefit test may seem to treat the defendant's subsequent dealing with the benefit as determining the defendant's enrichment. However, restricting the incontrovertible enrichment test to realised benefits should not be confused with an extant enrichment approach.[188] There is an objective transfer of value to the defendant at the moment of receipt of the benefit, but the need to prove *choice* of the benefit is only avoided when the defendant is incontrovertibly enriched by the realisation of the benefit in money. For instance, in the example of *Greenwood v Bennett* considered above,[189] the market value for Harper's services was £226, which increased the value of Bennett's vehicle by £325. If Bennett subsequently chooses to sell the car, the transfer of value is the £226 in services which Harper provided, not the increased value subsequently realised.[190] Of course, if Bennett had realised less than the market value of the service, the benefit is only incontrovertibly enriching up to the amount realised. So, if the repairs had only increased the value of the car when sold by £50, instead of £325, it cannot be said that the defendant is incontrovertibly enriched by any more than £50. That is the extent to which the benefit has been turned into money. To recover any more, the claimant would need to establish enrichment on a different basis, such as choice of the benefit.

Finally, the 'tactical stances and manoeuvring' that concerned Mance LJ do not present an insurmountable difficulty. Where the claimant can establish enrichment on another basis, for example choice of the benefit, then enrichment can be proved irrespective of realisation. Where choice of the benefit cannot be established, the claimant will have to wait until the benefit becomes

[187] Virgo, *The Principles of the Law of Restitution* (2006) (n 3) 81.

[188] *Cf* ibid 99.

[189] See above nn 177–78 and accompanying text.

[190] See Mitchell, Mitchell and Watterson, *Goff & Jones The Law of Unjust Enrichment* (2011) (n 3) §4-15.

incontrovertible. However, the date of trial and limitation periods do not present insuperable practical difficulties because the cause of action in unjust enrichment will only crystallise when the element of enrichment is satisfied, which—on the approach in chapter seven of this book—is only when the benefit is subsequently realised. The defendant will have received an immediate transfer of value at the moment of receipt, but the enrichment requirement will not be satisfied until the freedom of choice limb of the enrichment inquiry is also satisfied, meaning the cause of action will only be actionable when the benefit is realised and the limitation period will then run.

Alternatively, although there is no authority on point, it may be preferable to order a lien over the benefit that entitles the defendant to recover the value transferred from the proceeds of sale only when the benefit is later sold.[191] Such a lien could be ordered by analogy with the award of security interests in other cases with the purpose of preventing the unjust enrichment of the defendant upon realisation of the benefit in money.[192] The defendant would come under a personal obligation to make restitution of the value originally received (but not exceeding the amount actually realised) upon sale of the benefit, secured by an equitable right to the benefit and its proceeds.

### *(ii) Principal Sum and Use Value*

As the receipt of money and 'money-like' benefits is incontrovertibly enriching, no freedom of choice question arises where the claim is for the principal sum. Accordingly, the choice of benefit test does not apply. As money is a measure and store of value, the individual defendant has received an objective transfer of value and cannot object that he or she did not choose the receipt. The defendant must make restitution of the value received or plead a defence, such as change of position, if the money has been dissipated. Take the example of a defendant who is unaware of a mistaken payment of money when that money is subsequently stolen. In these circumstances, as long as the money is 'received' by the defendant,[193] the defendant is enriched by the value of the receipt. As is explained in chapter seven, enrichment by the receipt of money is determined at the moment of receipt. Suggesting that the defendant is not enriched because the money is subsequently stolen confuses enrichment and change of position by adopting an extant enrichment approach that is not part of the English law of unjust enrichment. The theft of the money is a question for the defence of change of position and the answer depends on the scope of the defence in circumstances involving 'independent' changes of position.[194]

[191] See *Re Gareau Estate* (1995) 9 ETR (2d) 25 (ONCJ); Mitchell, Mitchell and Watterson, *Goff & Jones The Law of Unjust Enrichment* (2011) (n 3) §§4-17, 27-16.

[192] For a discussion of equitable liens in unjust enrichment, see ch 5, s IV.B.

[193] *Marsh v Keating* (1834) 1 Bing NC 198, 131 ER 1094; *National Commercial Banking Corp of Australia v Batty* (1986) 160 CLR 251 (HCA) 265–69 (Gibbs CJ) 269–70 (Wilson J) 276–80 (Brennan J).

[194] E Bant, *The Change of Position Defence* (Oxford, Hart, 2009) 145–47.

A different position obtains in respect of use value claims because the use of money is not incontrovertibly enriching. The use of money is a non-money benefit which, although it can be (and often is) realised in money, is not equivalent to money within the category of M4. While it is irrelevant what the defendant actually does with the money received, as the majority held in *Sempra*,[195] a defendant who does not choose the use of the money, for example because he does not know of the mistaken payment into his account, is not enriched by that use unless it becomes incontrovertible. Take the above example of the unknowing recipient of a mistaken payment into a bank account: where the deposit yields interest from the bank, then the use of the money has been realised in money and is incontrovertible to that extent; whereas, if the account is not interest-bearing and the defendant does not actually use the money, then he may legitimately assert that he did not choose it and restitution of compound interest on the principal sum infringes his freedom of choice. By contrast, in *Sempra*, the Revenue, having demanded the sums paid as advanced corporation tax, chose the receipt and therefore could not object to the use value claim on the grounds it infringed its freedom of choice.

Therefore, the incontrovertible enrichment or choice of the benefit test must be satisfied to establish enrichment by the use of money. The incontrovertible enrichment test will be satisfied whenever the defendant has turned that use into money, through interest or investment or otherwise. The choice of the benefit test will be satisfied where the defendant: (i) requested the money, as in *Sempra*; (ii) knew about the receipt and could readily have returned the money but refused to make it available to the defendant; or (iii) failed to take a reasonable opportunity to reject the continued use of the money. In circumstances where a defendant has chosen the use of money, the opportunity of use is a valuable benefit and constitutes an enriching transfer of value to the defendant. If the defendant then does not invest the money or invests it poorly, he or she is no less enriched by that use: the defendant had 'the opportunity to turn it to account' at no cost, which is an 'interest-free loan' from the claimant. For this reason, the majority in *Sempra* was entirely correct to reject the minority view that evidence as to what the Revenue did with the tax payments was required to prove enrichment. The Revenue had chosen the use of the money and was therefore enriched by the value of that use.

## C. Incontrovertible Enrichment and Subjective Devaluation

Burrows suggests that there may be circumstances in which objectively 'incontrovertible' benefits may not enrich the particular defendant because it may be reasonable to deny that the benefit is enriching in the circumstances. For example, even the receipt of money by D from C may not be unquestionably enriching where D would have received the same amount from X but for the receipt of money from C. *Ministry of Defence v Ashman*,[196] a trespass case, may arguably be

[195] See ch 7, fns 21–24 and accompanying text.

[196] *Ministry of Defence v Ashman* (1993) 66 P&CR 195 (CA).

an example. Ashman was saved the necessary expense of paying for accommodation and was therefore incontrovertibly enriched. However, she could 'subjectively devalue' the accommodation received as, but for the concessionary rate, she would not have chosen to live in the more expensive Ministry of Defence housing. She was thus only required to make restitution of the value of alternative low cost housing. Burrows describes this as 'subjective devaluation of an incontrovertible benefit',[197] but this terminology is contradictory and should be avoided.

The concern Burrows articulates is that a defendant who receives an 'incontrovertible benefit' may not be enriched by it because he would have received the same benefit for less or for free. In the example where C discharges D's liability to pay £1,000 with the effect that D's wealthy uncle, X, does not gratuitously discharge the same liability, D has been saved a necessary expense but would have been saved the same expense without any obligation to make restitution. Arguably, on the approach the Court of Appeal took in *Ministry of Defence v Ashman*, although Ashman would necessarily have spent money on accommodation, the case was decided as if Ashman would have been housed elsewhere for less. Two points should be made in respect of these examples. First, as Burrows points out, the House of Lords in *Foskett v McKeown*[198] did not regard it as relevant that the defendant would have been paid out under the policy of insurance irrespective of the payment of some of the premiums with the claimant's trust money. Although the House of Lords did not decide *Foskett v McKeown* as an unjust enrichment case, but one of 'hard-nosed property rights', their Lordships' reasoning on this point was shown to be fallacious in chapter three.[199] If the defendant would have been enriched in any event, then *Foskett v McKeown* provides support for the proposition that a defendant cannot deny that an incontrovertible benefit is enriching on the basis that he would have received the same benefit for less or for free.

Second, these cases really raise questions of change of position.[200] The issue is not that the defendant did not choose or value the benefit, but rather that receipt of the benefit prevented the defendant from receiving the benefit at a lower cost or gratuitously. The defendant undoubtedly subjectively values the discharge of a necessary expense or the receipt of money. If D receives money from C, D's subjective valuation of money does not change simply because it has the effect of preventing X from paying D the same amount. Rather, the receipt of the benefit alters the defendant's position such that he is worse off if he is required to make restitution of the benefit than if he had never received it. This is a case of what Bant describes as 'independent', as opposed to defendant-instigated, change of position.[201] As she explains, there is no requirement of reliance in such cases and the defendant in these examples will have a change of position defence provided the other requirements of the defence are satisfied.

[197] Burrows, *The Law of Restitution* (2010) (n 51) 50–51.
[198] *Foskett v McKeown* [2001] 1 AC 102 (HL).
[199] See ch 3, s III.A.
[200] This appears to be accepted by Burrows in his most recent edition: Burrows, *The Law of Restitution* (2010) (n 51) 50–51.
[201] Bant, *The Change of Position Defence* (2009) (n 194).

## IV. Conclusion

Chapter six explored the protection of the defendant's freedom of choice in the law of unjust enrichment. It was suggested that liability to make restitution in unjust enrichment avoids infringement of the defendant's freedom of choice in two ways: first, through the requirement of choice of the benefit in the enrichment inquiry; and, second, through the defence of change of position. Only the former is relevant to this book. It was argued that proof of enrichment requires objective proof of choice of the benefit by the defendant manifesting an assumption of responsibility to pay for the benefit. On the basis of the historical position and modern authority, this question is best considered part of the enrichment inquiry.

Theories based on subjective devaluation were rejected for four reasons. First, it was argued that the request requirement does not provide an historical warrant for subjective devaluation and that, in fact, the forms of action applied an objective, reasonable valuation. Second, it was argued that the cases do not support subjective devaluation. On the contrary, the cases predominantly use the language of 'acceptance' or 'rejection' of the benefit and are better explained as turning on acceptance of the benefit where that choice objectively manifests an assumption of responsibility to pay. Third, it was suggested that both the 'strong' and 'weak' forms of subjective devaluation are incompatible with the concept of relational value that underpins the enrichment inquiry. Finally, on philosophical grounds, it was argued the defendant's free choice does not shape the defendant's obligation to make restitution, but rather negatives an objection to liability in unjust enrichment. It was then demonstrated that a defendant who chooses a benefit in circumstances that assume financial responsibility cannot object to restitution on freedom of choice grounds.

Under the choice of benefit model, therefore, the particular defendant will be factually enriched where: (i) there is proof of choice of the benefit by the defendant; or (ii) the benefit is incontrovertibly enriching. Under the choice of benefit test, it was argued that, where the defendant raises evidence that he did not choose the benefit, the claimant must prove: (i) choice of the benefit; and (ii) an assumption of responsibility to pay for the benefit. This commonly (although not exclusively) occurs in three situations: (i) where the defendant requests the benefit; (ii) where the benefit is readily returnable and the defendant refuses to make it available to the claimant; and (iii) where, and to the extent that, the defendant freely accepts the benefit. Under the incontrovertible enrichment test, a benefit will be incontrovertibly enriching where, by its very nature, an obligation to make restitution of its value in money will not infringe the defendant's freedom of choice. This occurs in two common situations: (i) where the benefit saves the defendant a legally or factually necessary expenditure; or (ii) where the benefit is money or money-like.

# 7

# Immediate and Extant Enrichment

One of the key consequences of the conflation of factual and legal enrichment is confusion about the moment of enrichment. As the claimant can sometimes obtain restitution of a specific right that may have changed in value since the moment of receipt, commentators and courts have sometimes confused the point of enrichment in factual enrichment cases with the date of judgment,[1] with profound implications for valuation. The value of a benefit at the moment the defendant is enriched and the value of the benefit retained by the defendant at the date of judgment may vary considerably and the choice between the 'immediate' enrichment and 'extant' enrichment approaches merits careful attention. Unfortunately, the failure to identify the moment of enrichment is a grave lacuna in the existing literature on unjust enrichment and the cases do not always adopt a consistent approach.

The immediate and extant enrichment approaches emerge from two different starting points: first, those who take the view that unjust enrichment involves the reversal of defective transfers; and, second, those who understand unjust enrichment as the restitution of extant gains. Unjust enrichment concerns both of these, but the different emphasis is important because it underlies two radically different approaches to the identification of the defendant's enrichment and the division of the primary claim and the defences to it. Viewing unjust enrichment as the reversal of defective transfers leads to a transactional approach that identifies the enrichment to be given up as the enrichment immediately received, whereas understanding unjust enrichment as the giving up of extant gains leads to a focus on what the defendant still holds. This is the fundamental distinction between the 'immediate enrichment' and 'extant enrichment' approaches.

In factual enrichment cases, this book maintains that the 'moment of enrichment' is the moment when the two limb inquiry outlined in chapter three is satisfied. The moment of enrichment is the relevant point of valuation. In legal enrichment cases, the moment of enrichment is when the right is acquired or the obligation released in the defective transaction. Enrichment is concerned, therefore, with the value received or right or release obtained in the defective transaction, not what the defendant still holds. Of course, the law of unjust enrichment takes account of what survives in the defendant's hands, but this represents the principled distinction between the enrichment inquiry and the defence of change of position. Furthermore, it is argued that the focus on immediate enrichment

[1] For an example, see below nn 7–9 and accompanying text.

defended in this chapter is mandated by the 'at the expense of' requirement, which connects the two parties to the defective transaction.

# I. Immediate Enrichment in Factual Enrichment Cases

In chapter three, it was contended that factual enrichment requires proof that:

(i) the defendant received value; and
(ii) the defendant chose the benefit or it is 'incontrovertibly enriching'.

The defendant is enriched by the value received in the defective transaction only when *both* elements of the enrichment inquiry are established. Contrary to the suggestion that the change of position defence has shifted the enrichment inquiry away from value received to value surviving,[2] the recognition of the defence has enabled a strict approach to identifying the defendant's enrichment as the value received at the moment of enrichment. However, this book must confront the various 'extant enrichment' approaches that suggest the enrichment inquiry is concerned with what the defendant still holds. Sub-section A outlines and rejects three possible versions of the 'extant enrichment' thesis. Sub-section B makes the case for an immediate enrichment approach, arguing that it is consistent with the case law and the theoretical basis of unjust enrichment claims as an instantiation of corrective justice. Sub-section C then explains that the moment of enrichment is the immediate receipt of value by the defendant at the claimant's expense, except in those circumstances where the benefit is chosen or becomes incontrovertible after the initial transfer of value. Where the second limb is satisfied only subsequently, the enrichment is limited to the value of the benefit chosen, or the extent to which the benefit is incontrovertible.

## A. Extant Enrichment Approaches

While it is generally accepted that enrichment is measured at the moment of the enrichment of the defendant at the claimant's expense, much confusion has resulted from not taking this point seriously. In different ways, commentators have considered what happens after the defendant is enriched to be relevant to the identification and valuation of the defendant's enrichment. For example, some

[2] See *Commerzbank AG v Price-Jones* [2003] EWCA Civ 1663; P Birks, 'Change of Position and Surviving Enrichment' in W Swadling (ed), *The Limits of Restitutionary Claims: A Comparative Analysis* (Glasgow, The United Kingdom Committee of Comparative Law, 1997); P Birks, *Unjust Enrichment*, 2nd edn (Oxford, Clarendon Press, 2005) 62–63, 208–09; R Chambers, 'Two Kinds of Enrichment' in R Chambers, C Mitchell and J Penner (eds), *Philosophical Foundations of the Law of Unjust Enrichment* (Oxford, Oxford University Press, 2009) 247–49.

commentators and courts have suggested that unjust enrichment is concerned with the value 'surviving'[3] in the defendant's hands or the 'factual benefit'[4] to the defendant. Theories that define enrichment by reference to what occurs after the moment of enrichment are collectively termed 'extant enrichment' theories in this book, but this is undoubtedly an ambiguous description that captures at least three different meanings in factual enrichment cases: (i) the present value of the benefit at the date of judgment; (ii) the value subsequently derived from the benefit by the defendant; and (iii) the value surviving after taking into account the defendant's changed position. This sub-section considers and rejects these extant enrichment approaches and contends that the enrichment inquiry is always focussed on the moment of enrichment. As we shall see, this has tremendous importance because a focus on subsequent events and what survives in the defendant's hands incorrectly quantifies the factual enrichment and confuses restitution and disgorgement.[5]

### *(i) Present Value*

The first possible extant enrichment approach turns on the distinction between the value of the benefit at the moment of enrichment and its present value at the date of judgment. If the law of unjust enrichment were really concerned with the giving up of extant gains still held by the defendant, then the date of judgment would be the date of valuation of the defendant's enrichment. This is not the case. It is clear from the cases examined below that the law of unjust enrichment focuses on the value at the moment of enrichment, not the present value. For example, the law regularly confronts the date of valuation question in making quantum meruit awards for unjust enrichment and the position is unequivocal: the services are valued at the date they enrich the defendant.[6]

However, the decision in *Cheese v Thomas* is an example where the valuation was not made at the time of transfer.[7] The claimant, Cheese, and his great-nephew, Thomas, purchased a house, which declined in value. Cheese sought to recover the value of his contribution to the purchase price on the basis of undue influence, which was admitted. This was a claim for restitution of the value of the £43,000 contribution received by Thomas from Cheese. However, the Court of Appeal held that the fall in value should be borne by both parties

[3] See ibid.

[4] See R Stevens, *Torts and Rights* (Oxford, Oxford University Press, 2007) 61. Although he uses this terminology in relation to torts, Stevens takes the same view in respect of gains from unjust enrichment: R Stevens, 'Three Enrichment Issues' in A Burrows and A Rodger (eds), *Mapping the Law: Essays in Memory of Peter Birks* (Oxford, Oxford University Press, 2006) 53 *cf* J Edelman, 'The Meaning of Loss and Enrichment' in R Chambers, C Mitchell and J Penner (eds), *Philosophical Foundations of the Law of Unjust Enrichment* (Oxford, Oxford University Press, 2009) 224–25.

[5] See above ch 1, s II.

[6] C Mitchell, P Mitchell and S Watterson, *Goff & Jones The Law of Unjust Enrichment*, 8th edn (London, Sweet & Maxwell, 2011) §4-34. See discussion of quantum meruit awards below in s I.B. of this chapter.

[7] *Cheese v Thomas* [1994] 1 WLR 129 (CA).

in proportion to their contributions, a conclusion that is not consistent with the immediate enrichment thesis. Thomas's immediate enrichment was the value of Cheese's initial contribution to the purchase price, not the present value of that contribution after the diminution in the price. The justification offered by Sir Donald Nicholls V-C is that, while the 'basic objective of the court is to restore the parties to their original positions', the court had discretion to achieve 'a practically just outcome'.[8] As the purchase was in the nature of a joint venture, the court held that the valuation should be at the later date.

The conclusion reached in *Cheese v Thomas* cannot be supported and should not be followed in subsequent cases. If Cheese laboured under undue influence, his contribution to the purchase price unjustly enriched Thomas at his expense. Thomas was enriched by the value received at the point of receipt. Indeed, it is surprising that the fact that the arrangement was in the nature of a joint venture is considered relevant, since the very existence of the joint venture arrangement depended on the undue influence. The better view is that the great-nephew was enriched by the immediate value of the contribution and the question before the court should have been whether the great-nephew could rely on the change of position defence to the extent of the decline in value.[9]

### *(ii) Subsequent Value*

The second extant enrichment approach views the defendant's enrichment as the gain causally derived from the benefit initially received. This is the approach supported by Stevens.[10] In the law of torts, Stevens's approach to the identification of gains in *Torts and Rights* is to ask whether the defendant is 'factually better off as a result of the wrong?'[11] In relation to the law of unjust enrichment, it is clear from 'Three Enrichment Issues'[12] that Stevens's conception of enrichment is similarly focussed on what occurs after the moment of enrichment: a defendant is not enriched unless he is factually better off as a result of the benefit conferred. He advocates an apportionment of the subsequent factual benefit between the various causal contributions to the gain actually derived; the defendant's enrichment is that part of the gain causally derived at the claimant's expense.[13] As we shall see below, this approach is inconsistent with the cases, but it is rejected here as a matter of principle.

The distinction between immediate and subsequent enrichment is a distinction based on timing, but it has normative implications. The immediate enrichment

[8] Ibid 43 (Nicholls V-C).

[9] See discussion of change of position in *Cheese v Thomas* in M Chen-Wishart, 'Loss Sharing, Undue Influence and Manifest Disadvantage' (1994) 110 *LQR* 173, 177–78; N Nahan, 'Rescission: A Case for Rejecting the Classical Model?' (1997) 27 *University of Western Australia Law Review* 66, 84–85 *cf* Mitchell, Mitchell and Watterson, *Goff & Jones The Law of Unjust Enrichment* (2011) (n 6) §4-40.

[10] Stevens, 'Three Enrichment Issues' (2006) (n 4).

[11] Stevens, *Torts and Rights* (2007) (n 4) 61.

[12] Stevens, 'Three Enrichment Issues' (2006) (n 4) 53.

[13] Ibid 53, 55–57.

measure is the value received by the defendant at the moment he is enriched by the relevant benefit; the subsequent value measure is that portion of the gain made by the defendant that is causally attributable to the benefit received. For instance, in *Craven-Ellis v Canons*,[14] the management services provided by the claimant were the immediate enrichment: the defendant company received value through the defendant's labour, time and skill. The request was for the performance of management services and the benefit conferred on the company was the requested performance. However, if we imagine that the defendant company had landed a multi-million pound contract solely due to the claimant's management services, some portion of the profits from that contract represent subsequent value derived from the benefit conferred by the claimant. In this scenario, is the claimant only entitled to the market value of his labour and management skills or can he claim whatever portion of the profits are attributable to his skills and labour?

It is suggested that the claimant would only be entitled to the immediate enrichment in the defective transaction between the company and its director: the value of the management services at the time they were rendered. As highlighted by the *Craven-Ellis v Canons* example, in services cases the defendant is enriched by the value of the claimant's labour, time and expertise. If the defendant reaps large profits as a result of those services, those profits represent a subsequent gain: while the profits are causally connected to the claimant's skills and labour, they flow from the company's subsequent use of that benefit rather than being constitutive of it. The distinction is well illustrated by money: the immediate enrichment is the capital sum and the opportunity to use the money; the subsequent value of the benefit depends on the gains derived from the actual use of the money. The majority in *Sempra* made it clear that subsequent gains causally derived from the benefit conferred in the defective transaction are not recoverable in unjust enrichment,[15] although the claimant may have a right to claim such gains if the claim can be based on a wrong.[16]

### *(iii) Surviving Value*

The third possible extant enrichment approach takes into account changes in the defendant's position following the moment of enrichment. This is the approach suggested by Chambers, who treats changes of position after the receipt of the benefit as effectively being part of the 'enrichment' question, rather than a separate defence. As the editors of *Philosophical Foundations of the Law of Unjust Enrichment* explain:[17]

> [I]f the essence of the claimant's claim is for restitution of the defendant's actual enrichment, and the purpose of the 'defence' is to reflect how much the defendant

[14] *Craven-Ellis v Canons Ltd* [1936] 2 KB 403 (CA).
[15] See below nn 21–24 and accompanying text.
[16] See Edelman, 'The Meaning of Loss and Enrichment' (2009) (n 4) 225, 240–41.
[17] R Chambers, C Mitchell and J Penner, *Philosophical Foundations of the Law of Unjust Enrichment* (Oxford, Oxford University Press, 2009) 16.

> *remains* enriched at the time of the claim, then the claim, properly made, simply cannot be for the value received ... on Chambers's formulation of the causative event, the causative event is not the impugned transaction, but the enrichment it causes, or rather, sets in train, which begins at the level of value received, but diminishes when the defendant innocently invites another twenty guests to his daughter's wedding or lavishly benefits a charity.

An approach with similar implications has been articulated by Birks.[18] However, it is clear from the immediate enrichment approach advanced in this chapter that viewing the defendant's enrichment as the value received at the moment of enrichment does not necessitate collapsing the enrichment and change of position enquiries as Birks and Chambers suggest. On an immediate enrichment approach, the changed state of affairs at date of judgment is a matter for the defence. Consequently, proof of surviving value is not a necessary precondition to the restitution of the immediate factual enrichment: the cause of action 'does not depend on the continued retention of the [benefit] by the defendant'.[19] The defendant need not retain an extant benefit in order to be liable for restitution of the value received, although dissipation of that value will be relevant to the defence of change of position.

## B. Immediate Value

In factual enrichment cases, the immediate enrichment thesis holds that the enrichment is the 'immediate value' of the benefit received in the defective transaction, subject to the limitations imposed by the protection of freedom of choice. The immediate value restriction excludes subsequent events and conduct, as well as antecedent or simultaneous events and conduct, that are extraneous to the receipt of value in a defective transaction factually enriching the defendant at the expense of the claimant. The immediate enrichment thesis is supported here for three main reasons: first, this approach fits the existing body of case law, in particular the preponderance of those cases awarding money had and received, quantum meruit and quantum valebat, which are almost all valued at the moment of receipt; second, the 'at the expense of' requirement limits restitutionary liability to the immediate enrichment received; and, third, the immediate enrichment approach is consistent with the theoretical underpinnings of unjust enrichment as an instantiation of corrective justice.

### *(i) Fit with Existing Cases*

The immediate enrichment approach advocated in this book best fits and explains the cases.[20] Recently, this issue came before the House of Lords in *Sempra Metals* and the

[18] Birks, 'Change of Position and Surviving Enrichment' (1997) (n 2).

[19] *Portman BS v Hamlyn Taylor Neck* [1998] 4 All ER 202 (CA) 207 (Millett LJ).

[20] See, eg *Guardian Ocean Cargoes Ltd v Banco do Brasil SA (No 3)* [1992] 2 Lloyd's Rep 193 (QB); *Sempra Metals Ltd v IRC* [2007] UKHL 34, [2008] 1 AC 561; *Benedetti v Sawiris* [2010] EWCA Civ

majority sided with the immediate enrichment approach over an extant enrichment approach. Lord Hope,[21] Lord Nicholls[22] and Lord Walker[23] all held that the claimants were entitled to the use value of the Advance Corporation Tax payments irrespective of the subsequent use of the money by the IRC. As Lord Hope put it:[24]

> [M]oney has a value, and in my opinion the measure of the right to subtraction of the enrichment that resulted from its receipt does not depend on proof by Sempra of what the revenue actually did with it. It was the opportunity to turn the money to account during the period of the enrichment that passed from Sempra to the revenue.

The minority—Lord Scott[25] and Lord Mance[26]—preferred an extant enrichment approach. Their Lordships held that the award of compound interest for the use of the money must turn on what the IRC did with the advanced tax payments. The minority's focus on the value that the IRC obtained through subsequent use of the tax payments is inconsistent with the immediate enrichment approach adopted in the law of unjust enrichment generally. Furthermore, in the more recent decision in *Yeoman's Row Management v Cobbe*, Lord Scott takes an immediate enrichment approach, finding that the defendant was enriched by the services Cobbe provided in obtaining the grant of the permission. Lord Scott gives the example of a locksmith asked to fashion a key to a cabinet believed to be full of treasures. He concludes that the enrichment is the value of the services, not a share in the value of the treasures that those services unlocked.[27] On Lord Scott's own reasoning, the conclusion could hardly be otherwise if the cabinet were empty. The same approach was taken by all members of the Court of Appeal in *Benedetti v*

1427. In Canada, the preference for a 'value received', not 'value surviving', approach is explicit: *Peter v Beblow* [1993] 1 SCR 980 (SCC) [32] (McLachlin J); *Bell v Bailey* (2001) 203 DLR (4th) 589 (ONCA); *Wylie v Leclair* (2003) 226 DLR (4th) 439 (ONCA); *Vanesse v Seguin* [2009] ONCA 595, (2009) 96 OR (3d) 321 [7]–[10]. Australian authority generally favours an immediate value approach: *David Securities Pty Ltd v Commonwealth Bank of Australia* (1992) 127 CLR 353 (HCA) 378–79, 385 (Mason CJ, Deane, Toohey, Gaudron and McHugh JJ); *Coshott v Lenin* [2007] NSWCA 153; *Sharjade Pty Ltd v RAAF* [2008] NSWSC 1003; *Adamson v Miller* [2008] FMCA 1173 but *cf Heperu Pty Ltd v Belle* [2009] NSWCA 252 [145]–[153] (Allsop P), which explicitly favoured a 'value surviving' approach.

[21] *Sempra Metals Ltd v IRC* [2007] UKHL 34, [2008] 1 AC 561 [32] (Lord Hope): 'Disgorgement would be appropriate if the claimant was seeking to recover the actual profits that the defendant had made as a result of the enrichment. But Sempra does not ask for an account of profits, nor does it invite the court to look at the use, if any, to which the money was actually put by the revenue'.

[22] Ibid [117] (Lord Nicholls): 'The time value of money, measured objectively in this way, is to be distinguished from the value of the benefits a defendant actually derived from the use of the money. The latter value is not in point in the present case'.

[23] Ibid [178], [180] (Lord Walker): 'income benefits are more accurately characterised as an integral part of the overall benefit obtained by a defendant who is unjustly enriched …. [Proprietary claims and account of profits are to be distinguished from] personal claims for interest which represents (in a more or less conventional way) the benefit which the defendant is presumed to have derived from money in his hands'.

[24] Ibid [33] (Lord Hope).

[25] Ibid [132], [146] (Lord Scott).

[26] Ibid [231] (Lord Mance).

[27] *Yeoman's Row Management Ltd v Cobbe* [2008] UKHL 55, [2008] 1 WLR 1752 [40]–[41] (Lord Scott).

*Sawiris*,[28] relying on Lord Scott in *Yeoman's Row Management v Cobbe*. Thus, enrichment does not turn on the subsequent financial position of the defendant or any extant enrichment retained.

### Money Had and Received

It is clear that restitution for money had and received is determined at the moment of receipt because money is incontrovertibly enriching. In *Baker v Courage & Co*,[29] money was paid under a mistake of fact. The court held that the cause of action was complete the moment the money was paid. The principle that the enrichment arises at the moment of receipt in money cases has since been reaffirmed by the House of Lords in *Kleinwort Benson Ltd v Lincoln CC*.[30] However, the Court of Appeal decision in *Jones & Sons (Trustee) v Jones*[31] may appear to be inconsistent with an approach measuring restitution of money at the moment of receipt. The defendant acquired £11,700 belonging, by virtue of the doctrine of relation back, to the claimant trustee in bankruptcy, which the defendant invested in potato futures. The investment was successful and the defendant's deposit account stood at £50,760 when the trustee demanded this sum from the defendant's bank. The bank interpleaded and paid the sum into court. The Court of Appeal held that the claimant had a common law claim to the £50,760 standing in the deposit account. Importantly, Millett LJ explicitly held that it was not an action in money had and received for the profits made by Mrs Jones, and went on to say that:[32]

> [I]n an action for money had and received it would be irrelevant what the defendant had done with the money after she received it. Her liability would be based on her receipt of the money, and she would be personally liable to a money judgment for £11,700. But, while the trustee would be entitled to a money judgment for that sum, he would not be entitled to any particular sum of £11,700 such as the money in court in specie.

Instead, Millett LJ found that the bank owed the debt represented by the bank account *to the trustee*. Smith rightly criticises this conclusion as a court-ordered redistribution of rights under a contract,[33] a finding which has no precedent at law. Nonetheless, the decision is explicitly rights-based, not value-based. Millett LJ viewed the defendant's enrichment as the right received at the claimant's expense and understood the action to reverse a rights-based enrichment. Whether or not

[28] *Benedetti v Sawiris* [2010] EWCA Civ 1427 [60], [80] (Arden LJ) [140], [145], [153] (Etherton LJ) [172] (Rimer LJ).

[29] *Baker v Courage & Co* [1910] 1 KB 56 (KB).

[30] *Kleinwort Benson Ltd v Lincoln CC* [1999] 2 AC 349 (HL). See also *El Ajou v Dollar Land Holdings plc* [1993] 3 All ER 717 (Ch) 757 (Millett J); *Fuller v Happy Shopper Markets Ltd* [2001] EWHC 702 (Ch), [2001] 1 WLR 1681 [12]–[18]; *Fea v Roberts* [2005] EWHC 2186 (Ch) [61]; Mitchell, Mitchell and Watterson, *Goff & Jones The Law of Unjust Enrichment* (2011) (n 6) §4-34.

[31] *Jones & Sons (a firm) (Trustee) v Jones* [1997] Ch 159 (CA).

[32] Ibid 168 (Millett LJ).

[33] L Smith, *The Law of Tracing* (Oxford, Oxford University Press, 1997) 327–28. For an argument for using money had and received to effect specific restitution of a right to money at law, see L Smith, 'Simplifying Claims to Traceable Proceeds' (2009) 125 *LQR* 338.

*Jones* is correctly decided, it is not a factual enrichment claim and it does not undermine the general rule that restitution of money had and received is measured at the moment of enrichment.

Quantum Meruit Awards

The immediate enrichment approach draws support from the assessment of quantum meruit awards. In quantum meruit awards for unjust enrichment,[34] effectively the award of restitution where the benefit conferred is a service,[35] the services are valued at the date they were rendered.[36] For example, the claimant in *Greenwood v Bennett*[37] was awarded the market value of the service rendered, not the gain realised by the subsequent sale of the car. Although the value of the service only became incontrovertible when it was realised in money, it will be explained below that the claimant cannot recover more than the value the defendant received *from* the claimant, that is the value of the service rendered.[38] Robert Goff J reached the same conclusion in *BP Exploration Co (Libya) Ltd v Hunt (No 2)*.[39] The gain that the defendants subsequently received as a result of the exploration of the concession was the vastly increased value of the concession, but the award was limited to an assessment of the value of the exploration work. Stevens explains both *Greenwood v Bennett* and *BP Exploration* as an apportionment of gain between the inherent value of the asset and the work done by the claimant,[40] but this is manifestly not the process by which Robert Goff J calculated the 'just sum' under section 1(3) of the Law Reform (Frustrated Contracts) Act 1943. Rather, Goff J considered the section to be a statutory application of the law of unjust enrichment,[41] and he stated that, but for the statute, he would have construed the exploration services themselves as the enrichment.[42]

In *Craven-Ellis*, the claimant was not awarded his personal losses as a result of performing the management services, nor was he awarded the gains made by the company as a result of his work; he was awarded the value of the management services he performed.[43] As the services had been requested, the right to restitution arose at the moment the services were provided.[44] In *Pavey & Matthews v Paul*, the builders were awarded $26,945.50, being 'a reasonable sum for the work

[34] As distinguished from contractual quantum meruit claims, see, eg *Foley v Classique Coaches Ltd* [1934] 2 KB 1 (CA); *J&J Penner Construction Ltd v Cringan* (1994) 93 Man R (2d) 252 (MBQB); G Fridman, 'Quantum Meruit' (1999) 37 *Alberta Law Review* 38.

[35] See ch 4, s III.A.

[36] *Sydney CC v Woodward* [2000] NSWCA 201 [94]; *Abigroup Contractors Pty Ltd v Peninsula Balmain Pty Ltd (No 2)* [2001] NSWSC 1016 [25]–[34]; *Coshott v Lenin* [2007] NSWCA 153 [17]. See Mitchell, Mitchell and Watterson, *Goff & Jones The Law of Unjust Enrichment* (2011) (n 6) §4-34.

[37] *Greenwood v Bennett* [1973] QB 195 (CA).

[38] See below n 66 and accompanying text.

[39] *BP Exploration Co (Libya) Ltd v Hunt (No 2)* [1979] 1 WLR 783 (QB).

[40] Stevens, 'Three Enrichment Issues' (2006) (n 4) 53, 55–57.

[41] *BP Exploration Co (Libya) Ltd v Hunt (No 2)* [1979] 1 WLR 783 (QB) 799 (Robert Goff J).

[42] Ibid 802 (Robert Goff J).

[43] *Craven-Ellis v Canons Ltd* [1936] 2 KB 403 (CA) 412 (Greer LJ).

[44] Ibid 409–12 (Greer LJ).

done and materials provided',[45] not the value of the house they had built or the costs they had incurred in doing so. The same is true of *William Lacey (Hounslow) Ltd v Davis*,[46] where the defendant had benefited in his negotiations with the War Damage Commission from preparatory work done by the claimants in anticipation of a contract that never eventuated. The claimant received the value of the services provided to the defendant, not the increased amount the defendant obtained from the War Damage Commission as a result. The effect of the quantum meruit award in all these cases is to reverse the immediate enrichment of the defendant, not the extant enrichment retained by the defendant.

However, a difficulty arises in some cases where the quantum meruit is assessed on a commission basis. There is a suggestion in the decision of Jacobs J in *Vedatech Corp v Crystal Designs (UK)*[47] that, where the industry practice is to remunerate services by commission rather than on a fee or cost-plus basis, the commission should be calculated as a percentage of the subsequent profits made.[48] Jacobs J did not have to decide the question of quantum in *Vedatech* and his obiter remarks are equivocal about the relevance of the profit figure, but his suggestion should not be followed. In *Way v Latilla*, Lord Atkin made the point that the court could take into account pre-contractual negotiations between the parties 'not with a view to completing the bargain for them, but as evidence of the value which each of them puts upon the services'.[49] The difficulty with the suggestion that the commission should be based on the subsequent profits in *Vedatech* is that such a quantum meruit award *would* complete the bargain between the parties. Vedatech should only have been entitled to a percentage of the profits made if it had secured a contract to that effect; conversely, had the transaction not been successful and no commission were payable, the defendants should not have been entitled to request and take the benefit of Vedatech's work without paying for it unless a contract so provided. As Judge LJ put it in *Sharab v Salfiti*, 'the valuation of the services rendered should [not] be affected by the use to which the recipient subsequently puts them, and in particular whether that use results in a business triumph or financial disaster'.[50] On the approach defended in this book, a commission based on the *reasonable expected profits* should have been awarded.

That the commission should properly be calculated on the *reasonable expected profits* is clear from *Benedetti v Sawiris*.[51] It was common ground between the parties that Benedetti was entitled to be remunerated on a quantum meruit basis. However, at first instance Patten J awarded a quantum meruit based on the valuation Sawiris placed on Benedetti's services after the transaction (€75.1

[45] *Pavey & Matthews v Paul* (1987) 162 CLR 221 (HCA) 225 (Mason and Wilson JJ).
[46] *William Lacey (Hounslow) Ltd v Davis* [1957] 1 WLR 932 (QB).
[47] *Vedatech Corp v Crystal Decisions (UK) Ltd* [2002] EWHC 818 (Ch).
[48] Ibid [76], [86], [90], [94] (Jacobs J).
[49] *Way v Latilla* [1937] 3 All ER 759 (HL) 764 (Lord Atkin).
[50] *Sharab v Salfiti* [1996] EWCA Civ 1189.
[51] *Benedetti v Sawiris* [2009] EWHC 1330 (Ch). See A Lodder, 'Unjust Enrichment and the Assessment of Quantum Meruit Awards' (2010) 126 *LQR* 42.

million), rather than the 'market value' of the services assessed by the industry standard commission of 0.3 per cent of the transaction value (€36.3 million).[52] Patten J's judgment was rightly overturned on this point in the Court of Appeal.[53] As Sawiris requested the services, the correct award was the market value at the time the services were performed. Arden LJ was perfectly clear that the 'services have to be valued as at the date when the services had been fully provided'[54] and 'the amount of the award will not necessarily be on the scale of the profit made by the respondents'[55] from the acquisition. Arden LJ was concerned to avoid a 'windfall'[56] to Benedetti if the award were based on Sawiris's valuation of those services after the fact and with hindsight of the profits actually made. The Court of Appeal's conclusion is only consistent with an approach that values the services the defendants received from Benedetti at the time the services were rendered.

*Way v Latilla*,[57] relied on extensively in *Benedetti*, is itself an example of the immediate enrichment approach supported in this book. Way provided Latilla with information about gold mines and concessions in West Africa in return for a reasonable sum and a share of the concessions. There was no concluded contract, but Way recovered a quantum meruit award for the services he had performed. At first instance, the court found there was a contract and awarded Way three per cent of Latilla's profits, which amounted to an award of £30,000. In the Court of Appeal, the finding that there was a contract was overturned. On appeal to the House of Lords, Way was awarded a quantum meruit. Latilla's profits were irrelevant to the calculation of the award. Way was instead awarded £5,000 assessed as a 'participation', which amounted to a commission.[58] Lord Atkin accepted the trial judge's valuation of the participation of £5,000 rather than awarding a percentage of the subsequent profits (ie the £30,000 award at trial):[59]

> It is true that there is evidence that Mr Latilla made very large profits. On the other hand, this amount was very favourably affected by this country's financial policy in respect of gold, which was altered some time after the services were rendered. Mr Way does not profess to have discovered the line of reef on which the concessions lay, and some of them at least were in respect of abandoned workings. These concessions had to be financed for some years, and other interests had to be satisfied.

The factors identified by Lord Atkin highlight why the commission is not to be calculated by reference to the subsequent profits. If the court is to assess the quantum meruit when the defendant is enriched, the valuation should not turn on when the claim is brought and whether there is evidence of the subsequent

52 *Benedetti v Sawiris* [2009] EWHC 1330 (Ch) [567]–[571] (Patten J).
53 *Benedetti v Sawiris* [2010] EWCA Civ 1427.
54 Ibid [80] (Arden LJ).
55 Ibid [60] (Arden LJ).
56 Ibid [80], [85] (Arden LJ).
57 *Way v Latilla* [1937] 3 All ER 759 (HL).
58 Ibid 764 (Lord Atkin). See also *Benedetti v Sawiris* [2009] EWHC 1330 (Ch) [531] (Patten J).
59 *Way v Latilla* [1937] 3 All ER 759 (HL) 764–65 (Lord Atkin).

profits made or not. The surviving value is irrelevant to a claim that is based on the immediate enrichment conferred by the provision of the services.

In *BP Exploration v Hunt (No 2)*, Robert Goff J took the view that where a contract:[60]

> [P]rovided that [the defendant] was to receive a stake in the concession, then the just sum might be enhanced on the basis that, in all the circumstances, a reasonable sum should take account of such a factor.

So, in circumstances where a commission is usual and the claimant risks making nothing or possibly sharing in huge profits, a restitutionary award calculated by reference to the market value of the services must take account of the relevant risks and rewards and be discounted or adjusted accordingly. However, there is no suggestion that the commission envisaged by the parties should be applied to the actual profits subsequently made. If it were otherwise, a claim for quantum meruit in relation to a transaction where the profit made is unforeseeably 100-fold larger than expected would entitle the claimant to a huge windfall without a contract. This is not the law.

Quantum Valebat Awards

The same rule applies to quantum valebat awards where, instead of a service, the benefit conferred is a good.[61] An example is the delivery of the steel nodes in *British Steel Corp v Cleveland Bridge and Engineering Co*.[62] Robert Goff J, treating the measure of recovery in the alternative quantum meruit and quantum valebat claims together, awarded the claimants 'a reasonable sum' calculated by reference to the price of the nodes at the time of delivery. Likewise, in *BP Exploration v Hunt (No 2)*, Robert Goff J assessed the 'just sum' under the Law Reform (Frustrated Contracts) Act 1943 for the farm-in oil delivered to Hunt 'in the nature of a *quantum valebat*' as the 'market value of the benefit itself' when received.[63]

### *(ii) 'At the Expense of'*

Although the 'at the expense of' requirement is beyond the scope of this book, it is suggested here that this requirement provides a second reason in support of the immediate enrichment approach over the extant enrichment approach. As Lord Atkin made clear in *Way v Latilla*,[64] it makes no sense to view the defendant's enrichment as the value in the defendant's hands as a result of events extraneous to the defective transaction. In the example of *Craven-Ellis v Canons Ltd*[65]

60 *BP Exploration Co (Libya) Ltd v Hunt (No 2)* [1979] 1 WLR 783 (QB) 805 (Robert Goff J).

61 Ibid 836 (Robert Goff J); *Dowell v Custombuilt Homes Pty Ltd* [2004] WASCA 171 [98] (Murray J). See Mitchell, Mitchell and Watterson, *Goff & Jones The Law of Unjust Enrichment* (2011) (n 6) §4-34.

62 *British Steel Corp v Cleveland Bridge and Engineering Co Ltd* [1984] 1 All ER 504 (QB).

63 *BP Exploration Co (Libya) Ltd v Hunt (No 2)* [1979] 1 WLR 783 (QB) 839 (Robert Goff J).

64 *Way v Latilla* [1937] 3 All ER 759 (HL) 764–65 (Lord Atkin).

65 *Craven-Ellis v Canons Ltd* [1936] 2 KB 403 (CA).

considered above, the immediate enrichment to the company was the management services provided by Craven-Ellis while his contract of employment was void. However, the value that survived is the present value of all profits causally attributed to Craven-Ellis's management, irrespective of the influence of extraneous factors such as movements in supply and demand, altered market conditions and so on. In *Greenwood v Bennett*,[66] Harper provided £226 worth of labour and materials to repair Bennett's car. The increase in the value of the car as a result was £325. Virgo reaches the conclusion that the defendant's enrichment is the £325 increase in the value of the car.[67] However, the Court of Appeal rightly awarded £226, which is the value received by the defendant from the claimant in the defective transaction. The increase in the value of the car is due to reasons extraneous to the defective transaction, including the inherent potential value of the car. Thus, the entire £325 is not 'at the expense of' the claimant.

The extant enrichment approach incorporates arbitrary factors that may cause fluctuating market values, such as supply and demand factors, seasonal factors, systemic factors and other variables, which have little to do with proving the defendant's enrichment 'at the claimant's expense'. Consequently, the extant enrichment approach relies on an attenuated notion of 'at the expense of' that looks beyond the defective transaction at a state of affairs that is unrelated to the transfer of value between the claimant and defendant. This cannot be right. The 'at the expense of' requirement mandates an immediate enrichment approach.

### *(iii) Corrective Justice*

The focus on immediate value transferred derives normative force from the conception of 'corrective justice' advocated by commentators such as Weinrib[68] and Smith,[69] which is often said to underpin liability in unjust enrichment. Indeed, the Supreme Court of Canada in *Kingstreet Investments v New Brunswick* held that:[70]

> Restitution is a tool of corrective justice. When a transfer of value between two parties is normatively defective, restitution functions to correct that transfer by restoring the parties to their pre-transfer positions.

[66] *Greenwood v Bennett* [1973] QB 195 (CA).

[67] G Virgo, *The Principles of the Law of Restitution*, 2nd edn (Oxford, Oxford University Press, 2006) 99.

[68] E Weinrib, *The Idea of Private Law* (Cambridge, Harvard University Press, 1995); E Weinrib, 'The Normative Structure of Unjust Enrichment' in C Rickett and R Grantham (eds), *Structure and Justification in Private Law* (Oxford, Hart, 2008); E Weinrib, 'Correctively Unjust Enrichment' in R Chambers, C Mitchell and J Penner (eds), *Philosophical Foundations of the Law of Unjust Enrichment* (Oxford, Oxford University Press, 2009).

[69] L Smith, 'Restitution: The Heart of Corrective Justice' (2001) 79 *Texas Law Review* 2115; L Smith, 'Unjust Enrichment: Big or Small?' in S Degeling and J Edelman (eds), *Unjust Enrichment in Commercial Law* (Sydney, Lawbook Co, 2008).

[70] *Kingstreet Investments v New Brunswick (Department of Finance)* [2007] 1 SCR 3 (SCC) [32].

Corrective justice is predicated upon the fundamental purpose of restoring equality in the bilateral relationships that underpin the private law.[71] The law of unjust enrichment operates to restore parties' pre-transactional normative positions.[72] On the enrichment model advanced here, the law of unjust enrichment focuses on normatively defective transfers of value and the link between the claimant and defendant is transactional: the law is responding to a transaction between the claimant and defendant involving a transfer of value.

This is sometimes expressed as the difference between 'normative' and 'material' gains and losses, but it is better understood as the difference between a transfer of value and an accretion to wealth, which was examined in chapter two.[73] Value is not the same as wealth and the focus on surviving enrichment looks to the defendant's wealth rather than the value transferred at the claimant's expense. The law of unjust enrichment has always been concerned primarily with the moment of the event altering the parties' rights. For this reason, the law only requires the defendant to give up the immediate enrichment received, not a gain subsequently derived from that receipt.[74] Leaving aside the defence of change of position, this logic must apply equally when the value received is dissipated: the defendant is enriched by the value received, not the diminished value of whatever part of the benefit survives in the defendant's hands. Corrective justice is inherently bilateral and transactional and, if unjust enrichment can usefully be explained as an instantiation of corrective justice, it is the defendant's immediate enrichment that represents the normative 'plus' to be corrected. The transfer of value to the defendant at the claimant's expense provides the normative link between the claimant and the defendant that is reversed by corrective justice.

## C. Identifying the Point of Enrichment

The protection of freedom of choice in factual enrichment cases raises difficult questions about the point at which a defendant is enriched by the receipt of a benefit. This is because of the two ways in which a defendant's objection from freedom of choice can be overcome: proof of choice of the benefit and incontrovertible enrichment. The point at which a transfer of value takes place and the point at which a defendant chooses the benefit or the benefit becomes incontrovertible will often not be the same. Most commonly, the defendant will request a

[71] Aristotle, *Nicomachean Ethics* (London, JM Dent & Sons, 1911) vol V, Ch IV; H Hart, *The Concept of Law*, 2nd edn (Oxford, Clarendon Press, 1997) 159; Smith, 'Unjust Enrichment: The Heart of Corrective Justice' (2001) (n 69) 2118; K Barker, 'Understanding the Unjust Enrichment Principle in Private Law' in J Neyers, M McInnes and S Pitel (eds), *Understanding Unjust Enrichment* (Oxford, Hart, 2004) 97.

[72] Smith, 'Unjust Enrichment: The Heart of Corrective Justice' (2001) (n 69) 2118.

[73] See ch 2, s IV.B.

[74] M McInnes, '"At the Plaintiff's Expense": Quantifying Restitutionary Relief' [1998] *CLJ* 472; M McInnes, 'Interceptive Subtraction, Unjust Enrichment and Wrongs—A Reply to Professor Birks' [2003] *CLJ* 697.

benefit before it is conferred and it is obvious that the defendant is enriched only by the value received when the benefit is conferred. However, proof of choice of the benefit may occasionally occur subsequently, most often when the defendant is not aware of the receipt of the benefit at the time it is conferred. In these cases, the factual enrichment is limited by the value of *the benefit chosen* by the defendant at the date of acceptance of the benefit. Likewise, a benefit may only become incontrovertibly enriching when it is subsequently realised in money. In these cases, the factual enrichment is the lesser of the value of the benefit received and the gain realised. In all cases, the moment of enrichment is the moment when both limbs of the enrichment inquiry are satisfied.

Understanding this relationship between the receipt of value and the tests for freedom of choice is critical. The choice of benefit and incontrovertibility tests go to protecting the defendant's freedom of choice, not to the receipt of a benefit transferring value to the defendant. Where the defendant receives a valuable right from the claimant or is the recipient of a service performed by the claimant, there is a transfer of value to the defendant. Whether the defendant chose the good or service is irrelevant to the existence of this objective transfer of value. However, the particular defendant is not automatically enriched by *any* value received; the value is only *potentially* enriching, depending on whether the second limb is satisfied. The defendant is only enriched when the benefit is chosen by the defendant or when the benefit becomes incontrovertible, and then only to the extent of the value of the benefit chosen or its incontrovertibility. Thus, the first limb of the factual enrichment inquiry identifies the value transferred to the defendant, but the second limb limits the enrichment to the value of the benefit at the moment of enrichment.

### *(i) Choice of Benefit Cases*

In cases satisfying the choice of the benefit test, the defendant's enrichment is always the moment of the transfer of value, unless the choice of the benefit takes place subsequently. There are two possible scenarios. First, the defendant may have chosen the benefit before the point of receipt of the benefit, which is typical in request cases. If the defendant requests services that the claimant never provides, it is obvious that the defendant is not enriched simply because the defendant chose the benefit. The mere request, without any part of the requested performance, does not constitute a benefit. The absence of a transfer of value to the defendant from the claimant precludes a finding of enrichment. The defendant will be enriched if and when the benefit is received.

The second, less common, scenario is where the choice of the benefit takes place after the point of receipt. One circumstance when this will be the case is where the benefit is readily returnable but the defendant refuses to return the benefit to the claimant, as occurred in *McDonald v Coys of Kensington*.[75] Although McDonald's

[75] *McDonald v Coys of Kensington* [2004] EWCA Civ 47, [2004] 1 WLR 2775.

factual enrichment could be easily established on the facts, Mance LJ would have been prepared to conclude that McDonald was enriched simply because he refused to return the mark to Cressman even though it was 'readily returnable'. Where the value of the benefit has changed before the defendant exercises a choice not to make it available to the claimant on request, this will make a difference to the defendant's factual enrichment: the defendant is not factually enriched until the choice of benefit test is satisfied. For instance, if McDonald were not aware of the transfer of the registration mark to him under the statutory scheme in 2000, but refused to return it when alerted to this fact in 2004 after the widespread introduction of personalised marks had greatly reduced its value, his refusal to return the benefit amounts to a choice of the benefit in 2004, not 2000. He is only enriched at the date he chooses the benefit. On these facts, McDonald would only be enriched by the value of the mark once he chose it in circumstances that assumed financial responsibility to pay for it under the test enunciated in chapter six.[76] Although it is theoretically possible in certain exceptional situations, a choice of a benefit will not usually be a choice to assume financial responsibility retrospectively.

However, what if the mark, instead of declining in value, was worth considerably more at the date the benefit was chosen? It is critical to remember that the first limb identifies the transfer of value from the claimant to the defendant, which occurs when the mark is first transferred to McDonald under the statutory scheme in 2000. In the same way that the choice of benefit requirement limits the claim to the value of the benefit when chosen, the first limb of the factual enrichment inquiry limits the enrichment to the value received *from the claimant* in the defective transaction. Accordingly, the claim would be for the value immediately transferred upon receipt of the benefit, not the increased value of the benefit at the moment of enrichment. This is the true explanation for why so-called 'subjective devaluation' does not entail 'subjective revaluation'[77] of the benefit where the benefit increases in value.[78] The second limb of the factual enrichment inquiry qualifies the defendant's enrichment from a transfer of value that occurs at the moment of receipt; the transfer of value does not take place at the moment of choice.

### *(ii) Incontrovertible Enrichment Cases*

It was argued in chapter six that a benefit may be incontrovertible when it is money or money-like or when it saves a necessary expenditure. In most of these cases, the benefit is incontrovertible from the moment it is received, for example where the defendant receives money. However, the benefit may become incontrovertible

[76] See ch 6, s II.A.

[77] *Cf* M Garner, 'The Role of Subjective Benefit in the Law of Unjust Enrichment' (1990) 10 *OJLS* 42, 43; Virgo, *The Principles of the Law of Restitution* (2006) (n 67) 88–89; Mitchell, Mitchell and Watterson, *Goff & Jones The Law of Unjust Enrichment* (2011) (n 6) §4-11.

[78] For a possible example of subjective revaluation, see *Benedetti v Sawiris* [2009] EWHC 1330 (Ch), which was reversed on this point in *Benedetti v Sawiris* [2010] EWCA Civ 1427. See Lodder, 'Unjust Enrichment and the Assessment of Quantum Meruit Awards' (2010) (n 51) 46–47.

after the transfer of value, such as where the benefit is subsequently realised in money. As explained above, the defendant will only be enriched when the second limb of the factual enrichment inquiry is satisfied, that is when the benefit is realised in money. Further, as with the choice of benefit test, the claimant is not entitled to the realised gain; rather, under the first limb of the factual enrichment inquiry, the claimant is limited to the value transferred to the defendant in the defective transaction.

Where the claimant repairs a motor vehicle by mistake, the claimant may recover the reasonable value of the services or the increased value of the car, *whichever is the lower figure*. The immediate value the defendant has received is the value of the service when rendered, but the defendant is only incontrovertibly enriched when the service is later realised in money. So, where the claimant carries out repairs worth £226 that increase the value of the defendant's car by £325, if the defendant subsequently chooses to sell the car, the benefit is the £226 in services that the claimant provided, not the increased value realised. Of course, if the benefit is realised for less than the market value of the service, the service is only incontrovertibly enriching up to the amount realised. For example, if the repairs in *Greenwood v Bennett* had only increased the value of the car when sold by £50, it cannot be said that the defendant is incontrovertibly enriched by any more than £50 because that is the extent to which the benefit has been turned into money. The £50 award should not be confused with the restitution of surviving value; it is the restitution of the immediate value transferred to the extent that it is incontrovertible. For instance, were there evidence that the defendant had requested the repairs, there can be no doubt that the claimant could recover the £226 market value of the services even though the realised gain is £50.

## II. Immediate Enrichment in Legal Enrichment Cases

The difference between the immediate and extant enrichment approaches has a different significance in legal enrichment cases as there is no question of valuation and thus no need to identify a point in time for valuing the enrichment. However, although it is irrelevant for valuation purposes, it is nevertheless important to identify the point of enrichment in legal enrichment cases because it goes to the consistency of the immediate enrichment approach across the case law. The theoretical coherence of the immediate enrichment thesis would, to some extent, be undermined if a different approach were taken to legal enrichment.

It is contended in this section that, although the logic of the claim in legal enrichment cases depends upon the defendant's still holding the right claimed or remaining amenable to the obligation released, these cases are nonetheless consistent with the immediate enrichment approach. The defendant is immediately enriched from the moment a right is acquired or an obligation released in a defective transaction at the claimant's expense. As the relevant enrichment is the right or release, not its value, subsequent events that affect the value of the right or release do not alter the defendant's legal enrichment. This is why appreciation or diminution in the value of the right or obligation is not relevant to the proof of enrichment: all that matters for legal enrichment is that the defendant received the relevant right or release at the claimant's expense and either continues to hold the right or to be capable of being subject to the obligation. As explained in chapter five, reversal of a legal enrichment occurs in four common situations: resulting trusts, rescission, rectification and restitutionary subrogation. This section argues that all four situations are consistent with the immediate enrichment approach adopted above in relation to factual enrichment claims.

## A. Resulting Trusts

It was argued in chapter five that (at least some) resulting trusts are a form of specific restitution of rights. In particular circumstances, where the defendant is unjustly enriched by the acquisition of a right at the claimant's expense, restitution will take the form of a resulting trust of that right. The defendant will hold the right on trust for the claimant, who may collapse that trust and obtain restitution of the right from the defendant. For example, where the defendant is a trustee enriched by a legal right conferred by the settlor upon a trust that fails, a resulting trust arises in favour of the settlor, who has a power to obtain restitution of the right held on trust.

In these circumstances, the mechanism of trust is used to give the claimant the power to obtain restitution of the right that unjustly enriches the defendant. As with other enrichment by rights cases, the defendant is enriched from the moment of creation of the relevant right. It does not matter that the defendant may have always held the legal right subject to a trust because the relevant enrichment is characterised legally, not in value terms; the defective transaction enriched the defendant by the creation of the right and the fact that the right may have been held for the benefit of the transferor since receipt is irrelevant for the purpose of legal enrichment. The constrained use or subjective value of the right to the defendant is irrelevant for the purpose of a finding of enrichment based simply on the acquisition of a right by the defendant at the claimant's expense. As the defendant is enriched from the moment of creation of the right, the resulting trust cases are consistent with the immediate enrichment thesis.

## B. Rescission

Rescission cases are entirely consistent with the immediate enrichment analysis. As explained in chapter five, when a transaction is rescinded, there are three potential scenarios: (i) a purely executory contract; (ii) a partly or fully-executed contract where no property rights have been created; and (iii) a partly or fully-executed contract where a property right has been created. It is argued that, in all three cases, the defendant is immediately enriched by the contractual rights created, as well as by the value of any performance or the creation of any property rights by reason of the contract.

### *(i) Purely Executory Contracts*

It was shown in chapter five that rescission of a purely executory contract is restitutionary because setting aside the contract reverses the unjust creation of contractual rights. However, there is no doubt that the defendant is enriched by the contractual rights at the moment they are created. As explained in chapter three,[79] contractual rights are rights capable of constituting an enrichment. These rights must enrich the defendant from the outset, not simply when performance commences or the contract is fully executed. For instance, contractual rights can be assigned for value prior to execution. The notion that a contractual right only becomes enriching on performance confuses factual and legal enrichment: for legal enrichment purposes, the enrichment is the contractual right itself, not its value. There is no doubt that the defendant obtains the right at the moment the contract is concluded. Performance will be relevant to any transfer of value under the contract, but the defendant is enriched by the creation of the right, even where the contract is purely executory.

### *(ii) Partly or Fully-executed Contracts Where no Property Rights have been Created*

As outlined in chapter five, setting aside contractual rights and obligations by rescission, without more, does not reverse value transferred by subsequent performance of the contract. Rescission does not automatically restore money paid or the value of work done under the contract. Rather, the rescission of the contract is only a part of restitution (and counter-restitution) of value transferred under an executed contract. For example, in a contract for services, the claimant is entitled to restitution of the value of work done under the contract, subject to a counter-claim for restitution of any money paid by the defendant. As with quantum meruit awards generally, the value of the work done is assessed at the time of performance, not at the point when the contract is rescinded.[80] Of course, the defences to rescission, such as the requirement that *restitutio in integrum* be possible, take into account what happens after that point, but it cannot be doubted that the relevant points of enrichment are the moment of the creation of the contractual right and the moment of receipt of value by performance.

### *(iii) Rescission Where Property Rights have been Created*

The situation is identical in circumstances where the contract creates a property right held by the defendant. Rescission is part of a restitutionary response, but

[79] See ch 3, nn 118–20 and accompanying text.
[80] See ch 5, s II.C.

setting aside contractual rights and obligations does not itself effect restoration of property rights conferred under the rescinded contract.[81] Rather, the claimant has a right to restitution of the property right unjustly conferred under the contract. The defendant is enriched at the moment the property right is created by the voidable contract. The defendant is immediately enriched by that right, irrespective of the use of the property or the value he attaches to it: the right is the relevant enrichment, not its use or value to the defendant.

### C. Rectification

The same approach must logically apply to rectification in each case. It was submitted in relation to rescission that the creation of contractual rights is immediately enriching in all cases and the position cannot possibly differ where the remedy is rectification rather than rescission. Likewise, any performance under an unrectified contract must be immediately enriching at the time of that performance and any property rights created must be enriching from the moment of creation. Rectification poses no unique problems for the immediate enrichment thesis.

### D. Subrogation

The final form of restitution of a legal enrichment is restitutionary subrogation. In chapter five, it was explained that subrogation often reverses the defendant's enrichment by the release of a liability at the claimant's expense. The subrogation reinstates a liability formerly owed by the defendant but released by the payment or performance of the claimant. The immediate enrichment thesis holds in restitutionary subrogation cases: the defendant is immediately enriched by the release of the liability as the liability ceases to exist at the moment of release. Since legal enrichment is concerned with the legal position of the defendant, not the value of the release of the obligation, the enrichment does not arise only when the liability would have fallen due, but when the defendant's legal position is changed at the claimant's expense. It is clear that the defendant's enrichment arises immediately upon the release.

## III. Conclusion

This chapter has focussed on the point of enrichment in factual and legal enrichment cases. It critically examined and rejected views of the enrichment inquiry that determine the defendant's enrichment by reference to the extant gain retained

[81] See ch 5, s II.B.

by the defendant in favour of identifying the enrichment as the immediate value transferred, right created or duty released in the defective transaction, subject to the limitations imposed by the choice of benefit and incontrovertible enrichment tests in factual enrichment cases. The immediate enrichment thesis is preferable for three reasons: first, it provides a consistent explanation of the preponderance of cases that value the enrichment at the moment of enrichment; second, it makes sense of the requirement that the defendant's enrichment be 'at the expense of' the claimant; and, third, it fits with an explanation of unjust enrichment as an instantiation of corrective justice. Therefore, on the basis of both fit and justification, there is a strong normative foundation for identifying the point of enrichment as the moment of factual or legal enrichment.

# 8

# Conclusions and Implications

## I. Factual and Legal Enrichment

The central contribution of this book to the law of unjust enrichment is the bifurcation of the enrichment inquiry into factual and legal enrichment. This book shows that the law adopts two different characterisations of the defendant's enrichment and that different responses, requirements and considerations turn on that characterisation. Most commonly, the law adopts a factual characterisation of the benefit to the defendant in terms of economic value: the defendant is enriched by the value received at the claimant's expense. Although the defendant's enrichment in these cases can often be characterised legally, the alternative factual enrichment claim reverses the value of the defendant's acquisition of rights or release from obligations, not the change in the defendant's juridical relations. Accordingly, the law's response in these cases is not to reverse the legal position, but instead to award monetary restitution. In legal enrichment cases, by contrast, the law adopts a legal characterisation of the benefit because the claimant seeks to reverse the enrichment in law, not recover the value transferred. In these cases, it is the change in the juridical relations of the defendant that matters and the law's response is to reverse that change by awarding specific restitution of the right or specific reinstatement of the obligation.

At the outset, this book identified the absence of close theoretical examination of the enrichment inquiry as a critical lacuna in the law of unjust enrichment. Accordingly, chapter two of the book sought to remedy this deficiency in our existing understanding by clarifying the theoretical building blocks of the enrichment inquiry: value, rights and obligations. In relation to value, it was contended that the law adopts a relational theory of value in unjust enrichment. The superficial attraction of idiosyncratic approaches to value was debunked in favour of the economic analysis of value more commonly employed by the courts in factual enrichment cases. Furthermore, to provide the foundations of legal enrichment, chapter two adopted a strict Hohfeldian analysis of rights and obligations as a framework to conceptualise the defendant's enrichment in legal terms. The Hohfeldian analysis provided the theoretical basis for the division into 'enrichment by rights'—where the defendant is enriched by the acquisition of a claim-right or power—and 'enrichment by release'—where the defendant is enriched by the release of a duty or liability. Furthermore, the utility of the concept of wealth for explaining enrichment was disavowed.

The adoption of relational value theory and Hohfeldian analysis of rights and obligations provides the foundation of the central theoretical division of enrichment into factual and legal enrichment in chapter three. A defendant may be benefitted in a variety of different forms, but the characterisation of that enrichment is critical. Instead of asking whether the defendant is enriched and then determining whether restitution is monetary or proprietary, it is necessary to ascertain whether the claimant is asserting:

(i) that the defendant is enriched by the value of the benefit received and seeks monetary restitution of that value; or
(ii) that the defendant is enriched by the acquisition of a right or release of an obligation at the claimant's expense and seeks specific restitution of that right or reinstatement of the obligation.

In factual enrichment claims, which were examined in detail in chapter four, the receipt or use of money, the performance of a service, the receipt or use of goods or land, and the release of obligations is reduced to the single quantitative dimension of value. The defendant's enrichment *is* value and the claim is for the restitution of that value by the payment of money. By contrast, in the legal enrichment cases examined in chapter five, it is the legal effect of the defective transaction that matters. The defendant's enrichment is the right or release acquired and the claimant is asking that the enrichment be reversed in law by specific restitution of the right (whether by a resulting trust, rescission or rectification) or reinstatement of the liability (by subrogation).

## II. Consequences

The significance of the law's bifurcated characterisation of the defendant's enrichment in factual and legal terms is manifold. First, this bifurcation enables a revised analysis of the forms of restitution. This book defined restitution in an orthodox fashion as the 'reversal of the defendant's enrichment' but existing analyses of 'proprietary restitution' have not fully appreciated that the characterisation of the enrichment is intimately connected with the measure and form of the restitutionary response. Specific restitution of the defendant's enrichment is determined by the legal characterisation of the enrichment. As the law reverses legal enrichments in a variety of ways, the province of specific restitution is thus broader than previous analyses have suggested. On this approach, resulting trusts, rescission, rectification and subrogation are all forms of specific restitution that reverse a legal enrichment of the defendant. If this analysis is accepted, it is necessary to revise the existing understanding of restitution in a way that links the different characterisation of the enrichment to be reversed with the form of restitution.

Second, the division between factual and legal enrichment reveals that freedom of choice concerns in the enrichment inquiry arise because of the characterisation of the defendant's enrichment as value. Accordingly, it was concluded that freedom of choice concerns have no application in establishing enrichment in legal enrichment cases. Once freedom of choice is properly restricted to value cases and the relational nature of value is properly understood, it becomes clear that freedom of choice concerns can be met by an objective enrichment model coupled with the change of position defence. Accordingly, chapter six rejected 'subjective devaluation' and advanced an alternative, objective model of factual enrichment according to a 'choice of benefit' test aimed at identifying when holding a defendant to be enriched by the value of a benefit in kind will infringe his freedom of choice. It was contended that a defendant is factually enriched whenever two elements are satisfied:

(i) a transfer of value to the defendant; and
(ii) unless the benefit is 'incontrovertibly enriching', the defendant chose the benefit.

By contrast, in legal enrichment cases, the value of the enrichment is irrelevant to establishing enrichment, as this element is satisfied by proving that the defendant has acquired a right or the release of an obligation at the expense of the claimant.

Finally, in chapter seven, it was shown that the enrichment model proposed in this book clarifies the point at which enrichment occurs. Under the traditional approach, which conflates factual and legal enrichment claims, the courts have sometimes assessed enrichment at the point of receipt and sometimes at the date of judgment. By dividing the enrichment inquiry in two, this book reveals that the enrichment inquiry is always concerned with the immediate enrichment received by the defendant, whether that be the value received, the right acquired or the release obtained, subject to the limitations imposed by the requirement of choice of the benefit or incontrovertibility in factual enrichment claims. In legal enrichment cases, the claimant is seeking restitution of the specific right or reinstatement of the specific obligation, not the value of these benefits. Thus, it is misguided to confuse specific restitution in legal enrichment cases with valuation of a right or obligation at the date of judgment.

## III. Further Implications

The radical reappraisal of the enrichment inquiry suggested in this book has wide-ranging implications and raises novel questions for the future development of the law of unjust enrichment and other areas of private law. Several key implications are foreshadowed here. First, as the identification of a legal enrichment is necessary, but not sufficient, for specific restitution, when is specific restitution of a legal enrichment available? Second, if the division between factual and legal enrichment is adopted, when can value claims and legal enrichment claims be combined? Third, is the division between factual and legal enrichment replicated in the 'at the expense of' requirement? Fourth, in the unjust inquiry, does this book shed any light on Birks's suggestion that the English 'unjust factors' approach should be replaced by 'absence of basis'? Fifth, in relation to the most important defence to unjust enrichment claims, does the immediate enrichment thesis clarify the scope of the change of position defence? Finally, to what extent is the analysis in this book applicable in the law of wrongs?

### *(i) The Availability of Specific Restitution*

The question when specific restitution of a legal enrichment is available is beyond the confines of the enrichment inquiry and this book, but the analysis presented here shows that the existing model of finding the defendant to be enriched and then asking whether restitution should be personal or proprietary is unsatisfactory. Instead, where the defendant is legally enriched and specific restitution to reverse that enrichment remains possible, this book concluded that the defendant will have a power to obtain specific restitution *provided* the law recognises the existence of such a claim. Whether the law recognises specific restitution of a right was said to depend on the legal or equitable regime governing the specific right; unjust enrichment gives rise to a power to obtain specific restitution within the relevant rights regime and subject to its limitations.

However, the division between factual and legal characterisation of enrichment may have more far-reaching implications for the consistent answer to that question in the law. It may be that specific restitution should always prima facie be available in legal enrichment cases because it is 'the most perfect way to make restitution, since it most perfectly restores the *status quo ante*'.[1] A more calibrated position is suggested by Chambers[2] and McFarlane and Stevens.[3] They argue that, where it is the acquisition of the specific right that is unjust, rather than merely the receipt of the value of the right, then specific restitution should be available. For example, the transfer of a right to be held on trust is intended to create obligations in relation to a specific right, not merely its value, so where the trust fails the obligation to make restitution attaches to the specific right. Likewise, where a voidable contract creates rights and obligations in relation to a specific right, such as the transfer of land or an identified chattel, the purchaser is unjustly enriched by a specific right. By contrast, the vendor in such a case has contracted for a certain price, not a specific right, and so the vendor

[1] L Smith, 'Philosophical Foundations of Proprietary Remedies' in R Chambers, C Mitchell and J Penner (eds), *Philosophical Foundations of the Law of Unjust Enrichment* (Oxford, Oxford University Press, 2009) 294. See also R Chambers, 'Two Kinds of Enrichment' in R Chambers, C Mitchell and J Penner (eds), *Philosophical Foundations of the Law of Unjust Enrichment* (Oxford, Oxford University Press, 2009) 267.

[2] Chambers, 'Two Kinds of Enrichment' (2009) (n 1) 273–75.

[3] B McFarlane and R Stevens, 'The Nature of Equitable Property' (2010) 4 *Journal of Equity* 1, 18–20.

is unjustly enriched only by the value of the money, not the specific right to it. On this approach, the identification of the enrichment either factually or legally is critical to ascertaining whether the unjust factor relates to the specific right acquired or obligation released, or merely its value. The problem of identifying when specific restitution is available is not susceptible of easy answers and it has long bedevilled the law of unjust enrichment but, on the approach suggested by Chambers and McFarlane and Stevens, the bifurcated model of enrichment suggested in this book may help to resolve some of the difficult questions raised in this context.

### *(ii) Combining Value-based and Legal Enrichment Claims*

While this book argues that a benefit can be characterised in two different ways, it does not examine when the two kinds of claim can be brought together because the availability of specific restitution remains highly controversial and, as just mentioned, it is not resolved in this book. However, we saw that where the enrichment is a right to a car that has been driven by the defendant, a claimant can combine a legal enrichment claim for specific restitution of the right to the car with a value-based claim for the use value of the car. In relation to rescission, the claimant is entitled to seek specific restitution of the contractual rights by exercising the power of rescission and may also claim restitution of value transferred by performance under the contract.[4] The principle is that, provided the claimant is not seeking restitution of the same enrichment both by value and by rights and restitution of one would not incidentally achieve restitution of the other, the two kinds of claim may be combined. It is also clear that the claimant must elect between specific restitution of property transferred under the contract and restitution of the value of that property: you cannot get back both the right to the car and its value. Nonetheless, there will be no double recovery where the claimant seeks restitution of a property right acquired by the defendant under the contract and the value of its use. Similarly, there is no double recovery where the claimant seeks specific restitution of a property right and the diminution in the value of that right.[5]

Another example of concurrent legal and value claims considered in this book is restitutionary subrogation, where the legal enrichment claim is combined with a factual enrichment claim. In these cases, the defendant is enriched by both the release of a liability and the necessary expense saved as a result of the claimant's payment. The claimant thus has a factual enrichment claim, but also seeks security for that claim by subrogation. The exercise of the subrogated security right is conditional upon the non-payment of the underlying factual enrichment claim. Therefore, there is no double recovery.

[4] See ch 5, s II.C.

[5] See, eg *Erlanger v The New Sombrero Phosphate Co* (1878) 3 App Cas 1218 (HL) 1278.

### *(iii) At the Expense of*

As outlined in chapter one, the 'at the expense of' question is the second requirement of a cause of action in unjust enrichment: the relevant enrichment must be 'at the expense of the claimant'. The recognition of two different kinds of enrichment properly identifies *what* must be 'at the expense of' the claimant: in value cases, it is the value received that must be at the expense of the claimant; in legal enrichment cases, it is the right or release of an obligation that must be at the expense of the claimant.[6] Accepting this distinction is likely to have at least two implications for resolving a number of difficult questions in this inquiry. First, the understanding of transfers of value promoted in this book provides a normative link between claimant and defendant that is preferable to a crude requirement of a 'corresponding loss' to the claimant. Second, although the discussion in the book was limited to the simple two-party bilateral enrichment situation, the conclusions have obvious implications for more complex 'at the expense of' scenarios involving remote enrichees.

On the first point, if this book is correct to say that factual enrichment claims depend on a 'transfer of value' from the claimant to the defendant, then this should provide the normative link between claimant and defendant in the 'at the expense of' requirement. As explained in chapter two, a transfer of value is a transactional concept; it occurs when the defendant receives value from the claimant in a normatively defective transaction. The transfer of value provides the normative link between the claimant and the defendant and underpins the requirement that the defendant's enrichment comes 'at the claimant's expense'. In addition, when coupled with the immediate enrichment thesis in chapter seven, this transactional concept of value suggests that the 'at the expense of' requirement in value cases limits the claim to the value received by the defendant in the defective transaction. As Weinrib explains, the transfer of value ensures:[7]

> [T]he immediacy of the link between the parties as transferor and transferee of value. The notion of a transfer thereby defines the ambit of liability, preventing liability that is either too restrictive or too expansive … . Liability is too expansive when the plaintiff's claim is allowed even though the parties are not related as transferor and transferee.

Factual enrichment cases may thus be structurally limited to the transfer of value in the defective transaction between the parties. This does not require a corresponding loss to the claimant;[8] rather, it requires that any value received by

[6] The virtues of the factual–legal distinction for explaining the 'at the expense of' requirement are demonstrated by E Ball, '"At the Expense of the Claimant": Unpacking the Requirement' (M Phil thesis, University of Oxford, 2011).

[7] E Weinrib, 'Correctively Unjust Enrichment' in R Chambers, C Mitchell and J Penner (eds), *Philosophical Foundations of the Law of Unjust Enrichment* (Oxford, Oxford University Press, 2009) 37.

[8] The requirement of corresponding loss has been generally rejected: P Birks, *Unjust Enrichment*, 2nd edn (Oxford, Clarendon Press, 2005); J Edelman, 'The Meaning of Loss and Enrichment' in R Chambers, C Mitchell and J Penner (eds), *Philosophical Foundations of the Law of Unjust Enrichment* (Oxford, Oxford University Press, 2009).

the defendant comes from the claimant in a bilateral transfer. For example, in a standard services case, the cost to the claimant may be less than the value of the service received by the defendant, but what matters is that the value received by the defendant came from the claimant in the defective transaction.

Second, differentiating factual and legal enrichment helps makes sense of the operation of the 'at the expense of' requirement against remote enrichees. The importance of recognising the distinction is that, unlike transfers of value, which are abstract, rights and obligations are particular to persons: they exist in relationships between persons or, in the case of property rights, in relation to corporeal things. A person may retain a right to property despite the corporeal thing passing through numerous hands to a remote enrichee. Through the process of tracing through unauthorised substitutions, the property right may even be exigible in respect of a different thing.[9] The same persisting quality is a feature of persistent powers, like the beneficiary's power to collapse a trust. As a result, a legal enrichment might come 'from' the claimant even though the subject matter of the right is received from a third party. As a result, a bilateral transfer of value may be present where D's enrichment is at C's expense even though the enrichment is conferred by X.[10] For example, in situations of 'interceptive subtraction' and 'leapfrogging'[11] it may be correct to view the transaction as involving a transfer of *value* between C and D, even though X confers the legal enrichment. Thus, in both factual and legal enrichment claims, the 'at the expense of' question may be better understood by separating the legal effect of the transaction and the factual transfer of value.

Critically, however, although the enrichment can be characterised in two different ways, this does not imply a strict bifurcation of the 'at the expense of' requirement. For instance, where the defendant acquires a right, that right may be characterised in two different ways, but the right has no less come 'from' the claimant because it is characterised legally rather than factually. So, where the defendant has acquired a right or the release of an obligation, how that benefit is characterised does not determine whether the benefit is at the claimant's expense. Rather, a focus on the difference between the legal characterisation of the benefit and the factual transfer of value may help explain the operation of the 'at the expense of' requirement against remote enrichees in both factual and legal enrichment cases.

### *(iv) Absence of Basis*

In his final work, Birks suggested that the law of unjust enrichment can be better understood in terms of a civilian-inspired 'absence of basis' approach,[12] rather

[9] See generally *Boscawen v Bajwa* [1996] 1 WLR 328 (CA) 334 (Millett LJ); L Smith, *The Law of Tracing* (Oxford, Oxford University Press, 1997).

[10] See P Birks, *Unjust Enrichment*, 2nd edn (Oxford, Clarendon Press, 2005) 78–82.

[11] See ibid ch 4.

[12] See ibid 101–60.

than the orthodox unjust factors approach still applied in England (and presumed in this book).[13] According to Birks, restitution follows where an enrichment has no legal basis. An unjust factor may provide a reason why an apparent legal basis does not exist,[14] but it is not necessary to point to an unjust factor where there is no purported legal basis for an enrichment at all. The bifurcation of the enrichment inquiry suggested in this book does not imply that the unjust question is to be resolved differently depending on the characterisation of the defendant's enrichment; on the contrary, the fact that the same unjust factors give rise to restitutionary responses with the same purpose and effect was an explicit reason for gathering factual and legal enrichment claims together in unjust enrichment. Thus, it seems likely that whichever model prevails will encompass both kinds of enrichment.

However, the enrichment model presented in this book casts doubt on the absence of basis thesis in two fundamental respects. First, in factual enrichment cases, the receipt of value by the defendant, not the legal effect, is the foundation of the claim. There are various examples where there is no legal right acquired or obligation released, for instance quantum meruit awards. Indeed, this book suggests that a transfer of value may take place without a corresponding transfer of the underlying right, as occurs where the defendant acquires possession of a chattel and title does not pass. The absence of basis theory is most plausible where what is in need of explanation is a legal right or the release of a legal obligation, but the theory provides no reason for concluding that the receipt of *value* requires a legal basis.[15] By contrast, the unjust factors model assumes that it is the *restitution* of value that requires a justification, not the *receipt* of value. As such, absence of basis theories are forced to claim that all transfers of value require a legal basis, which is difficult to square with the conclusion in this book that transfers of value can occur without the transfer of any underlying legal right or the release of a legal obligation.

Second, if this book correctly classifies rescission and rectification on particular grounds as being restitutionary responses to unjust enrichment, it is very difficult to explain these cases on an absence of basis approach. In rescission, that the contract is voidable because of an unjust factor, as opposed to void, assumes that a valid basis for the defendant's enrichment exists until the power is exercised. In rectification cases, the contract, including the unrectified terms, is valid until rectified. In both cases, the power arises immediately upon the defendant's unjust

[13] See *Deutsche Morgan Grenfell plc v IRC* [2006] UKHL 49, [2007] 1 AC 558 [21] (Lord Hoffmann); *Sempra Metals Ltd v IRC* [2007] UKHL 34, [2008] 1 AC 561. Australia: *David Securities Pty Ltd v Commonwealth Bank of Australia* (1992) 127 CLR 353 (HCA) *cf* Canada: *Garland v Consumers' Gas Co* [2004] SCC 25, [2004] 1 SCR 629 (SCC); *Pacific National Investments Ltd v City of Victoria* [2004] SCC 75, [2004] 3 SCR 545 (SCC).

[14] Birks, *Unjust Enrichment* (2005) (n 10) 116.

[15] K Barker, 'Responsibility for Gain: Unjust Factors or Absence of Legal Ground? Starting Points in Unjust Enrichment Law' in R Grantham and C Rickett (eds), *Structure and Justification in Private Law* (Oxford, Hart, 2008).

enrichment, even though there is, by definition, a valid basis for the enrichment until the claimant's election to rescind. Thus, the inclusion of rescission and rectification as restitutionary responses to unjust enrichment suggests that the absence of basis model does not accurately reflect English law.

### *(v) Change of Position*

It is suggested in this book that there are three points of intersection between the enrichment inquiry and the change of position defence: the first is the relationship between immediate enrichment and subsequent or anticipatory changes of position; the second is the interaction between the protection of the defendant's freedom of choice afforded by the enrichment inquiry and the protection of freedom of choice in the change of position defence; and the final point of intersection is the applicability of the defence to legal enrichment claims.

In respect of the first point of intersection, the immediate enrichment thesis advanced in chapter seven suggests that there is a principled distinction between the enrichment inquiry and the operation of the change of position defence. This is a vital rejoinder to those who adopt an extant enrichment approach. For example, in the introduction to *Philosophical Foundations of the Law of Unjust Enrichment*, his fellow editors question Chambers's focus on surviving enrichment and suggest that it may break down the distinction between enrichment and change of position. This book concurs with their assessment that Chambers's analysis 'strongly suggests that the change of position defence is not really a defence … and the purpose of the "defence" is to reflect how much the defendant *remains* enriched'.[16] This problem was highlighted in the recent decision in *Heperu v Belle*,[17] where the Court of Appeal of New South Wales adopted a surviving enrichment approach and failed to appreciate the role of change of position.

If the immediate enrichment thesis defended in chapter seven is correct, it suggests a principled distinction between the enrichment inquiry and change of position: the enrichment inquiry is concerned with the value transferred, rights created and duties released in the defective transaction, whereas the change of position defence is concerned with extraneous events or conduct of the defendant in reliance on, or in anticipation of, receipt of the enrichment that either diminishes or extinguishes the enrichment. The immediate enrichment thesis introduces a distinction based not only on timing, but on normative grounds for segregating primary liability for restitution from a defence that has a separate substantive justification from the primary claim. This may provide one basis for concluding that the defence of change of position is not simply the negation of the enrichment inquiry (ie it is not simply a 'disenrichment' defence),[18] but rather

[16] R Chambers, C Mitchell and J Penner, *Philosophical Foundations of the Law of Unjust Enrichment* (Oxford, Oxford University Press, 2009) 16.

[17] *Heperu Pty Ltd v Belle* [2009] NSWCA 252 [145]–[157] (Allsop JA).

[18] *Cf* Birks, *Unjust Enrichment* (2005) (n 10) 208–12; A Burrows, *The Law of Restitution*, 3rd edn (Oxford, Oxford University Press, 2010) 526–27.

relies on events that are extraneous to the defective transaction and the defendant's conduct in response to, or in anticipation of, receipt of that enrichment.[19]

In respect of the second point of intersection, the notion that the protection of the defendant's freedom of choice is provided by the defence of change of position was floated in *Sempra Metals Ltd v IRC*.[20] In *Sempra Metals*, the House of Lords found that the Revenue was enriched by the use value of the advanced corporate tax payments they received. However, the Revenue was not required to make restitution at commercial rates of interest because it had instead discharged public sector borrowing at government rates. Lord Nicholls expressly left open the question of whether this so-called 'subjective devaluation' is to be 'characterised as part of the "change of position" defence available in restitution'.[21] On the approach in chapter six, the law should follow his Lordship's intriguing suggestion only part of the way. The defendant's freedom of choice is relevant to liability in two ways: first, the defendant's freedom of choice is relevant to establishing factual enrichment; and, second, it is relevant to what the defendant chooses to do in reliance on the benefit or anticipated benefit. Accordingly, in value cases, the law protects the defendant's freedom of choice in two ways: (i) by the second limb of the enrichment inquiry, that is proving that the particular defendant chose the benefit; and (ii) by the defence of change of position. The precise role of freedom of choice in the defence of change of position is beyond the scope of this work, but it is important to appreciate that the enrichment inquiry does not bear the entire burden of protecting the defendant's freedom of choice.

Finally, unresolved issues arise in respect of whether a defendant is entitled to the change of position defence in legal enrichment cases.[22] To some extent, changes of position exclude legal enrichment claims, as specific restitution requires the defendant to retain the right acquired or remain amenable to the obligation released. So, if the defendant no longer has the right, or the obligation cannot be reinstated because of a change of circumstances, then specific restitution will be denied. However, it is not clear whether the change of position defence applies when the defendant changes her position by giving up a *different* right or by dissipating value in good faith reliance on the security of the right acquired or release obtained. Specific restitution may seem a harsh result. For example, if the defendant acquires title to the claimant's car by mistake and, in good faith, makes a gift of her old car to a third party, this should arguably constitute a change of

[19] J Edelman and E Bant, *Unjust Enrichment in Australia* (Oxford, Oxford University Press, 2006) 319–23; E Bant, *The Change of Position Defence* (Oxford, Hart, 2009) ch 8.

[20] *Sempra Metals Ltd v IRC* [2007] UKHL 34, [2008] 1 AC 561.

[21] Ibid [119] (Lord Nicholls). See also [232] (Lord Mance).

[22] P Birks, 'Change of Position: The Nature of the Defence and its Relationship to other Restitutionary Defences' in M McInnes (ed), *Restitution: Developments in Unjust Enrichment* (North Ryde, LBC Information Services, 1996) 55–56; P Birks, 'Change of Position and Surviving Enrichment' in W Swadling (ed), *The Limits of Restitutionary Claims: A Comparative Analysis* (Glasgow, The United Kingdom Committee of Comparative Law, 1997) 43; C Rotherham, 'Tracing Misconceptions in *Foskett v McKeown*' [2003] *RLR* 57, 73–76; Bant, *The Change of Position Defence* (2009) (n 19) 204–09; Burrows, *The Law of Restitution* (2010) (n 18) 547–48.

position. The bifurcation of enrichment in this book suggests that the defence of change of position may apply to legal enrichment cases, as the difference is simply one of characterisation of the benefit. Indeed, there are cases treating a change of position as a defence to legal enrichment claims,[23] especially in the context of rescission.[24] Conversely, there are countervailing considerations where a claimant has a 'proprietary' interest, as the protection of property typically overrides any concern for the defendant.[25] Ultimately, whichever conclusion is reached, the division between factual and legal enrichment is critical to resolving the boundaries of the change of position defence in claims for specific restitution.

*(vi) Wrongs*

This book is confined to the analysis of the principles of enrichment in the law of unjust enrichment, but much of the analysis is equally relevant to the law of restitution for wrongs. For instance, it must be the case that the enrichment inquiry is bifurcated in both unjust enrichment and wrongs cases. More generally, however, it is not clear whether the principles of enrichment are, or should be, equivalent in wrongs cases, and one area of potential difference is the role of freedom of choice. In relation to unjust enrichment, this book suggested that the choice of the benefit was a necessary aspect of establishing factual enrichment, but the same may not hold true in wrongs cases. It may be that the receipt of value is enriching even in circumstances where the defendant did not choose the benefit and it is not incontrovertibly enriching. On the other hand, *Ministry of Defence v Ashman*[26] and *Ministry of Defence v Thompson*,[27] both wrongs cases, suggest a concern to protect the defendant's freedom of choice in the case of trespass to land. In the absence of further authority, it remains to be seen whether the law will adopt the same principles of enrichment in wrongs cases more generally, but it is likely that the enrichment model proposed in this book will assist in the analysis of restitution for wrongs.

## IV. Conclusion

The increasing complexity of unjust enrichment analysis since the publication of *An Introduction to the Law of Restitution* is to be welcomed. In the decades since Birks's seminal text, many of the orthodoxies that emerged from his groundbreaking work have been challenged and overturned, often by Birks himself. However, the original abstraction from the core case of a mistaken payment of money to

[23] Eg *Allcard v Skinner* (1887) 36 ChD 145 (CA); *Gertsch v Atsas* [1999] NSWSC 898.
[24] See Bant, *The Change of Position Defence* (2009) (n 19) 102–14.
[25] See D Fox, 'Legal Title as a Ground of Restitutionary Liability' [2000] *RLR* 465, 488.
[26] *Ministry of Defence v Ashman* (1993) 66 P&CR 195 (CA).
[27] *Ministry of Defence v Thompson* (1993) 25 HLR 552 (CA).

'enrichment' has largely escaped close scrutiny. This book aims to remedy this relative lack of detailed study by undertaking the first comprehensive analysis of the theoretical structure and role of enrichment in the law of unjust enrichment.

The bifurcated model of the enrichment inquiry proposed here is undoubtedly a radical departure from the prevailing unitary definition of enrichment, but it is a recasting of the theoretical framework that better explains and justifies the cases because it abstracts less indiscriminately and incorporates greater nuance and complexity than prevailing accounts. Moreover, it has been shown that the division between factual and legal enrichment has substantive consequences, not just for the enrichment inquiry, but for the law of unjust enrichment and beyond. If the law of unjust enrichment is to develop coherent and defined boundaries, the enrichment inquiry cannot generalise too much and must deal in differences that matter. Consequently, the law of unjust enrichment should differentiate between factual and legal enrichment, both to acknowledge the substantive differences between each type of claim and to ensure like claims are treated alike.

# Bibliography

## I. Texts, Digests and Restatements


American Law Institute, *Restatement of the Law of Restitution*, 1st edn (American Law Institute, 1937).

——, *Restatement (Second) of Contracts*, 2nd edn (American Law Institute, 1981).

Ames, A, *Lectures on Legal History and Miscellaneous Legal Essays* (Harvard University Press, 1913).

Aristotle, *Nicomachean Ethics* (JM Dent & Sons, 1911).

Austin, J, *Lectures on Jurisprudence or the Philosophy of Positive Law*, 5th edn (London, John Murray, 1885).

Baker, J (ed), *The Reports of Sir John Spelman* (Publications of the Selden Society, Selden Society, 1978).

——, *An Introduction to English Legal History*, 3rd edn (Butterworths, 1990).

——, *An Introduction to English Legal History*, 4th edn (Butterworths, 2002).

—— and Milsom, S, *Sources of English Legal History: Private Law to 1750* (Butterworths, 1986). Ball, E, '*"At the Expense of the Claimant": Unpacking the Requirement*' (M Phil thesis, University of Oxford, 2011).

Baloch, T, *Unjust Enrichment and Contract* (Oxford, Hart, 2009).

Bant, E, *The Change of Position Defence* (Oxford, Hart, 2009).

Beale, H, *Chitty on Contracts*, 29th edn (London, Sweet & Maxwell, 2004).

Beatson, J, *The Use and Abuse of Unjust Enrichment* (Oxford, Clarendon Press, 1991).

Bentham, J, *An Introduction to the Principles of Morals and Legislation* (Athlone Press, 1970).

Berle, A and Means, G, *The Modern Corporation and Private Property*, revised edn (Harcourt, Brace & World, 1968).

Birks, P, *An Introduction to the Law of Restitution*, 1st edn (Oxford, Clarendon Press, 1985).

——, *An Introduction to the Law of Restitution*, revised edn (Oxford, Clarendon Press, 1989).

——, *Unjust Enrichment*, 2nd edn (Oxford, Clarendon Press, 2005).

—— and R Chambers, *The Restitution Research Resource* (Mansfield, 1994).

—— and F Rose, *Restitution and Equity* (Mansfield, 2000).

Black, H, *Black's Law Dictionary*, 5th edn (West Publishing Company, 1979).

Bridge, M, *Personal Property Law*, 3rd edn (Oxford, Oxford University Press, 2002).

Burrows, A, *The Law of Restitution*, 3rd edn (Oxford, Oxford University Press, 2010).

—— and McKendrick, E, *Cases and Materials on the Law of Restitution* (Oxford, Oxford University Press, 1997).

——— and Edelman J, *Cases and Materials on the Law of Restitution*, 2nd edn (Oxford, Oxford University Press, 2007).

Chambers, R, *A Course of Lectures on English Law* (Oxford, Clarendon Press, 1986).

——, *Resulting Trusts* (Oxford, Clarendon Press, 1997).

——, *An Introduction to Property Law in Australia*, 2nd edn (Sydney, Lawbook Co, 2008).

——, Mitchell, C and Penner, J, *Philosophical Foundations of the Law of Unjust Enrichment* (Oxford, Oxford University Press, 2009).

Chen-Wishart, M, *Contract Law*, 2nd edn (Oxford, Oxford University Press, 2007).

Cheshire, G, Fifoot, C and Furmston, M, *Law of Contract*, 13th edn (Butterworths, 1996).

Dugdale, A, *Clerk & Lindsell on Torts*, 18th edn (London, Sweet & Maxwell, 2000).

Edelman, J, *Gain-Based Damages: Contract, Tort, Equity and Intellectual Property* (Oxford, Hart, 2002).

—— and Bant, E, *Unjust Enrichment in Australia* (Oxford, Oxford University Press, 2006).

Fifoot, C, *History and Sources of the Common Law: Tort and Contract* (London, Stevens & Son, 1949).

Gilbert, J, *Gilbert on Contracts* (BL MS Hargrave 265, fo 93 c 1705).

Goff, R and Jones, G, *The Law of Restitution*, 4th edn (London, Sweet & Maxwell, 1993).

———, *The Law of Restitution*, 6th edn (London, Sweet & Maxwell, 2002).

Goode, R, *Commercial Law* (Penguin, 2004).

Grantham, R and Rickett, C, *Enrichment and Restitution in New Zealand* (Oxford, Hart, 2000).

Gray, H, *Garrow and Gray's Law of Personal Property in New Zealand*, 5th edn (Butterworths, 1968).

Gummow, W, *Change and Continuity: Statute, Equity and Federalism* (Oxford, Oxford University Press, 1999).

Häcker, B, *Consequences of Impaired Consent Transfers* (Mohr Siebeck, 2009).

Hammond, R, *Personal Property: Commentary and Materials*, revised edn (Oxford, Oxford University Press, 1992).

Harris, J, *Property and Justice* (Oxford, Clarendon Press, 1996).

Hart, H, *The Concept of Law*, 2nd edn (Oxford, Clarendon Press, 1997).

Hegel, G, *Elements of the Philosophy of Right* (Cambridge, Cambridge University Press, 1991).

Hicks, J, *Value and Capital* (Oxford, Oxford University Press, 1939).

Hobbes, T, *Leviathan* (Andrew Crooke, 1651).

Hohfeld, W, *Fundamental Legal Conceptions as Applied in Judicial Reasoning* (Yale University Press, 1923).

Holdsworth, W, *A History of English Law*, 5th edn (London, Sweet & Maxwell, 1942).

Ibbetson, D, *A Historical Introduction to the Law of Obligations* (Oxford, Oxford University Press, 1999).

Jackman, I, *The Varieties of Restitution* (Sydney, Federation Press, 1998).

Jackson, R, *The History of Quasi-Contract in English Law* (Cambridge, Cambridge University Press, 1936).

Jaffey, P, *The Nature and Scope of Restitution: Vitiated Transfers, Imputed Contracts and Disgorgement* (Oxford, Hart, 2000).

Jones, G (ed), *Goff & Jones The Law of Restitution*, 7th edn (London, Sweet & Maxwell, 2007).

Keener, W, *A Treatise on the Law of Quasi-Contracts* (Baker and Voorhis & Co, 1893).

Kimel, D, *From Promise to Contract: Towards a Liberal Theory of Contract* (Oxford, Hart, 2003).
Krebs, T, *Restitution at the Crossroads: A Comparative Study* (London, Cavendish, 2001).
Langdell, C, *Summary of the Law of Contracts*, 2nd edn (Boston, Little, Brown & Co, 1880).
Locke, J, *Two Treatises of Government* (Awnsham and John Churchill, 1698).
Maddaugh, P and McCamus, J, *The Law of Restitution* (Canada Law Book, 1990).
Maitland, F, *The Forms of Action at Common Law*, reprinted edn (Cambridge, Cambridge University Press, 1968).
Mason, K and Carter, J, *Restitution Law in Australia* (Sydney, Butterworths, 1996).
McFarlane, B, *The Basic Structure of Property Law* (Oxford, Hart, 2008).
Meagher, R, Heydon, D and Leeming, M, *Meagher, Gummow & Lehane's Equity: Doctrines & Remedies*, 4th edn (LexisNexis Butterworths, 2002).
Millett, P, *On Villainy* (University of Queensland Press, 2007).
Mitchell, C and Watterson, S, *Subrogation Law and Practice*, revised edn (Oxford, Oxford University Press, 2007).
——, Mitchell, P and Watterson, S, *Goff & Jones The Law of Unjust Enrichment*, 8th edn (London, Sweet & Maxwell, 2011).
Myrdal, G, *The Political Element in the Development of Economic Theory* (Routledge, 1969).
Neyers, J, McInnes, M and Pitel, S, *Understanding Unjust Enrichment* (Oxford, Hart, 2004).
Nicholas, B, *An Introduction to Roman Law* (Oxford, Clarendon Press, 1962).
O'Sullivan, D, Elliott, S and Zakrzewski, R, *The Law of Rescission* (Oxford, Oxford University Press, 2008).
Palmer, G, *The Law of Restitution* (Little Brown, 1978).
Peel, E, *Treitel on the Law of Contract*, 12th edn (London, Sweet & Maxwell, 2007).
Penner, J, *The Idea of Property in Law* (Oxford, Clarendon Press, 1997).
Pollock, F and Wright, R, *An Essay on Possession in the Common Law* (Oxford, Clarendon Press, 1888).
Ricardo, D, *On the Principles of Political Economy and Taxation*, 3rd edn (London, John Murray, 1821).
Sheppard, W, *A Grand Abridgement of the Common and Statute Law of England* (Flesher, Streater and Twyford, 1675).
Simpson, A, *History of the Common Law of Contract* (Oxford, Clarendon Press, 1975).
Skelton, A, *Restitution and Contract* (Mansfield, 1998).
Smith, A, *The Wealth of Nations*, 11th edn (Cooke & Hale, 1818).
Smith, L, *The Law of Tracing* (Oxford, Oxford University Press, 1997).
Stephen, H, *A Treatise on the Principles of Pleading in Civil Actions*, 2nd edn (Joseph Butterworth & Son, 1827).
Stevens, R, *Torts and Rights* (Oxford, Oxford University Press, 2007).
Street, T, *Foundations of Legal Liability* (Edward Thompson, 1906).
Swadling, W (ed), *The Quistclose Trust: Critical Essays* (Oxford, Hart, 2004).
Thomas, J, *Textbook of Roman Law* (North-Holland, 1976).
Virgo, G, *The Principles of the Law of Restitution*, 2nd edn (Oxford, Oxford University Press, 2006).
Von Savigny, F, *Von Savigny's Treatise on Possession*, 6th edn (London, Sweet & Maxwell, 1979).

Weinrib, E, *The Idea of Private Law* (Harvard University Press, 1995).
Winfield, P, *Province of the Law of Tort* (Cambridge, Cambridge University Press, 1931).
——, *The Law of Quasi-Contracts* (London, Sweet & Maxwell, 1952).
Wood, T, *Institute of the Laws of England* (Garland, 1724).
Woodley, M (ed), *Osborn's Concise Law Dictionary*, 10th edn (London, Sweet & Maxwell, 2005).
Worthington, S, *Personal Property: Cases and Materials* (Oxford, Hart, 2000).
Zakrzewski, R, *Remedies Reclassified* (Oxford, Oxford University Press, 2005).

## II. Journal Articles and Book Chapters

Ames, J, 'The History of Assumpsit: Implied Assumpsit' (1888) 2 *Harvard Law Review* 53.
Baker, J, 'The Use of Assumpsit for Restitutionary Money Claims' in Schrage, E (ed), *Unjust Enrichment: The Comparative Legal History of the Law of Restitution* (Duncker & Humblot, 1995).
——, 'The History of Quasi-Contract in English Law' in Cornish, W et al (eds), *Restitution: Past, Present and Future* (Oxford, Hart, 1998). Ball, S, 'Work Carried Out Pursuant to Letters of Intent—Contract or Restitution' (1983) 99 *LQR* 572.
Barker, K, 'Understanding the Unjust Enrichment Principle in Private Law' in Neyers, J, McInnes, M and Pitel, S (eds), *Understanding Unjust Enrichment* (Oxford, Hart, 2004).
——, 'Responsibility for Gain: Unjust Factors or Absence of Legal Ground? Starting Points in Unjust Enrichment Law' in Grantham, R and Rickett, C (eds), *Structure and Justification in Private Law* (Oxford, Hart, 2008).
Barton, J, 'Contract and Quantum Meruit: The Antecedents of *Cutter v Powell*' (1987) 8 *Journal of Legal History* 48.
Beatson, J, 'The Temptation of Elegance: Concurrence of Restitutionary and Contractual Claims' in Swadling, W and Jones, G (eds), *The Search for Principle: Essays in Honour of Lord Goff of Chieveley* (Oxford, Oxford University Press, 1999).
—— and Virgo, G, 'Contract, Unjust Enrichment and Unconscionability' (2002) 118 *LQR* 352.
Benson, P, 'Abstract Right and the Possibility of a Nondistributive Concept of Contract: Hegel and Contemporary Contract Theory' (1989) 10 *Cardozo Law Review* 1077.
——, 'The Unity of Contract Law' in Benson, P (ed), *The Theory of Contract Law: New Essays* (Cambridge, Cambridge University Press, 2001).
Birks, P, 'Restitutionary Damages for Breach of Contract' (1987) *Lloyd's Maritime and Commercial Law Quarterly* 421.
——, 'In Defence of Free Acceptance' in Burrows, A (ed), *Essays on the Law of Restitution* (Oxford, Clarendon Press, 1991).
——, 'The English Recognition of Unjust Enrichment' (1991) *Lloyd's Maritime and Commercial Law Quarterly* 473.
——, 'Restitution and Resulting Trusts' in Goldstein, S (ed), *Equity and Contemporary Legal Developments* (Harry and Michael Sacher Institute for Legislative Research and Comparative Law, 1992).

——, 'Change of Position: The Nature of the Defence and its Relationship to Other Restitutionary Defences' in McInnes, M (ed), *Restitution: Developments in Unjust Enrichment* (LBC Information Services, 1996).
——, 'Equity in the Modern Common Law: An Exercise in Taxonomy' (1996) 26 *University of Western Australia Law Review* 1.
——, 'Trusts Raised to Reverse Unjust Enrichments: The *Westdeutsche* Case' (1996) *Restitution Law Review* 3.
——, 'Change of Position and Surviving Enrichment' in Swadling, W (ed), *The Limits of Restitutionary Claims: A Comparative Analysis* (United Kingdom Committee of Comparative Law, 1997).
——, 'On Taking Seriously the Difference Between Tracing and Claiming' (1997) 11 *Trust Law International* 2.
——, 'Property and Unjust Enrichment: Categorical Truths' (1997) *New Zealand Law Review* 623.
——, 'Unjust Factors and Wrongs: Pecuniary Rescission for Undue Influence' (1997) *Restitution Law Review* 72.
——, 'Misnomer' in Cornish (ed), *Restitution: Past, Present and Future* (Oxford, Hart, 1998).
——, 'Equity, Conscience and Unjust Enrichment' (1999) 23 *Melbourne University Law Review* 1.
——, 'Property, Unjust Enrichment and Tracing' (2001) 54 *Current Legal Problems* 231.
——, 'Unjust Enrichment and Wrongful Enrichment' (2001) 79 *Texas Law Review* 1767.
——, 'Retrieving Tied Money' in Swadling, W (ed), *The Quistclose Trust: Critical Essays* (Oxford, Hart, 2004).
Burrows, A, 'Free Acceptance and the Law of Restitution' (1988) 104 *LQR* 576.
——, 'Quadrating Restitution and Unjust Enrichment: A Matter of Principle?' (2000) 8 *Restitution Law Review* 257.
——, 'Proprietary Restitution: Unmasking Unjust Enrichment' (2001) 117 *LQR* 412.
——, 'Construction and Rectification' in Burrows, A and Peel, E (eds), *Contract Terms* (Oxford, Oxford University Press, 2007).
——, 'The Relationship Between Unjust Enrichment and Property: Some Unresolved Issues' in Edelman, J and Degeling, S (eds), *Unjust Enrichment in Commercial Law* (Sydney, Lawbook Co, 2008).
Chambers, R, 'Resulting Trusts in Canada' (2000) 38 *Alberta Law Review* 378.
——, 'Resulting Trusts and Equitable Compensation' (2001) 15 *Trust Law International* 2.
——, 'Resulting Trusts' in Burrows, A and Rodger, A (eds), *Mapping the Law: Essays in Memory of Peter Birks* (Oxford, Oxford University Press, 2006).
——, 'Two Kinds of Enrichment' in Chambers, R, Mitchell, C and Penner, J (eds), *Philosophical Foundations of the Law of Unjust Enrichment* (Oxford, Oxford University Press, 2009).
Chen-Wishart, M, 'Loss Sharing, Undue Influence and Manifest Disadvantage' (1994) 110 *LQR* 173.
Dawson, F, 'Rescission and Damages' (1976) 39 *MLR* 214.
Dawson, J, 'Erasable Enrichment in German Law' (1981) 61 *Boston University Law Review* 217.
Denning, A, 'Quantum Meruit and the Statute of Frauds' (1925) 41 *LQR* 82.
Edelman, J, 'Unjust Enrichment, Restitution and Wrongs' (2001) 79 *Texas Law Review* 1869.
——, 'Gain-Based Damages: Development and Reflections' in Burrows, A and Rodger, A (eds), *Mapping the Law: Essays in Memory of Peter Birks* (Oxford, Oxford University Press, 2006).

——, 'Review: The Law and Ethics of Restitution' (2006) 69 *MLR* 131.

——, 'The Meaning of Loss and Enrichment' in Chambers, R, Mitchell, C and Penner, J (eds), *Philosophical Foundations of the Law of Unjust Enrichment* (Oxford, Oxford University Press, 2009).

Eleftheriadis, P, 'The Analysis of Property Rights' (1996) 16 *Oxford Journal of Legal Studies* 31.

Fox, D, 'Legal Title as a Ground of Restitutionary Liability' (2000) *Restitution Law Review* 465.

——, 'The Transfer of Legal Title to Money' (1996) 4 *Restitution Law Review* 60.

Fridman, G, 'Quantum Meruit' (1999) 37 *Alberta Law Review* 38.

Fuller, L and Perdue, W, 'The Reliance Interest in Contract Damages' (1936) 46 *Yale Law Journal* 52.

Garner, M, 'The Role of Subjective Benefit in the Law of Unjust Enrichment' (1990) 10 *Oxford Journal of Legal Studies* 42.

Gautreau J, 'When Are Enrichments Unjust?' (1988–89) 10 *Advocates' Quarterly* 258.

Grantham, R and Rickett, C, 'Restitution, Property and Ignorance—A Reply to Mr Swadling' (1996) *Lloyd's Maritime and Commercial Law Quarterly* 463.

—— ——, 'Property and Unjust Enrichment: Categorical Truths or Unnecessary Complexity?' (1997) *New Zealand Universities Law Review* 668.

—— ——, 'Restitution, Property and Mistaken Payments' (1997) *Restitution Law Review* 83.

—— ——, 'Resulting Trusts—A Rather Limited Doctrine' in Birks, P and Rose, F (eds), *Restitution and Equity, vol 1: Resulting Trusts and Equitable Compensation* (Mansfield Press, 2000).

—— ——, 'Property Rights as a Legally Significant Event' (2003) 62 *Cambridge Law Journal* 717.

Häcker, B, 'Rescission and Third Party Rights' (2006) *Restitution Law Review* 1.

——, 'Proprietary Restitution After Impaired Consent Transfers: A Generalised Power Model' (2009) 68 *Cambridge Law Journal* 324. Harris, D, 'The Concept of Possession in English Law' in Guest, A (ed), *Oxford Essays in Jurisprudence* (Oxford, Clarendon Press, 1961).

Ho, L and Smart, P, 'Reinterpreting the Quistclose Trust: a Critique of Chambers' Analysis' (2001) 21 *Oxford Journal of Legal Studies* 267.

Hohfeld, W, 'Some Fundamental Legal Conceptions as Applied in Judicial Reasoning' (1913) 23 *Yale Law Journal* 16.

Honoré, A, 'Ownership' in Guest, A (ed), *Oxford Essays in Jurisprudence* (Oxford, Clarendon Press, 1961).

Jaffey, P, 'Two Theories of Unjust Enrichment' in Neyers, J, McInnes, M and Pitel, S (eds), *Understanding Unjust Enrichment* (Oxford, Hart, 2004).

Klimchuk, D, 'Unjust Enrichment and Corrective Justice' in Neyers, J, McInnes, M and Pitel, S (eds), *Understanding Unjust Enrichment* (Oxford, Hart, 2004).

Kovacic, C, 'A Proposal to Simplify Quantum Meruit Litigation' (1985) 35 *Auckland University Law Review* 547.

Lodder, A, 'Unjust Enrichment and the Assessment of Quantum Meruit Awards' (2010) 126 *LQR* 42.

McFarlane, B and Stevens, R, 'The Nature of Equitable Property' (2010) 4 *Journal of Equity* 1.

McGhee, J, 'The Nature of the Enrichment Enquiry' in Edelman, J and Degeling, S (eds), *Unjust Enrichment in Commercial Law* (Sydney, Lawbook Co, 2009).

McInnes, M, '"At the Plaintiff's Expense": Quantifying Restitutionary Relief' (1998) *Cambridge Law Journal* 472.

——, 'Restitution, Unjust Enrichment and the Perfect Quadration Thesis' (1999) *Restitution Law Review* 118.
——, 'The Measure of Restitution' (2002) 52 *University of Toronto Law Journal* 163.
——, 'Interceptive Subtraction, Unjust Enrichment and Wrongs—A Reply to Professor Birks' (2003) *Cambridge Law Journal* 697.
——, 'Enrichment Revisited' in Neyers, J, McInnes, M and Pitel, S (eds), *Understanding Unjust Enrichment* (Oxford, Hart, 2004). McKendrick, E, 'The Battle of the Forms and the Law of Restitution' (1988) 8 *Oxford Journal of Legal Studies* 197.
Millett, P, 'The Quistclose Trust: Who Can Enforce It?' (1985) 101 *LQR* 269.
——, 'Restitution and Constructive Trusts' (1998) 114 *LQR* 399.
——, 'Pension Schemes and the Law of Trusts' (2000) 14 *Trust Law International* 66.
——, 'Proprietary Restitution' in Degeling, S and Edelman, J (eds), *Equity in Commercial Law* (Sydney, Thomson LBC, 2005).
Mitchell, C, 'Subrogation, Tracing and the *Quistclose* Principle' (1995) *Lloyd's Maritime and Commercial Law Quarterly* 451.
——, 'Subrogation: Persistent Misunderstandings' in Burrows, A and Rodger, A (eds), *Mapping the Law: Essays in Memory of Peter Birks* (Oxford, Oxford University Press, 2006).
——, 'Restitutionary Claims for Services: Principles of Quantification' in Edelman, J and Degeling, S (eds), *Unjust Enrichment in Commercial Law* (Sydney, Lawbook Co, 2008).
—— and Mitchell, P, '*Planché v Colburn*' in Mitchell, C and Mitchell, P (eds), *Landmark Cases in the Law of Restitution* (Oxford, Hart, 2006).
Nahan, N, 'Rescission: A Case for Rejecting the Classical Model?' (1997) 27 *University of Western Australia Law Review* 66.
Nicholls, L, 'My Kingdom for a Horse: The Meaning of Words' (2005) 121 *LQR* 577.
Nolan, R, 'Dispositions Involving Fiduciaries: The Equity to Rescind and the Resulting Trust' in Birks, P and Rose, F (eds), *Restitution and Equity* (Mansfield Press, 2000).
——, 'Equitable Property' (2006) 122 *LQR* 232.
O'Dell, E, 'The Resulting Trust' in Grantham, R and Rickett, C (eds), *Structure and Justification in Private Law* (Oxford, Hart, 2008).
O'Sullivan, J, 'Rescission as a Self-help Remedy: A Critical Analysis' (2000) 59 *Cambridge Law Journal* 509.
Penner, J, 'The Bundle of Rights Picture of Property' (1996) 43 *University of California at Los Angeles Law Review* 711.
Raz, J, 'Promises in Morality and Law' (1982) 95 *Harvard Law Review* 916.
Rickett, C, 'Different Views on the Scope of the Quistclose Analysis' (1991) 107 *LQR* 608.
——, 'Old and New in the Law of Tracing' in Edelman, J and Degeling, S (eds), *Equity in Commercial Law* (Sydney, Lawbook Co, 2005).
Rose, F, 'Restitution for the Rescuer' (1989) 9 *Oxford Journal of Legal Studies* 167.
Rotherham, C, 'Tracing Misconceptions in *Foskett v McKeown*' (2003) *Restitution Law Review* 57.
Rudden, B, 'Things as Things and Things as Wealth' (1994) *Oxford Journal of Legal Studies* 81.
Scott, A, 'The Nature of the Rights of the "Cestui Que Trust"' (1917) 17 *Columbia Law Review* 269.
Scott, S, 'Restitution and the Argument of Subjective Devaluation' (1993) 15 *New Zealand Universities Law Review* 246.
Sheinman, H, 'Contractual Liability and Voluntary Undertaking' (2000) 20 *Oxford Journal of Legal Studies* 205.

Smith, L, 'Three-Party Restitution: A Critique of Birks's Theory of Interceptive Subtraction' (1991) *Oxford Journal of Legal Studies* 481.

——, 'The Province of the Law of Restitution' (1992) 71 *Canadian Bar Review* 672.

——, 'Unjust Enrichment, Property and the Structure of Trusts' (2000) 116 *LQR* 412.

——, 'Restitution: The Heart of Corrective Justice' (2001) 79 *Texas Law Review* 2115.

——, 'Unravelling Proprietary Restitution' (2004) *Canadian Business Law Journal* 317.

——, 'Tracing' in Burrows, A and Rodger, A (eds), *Mapping the Law: Essays in Memory of Peter Birks* (Oxford, Oxford University Press, 2006).

——, 'Unjust Enrichment: Big or Small?' in Degeling, S and Edelman, J (eds), *Unjust Enrichment in Commercial Law* (Sydney, Lawbook Co, 2008).

——, 'Philosophical Foundations of Proprietary Remedies' in Chambers, R, Mitchell, C and Penner, J (eds), *Philosophical Foundations of the Law of Unjust Enrichment* (Oxford, Oxford University Press, 2009).

——, 'Simplifying Claims to Traceable Proceeds' (2009) 125 *LQR* 338. Smith, S, 'Concurrent Liability in Contract and Unjust Enrichment: The Fundamental Breach Requirement' (1999) 115 *LQR* 245.

Stevens, R, 'Three Enrichment Issues' in Burrows, A and Rodger, A (eds), *Mapping the Law: Essays in Memory of Peter Birks* (Oxford, Oxford University Press, 2006).

——, 'Is There a Law of Unjust Enrichment?' in Degeling, S and Edelman, J (eds), *Unjust Enrichment in Commercial Law* (Sydney, Lawbook Co, 2008).

Swadling, W, 'A Claim in Restitution?' (1996) *Lloyd's Maritime and Commercial Law Quarterly* 63.

——, 'A New Role for Resulting Trusts' (1996) 16 *Legal Studies* 110.

——, 'Property and Unjust Enrichment' in Harris, J (ed), *Property Problems: From Genes to Pension Funds* (Kluwer Law International, 1997).

——, 'A Hard Look at *Hodgson v Marks*' in Birks, P and Rose, F (eds), *Restitution and Equity* (Mansfield Press, 2000).

——, 'Property: General Principles' in Birks, P (ed), *English Private Law*, 1st edn (Oxford, Oxford University Press, 2000).

——, 'Rescission, Property and the Common Law' (2005) 121 *LQR* 123.

——, 'Unjust Delivery' in Burrows, A and Rodger, A (eds), *Mapping the Law: Essays in Memory of Peter Birks* (Oxford, Oxford University Press, 2006).

——, 'Explaining Resulting Trusts' (2008) 124 *LQR* 72. Tarrant, J, 'Property Rights to Stolen Money' (2005) 32 *University of Western Australia Law Review* 234.

Tettenborn, A, 'Misnomer—A Response to Professor Birks' in Nolan, R (ed), *Restitution: Past, Present and Future* (Oxford, Hart, 1998).

——, 'Subsisting Contracts and Failure of Consideration: A Little Skepticism' (2002) *Restitution Law Review* 1.

Trukhtanov, A, 'The Irreducible Core of Trust Obligations' (2007) 123 *LQR* 342.

Watts, P, 'Subrogation: A Step Too Far?' (1998) 114 *LQR* 341.

Weinrib, E, 'The Normative Structure of Unjust Enrichment' in Rickett, C and Grantham, R (eds), *Structure and Justification in Private Law* (Oxford, Hart, 2008).

——, 'Correctively Unjust Enrichment' in Chambers, R, Mitchell, C and Penner, J (eds), *Philosophical Foundations of the Law of Unjust Enrichment* (Oxford, Oxford University Press, 2009).

Wilmot-Smith, F, 'Replacing Risk Taking Reasoning' (2011) 27 *LQR* 61.

Worthington, S, 'Restitution and Insolvency' in Rose, F (ed), *Restitution and Insolvency* (Mansfield Press, 2000).

Zimmerman, R and Du Plessis, J, 'Basic Features of the German Law of Unjustified Enrichment' (1994) *Restitution Law Review* 14.

# INDEX

www.ingramcontent.com/pod-product-compliance
Ingram Content Group UK Ltd.
Pitfield, Milton Keynes, MK11 3LW, UK
UKHW020832290926
15470UKWH00009B/1855/J

9 781849 463294